COMMUNITIES OF CARE

Communities of Care

THE SOCIAL ETHICS
OF VICTORIAN FICTION

Talia Schaffer

PRINCETON UNIVERSITY PRESS
PRINCETON & OXFORD

Copyright © 2021 by Princeton University Press

"Small Kindnesses" from *Bonfire Opera* by Danusha Laméris, © 2020. Reprinted by permission of the University of Pittsburgh Press.

Princeton University Press is committed to the protection of copyright and the intellectual property our authors entrust to us. Copyright promotes the progress and integrity of knowledge created by humans. Thank you for supporting free speech and the global exchange of ideas by purchasing an authorized edition of this book. If you wish to reproduce or distribute any part of it in any form, please obtain permission.

Requests for permission to reproduce material from this work should be sent to permissions@press.princeton.edu

Published by Princeton University Press
41 William Street, Princeton, New Jersey 08540
99 Banbury Road, Oxford OX2 6JX

press.princeton.edu

GPSR Authorized Representative: Easy Access System Europe - Mustamäe tee 50, 10621 Tallinn, Estonia, gpsr.requests@easproject.com

All Rights Reserved
First paperback printing, 2025
Paperback ISBN 9780691271101
Cloth ISBN 9780691199634
ISBN (e-book) 9780691226514
LCCN: 2022275460

British Library Cataloging-in-Publication Data is available

Editorial: Anne Savarese and James Collier
Production Editorial: Sara Lerner
Jacket/Cover Design: Pamela L. Schnitter
Production: Erin Suydam
Publicity: Alyssa Sanford and Amy Stewart
Copyeditor: Cynthia Buck

Jacket/Cover Credit: Ford Madox Brown, *Henry Fawcett; Dame Millicent Fawcett*, 1872. Oil on canvas, 42 3/4 in. × 33 in. (1086 mm × 838 mm). Bequeathed by Sir Charles Wentworth Dilke, 2nd Bt, 1911. © National Portrait Gallery, London

This book has been composed in Miller

Dedicated to the friends who have sustained me,
especially Nicole, who for the past twenty years
has been a care community in herself

.

Small Kindnesses

*I've been thinking about the way, when you walk
down a crowded aisle, people pull in their legs
to let you by. Or how strangers still say "bless you"
when someone sneezes, a leftover
from the Bubonic plague. "Don't die," we are saying.
And sometimes, when you spill lemons
from your grocery bag, someone else will help you
pick them up. Mostly, we don't want to harm each other.
We want to be handed our cup of coffee hot,
and to say thank you to the person handing it. To smile
at them and for them to smile back. For the waitress
to call us honey when she sets down the bowl of clam chowder,
and for the driver in the red pick-up truck to let us pass.
We have so little of each other, now. So far
from tribe and fire. Only these brief moments of exchange.
What if they are the true dwelling of the holy, these
fleeting temples we make together when we say, "Here,
have my seat," "Go ahead—you first," "I like your hat."*

—DANUSHA LAMÉRIS, *BONFIRE OPERA*

CONTENTS

Preface and Acknowledgments · xi

	Introduction: Care Communities Today	1
CHAPTER 1	Ethics of Care and the Care Community	28
CHAPTER 2	Austen, Dickens, and Brontë: Bodies before the Normate	60
CHAPTER 3	Global Migrant Care and Emotional Labor in *Villette*	88
CHAPTER 4	Beyond Sympathy: The State of Care in *Daniel Deronda*	117
CHAPTER 5	Care Meets the Silent Treatment in *The Wings of the Dove*	140
CHAPTER 6	Composite Fiction and the Care Community in *The Heir of Redclyffe*	160
	Epilogue: Critical Care	189

Notes · 219
Works Cited · 243
Index · 267

PREFACE AND ACKNOWLEDGMENTS

THERE ARE SEVERAL STORIES I could tell about how this book came to be, all of them true.

I could describe how a talk I gave on care and disability in *Our Mutual Friend* received a startlingly enthusiastic reception at Dickens Universe in 2014, making me realize that people craved more work on this subject. At the time I'd had no intention of doing a book on ethics of care, which I thought I'd already treated fully enough in *Romance's Rival*, but in response to the Dickens Universe audience, I began to imagine how I might expand this material. The result is the book you see before you. Dickens Universe audiences include both community members and scholars, and so, from its very inception, I imagined this project as reaching out to a wider and more public audience than academics usually target.

I could describe how, after writing a lengthy, historically oriented book, I thought it would be a good challenge to try to do a shorter, more tightly focused theoretical manifesto. However, both *Romance's Rival* and *Communities of Care* ended up blending historical and theoretical work, although in opposite sequences. For *Communities of Care*, I wanted to provide historical information to enrich the already philosophical forum of ethics of care. However, for *Romance's Rival*, I aimed to introduce theoretical categories to help organize well-known historical information. If I started with a hope that this would be my "theory book," whereas the last was my "history book," I now realize that all books should be theory books and history books alike, for theory written without historical awareness will be ill informed, while history written without a conscious theoretical framework will meander into cultural assumptions it mistakes for truth.

Nevertheless, my initial intention to write a manifesto has left at least two marks on this volume that differentiate it from conventional literary critical books. One is the structure of multiple short chapters rather than the usual fewer, longer chapters, a writing exercise designed to ensure conciseness. The other relic is a slightly jauntier style, more oriented toward popular writing, lived reality, and contemporary politics. I directly address the reader (hi, reader!) and use contractions and second-person pronouns. I have tried to make this a hybrid project, with a composite voice.

I could also mention that I like to see my work in terms of overall patterns. Having written two books on nineteenth-century aesthetics and material culture, *The Forgotten Female Aesthetes* and *Novel Craft*, I liked the idea of doing another pair of books on social relations, so that I'd have *Communities of Care* alongside *Romance's Rival*. In each case, the second book grew out of material in the first. Instead of paired books, however, the story of a different pattern has emerged: a quartet. All four of my monographs, *Communities of Care, Romance's Rival, Novel Craft,* and *The Forgotten Female Aesthetes,* work the same way. All four reconstruct a moment in the nineteenth century when some mode of thought flourished and then gradually ebbed, leaving residual practices by which we can trace its original contours. These phenomena meant something in their own time, and recovering their meanings can offer us alternatives to conceptual assumptions we now take for granted. This idea of slow, entangled change is the only way to do justice to the complications of the past, and it is a way to awaken ourselves to what that past can offer us.

But the story I most want to tell here is that I began writing this book as a reaction to the catastrophic US election of 2016 and finished writing it in the cataclysmic summer of 2020, with its global pandemic and racial justice convulsions. The four years of this book's writing meant consciously foregrounding an agenda of care over and against a nonstop news background of astonishing cruelty, racism, sexism; the trampling of basic rights; the evisceration of the environment; the human rights outrages against people of color, immigrants, and trans people; and the destruction of ethical norms in government, public speech, and basic conduct. At the same time, of course, my world of academia has been imploding, dynamited by the crisis of contingent faculty hiring, which has destroyed a generation of our best thinkers and eviscerated our departments, and as I write this in 2020, academia has been decimated even further by the massive economic collapse of the pandemic. Never has care been more necessary, or more part of public awareness.

I'm a Victorianist; I'm not used to writing on a topic that is dominating the news. So it was strange for me to discover that care was everywhere in 2020. Facebook introduced a "care" emoji. Daily I ran across articles about care in venues like *Medium, Avidly, The Nation,* and *The New Yorker,* and I have used the opportunity of this book to amplify these voices alongside more traditional academic sources. At the height of the pandemic, people applauded caregivers, particularly health care workers, at 7:00 every evening. Caregivers were hailed as heroes. As I complete this book in the autumn of 2020, the media is full of speculations about how to provide a sense of community in newly remote classrooms and among people suffering through months of social isolation. For a Victorianist, it certainly is a strange feeling to be timely.

And yet I didn't feel I had a choice. I felt, at first dimly and then with growing certainty, that the only kind of scholarship I could muster in an ethical crisis was to write about ethics as well as I could, in the most historically nuanced, theoretically lucid, and pragmatically usable form possible. I felt that the best way I could turn my critical skills to our current need was to use them to build a kind of reparative reading we could use, a rigorous and persuasive protocol. I can't institute decent governance, I can't restore voting rights or choice or civility or climate, and I can't make decent work conditions happen. I am a literary critic, and what I can do is to try to produce the kind of criticism that can guide us to endure, understand, and shape a usable response.

You who read this, hopefully from a different national and professional situation in the future, know that this book emerged in the crucible of an ethical emergency, and that my response to my sense of horror was to make it as strong as possible, to reinforce its walls and insulate its apertures with every piece of theoretical and historical and critical plating I could find. The result is that this book is a denser and more thickly citational piece of writing than the manifesto I initially imagined. I began by simply trying to write with clarity, but I ended up needing to generate strength. This book cannot do other than express the traumatic national situation in which it took shape, and if conditions have changed by the time you read this, perhaps *Communities of Care*'s capacity to communicate the feeling of this era is not the least useful of its functions. I wrote this book to be theory. But I would like nothing better than for it to become history too.

I have a lot of people to thank. Most books develop in a communal nexus, but given the topic of *Communities of Care*, I have been particularly aware of the way these ideas develop through the help of others.

Some profoundly intelligent comments from listeners at the University of Illinois at Urbana-Champaign as far back as 2013 led me to fundamental rethinking of care ethics. The surprising reaction at Dickens Universe the following year convinced me to make it into a book of its own, and along the way the audiences at many talks helped me understand what needed to be explained and prompted me to articulate what I was really saying. Thank you to the people who came to hear this work between 2014 and 2019 at Harvard, Princeton, Columbia, the University of Tennessee at Knoxville, the University of Louisville, the College of Charleston, Aston University, the University of Kansas, Emory University, George

Washington University, and the University of Indiana. I am particularly grateful for feedback from Deidre Lynch at Harvard, Nancy Henry at the University of Tennessee, Deborah Lutz at the University of Louisville, Timothy Carens and Kathleen Beres Rogers at the College of Charleston, Anna Neill and Ann Wierda Rowland at the University of Kansas, Paul Kelleher and Rosemarie Garland Thomson at Emory, Maria Frawley at George Washington University, and Rae Greiner, Ivan Kreilkamp, and Lara Kriegel at the University of Indiana. I also want to thank the audiences at NAVSA, MLA, and the Society for Novel Studies over the past few years, who have heard many, many talks on Charlotte Yonge without complaining (much).

The theoretical foundation of this book was constructed during my experience in 2018–2019 as a Rockefeller Fellow at the University Center for Human Values at Princeton, whose members were patient and kind to a literary scholar trying to make her way in philosophy. Thank you to my fellow Fellows and friends, Macalester Bell, Susan Brison, Lara Buchak, Benjamin Burger, Joseph Chan, Amanda Greene, Matthew Landauer, Melissa Lane, Tori McGeer, Tom Parr, Adam Potkay, Nelson Tebbe, Stephen White, and Annette Zimmerman, and I also thank my friends in the Princeton English Department for their hospitality: Meredith Martin, Deborah Nord, Diana Fuss, Claudia Johnson, and Susan Wolfson. I am grateful that the program introduced me to the work of Miranda Fricker, Sally Haslanger, and Kate Manne. Eva Feder Kittay and Virginia Held were generous and encouraging as I worked on this book. The UCHV program's loan of an extra laptop for six strenuous weeks when my own was in the shop and I had a major deadline made all the difference.

Thank you to the wonderful members of the Victorianist community all over the globe. I have mentioned many of them already, but I want to name some people whose support has sustained me for decades: Elaine Freedgood, Pamela Gilbert, Shuchi Kapila, Diana Maltz, Elsie Michie, Deborah Denenholz Morse, Anna Neill, Pam Thurschwell, and Tamara Silvia Wagner. I am especially grateful to Kathy A. Psomiades for writing an article about feminist work in *Criticism* that showed me my own historical investments better than I could have seen them myself. A special shout-out to Dennis Denisoff, with whom I was coediting *The Routledge Companion to Victorian Literature* while finalizing this book, and whose encouraging, patient, kind friendship is as valuable as his endless capacity for attentive hard work. There are too many helpful, inspirational people in my field to list here, even if I had ten volumes, but please know that if I've corresponded with you, joked with you, responded to your posts, enjoyed your conference papers, retweeted you, or written for you. I thank you here for making my world better over the past few years.

Some of my friends did serious labor on this manuscript. I want to give special thanks to Tim Alborn, who read an early draft of the epilogue and talked to me about assessments; to Matt Gold, who generously shared work on ethics of care in digital humanities with me; and to Lauren Goodlad and Zarena Aslami, incisive and generous readers of three chapters of the nearly finished manuscript. Carolyn Betensky confessed that she was Reader One, and nothing could have pleased me more than to owe some astute edits to her fine observation. Whoever Reader Two is, I salute you.

It is a special joy to recognize my inspirational colleagues at CUNY. Thank you to the incomparable Nicole Cooley, who is always intensely sympathetic, who is more entertaining when exasperated than anyone else I know, and who continues to help me make sense of home and work and the commute between them. Everyone should have a chair who, when you present something at a department reading group and say, "I don't know where to place this," suggests that maybe you could publish it in the special issue she is editing right now. Thank you, Karen Weingarten, for giving this theory a home in *South Atlantic Quarterly*, and thank you, Glenn Burger, for your steady, wise leadership of the department over many years. Annmarie Drury used the opportunity of a sociable lunch to propose nominating me for a major honor, an act of kindness that still floors me whenever I think about it. Kandice Chuh led the Graduate Center through an impossible time with sympathy, vision, and, somehow, even joy. At Queens and the Graduate Center, I am honored to have colleagues who include Tanya Agathocleous, Seo-Young Chu, Annmarie Drury, Gloria Fisk, Miles Grier, Caroline Hong, Briallen Hopper, Steve Kruger, Cliff Mak, Bill Orchard, Tanya Pollard, Caroline Reitz, Siân Silyn Roberts, Veronica Schanoes, Roger Sederat, Jason Tougaw, and Amy Wan. To the dissertating graduate students I have worked with over these past four years: thank you for your inspirational passion, insight, political principle, teaching skills, and mutual care. These extraordinary scholars and colleagues include Anick Boyd, Christine Choi, Laura Eldridge, Ryan Everitt, Julie Fuller, Aaron Ho, Miciah Hussey, Lindsay Lehman, Christian Lewis, Elissa Myers, Rose O'Malley, Jon Rachmani, Zach Samalin, Erin Spampinato, Emily Stanback, Anastasia Valassis, and Livia Woods.

Many institutions generously made this book possible. CUNY awarded me a Book Completion Award, which paid for the new computer that finally replaced the one that failed at Princeton. Earlier versions of material in this book originally appeared in *South Atlantic Quarterly*, *Novel*,

Victorian Literature and Culture, Henry James Review, Victorian Review, and *Approaches to Teaching Jane Austen's Persuasion*. I am grateful to those presses for permission to reprint, and for the editorial assistance that helped refine key ideas in this book. Specifically:

- An earlier version of part of chapter 1 appeared as "Care Communities: Ethics, Fictions, Temporalities," originally published in *South Atlantic Quarterly*, vol. 118, no. 3, pp. 521–42. © 2019, Duke University Press. All rights reserved. Republished by permission of the rightsholder and present publisher, Duke University Press. www.dukeupress.edu.
- Some material in chapter 2 appeared in "The Medical Context: Disability, Injury, Illness, and Nursing in *Persuasion*," published in Marcia McClintock Folsom and John Wiltshire, eds., *Approaches to Teaching Austen's Persuasion* (MLA, 2021). Republished by permission.
- An earlier version of chapter 3 appeared as "Why Lucy Doesn't Care: Migration and Emotional Labor in Villette," originally published in *Novel* 52:1 (2019): 84–106. (c) 2019, *Novel*, Inc. All rights reserved. Republished by permission of the rightsholder and present publisher, Duke University Press. www.dukeupress.edu.
- An earlier version of chapter 5 appeared as "The Silent Treatment of the Wings of the Dove: Ethics of Care and Late-James Style," originally published in *Henry James Review* 37:3 (Fall 2016): 233–45. Republished by permission.
- An earlier version of chapter 6 appeared as "Victorian Feminist Criticism: Recovery Work and the Care Community," in *Victorian Literature and Culture* 47:1 (Spring 2019): 63–91. Republished by permission.
- I am also grateful to the University of Pittsburgh Press for permission to reprint Danusha Laméris's poem, "Small Kindnesses."

Princeton University Press has been an exemplary press to work with. Anne Savarese is such a deft editor that she ushered this book under contract before I knew it had happened, Sara Lerner and James Collier made it all work, and Cynthia Buck copyedited the manuscript with sympathy and finesse. Thank you to Pamela L. Schnitter, who designed the cover, featuring Ford Madox Brown's portrait of Millicent Garret Fawcett and Henry Fawcett, a painting that beautifully combines all the themes of this book: political activism, collaborative writing, and mutual care.

This book is, fittingly, dedicated to the communities of care that have kept me going over the past several years. Thank you to the intellectual and spiritual nourishment of B'nai Keshet; how lucky am I to have a synagogue with a Levinas reading group? Thank you to the selfless, hardworking people at Glen Ridge High School who got us through the lockdown by reaching out to each student, staff, and faculty member. Thank you to my warm local friends, Lee Behlman, Wendy Xin, and the stalwart feminist squad of LoriJeane Moody, Jane Marcus, and Sarah Scalet. I owe a great deal to the loving families of the Schaffer and Musser clans, for many backyard meals, long conversations, parties, and support, and for emails around the world and country that kept us together when we were stuck apart.

Having spent this year at home, I am very lucky to have a home that includes these beloved beings: George, Eliana, and now Milo, who taught me about cross-species communication, and who always knew when I needed to go out for a walk. Eliana Musser has grown into a wise, steady, wry young adult, a sensitive and sensible person, and we have been proud to watch her discover her passions and find the person she was always meant to be. We can't wait to see where her intellect, insight, and humor will take her. As for George Musser—thank you for hours spent trudging around town thrashing out ideas, thank you for liking whatever I cooked, and thank you for making me update my computer. Two decades ago our book projects could not have been further apart: I was working on amateur Victorian handicrafts and you were working on string theory (but not the kind with actual strings, which would have been more relevant). Today we find ourselves converging. To our mutual surprise, both of us are working on books that centrally involve disability studies, panpsychism, and philosophy. It has been a new and touching pleasure to find you as an invaluable colleague in the life of the mind, as well as the life of our family and home.

COMMUNITIES OF CARE

INTRODUCTION

Care Communities Today

I am cognizant of the interrelatedness of all communities and states. . . . Injustice anywhere is a threat to justice everywhere. We are caught in an inescapable network of mutuality, tied in a single garment of destiny. Whatever affects one directly, affects all indirectly.

—MARTIN LUTHER KING JR., "LETTER FROM
A BIRMINGHAM JAIL" (1963)

READER, I WANT TO WARN YOU from the start: although this book has a title featuring the word "care," it is not going to be pleading for us all to care more about each other, nor will it be praising Victorian characters for truly caring. Forget the pleasant platitudes of care. Think of care as a practice—a difficult, often unpleasant, almost always underpaid, sometimes ineffective practice, but nonetheless an activity that defined the lives of nineteenth-century subjects, particularly female subjects, and that I assert helps define our lives today. As Florence Nightingale famously wrote in 1860, "Every woman, or at least almost every woman, in England has, at one time or another of her life, charge of the personal health of somebody, whether child or invalid,—in other words, every woman is a nurse."[1] Even more common is care in the larger sense: acts of friendship, parenting, mentoring. In looking at Victorian subjects, we might ask: why was caregiving so widespread in the nineteenth century, and how might caregiving have affected people's ideas of subjectivity, writing, and social relations? In looking at our own needs as readers, critics, teachers, and citizens, we might ask a different question: how can an understanding of care principles help us rethink what we are doing?

In *Communities of Care: The Social Ethics of Victorian Fiction*, I am aiming to develop a literary criticism that is predicated on care. This book makes no sentimental appeal to anyone's feelings. It stakes a claim that is as rigorous, textually embedded, philosophically abstract, and historically based as I could manage. Orienting us toward social relationality and action instead of individual psychology and deep motives, care ethics, I argue, can give us new understanding of our reading practices and strengthen alliances in our own lives.

This introduction demonstrates how to use care as the basis of a theory of reading, with special attention to ideas of character, and how to understand relationality as a powerful tool developed by global, indigenous, and queer communities. We can see care as a lens through which to view relationships, behaviors, and persons. Although it's common to refer to theory as a lens, I want to activate the material qualities of the metaphor.[2] A lens is a visual prosthesis that extends our sight, introducing close-ups, distortions, breakages, frames, and distances that can make us see the familiar anew. Because my work is so indebted to disability studies, I want to maintain that sense of the lens as extended prosthetic capability, rather than the medical correction of a flawed view. In other words, the lens of care doesn't fix a problem so much as it enhances our abilities.

Specifically, this book aims to develop the category of "communities of care." It does so by combining the feminist philosophy of "ethics of care" with particular examples in Victorian fiction, the incidences of voluntary carers who coalesce around someone in need, like the characters who flock to Louisa Musgrove's bedside after her fall, surround Esther Summerson in her great illness, and wait at Ralph Touchett's deathbed. I am using this small social formation, the care community, both to develop a relational reading of the fiction in which it is omnipresent and to model social networks in ways we can use ourselves.

Communities of Care is trying to do a lot of tasks at once, but like that lens, it aims to focus its multiple facets together into one vista. In making ethics of care theory speak to Victorian fiction, I hope to enrich both. I want to expand ethics of care by introducing the historical evidence of another culture's forms of care. The philosophy tends to assume contemporary Western conditions, and I join the efforts of critics like Vrinda Dalmiya and Oche Onazi in trying to diversifying its purview, although I do so through introducing historical rather than global alternatives.[3] I also want us to use care theory to rethink our lives as academics, to reimagine what we do as teachers and scholars and service workers, to envision even the basic act of reading as a mode of repairing, sustaining, and maintaining an other.

Finally, I aim to help literary scholars address the communal structures of Victorian texts. As Alicia Christoff points out, Victorian novel criticism "has to some extent resisted relationality—perhaps inevitably, and perhaps without our knowing. We have insisted on firm divides between characters, narrators, readers, and authors rather than theorizing their interrelation."[4] I join Christoff in developing a relational theory that will help us think about not only how characters connect (as in *Daniel Deronda*), but also how readers get drawn into communion with the text (in *The Wings of the Dove*) and how authors may be read as composite, collaborative makers (in *The Heir of Redclyffe*). To do this properly, however, literary critics need to stop invoking "care" as a vaguely altruistic principle and instead access the full capacity of a modern, precise, grounded, politically aware theory of care.

In this introduction, I situate this project in twenty-first-century issues, while the epilogue proposes explicit lessons that readers can implement. Bookending the volume, these two chapters speak to an ethics of care as an immediate, pragmatic, urgently necessary practice, in literary criticism, in teaching, in academia, and in the social world in which we live. Between these two framing chapters, I tease out how care communities work by looking at some exceptionally well-developed examples produced before professional medical care became the norm. The case studies in Dickens, Eliot, Brontë, Yonge, and James show us how care communities operate and why they fail, and we can use them to deduce principles to guide us when we attempt to foster such communities ourselves.

I begin this introduction by analyzing how care's communal dynamics might inform our reading practices and our understanding of character formations. I explain why it matters to understand care as an action rather than a feeling, and then I develop my key term, the "care community," by showing its roots as a mechanism for survival among people of color, queer people, disabled folks, and radical activists. Just as characters can be understood relationally, not only as individuals, so too human flourishing can be read in terms of care communities, not only nuclear families. Using a wider lens can show us more ways of envisioning people in combination with one another.

Care and Theories of Reading

Communities of Care originally formed amid a body of criticism that seeks to produce an ethical, positive, creatively affirming form of reading.[5] Eve Kosofsky Sedgwick began this trend in "Paranoid Reading and Reparative Reading," where she refashioned Melanie Klein's theory of paranoid and depressive states into what she called paranoid and reparative readings.[6]

Having replaced "depressive state" with "reparative reading," however, Sedgwick found it difficult to define reparative reading practices without sounding "sappy, aestheticizing, defensive, anti-intellectual, or reactionary."[7] Today reparative reading is associated with what David Kurnick describes as a "hortatory, cheeriness-mandating critical tradition . . . that sometimes appears to operate as if the announcement that one speaks reparatively were sufficient to repair anyone in hearing range." The aim of this book is to make reparative reading into a rigorous practice.[8]

One way to define reparative reading is to compare it with its opposite, paranoid reading: for each trait of paranoid reading, there must be a corresponding reparative function.[9] Paranoid reading is a strong tautological reading that treats everything as proof for its conclusions, implying that reparative reading would need to be a weak reading that admits case-by-case divergences and requires individualized applications. Sedgwick posits paranoid reading as anticipatory, reflexive, mimetic, relentlessly seeking and predicting problems, so reparative reading ought to be other-directed and open to unpredictability and alterity.[10] Paranoid reading litigates a repetitive temporality of sameness, so reparative reading ought to allow for subjectively diverse, multiple, creative experiences of time.[11] Paranoid reading works according to a logic of rigorous public exposure, so reparative reading might privilege private understandings, discursive exchanges, and immersion in others' feelings.[12]

In these respects, paranoid reading sounds like the diagnostic medical gaze, seeking individual flaws in otherwise similar bodies, while reparative reading resembles care.[13] I mean no disrespect for paranoid reading. I respect and try to practice the intensive, professional attention it requires. But this book explores the other side, the reparative practice of care, and the very fact that Sedgwick did not define reparative reading offers us an opportunity to imagine the range of alternative, creative practices affiliated with caregiving.

We might start with the term "reparative." Steven Jackson defines "repair" as "the subtle acts of care by which order and meaning in complex sociotechnical systems are maintained and transformed, human value is preserved and extended, and the complicated work of fitting to the varied circumstances of organizations, systems, and lives is accomplished."[14] Similarly, the disability activist Eli Clare calls for "restoration" as an alternative to "cure," highlighting restoration as a complex, responsive, dynamic interaction.[15] Clare's "restoration" and Jackson's "repair" require thinking of breakage as something that affords opportunity, not as a defect to be fixed. In this respect, Jackson's theory is indebted to the Heideggerian concept of "tool-being": only when objects break do we become aware of their being, their qualities and materials.[16] Lenses that work are transparent; lenses that break make us conscious of the way glass cracks. We stop taking them for granted.[17] The broken tool requires us to adjust, extend, and maintain systems. Moreover, breakage can be valuable in another way: it stops an abusive system. As Sara Ahmed points out, "To transform a system we have to stop it from working."[18] Breakage offers a kind of creative refresh. Thus, valuing repair also means seeing the beauty of breakage, loving the bodyminds that behave differently, noticing the creative potential in their play against norms. To repair is not to erase, but to think deeply about the usability of an older, inherited mode: to think about what it offered, why it ceased to function, what can be maintained or transformed for later use. In that sense, repair is a temporal bridge that connects the past to the future.[19]

A reparative reading, then, would update, preserve, translate, and explain the past to a new audience. It would seek the cruxes, knots, or gaps that critics are trained to spot. It is, in Jackson's nice phrase, "articulation work": fitting parts to wholes, calibrating and adjusting.[20] This idea turns what is broken into an opportunity for repairing and reaching out, and it positions us, perhaps, as the restorers of literary, formal, and cultural knowledge that is disintegrating. We literary critics do "articulation work" when we explicate a historical discourse to a modern reader. A reparative reading is historical criticism as a form of care.

If we want to do reparative reading, then, we need to embrace a carefully attuned relation with each particular text in which we can value what is broken, be patient with the past, and repair it to survive for future others to enjoy. It is a protocol. It is a methodology.

This introduction is not the place for a point-by-point definition of care—that will come in chapter 1—but I want to posit two important definitions for now. First: care is an action, not a feeling. Reparative readers attend to the needs of the text no matter how they feel about it. In ordinary life, we have all given care because we cared about the recipients, but we have also given care because we were paid to do it, because we had to do it as part of a job, or because there was simply nobody else around who could. "Caregiving" differs from, and need not derive from, "caring." The acts and the feelings run on different tracks, and although they can intertwine and produce each other, they can also remain separate. Sometimes the feeling comes first: parental love can motivate you to change the diaper. But sometimes the action performatively generates the feeling: change enough diapers, and you may come to care about the person you are helping. Care actions and caring feelings can also remain distinct, as in the case of therapists or medical personnel who try to keep their feelings detached from their work. In short, while care actions and caring feelings are intimately intertwined, they are not the same, and we can't always predict which will produce the other.

Second, good care is fluid; "parties are not stuck in their positions as carers or cared fors."[21] Marian Barnes explains that in a care network responsibilities operate among all members, for "interdependency is multidirectional."[22] The care dynamic is a complicated, flexible set of actions among multiple actors in a social relationship. Crucially, the fluidity occurs through communication (which may, of course, be nonverbal): the carer tries to ascertain whether an action will work, and the cared-for acknowledges it; when the care has been extended and acknowledged, someone else's needs can spring up, to be in turn queried, met, and acknowledged. In reparative reading, a text can meet our needs by comforting us, and we can meet its needs by explaining its qualities to others. Socializing can be a constant exchange of microcaring acts.

For instance, think about how the carer and cared-for roles slip around in a familiar situation from academic life: a question-and-answer period after a talk. A questioner may need the speaker's help to understand the argument, but the speaker also needs the feedback provided by the questioner. If this exchange goes well, both sides will be both giving and receiving care, in a fluid dance performed without conscious effort, the only indicator of successful mutual care being each participant's sense of tacit satisfaction.

However, such nicely mutual relations belie real labor conditions. The case of the talk is no exception. Here the cleaning staff has prepped the room for the comfort of the speaker and audience, who do not return care to the cleaners. (If anything, they leave behind more mess to clean up.) There is no mutuality in this scene; indeed, they will probably not even meet one another. The cleaners' work is invisible labor. Susan Leigh Star and Anselm Strauss have explained that two ways to invisibilize work are rendering the worker unseen (the attendees at the talk do not see the cleaners) and teaching people to take the work for granted (since attendees expect the floor to be clean, they don't notice that it is).[23]

Invisibilized work is a big part of care, and this book attends to the conditions of mechanized labor, service work, and global migration that constitute the reality of paid caregiving today, along with the more mutual bonds of voluntary communal care. A successful theory of care needs to account for exploitative power dynamics as well as egalitarian mutual care. Here it proves helpful to stress care's status as an *action*. As such, it can be contractually protected and adequately renumerated, whereas it is much harder to recompense a vaguely generous, sentimental impulse. If care is a thing you do, it can be subject to regulations. Sympathy is harder to itemize.

Activity can also point us toward interesting ways of reading personhood. Literary critics are used to imagining that a character's acts reveal a deeper inner self, but for caregivers, feelings can develop in antagonism with public acts, or in ways that are intimately shaped by those acts or remain quite independent of them. In other words, a character's acts do not necessarily reveal a deeper self. And what is true of caregivers may be true of all characters (perhaps we should call them "care-actors").[24] We need to read in a way that diverges from the surface/depth model, exploring ideas of character that are performative, accumulative, diffused, fractured, interdependent, generic—that is, reading character without the concept of the unique inner core. Moreover, the fluidity of care invites us to read relationships rather than people, interpolating even readers and authors in a constant dance of mutual attendance.

This expanded idea of character may be clearer if we return to the vignette of the speaker and the audience. On the one hand, we need to note that care occurs without much regard to the participants' specific identities—anyone could be the speaker, the questioner, the cleaner. Care theorists call them carers and cared-fors, stressing that anyone can step into and out of those roles. The slots of "speaker," "questioner," "cleaner," and "audience member" are simply placeholders that anyone could occupy. Yet at the same time, we all know that their specific subject position does matter. White men are still more likely to be the speakers, while women of color are more likely to be invisibilized cleaners. In assessing such scenes, we need to assume that these slots are fundamentally open—we can't argue that different bodies should step into those roles unless we believe these roles ought to be genuinely available—but at the same time we need to acknowledge the historically determined specificity of the bodies that are allowed to inhabit each role in reality. The lenses through which we read are actually giving us binocular vision, simultaneously registering the formal openness of the slot and the actual identity of the person. They feed one another. This person is a professor; professors look like this sort of person.

However, we experience binocular vision only when the two lenses are in balance. When there is a fracture, when the specific person actually clashes with the general role, that is the kind of creative breakage that makes us notice the system's failure and prompts us to begin reparative work. A good breakage happens when the person who is a professor is darker, younger, more female, more trans, than the generic idea of a professor.²⁵ The space between the type and the individual is what provokes political action.

In conventional literary studies, character as generic type is often assumed to be an early model, later superseded by the rise of the individual. Critics generally agree that medieval literature used allegorical characters embodying qualities, and that many early modern characters were not full psychological beings in the modern sense. Michael McKeon notes that

> before the modern period, the category of "personal identity" itself lacks the substance it has for us because people tend to conceive of themselves less as individual persons who join together to make social wholes than as components of social wholes that are already given. Character is a primarily a fact of kinship, family, clan, tribe, lineage.²⁶

During the eighteenth century, however, interest shifted "from . . . characters that typify to those that specify—what literary critics and historians have identified as the rise of the individual and subjective interiority."²⁷

The emergence of the modern novel form facilitated the development of characters with unique, complex, deep psychology. In inventing the novelistic deep character, the story goes, we learned to see ourselves differently. Nancy Armstrong famously argues that fictional characters were the first modern subjects, and that readers learned to articulate their selves by reading the novel, while modern writers worked to elaborate the figure of the individual.²⁸ The novel's "primary criterion," insists Ian Watt, "was truth to individual experience—individual experience which is always unique and therefore new."²⁹ The conventional literary history I have been rehearsing lays out a progressive narrative—often encapsulated in "the rise of the novel" arguments—that starts with rudimentary types and rises to the climactic achievement of individuality in the modern novel form, although Deidre Shauna Lynch shrewdly argues for reading the shift to unique, individual character as a consumer choice rather than a cultural achievement. She argues that it became a kind of status symbol for readers to show they were capable of eliciting the subtle elements of deep character, so the invention of this form can be read as a market development rather than an advance toward the recognition of an innate reality.³⁰

Yet through the nineteenth century, allegorical types still haunt character, in spite of the presumed primacy of individualism. In *The Historical Novel*, Georg Lukács famously argues that Sir Walter Scott used characters who were representative human types to show how historical forces affected people, and he ascribes this style to fiction written before 1848.[31] Recent research on Chartist fiction, the industrial novel, and the social problem novel confirms that these genres produced from the 1820s to the 1840s tend to feature types rather than unique individuals, partly because of their strong links to the radical press.[32] We recognize this generic tendency in Dickens, who so often wrote characters as types (probably because he was so influenced by melodrama), as in *Our Mutual Friend*'s trio of dinner guests, Brewer, Boots, and Buffer. In nineteenth-century fiction, men are often deployed in vocational identities—the industrialist, the worker, the organizer, the clergyman—while women tend to disappear into service roles like housekeeper and governess. Daniel M. Stout aims to

> steer us away from a view of the period as one in which a monolithic individualism replaced the older forms of a collective England. Certain forms of collectivity (for example, Chartism, the aristocracy) were undoubtedly in or on the brink of decline in the early nineteenth century, but other forms of collectivity were also appearing in the period ... like the business corporation or the romantic nation.[33]

Not only did collective forms persist, but new ones emerged, like pollution; as Stout points out, how do you hold a specific agent liable for fogs, or clouds, or dirt, or contagion?[34]

Collective action and corporate personhood remained integral to thinking about character in the nineteenth century, often coexisting with the realist model of interiority, making the reader toggle between seeing figures as specific persons and as types. In *Bleak House* (1853), Mrs. Jellyby and Mrs. Pardiggle may be named individuals, but they represent types of philanthropic action; Jo is both an individual with a particular personality and a generic representative of a category of indigent children who were "dying thus around us every day."[35] Catherine Gallagher's reading of *Middlemarch* (1871–1872) brilliantly evinces this dual movement, as Eliot constantly negotiates "the strife between type and instance, between reference and realization."[36] Eliot constructed her characters both as examples of types, like Saint Theresa, and as atypical selves, people who have particular lots. We need to be able to affiliate Dorothea with a category in order to understand her, but we need to see how she differs in order to believe in her.[37]

Instead of assuming that a unique inner self generates certain surface acts, so that the acts reveal the inner self, we might consider what happens if we move to the knottier, weirder psychologies visible through caregiving. What would that do to types and individuals? One possibility is that we learn to see them as simultaneously present. Stout sees a "permanent strain" between collective personhood and individualism, intertwined and inextricable, locked in the dynamic Gallagher describes.³⁸ Literary character, then, may not trace a historical progress from type to individual, but rather may be the arena in which both stand, a space defined by an ongoing relationship between the two sides. But another possibility is that one disrupts the other. What if repeated acts of caregiving do not reveal deeper feelings of caring at all? What if a character's public acts are detached from—or even at odds with—a real core self? How do we read a character if her public speeches and deeds conceal (instead of revealing) an inner, authentic core?

This problem is particularly true of caregivers in the nineteenth-century novel. In a good care dynamic, the roles of carer and cared-for constantly switch—but many care dynamics were not good in the nineteenth century, and they are not good now. Service workers may be structurally consigned to the exhausting carer role, while disabled people may be constantly forced into the disempowering role of cared-for. Getting stuck in those roles can damage one's selfhood. If a caregiver feels pressure to become invisible, the chance to develop (or to learn how to recognize or express) particular unique selfhood may be threatened. A cared-for who constantly receives personalized treatment may develop an excessive sense of centrality. Getting stuck in either a caregiver or cared-for role can wreck the psyche in different ways, as caregivers don't register their own individuality and cared-fors don't see themselves as types. These divergent ends are not accounted for by the balanced, binocular vision of the individual/type. Such care-actors need a different theory.

The most influential theory of fictional characters, Alex Woloch's, is based on an industrial model and thus does not quite account for the forms of subjectivity we see in caregiving. In brief, Woloch argues that the novel invokes minor characters in order to make them vanish, either by enfolding them or by expelling them. Minor characters, he famously claims, are "the proletariat of the novel," serving the needs of the protagonist and the narrative while their own selfhood gets suppressed.³⁹ Everyone strives for majorness, and the novel is the site of their battle for supremacy. For instance, here is Woloch's account of Dickens:

> The protagonist might be continually overwhelmed, but as long as he holds on to his position as central character, the world of minorness never *completely*, or substantially, overwhelms him. In all of Dickens's novels, minor characters persistently wrest attention away from any privileged, central figure—but they never *succeed* in destroying the asymmetric structure that condemns them to minorness.⁴⁰

This agonistic model matches the Victorian experience of industrialization, in which people were pressed into service as interchangeable cogs, serving the factory owner–protagonist at the top. This economic and political perspective is compelling. Nobody would quarrel with Woloch's assumption that people ought to be able to achieve a fuller human existence, nor that industrialization dehumanized its workers, and it is his humane insistence on this necessity—his insistence on imagining an ethical alternative all too infrequently present in the texts themselves—that qualifies *The One Versus the Many* as a form of reparative reading.

However, if we test Woloch's model with caregiving, we run into problems. Caregivers—and other nineteenth-century subjects—were not necessarily struggling to express unique selfhood. If anyone could do so, it would have been white, middle-class, male, liberal individuals, but even so, they often had to follow a cultural script to take the jobs their families secured them and to exercise the values of duty, earnestness, piety, prudence, and self-discipline. Nineteenth-century exhortations commonly insist on people learning to accept their roles so as to become content with the station in which God had seen fit to place them. If people did not want to be wives, mothers, soldiers, or servants, or to work in the inherited farm or business, that was their problem, and it was their duty to learn to conform and be grateful. Such acquiescence in one's own categorization needs to be taken into account when reading character. Minor characters might not be struggling to reach the top, but rather to come to terms with the type of their own minorness.

Service was one of the largest employment categories in Victorian Britain.[41] Work as a companion, a governess, a nurse, or a servant—or even as a shopkeeper—was a different kind of economic model from factory work. It required a performance of emotional affect, a public effort to demonstrate complaisance, affection, or respect that did not need to match the person's authentic emotion and would not have been necessary amid the roar of industrial machinery. If industrial labor featured the kind of physical struggle Woloch describes, service work depended on a private dynamic of feelings. Such caregiving did not usually eventuate in a battle for mastery but was more likely to produce an internal struggle, a desperation to sustain an authentic sense of self when the job made that self disappear. We might think, for instance, about the poignant fact that Grace Poole has so grim a life, so minimal a self, that it is nearly impossible for Jane Eyre to believe she is laughing. Grace, like other caregiver minor characters in Victorian fiction, is not struggling for primacy with the protagonist, but trying, like other companions, governesses, servants, and nurses, to survive in an economic regime of emotional labor.

Another salient fact about care work in the Victorian novel is that it normally is a group activity. In the fantasy world of the novel, caregivers often join a care community that mystifies their labor to refashion it as a voluntary, leisured, feminized activity, as in *Dombey and Son* (1848) when Susan Nipper's paid nursemaid job is superseded by her spontaneous adherence to her mistress. Mediating between the lonely individual and the indifferent crowds, the community offers a form of organization that is both emotionally gratifying and endlessly adaptable, for its members can shift among various tasks—ameliorating each other's condition, addressing internal dissensions, or acting in solidarity against outside threats—while its amorphous size and fluctuating nature allow the reader to imagine herself a part of the group.

What if, instead of looking at individual character, we consider community relations? What if we leave behind the particular character's type or individual problem in order to zoom out and pan over a larger field? We might then focus on the functions that different agents perform in the group, the way those relations shift, the development of feeling over time, or the way a person's place in a community might be consolidated not by whom that person is but by what that person does. Communities direct our attention to duration, disindividuation, performance, fluctuation, communication. These are very different qualities from what literary critics have traditionally sought in characters: depth, uniqueness, individuality, authenticity, and feeling. They are also very different qualities from those of the crowd, a newer subject of critical interest: flaneurship, population, biopolitics, and urbanism.[42] Between the individual and the crowd, the community lingers—a lived experience, a nostalgic vision, a fictional world.

Because care communities are flexible, they can operate across barriers. As we shall see in this book, care communities can link multiple authors from different eras. The diffuse sociability of the care community might include the fictional, the dead, the text, and the reader. For Victorian audiences, a successful novel might have counted as one that conjured up a community of texts. They might reach out toward the reader, perhaps even by direct address, demanding that we respond and intervene to save suffering children, to consider proper actions in an unhappy marriage, to find the information the detective requires. Instead of asking who a character truly is, we might start asking who cares for whom, and how—a question that may lead us to disregard the boundaries of the text. Breaking the fourth wall, the care community can alter what we imagine to be the components and personnel of the space of fiction.

Modern Care Communities

The communal structure of the Victorian novel is not foreign to us. Some of us live with extended family or in families of choice, and most of us spend the bulk of our daily lives in small groups of unrelated people working together: coworkers, classes, teams, departments, congregations, neighborhoods, colleagues, coalitions, unions, clubs, friends. Communities of care can form around any kind of need: a group working on a project, a team trying to win a game, students working on a final paper, contributors to a collection. In each case, people give mutual care for a shared aim. A good class can become a care community. One might even see the periodical, the conference, the coauthored work, or the collection as printed forms of communal labor, since they represent the mutual labor of multiple people working to fulfill a need. Watching workplace sitcoms with ensemble casts allows us to revel in a fantasy care community not unlike the groups that form in Dickens novels.

Care communities help us survive, as witnessed by the fact that we keep producing them. Many of us crave the sensation of being securely ensconced in a group whose members sustain one another, but it is rare to find explicit advice about how to make this group work.[43] Usually we figure it out experientially, but we can also absorb lessons from fiction. Think, for instance, of the contrasting cases of Mrs. Pardiggle and Esther in *Bleak House*. Both enter the bricklayer's cottage, but the residents are offended by Mrs. Pardiggle's domineering presence, her monologuing, and her inappropriate assigned reading, while Esther successfully activates the tools that characterize a care community: fluid discourse, mutual respect, and voluntary participation. Both produce these effects through acts, not preexisting feelings, for the bricklayer's family are strangers. To be clear, I am not advocating that each of us turn to Victorian fiction for life lessons, and I certainly would not advise anyone to take Esther Summerson as a role model. Rather, I want us to read care relations as foundational concerns of Victorian culture and to recognize the remarkably rich, complex representations of care relations in these novels, for they were produced in a culture whose members had lifelong experience with communities of care.

Also, please do not think I am hoping to transform all small groups into mutually loving care communities through the magic of Victorian fiction. I want to stress this: not all small groups can or should become communities of care. Some small groups need to focus on an external desideratum, not attend to each other. Think, for instance, of audience members watching a film, customers eating in a cafeteria, or passengers waiting to board a plane. People might also be enmeshed in hierarchical structures marked by obedience and deference, as in the military, or systematizing bureaucracies in which members are processed, as in a state agency. They might perform jobs at separate stations, like checkout clerks at a register. In such cases, the disposition of bodies is a giveaway: they are parallel or in a line, oriented toward the thing they want, not each other.[44] People coexist neutrally in such structures, or even compete, even though they are occupying the same space. More ambiguous cases can be found in collectives organized to express shared interests: political advocacy coalitions, book clubs, fan groups, knitting circles, sports teams, classes. These groups can easily transform into care communities as participants bond and start to take care of each other, but they can also remain friendly yet distant coalitions of people who continue to focus jointly on something beyond the group.

This is perfectly fine: many groups should not turn into care communities. In an urgent situation, or a situation where large numbers have to be managed, a streamlined protocol may be more efficient than the kind of free-flowing, egalitarian conversations that characterize a care community. In a case where efficiency is the goal, the slow, personalized adaptability of the care community may be exactly the wrong approach. If the goal is improvement of labor conditions, large-scale unionization is certainly a much more useful route. If the group wants to effect political change, a pragmatic coalition can work better than a social group with complicated internal relationships.[45] After all, care communities are small, personal groups that are not designed for external change but for individual members' comfort, and their tendency to dissension can make them inappropriate mechanisms for swift decision-making. Care communities are not good for generating major social or political change, but they are good for helping people thrive. And when enough people can thrive, they can produce change.

Given this book's immersion in Victorian texts, my readers might expect me to place this analysis in the context of the ideal of feminine service. The unpaid labor of the "angel in the house" is often mystified as voluntary, delightful self-sacrifice, while the physical work of care is represented as an unpleasant burden. The white, female, middle-class carer spreads sunbeams to the sick in her heavenly ministrations; meanwhile, another carer, very often a person of color, empties bedpans and wipes up vomit. These two roles, one fetishizing care and the other debasing it, may seem like polar opposites, but they operate together. In a kind of pincer move, both work to "enlist, elicit, or forcibly extract the unwaged labor of women and the many others (typically, but not always, people of color) from whom it has historically demanded uncompensated or barely compensated care work," writes Micki McGee.[46] Whether care floats loftily above renumeration or seems too debased to be worth much, people get it for free either way.

It is perhaps a sign of the value of a care community that its structure resists this dehumanizing version of care. A care community flourishes on the premise of fluid care among everyone in the group. This is true even in texts produced in the heyday of the feminized ideal. Florence Dombey, for instance, is an iconic "angel in the house," yet her care communities include Sol Gills, Cap'n Cuttle, Wal'r, Jack Bunsby, Mr. Toots, Susan Nipper, Edith Dombey, and the dog Diogenes—a group diverse in gender, class, age, and even species. Indeed, care communities in Victorian fiction often depict military men as better caregivers than mothers, showing that care communities can license a different way of imagining care beyond the ministering angel.[47] The rest of this book will show that Victorian care communities are diverse, fluid groups. Jane Eyre's care community includes the moon and the tall grasses. Miss Flite's has birds and scraps of papers. Maggie Tulliver has a particular volume of Thomas à Kempis. Victorian care communities are not sentimental retreats but sophisticated adumbrations of the comfort to be found in relation with the outside world: the nonhuman, the dead, the disabled, the trees, the sky, the voices of the past, the feel of a book, the imagined reader, the future.

Thus, while discussions of *care* need to address the history of care as a feminized, maternal practice, discussions of *communities of care* can take their warrant from other experiences, other ways of being in the world. And those other experiences offer hope: along with the many sustaining, supportive, diverse groups in Victorian experience, they include queer extended families, grassroots movements, radical coalitions, and indigenous and disability self-care collectives. Hiʻilei Julia Kawehipuaakahaopulani Hobart and Tamara Kneese stress that "care contains radical promise through a grounding in autonomous direct action and nonhierarchical collective work. Instead of only acting as a force for self-preservation, care is about the survival of marginal communities because it is intimately connected to modern radical politics and activism."[48] Care communities offer "the survival of marginal communities," however, not because of "modern radical politics," but rather, because of deep structural histories that have helped people survive for centuries. The care community is no modern innovation.

Care communities are not innovative substitutes for a white Western nuclear family norm. Rather, the nuclear family is an exception—a short twentieth-century blip—in the long-term, robust tradition of collective social life. In 2016, 20 percent of Americans lived in multigenerational households, and that number is on the rise.[49] In 2000, only 23 percent of households in the United Kingdom were traditional nuclear families that consisted solely of parents and children; patterns were similar in the United States, Europe, and Australia.[50] This is not a very different figure from the one in the 1851 census, in which 36 percent of English households contained only parents and children.[51] Thus, even for the past 150 years— even during the supposed heyday of the nuclear family—two-thirds of British people have been living in alternative social structures.

This book's account of care communities, then, is rooted in the forms of communal care that constituted ordinary life in the Victorian period, but we can also locate those forms in the strategies developed by people of color to survive enslavement and economic oppression; the long-standing practices of communal inclusivity practiced by indigenous people; the extended familial care expected in Asian and African cultures; the collectives of disabled advocates giving mutual aid; and the robust, joyful networks of queer families of choice. The particular culture I study has affinities to many, many others engaged in this widespread practice across space and time.

Care ethicists have a particular interest in care work in the global south and welfare issues in developing nations.[52] In cultures where care is understood as a shared responsibility rather than as a burden to be outsourced to an institution, people develop innovative care protocols. Asian cultures, for instance, strongly value care for elders, family members, and neighbors, as reflected in architecture that facilitates cross-generational relations, in the cultural value placed on respectful relations to objects, and in the Confucian value placed on mentorship.[53] Vrinda Dalmiya connects care theory with the Mahābhārata to develop a cross-cultural feminist epistemology, and Ocho Onazi uses an African relational community ideal as the basis of his proposals for legal philosophical reform.[54]

Queer families of choice—the voluntary bonds forged by queer people as alternatives to the nuclear family—may be the most recognizable mode of care communities in modern life. Kath Weston described the dynamic as long ago as 1991 in *The Families We Choose*.[55] As people reconfigure their lives around intimate relations with friends rather than biological kin, and scholars call for "a new sociology of affective life" that can "register a fuller range of practices of intimacy and care," the family of choice invites new ways of theorizing relationships.[56] Perhaps a relationship is what you make, not your bond to those to whom you were born. Perhaps relationships, like care, are performative: repeated acts actually build the feeling that we normally assume to have predated it. Rather than "be" kin, Elizabeth Freeman asks, "what would it mean to 'do kinship'?" Drawing on Bourdieu's model of "practical kinship," she concludes that "kinship is a set of *acts* that may or may not follow the officially recognized lines of alliance and descent, and that in any case take precedence over the latter in everyday life."[57] "Doing kin" is, of course, what happened when extended Victorian families took in poor relations, unmarried aunts, ex-servants, neighbors, friends, and apprentices. The queer family of choice allows us to think about temporality, relationality, and community in ways that will resound throughout this book.

Queer relationality builds on the well-known Black practice of generating "fictive kin"—naming some people as honorary relations. This is particularly visible in "other-mothering," a way of producing communal child-care arrangements that helped the children survive when Black mothers were forced to be absent.[58] Fictive kin and other-mothering extended, enhanced, and diffused family, directly combating enslavement's appalling redefinition of human beings as property, and of human relationships as ownership.[59] These honorific "mother" and "aunt" relationships recognized affinity, propinquity, and capacity to care, rather than biology. Indeed, "racial, ethnic, and working-class communities have maintained expansive notions of kinship that supersede the genealogical grid, a fact reflected in many ethnographic studies of these communities," writes Freeman.[60] Such care practices can even include the dead, as Ruha Benjamin explains: "In the broadest sense, what is at stake in the idea that Black Afterlives Matter is the practice of making kin, not only *beyond* biological relatives, but also *with* the materially dead/spiritually alive ancestors in our midst."[61] This evokes a continual communion that acknowledges but reaches beyond death itself, seen in the memorializing currents of Christina Sharpe's *In the Wake* and M. NourbeSe Philip's *Zong!*[62] A similar yearning for a continued interaction with the dead in daily life appears in Victorian ghost stories and mourning practices.

Indigenous cultures also maintain a robust tradition of communal care that transcends categories. Kim TallBear explains that her Dakota tribe's extended kin networks include sexual and spiritual relationships instead of monogamous pairings. Often indigenous relations to the natural world feature mutually respectful acknowledgment of and cooperation with nonhuman beings, for "indigenist ontology and epistemology . . . are based on an understanding that reality is relationships. We are our relationships: to self, family, Nations (other peoples), our environment, ideas, ancestors, the cosmos, everything that IS. . . . We are not all separate entities that are interacting within relationships—we are the relationships."[63] Relationships that include the ecological and the cosmic allow for vastly more inclusive notions of community.

This does not mean that communities are necessarily harmonious. Indeed, the term "community" can be misleading, sometimes referring to a larger population ("the queer community") rather than a small intimate network, so activists often choose other terms, such as "pods," "care webs," or "care collectives."[64] Moreover, when people imagine a community, they often tend to romanticize it. "'Community' is not a magic unicorn, a one-stop shop that always helps us do the laundry and be held in need," Leah Lakshmi Piepzna-Samarasinha reminds us.[65] In fact, a viable community must accommodate dissension. Its members have to communicate because tensions will always arise over whose needs come first, who gets resources, who requires more. In Audre Lorde's famous words, "Without community there is no liberation, only the most vulnerable and temporary armistice between an individual and her oppression. But community must not mean a shedding of our differences, nor the pathetic pretense that these differences do not exist."[66] Piepzna-Samarasinha chronicles the difficulties she encountered in trying to establish care collectives for queer disabled people of color, which sometimes disintegrated in exhaustion or painfully erupted in interpersonal conflict. Piepzna-Samarasinha also attests, however, to the radical building of joyful, mutual support when her care collectives throve. Her work was harder than that of my Victorian subjects, who were able to assemble care collectives amid a thorough cultural comprehension of their aim and structure. But Piepzna-Samarasinha's testimony shows that contemporary radical activists can produce better ways of living in the world by building on indigenous and Black relationality.

Such lessons were not lost on the activists of the spring of 2020 as they fought for racial justice and found ways to sustain one another amid the coronavirus pandemic, a systematic practice of "mutual aid," as Dean Spade has described it.[67] Activists harvested the results of decades of thinking about and practicing communal formations in the explosive growth of "self-organized voluntarism" like "informal child-care collectives, transgender support groups, and other ad-hoc organizations."[68] Small groups sprang up to help their neighborhoods, often keyed to individual blocks. These were the kinds of groups that Karma Chávez defines as coalitions—queer political activism enabled by different groups fluidly joining for strategic purposes.[69] But one revelatory aspect of the pandemic self-organizing was that it was practiced not just by radical activists, queer reformers, and people of color, but also by people who associated with mainstream causes: religious organizations, neighborhood associations, schools. In the absence of a national federal response to the pandemic, these local collectives provided care to their members. At the same time, a new language of appreciation for caregivers emerged to thank those invisibilized workers who continued to provide medical care, clean buildings, and deliver goods at significant risk to their own lives. The pandemic produced a better understanding of caregiving and a more pragmatic sense of the usefulness of care-community structures that may resound into our shared future.[70]

The Black Lives Matter protests in the early summer of 2020 taught people about another use of care communities: their role in criminal justice reform. Restorative justice circles offer an alternative to policing and incarceration.[71] As Danielle Sered explains, our culture focuses on punishment, but restorative justice instead defines crime as a harm to be repaired through meaningful work by the responsible party.[72] Educational reformers have also adapted the indigenous practice of talking circles to resolve school conflicts, arranging small groups in which everyone is on the same level and everyone must hear each other.[73] "No one is at the head of the table in a circle; no one is at the top. While the harmed party's voice is central, its centrality in no way diminishes the value or importance of the responsible party's voice—or the voices of support people who are present," Sered explains.[74] Restorative justice relies on guided communication among members to work out meaningful ways of coming to terms with the past, meeting each other's needs in the present, and building a better future.

Interestingly, talking circles demonstrate that communal solutions can be artificially imposed. They don't have to derive from inherent affinities. Other-mothering and queer families of choice unite people who already have common experiences and a desire to be together, but talking circles bring together people who have harmed each other and who are likely to feel fear, guilt, and dislike toward each other. Yet it turns out that by using the simple physical prompt of the circle, making sure that people are seated on the same level and in a configuration that orients them toward each other, one can facilitate the work of acknowledging, repairing, and reforming. Like care, like kinship, communality can begin as a series of repeated acts, with the feeling coming later, if at all.

We already live in multiple collectives, and many of them are online. Our social media circles can function as virtual care communities—after all, being virtual does not mean they are not real. We are already in personal networks (neighborhoods, departments, clubs, political coalitions), extended familial relationships (animist, queer families of choice, othermothering), and social media groups. The question is, do we want to push these groups to be care communities, remembering that the community of care can have disadvantages to counterbalance the meaningful emotional sustenance it provides? If so, how might we set out to repair these communities, to register their breakages, and to translate them into new forms for future use? Digital collectives already have many of the qualities necessary for viable care communities: fluidity, permeability, mobility, diffuseness, inclusivity, discursivity, egalitarianism. What they do not always have is care. Participants in a social media discussion are more likely to attack than help each other. We have a machine for communal relations that runs on anti-care, extremism, and hatred; how might we do reparative work instead, training users to see each other as subjects to whom they could extend care?

Beyond Living in Care Communities: How to Think with Care

My training equips me best to be a close observer of textual representation and analyst of cultural patterns, and those are the skills I hope to contribute to this shared endeavor of recognizing and sustaining care. We certainly need large-scale legislative and economic change. But the small care exchanges we all engage in multiple times a day form part of that mission. Studying the relationships in the literally thousands of literary care communities in the Victorian record can teach us how to do care, not only in the stories where care works, but also (perhaps especially) in the cases where care goes awry.

The theory I am drawing on in this book is called "ethics of care," and while most of the time I focus on its "care" component, here at the beginning I want to articulate that "ethics" fundamentally informs and motivates this project. I believe that care communities have an inherent ethical component because they are relational structures that require dialogue and respect for others and are driven by the ability to put someone else's welfare above one's own, even temporarily. Inherent in good care are concepts that I find profoundly valuable: attending to others, acknowledging others, helping others, respecting others.

We need a culture in which care is a shared responsibility, as well as supported, respected, and renumerated. We started to do this during the pandemic, applauding health care workers and thanking the delivery people, mail carriers, and grocery workers who literally kept us all alive; for the first time, the heroic quality of daily acts of care became obvious to an entire society. In this book I hope to contribute by helping us view our everyday activities through the magnifying lens of care, helping us isolate and intensify certain acts. I want us to learn to see the constant small acts of ordinary socializing as care: holding a door for someone carrying packages, offering a guest food, disciplining a child, mentoring an intern, fighting fires, greeting strangers, liking posts. Ethics of care argues that all social relations consist of care exchanges—care that is negotiated, refused, allowed, recalibrated, exchanged—and that it is crucial to see care as the connective tissue of social life. Care needs to be redefined as a practice we are all already enmeshed in, regardless of gender. But precisely because it has been historically practiced by women, treating care as significant is already feminist. Ethics of care is a lens that helps us see care everywhere, instead of viewing it as a form of traditional women's work, a burden consigned to underpaid, exploited workers who are overwhelmingly people of color, or a sentimental idealization of a white, feminized "angel in the house." Rather, care acts make social relations functional.

Care communities only work well if the members behave well, and there are particular forms of bad behavior—lying, silence, exploitation—that can destroy a community of care. Because we are all involved in such communities, it is crucial to understand what makes them function or causes them to fail, and to learn how we can intervene to correct the experience. Most of this book addresses Victorian fictions that feature problematic care, but one lesson these texts teach us is that even substandard caregiving can make all the difference. In reading these texts, I have been touched to notice over and over again that the honest attempt to care—no matter how ineptly executed or poorly planned—often seems to be enough to sustain people.

Such a vision of a voluntary care community that muddles through to help someone may well be precious to us today, held as we are in the grip of neoliberalism, global capitalism, police brutality, racial injustice, and ecological catastrophe. But it was also cherished by the Victorians, who themselves endured, and in some cases created, these threats. Victorian people lived in an infamously hierarchical and essentialist culture that remorselessly tracked people according to race, gender, and class, monitored their time and movements, and regulated their emotions. It is no wonder that they sustained a compensatory fantasy of a different kind of social relation. In canonical and noncanonical texts, in realism and sensation fiction, in Regency and fin-de-siècle writing, the community of care shows up, the persistent dream of a voluntary, cooperative, egalitarian group of helpers. The delineation of what Miriam Bailin calls the "tender, reciprocal, and mutually constitutive" relations between nurse and patient fulfilled a crucial role for Victorians, setting up an ideal that may or may not have been matched in actual experience.[75] And I have tried to respect this fantasy level in my account in this book, laying out what seem to be the optimal ways for care communities to work while remaining quite aware that hardly any actual care communities will succeed in matching the ideal, either in the nineteenth century or now.

For the failures matter too. The failures produce political action. Communities of care cannot do everything; private benevolence is not an answer, neither in Dickens's fervent dreams of a generous rich savior (a Cheeryble brother, a Jarndyce, a reformed Scrooge) nor in George Bush's infamous praise of "a thousand points of light." We need to do care communities right, and we need to have serious national, economic, and legal structures as well. I am interested in communities of care as part of a set of responses to modern life that ought also to include political actions and government initiatives. I hope I have made it clear that the care community is one form of social arrangement among others, and not always the best kind, but that it is a form with a global reach and a long history and a powerful appeal; it is also a form that is small and flexible and intimate enough to make real in our own lives, when prodding a government to act can seem impossible.

Reading for care is empowering. For literary critics, ethics of care can expand what we notice. If ethics of care is a lens, it is a fisheye lens, capturing the edges of the scene; if it is a microphone, it is one that picks up heretofore ambient noise. It reorients us from intensive deep focus on individual characters' deep psychology and personal erotic desires toward the larger purview of the group. Examining narratives for communal relationships, not individuals, can help literary criticism participate in a global re-centering of care that is also occurring in sociology, economics, philosophy, and political science, as later chapters will show. Enshrining relationality as the basis of civic society alters our ideas of value and our aims in reading. It can also help us survive, particularly those of us living on the margins (and these days, so many are living on the margins). I have mentioned that the care community was a compensatory fantasy for Victorians, a haven of tender, egalitarian, affiliative caregiving in a harshly stratified daily existence, but being a fantasy does not make it any less real, or any less necessary, as part of an ethical imagination of how to improve our own harsh world today.

The Chapters to Come

Although scenes of communal care are omnipresent in Victorian fiction, I have chosen particular texts for their chronological resonance, both in their authors' lives and in the period.

Many of the novels I address here are late works (*Daniel Deronda, Persuasion, The Wings of the Dove, Villette*), which often tend to include the most nuanced, complex depictions of care. We might adapt Joseph Straus's characterization of late-style music as "often including bodily features (fractured, fissured, compact, or immobilized)," perhaps "inscribing their shared experience of disability, of bodies and minds that are not functioning in the normal way."[76] So too with authors: returning to care scenes late in life, when they may be in need of care themselves and when they have experienced caring for others, they bring a complex, experiential knowledge to writing about care. In some cases, they are rewriting earlier work that had a much sunnier view of loving care communities, correcting them according to more sober later knowledge.

Many of these novels also date from midcentury, which was a significant turning point in Victorian thinking about bodies and minds. In the first decades of the nineteenth century, subjects tended to understand suffering as a natural part of human experience, ameliorated by ordinary people providing pleasant distractions. But around midcentury, a modern medical idea began to emerge. This new paradigm held a more dramatic view of suffering: a healthy body develops a catastrophic fault that requires a heroic intervention by an expert to cure it. (This might remind us of paranoid reading.) Moving from ordinary suffering to extraordinary pathology, from everyday caregiving to professional cure, the ways of thinking about bodies changed profoundly in the midcentury decades. I have chosen mainly novels that were published in the period of the 1840s to the 1860s, when models of care were changing drastically in ways that authors wanted to address and care communities, now slipping out of reach, were becoming the objects of renewed yearning and fresh visibility.

This is a hybrid project combining Victorian literary criticism with philosophical ethics and contemporary political claims, and I am aware that this multifaceted lens may feel anomalous to readers. I recognize that the multiple agendas at work here may interest some readers more than others, and I want readers to be prepared for variations in subject as we move from the philosophical first chapter to the historical second chapter, embark on three chapters with literary case studies, and then end up at a pragmatic and political epilogue.

I use chapter 1 as a theoretical introduction to the concept of a care community, drawing primarily on philosophy (feminist ethics) and sociology (theories of community). After explaining current work in ethics of care theory, I offer my own definition of care as something that "meets another's need." My hope is that this definition can help us conceptualize care relations not only among humans but also among nonhuman animals, ecosystems, the inanimate, and the ineffable. I stress that care communities require several factors: they must be performative, egalitarian, affiliative, and discursive. While I explain the rationale behind these factors, I also pay attention to their interplay and to the results when they fail. I use Jürgen Habermas's theory of the public sphere as a guide in outlining how care communities work. There are differences between Habermas's public sphere and the kinds of private collectives I am tracking, but they also have a surprising number of parallels that can be mutually informative.

If care communities can be abstracted as structural models, readers (particularly readers who come to *Communities of Care* from philosophy) may wonder: why ground this analysis in the Victorian era? I address this query in chapter 2. Because modern medical professionalism developed around the 1850s, studying this period allows us to see the domestic care arrangements and understanding of illness prior to modern ideas, then trace the slow, uncomfortable transition to those ideas. I offer a theory of "ordinary bodies," based on Rosemarie Garland Thomson's famous coinage "extraordinary bodies."[77] Ordinary bodies are economically marginal bodies ground down by Victorian conditions like industrial pollution, economic stress, adulterated food, and contagion. Chronic sufferers—debilitated people with "ordinary bodies" (invalids, convalescents, incurables)—experienced ameliorative care through their care communities, which devoted their efforts to long-term support rather than heroic cure. I demonstrate how Austen's *Persuasion* (1817) and "Sanditon" (1817) evince a premedical model that relied on communal care to help invalids. But this model was replaced at midcentury, as I show through a reading of Dickens's "A Christmas Carol" (1843), a transitional work that still residually relies on care communities while moving into the medical realm. Literature of the Victorian period thus provides an exceptionally rich trove of accounts of care communities and serves as a complex, varied, sensitive barometer of the lived reality and imaginative extension of a care-based system as it began to give way to modern medicine.

Living through that transition could be agonizing, as we see in *Villette* (1853), the subject of chapter 3. Here Lucy Snowe initially overidentifies in her caregiving but then swings to the other extreme, cultivating a form of caregiving that is wholly divorced from private feeling. While at first this change feels liberating, in the end Lucy begins to feel trapped in a world of fakery. Her caregiving is a performance, not performative, a crucial and nearly fatal distinction. I use Arlie Russell Hochschild's theory of emotional labor to read Lucy as an early instance of a global migrant caregiver in fiction. Reading Lucy as a practitioner of emotional labor can help us develop a new theory of character based not in psychological depth but in repetitive public actions geared to economic survival rather than authentic self-expression. Lucy Snowe, then, is a disindividuated type; as such, she requires a different reading protocol than the usual protagonist. Learning to decode Lucy can help us read Victorian figures who sell their performances of apparent caring, the governesses, companions, and nurses who are the caregivers of the nineteenth-century novel. These often unnamed representative figures require, I argue, an alternative reading strategy keyed to the way care labor affects the subject.

The most influential ethical thinker in Victorian literary work was George Eliot. Eliot stressed the need to learn to think through others' perspectives, a displacement of self that matches core tenets of modern care ethics. In chapter 4, I argue that in Eliot's late work she began to shift from her famous advocacy of sympathy toward something more like an ethic of care. This chapter interrogates how reading for sympathy might be shaping our interpretative practices, and how sentimentality might be differently legible if seen not as a continuation of sympathy but as a blockage of care. *Daniel Deronda* (1876) also demonstrates, however, what it might feel like to give care even if one is privately indifferent to or suspicious of the recipient, exploring how the performative act of caregiving ends up generating caring feeling. In other words, in this last finished novel, Eliot begins to see caring as the result of caregiving rather than as its initiatory motive, and she begins to ask what kind of political difference care might make on a global scale.

Chapters 3 and 4 take a primarily historical perspective on Victorians grappling with care ideas, but the book turns to more abstract theorizing in chapters 5 and 6, where I focus on care as a model for communicative work, asking how discourse generally—and writing and reading specifically—might be imagined according to the structure of care. In other words, if the first two case studies ask how Victorians conceptualized their own changing social relations, the last two ask how those social relations structured their understanding of their writing practice, and whether such a discursive communal model might help us understand literary style.

In chapter 5, I address *The Wings of the Dove* (1902), a novel that shows dramatically how necessary discursive regulation is for care, and just how much damage is done by silence. Initially, it looks as if James is setting up a classic care-community situation, with a dying young woman surrounded by a loving affiliative group ready to support her. But in this case, both sides fail to communicate about the situation. Milly refuses to admit she is ill, while her carers are actually conspiring to get her fortune, a secret plot about which they cannot speak. The silence ends up destroying their lives and relationships. *The Wings of the Dove* makes us think about reading itself as a form of care, in which we require the text to communicate with us as we interact with it. In this modernist text, I argue, the characters' failures of utterance force us to step in and become part of the community ourselves.

The readers' interpolation into care relations in *The Wings of the Dove* resembles the authorial self-image in Charlotte Yonge's *The Heir of Redclyffe* (1853), the subject of chapter 6, for in both cases the imperative to form community extends so far that it incorporates the reader and author. Yonge's novel demonstrates how we can use a care-community idea to think about literary influence in a radically atemporal style. What happens if a novelist imagines Milton, Byron, and Scott not as forefathers against whom she must rebel, but rather as members of an unruly virtual community whose work anyone can appropriate, rewrite, critique, edit, and adapt, regardless of when they lived? Such a communal synthesis is particularly appropriate for women's writing, which often seems to imagine itself as the junction of multiple voices. *The Heir of Redclyffe* not only exemplifies a synchronic, communal authorial voice but also addresses communal life diegetically, for its main character, Guy, has two families—an adopted family that functions as a care community, and a biological lineage that is hierarchical and patriarchal—and Guy's life mediates between them.

In the epilogue, I turn to the care communities of academia, answering this introduction with specific suggestions to generate more humane, mutually supportive practices for citational norms, departmental relationships, committee work, review practices, and teaching dynamics. I want to think about academic work not as a set of individual, entrepreneurial missions, but as a dynamic in which collaborative, synthesized communication makes functional social relations possible. Can we create an academic culture—and a social, political, and personal culture—that furthers the community of care?

Whatever your interest, then, my hope is that the pages to come will meet your need and guide us toward reparative and care-full critique. *Communities of Care* repairs and restores ethics of care philosophy by inserting the foreign matter of Victorian communal practice into the cracks, creating a hybrid theory. If it is an unwieldy, jerry-rigged contraption, all the better. A smoothly functioning tool is purely instrumental and we scarcely notice it, but the tool I am building is so miscellaneous that we cannot help but think of our own relation to it. I want to celebrate the lumpy oddness of a conglomeration of feminist philosophy, disability studies, modern sociology, nineteenth-century cultural history, and literary scenes. What kind of lens would this make? My hope is that care-community theory's components will give it what we need: the flexibility for wide applicability, the strength for reinforced evidentiary validity, the capacity for intense close focus, and the range for reaching to peripheral analogues. An instrument that is part fish-eye lens, part binoculars, part reading glasses, and part magnifying lens could give us all the views we need to achieve a genuinely reparative form of reading.

CHAPTER ONE

Ethics of Care and the Care Community

What would it mean, then, to acknowledge poems and paintings, fictional characters and narrative devices, as actors? How might our thinking change?
—RITA FELSKI, *THE LIMITS OF CRITIQUE*[1]

I at least have so much to do in unravelling certain human lots, and seeing how they were woven and interwoven, that all the light I can command must be concentrated on this particular web.
—GEORGE ELIOT, *MIDDLEMARCH*[2]

IN THIS CHAPTER, I lay out the theory of care communities that will guide us through the rest of the book. People usually understand "caring" as a feeling of affectionate concern, and a "caregiver" as someone who helps a disabled person, generally a home health aide or nurse. But in this book, I challenge the first meaning and radically expand the second. I define "caring" as an action rather than a feeling, and I argue for caregiving as one of the most fundamental forms of human relationality. To give care is to engage in transactions as ordinary as greeting a cashier, packing a child's lunch, or grading a paper.[3] This theory of care comes from the feminist philosophy known as "ethics of care," but I have also developed it by testing its limits, imagining what care relations might look like with the inanimate, the distant, and the self. Along with defining care, this chapter addresses the elements that generate a successful group dynamic. How might this community regulate itself? What does it feel like to participate? What kind of internal assumptions govern its relationships? Within that network, what happens to time, to discourse, to feeling?

If my idea of "care" comes from philosophy, my use of "community" derives from sociology. Modern sociologists have been studying virtual personal networks, a form of communion that depends on imagined ties rather than geographic proximity, and the virtual personal networks they describe fit fictional lives as well as digitally mediated ones. Sometimes community is in the mind. In figuring out how such care communities work, it's been helpful to compare these personally oriented networks with Jürgen Habermas's "public sphere," which is a publicly oriented network. These similarly structured social groups point in divergent directions but can overlap and infiltrate one another. As it turns out, both care communities and public spheres require the same three factors: they involve discursive participation, they insist that their subjects hold egalitarian status, and they operate through performative acts rather than deep feelings.

The care community, then, turns out to be a structure on which political theory, feminist philosophy, and sociological research converge; a structure that, as we saw in the introduction, we all inhabit; and a structure that, as we shall see in the rest of this book, Victorian writers limned in rich detail, drawing on and reimagining their own extensive experiences of caregiving.

What Is Care?

The theory of ethics of care argues that every one of us is alive because others care for us, from our helpless infancy onward, and that every one of us reaches out to help others, in ways as large as parenting and as small as greeting a crossing guard. Enmeshed as we are in networks of obligation, gratitude, and assistance, we need to recognize our own profound social ties. None of us are autonomous; our very selfhood is intermeshed with others. Scholars of ethics of care, including Nel Noddings, Virginia Held, and Eva Feder Kittay, understand caregiving to model the fundamental interdependency of human life and social organization. Aimee Carrillo Rowe puts it well: "The formation of the subject is never individual, but is forged across a shifting set of relations that we move in and out of, often without reflection. The politics of relation is a placing that moves a politics of location through a relational notion of the subject to create a subject who recognizes and works within the coalitional conditions that creates [*sic*] and might unmake her—and others."[4]

In the introduction, I used the metaphor of a lens to talk about using the theory of ethics of care, but in thinking about caregiving itself, we might instead use the idea of a cantilevered bridge, itself a nineteenth-century invention. Anchored to each shore, the cantilever stretches out horizontally into space. An 1889 article in *All the Year Round* explained the engineering marvel of the Forth Bridge: "The cantilever . . . is merely a bracket built out from the shore by welding iron beam on to beam until it meets a similar bracket sent out from the other side. The homely illustration has been used, and may here be repeated, that it is like two men on opposite sides of a stream stretching out their arms to join hands."[5] The cantilevered bridge, not complete until the connection is made, aptly conveys the foundational element of care: relationship. Each side must seek the other by reaching toward that other from its own anchorage, braving the risks of empty space.

If the *All the Year Round* writer imagined a manly handclasp, many care ethicists envisioned a different form of contact: a mother holding a child. Ethics of care's earliest theorists often treated care as a feminine maternal trait, but they were also constantly working to complicate that position. Carol Gilligan and Noddings first outlined ethics of care in the 1980s, and in the 1990s theorists argued that it was a feminist practice to validate and emulate maternal caregiving in particular.[6] Sara Ruddick's *Maternal Thinking* and Held's *Feminist Morality* (both published in the 1990s) use mothering as the master example of care. They are careful to define "mothering" as a practice available to men too, but they embrace the feminist project of celebrating a function traditionally ascribed to women.[7] Although maternalism was influential, some critics felt uncomfortable with what seemed like an endorsement of a domestic ideal steeped in racial and class privilege as well as heterosexist assumptions. Celebrating motherhood risked turning ethics of care "feminine" rather than "feminist."[8] Peta Bowden warns that "celebrations of caring reduce and simplify the range of women's moral possibilities to those displayed in practices of care, and further, that the analysis of caring itself tends to be reduced to romantic stereotypes of mothering—usually those emanating from Western, white, middle-class, domestic relations."[9]

Today the assumption that white women are glad to give unpaid care to beloved members of their family painfully coexists with the economic reality that many paid caregivers must leave their own families behind. A global care chain forms when migrant women hired to care for others have to employ someone themselves to take care of their own families.[10] (The care chain is like a beam welded onto a beam—a risky extension.) Thus, women of color, acutely aware of the history of their inscription as nannies and caregivers, alert to the experiences of deprivation, separation, and exile involved in paid care, may have a very different reaction to the imperative to extend care than middle-class white women. Early ethics of care theory far too often assumed the perspective of the privileged family woman—and what's more, often seemed to justify her self-sacrifice.

Ethics of care tends to cast women as the carers and men as the cared-fors, writes Barbara Houston.[11] If women are supposed to be grateful for long days of unpaid diaper-changing at home, if women are inherently the nurturers for everyone else in the family, then celebrating that "angel in the house" role only fixes them into a perennially subservient relation. Kate Manne points out that women are "positioned as human *givers* when it comes to the dominant men who look to them for various kinds of moral support, admiration, attention, and so on. She is not allowed to *be* in the same ways as he is. She will tend to be in trouble when she does not give enough, or to the right people, in the right way, or in the right spirit."[12] Misogyny is a way of policing that giving, making sure women remain in their subordinate relation to men.

Maternalism, however, can also be an instrument of control. It is a managerial technique by which employers use the performance of benevolence to control their employees. This goes back at least as far as the American Civil War, according to Rosemarie Garland Thomson, who analyzes the maternalist dynamic in which a white woman "rescues" a disabled, often Black, woman, as in *Uncle Tom's Cabin* (1852).[13] Today many live-in caregivers find that their employers offer friendship, gifts, and advice, but then demand information about their employees' private lives in return. It is hard to combat this dynamic in which apparently well-meant caregiving makes the employer feel entitled to interfere thereafter.[14]

Maternalism as sentimental self-subordination, maternalism as insidious emotional control—these are flip sides of a toxic power dynamic in which women get stuck. In the nineteenth century, this dynamic was writ large, onto the entire globe. In Victorian colonialist rhetoric, the idea of care was used to justify controlling a supposedly childlike indigenous population. Colonialism was "made morally palatable by the rhetoric of responsibility and care for enslaved and colonized Others," points out Uma Narayan.[15] Kipling's "The White Man's Burden" is perhaps the most famous example of this kind of care-based rhetoric, in its insistence that the colonizer would "serve your captive's need," patiently laboring to "seek another's profit / And work another's gain."[16] In works like "An ABC for Baby Patriots," women's maternal teaching was explicitly used to instill colonial infantilization.[17] It is no surprise that modern global care chains first formed during the nineteenth century, the first century with an industrialized labor force.[18]

The problematic power dynamic of caregiving, so visible in maternalism, is also well known in disability studies. An aide can overpower a person who is particularly vulnerable, but a caregiver can also be depleted by constant giving. A relationship of care may be incapable of becoming egalitarian. The best that a caregiver can do, perhaps, is to keep asking: Does this feel good? Can you move that more to the left? What if I put it over there? Communication can turn the carer–cared-for dynamic into a finely tuned, constantly adjusted, ongoing relationship rather than either the imposition of a strong caregiver's preferences on a helpless caredfor or a cared-for demanding exhausting impossibilities from the wrung-out carer. Nonetheless, the very existence of the intimate, ongoing carer/cared-for dynamic can make Westerners uneasy. It militates against the ideas of autonomy, liberty, independence, and self-reliance that are so enshrined in post-Enlightenment thought—and care thus challenges profound ideas about what it means to be a subject and what a successful life might look like.

Care also forces us to rethink the private subject in relation to the public good. Full-time caregiving is, as Eva Feder Kittay has written, "a costly morality."[19] Caregiving must be supported by institutional or governmental arrangements. No person should have to carry the full weight of another's well-being without help, and that help must involve structural legislation and financial arrangements. Care makes us rethink not only personal autonomy but also the function of the state.

It was this recognition that pushed ethics of care theorists into a more political stance around the turn of the century. Ethics of care theory really has two distinct "generations," explains Olena Hankivsky: an earlier, more essentialist mode and a later, more political one.[20] For as the 1990s moved into the 2000s, Held and Kittay began to turn their maternalist thinking in a different direction, exploring how care could operate as a feminist political theory.[21] Current theorists now use care ethics to rethink contemporary ideas of caretaking, citizenship, migration, and legislation. Daniel Engster sums up the modern political orientation of the theory:

> Because human beings universally depend upon one another for care, we all have moral obligations to care for others in need. While we can fulfill some of our obligations to others through personal caring relationships, we can fulfill many others only through collective caring institutions and policies. Our moral obligations to care for others thus generate collective responsibilities to organize our political, economic, international, and cultural institutions at least in part to support caring practices and care for individuals in need.[22]

Instead of enshrining maternal feeling, care ethicists now work to uphold the value of a practice traditionally associated with women. Care ethicists fight the assumption that caregiving should be an underpaid, undervalued chore outsourced to our most vulnerable workers and assert instead that caregiving is a crucial practice fundamental to a functional society. Many contemporary care ethicists try to develop ideas for supporting migrant care workers and home health aides. For instance, Kittay advocates a national program, *doulia*, that would support at-home caregivers by paying them, training them, and giving them sick leave and vacation time.[23] Fiona Robinson accurately explains:

> Care ethics is not a claim about women's essential nature, or about women's universal oppression. It is not an exhortation for us all to "care" more, or to be "more caring." Care ethics is a critical feminist theory that seeks to reveal the different forms of power that keep the values and activities of care hidden from "public" view, and to demonstrate the devastating effects that ensue when care is consistently devalued, sidelined, and subordinated to the higher values of profit and military power. As an antidote to the values of neoliberalism, care must be recognized as a social responsibility, an attribute of citizenship, and a basis of feminist solidarity.[24]

Robinson's argument shows how far ethics of care has moved from its early stages, and how different it is from the popular conception that caring is a nice feeling we extend to those we love. Instead, caregiving is a crucial activity in which we are all engaged, one that requires social, political, and governmental support.[25]

This interrelational idea breaks with three centuries of political thought.[26] Classic liberal theory relies on the assumption that people are "liberal individuals in the marketplace, independent, autonomous, and rational," able to make rational choices in everything from market behavior to votes.[27] However, Kittay argues that caring relationships are stronger than rational contracts, and that those care bonds actually "make civic order and civic friendship possible."[28] Interdependency constitutes not only personhood but also "all social organization."[29] The classic liberal monad is not our identity but an artificial construct that is "at best suitable for a restricted and limited part of human life," Held explains.[30] This is a profound idea. If care ethicists are right, then a good government should prioritize supporting social ties, not just aim to protect individual citizens' liberties. Similarly, if care ethicists are right, economic theory should highlight models of cooperative and sustainable economic behavior that includes maternal and domestic ties, rather than competitive resource-mining or neoliberal consumerism.[31] Care ethics, then, undergirds some radically innovative economic and political thought today.

At a more experiential level, however, care ethicists work to interrogate precisely how care operates. They ask questions like: Does care need to be motivated by genuine feeling? Does care need to be acknowledged by its recipient? Are people stuck in single roles, as either carers or cared-fors? How can we balance the imperatives of care and justice in a viable society? What makes care go wrong? Who offers care, and who or what supports them?

Good care requires specific behaviors. Joan Tronto has argued that an ethics of care must demonstrate attentiveness, responsibility, competence, and responsiveness—values that can help us frame the overall care work in a relationship.[32] Noddings has argued that bad care occurs when the carer treats the cared-for as an abstract problem to be manipulated, or treats all cared-fors with a universalist one-size-fits-all mentality.[33] It is also bad care to project one's own wishes onto the cared-for, assuming that the cared-for must necessarily want what the carer would want in her place.[34] Instead, Noddings argues, good care takes a flexible, contingent, case-by-case approach in which the carer practices "engrossment" in another's mindset, as well as "motivational displacement," in which she shelves her own intentions to enact another's.[35] The carer and the cared-for are in perpetual interchange, in a fluid and complex relationship. Jean Keller and Eva Feder Kittay explain that moral deliberation does not derive from the application of universal principles, but rather is "contextual and narrative in approach," "attend[ing] to the particular features of the situation."[36] Acknowledgment is also crucial: care must be completed by the recipient acknowledging that it has been received.

Much depends on how we define care. Some theorists use a virtue-based definition, focusing on whether the carer intends to help, although most use a practice-based definition, in which care means actively trying to help someone.[37] Tronto's practice-based account defines care as "everything that we do to maintain, continue, and repair our 'world' so that we can live in it as well as possible." In this vision, all reparative work is care and presumably includes such activities as cleaning up a riverbed. But at the other extreme, Diemut Bubeck claims a highly restricted case: "Caring for is the meeting of the needs of one person by another person, where face-to-face interaction between carer and cared-for is a crucial element of the overall activity and where the need is of such a nature that it cannot possibly be met by the person in need herself."[38] In Bubeck's definition, care is only care if it occurs between humans in physical proximity and if the carer does something otherwise impossible: feeding a child is care, but making dinner for an adult who is physically capable of cooking for himself is not.

In this book, I try to define care in a way that steers between these two extremes, while hopefully partaking of both Bubeck's precision and Tronto's generosity. Here's my definition: care is "meeting another's need."[39]

Like Bubeck, I stress the cared-for's *need*, not her desires, but this requires some explanation. "Need" must be worked out through dialogue (including nonverbal communication) in each care situation. After all, needs change all the time and vary even within a given task; moreover, as any therapist will attest, talking can make people aware of needs they had not consciously registered. Bubeck categorically states that doing favors is not caregiving, but in my view it is not always that simple, since doing a favor for a capable adult may be meeting a deeper need, like demonstrating affection.

It is important to remember that care is a spectrum, not an on-off switch. Food provides a good example. Weak care, for instance, might come from a food item produced in an assembly-line industrial kitchen, sold in a vending machine or in plastic clamshells in a cafeteria. It is still meeting the diner's need, but it meets only the physical need for caloric fuel. Somewhat stronger care would be a meal produced by a cook in a restaurant, which carries the cook's personal imprint and may meet aesthetic as well as physical needs if served in an attractive way. But the strongest care would be a meal made by a beloved person according to a much-loved recipe, perhaps served on meaningful tableware. The more needs it satisfies, the better the care will be. This beloved person's meal would satisfy emotional, physical, aesthetic, and nostalgic needs all at once, even if it is not professional-quality food. The meal may be inferior cuisine, but superior care.

As the food example shows, the very nature of "needs" resists definitive explanation. Jürgen Habermas points out that "needs and wants are interpreted in the light of cultural values. Since cultural values are always components of intersubjectively shared traditions, the revision of the values used to interpret needs and wants cannot be a matter for individuals to handle monologically."[40] Thus, different care situations need to establish their own goals.[41] For instance, even taking the strongest care in providing food—made from the beloved person's recipe and served on special tableware—can actually be an act of cruelty if extended to someone whose food requirements preclude eating this meal. Prefabricated food may be great care if it is offered to someone who is craving it, like a nostalgic candy associated with childhood.

Care relations are built around another's "need" *no matter what the "need" is*. Care ethics doesn't care why someone needs care. A person might need care for many reasons: sadness, the struggle of second-language learning, the anxiety of being lost or feeling sick. Even good news like acceptance into an elite program might trigger anxieties and self-doubt. Needs may be physical, such as a need for help going to the bathroom or help eating, or emotional, such as the need for reassurance, affection, or guidance. Often needs are both physical and emotional: the person who needs help going to the bathroom may also need reassurance that her dignity remains intact. Obviously, the best care will meet both emotional and physical needs (like the family recipe prepared by a loved one), but care that meets only one need (like the generic output of a commercial kitchen) is still better than no care at all. Care occupies a wide range. The strongest care meets the most needs at once, but weak care that meets just one need is better than nothing. As we shall see in the rest of this book, characters in Victorian fiction often offer weak, poor care that can nevertheless often be (just) enough to sustain its recipient. I am not trying to assure readers, in an inspirational-poster way, that all that matters is to try. Rather, I am saying that if a carer genuinely tries to figure out the cared-for's need, even an inept attempt will give some comfort to the cared-for, some sense that she has been seen.

One reason I am stressing "need" is that it has consequences for disability readings of literary characters. Care is a theory through which we can register that someone needs help and assess how well someone meets that need, instead of wondering precisely what afflicts the characters and trying to diagnose them. (As Michael Bérubé points out, we need "to cure disability studies of its habit of diagnosing fictional characters" and turn instead to the web of social relations in which those characters are enmeshed.[42]) Disability simply becomes a point on a spectrum of need, evoking a response just like any other need. Because everyone has needs, and because need fluctuates, a disabled person, like anyone else, can be seen as someone who needs help sometimes and not at other times. If everyone can need help, everyone can provide help, ranging from strong care (sating multiple needs) to weak care (allaying one need). Redefining the issue as "need" rather than "ability" works against the notion that disability is a particular identity permanently inherent in some people (and determining everything about them) and not at all present in others. It makes disability merely one example of need among others, not an essential identity.

The word "meeting" in my definition of "care" emphasizes that care is an ongoing action, a practice repeated over time. As we shall see, that iterability is crucial to understanding care. Additionally, the word is not "solve" or "assuage"—it does not promise to make the cared-for feel good or to get rid of the problem, but simply to meet the cared-for's need at the time.

To be sure, "meeting" is difficult: it is not always easy to know whether a carer is meeting a need or simply overruling the cared-for. A care relation risks disempowering the participants and provoking conflict. Parents need to be able to say no, teachers need to be able to give a bad grade, and guardians need to withhold the substance that an addict is craving. On the other side, children, students, and patients need to be able to ask for something with the sense that their demands will be heard (if not necessarily granted). It must be possible for a bad grade to be corrected, or a parental refusal to be mitigated; otherwise, the relation becomes tyrannical. Hence the immense importance of dialogue in a care relation. Dialogue is the mechanism by which the carer and the cared-for can curb each other's bad tendencies and collude on a shared protocol, or at least justify their actions.[43] Each must express needs, and the other must listen carefully, attentively, and receptively.[44] Dialogue is how the two arms of the cantilevered bridge can angle accurately and unite properly.

When discourse is not enough to establish genuine "meeting," some form of justice is required. The relation of justice to care has been extensively canvassed, and there is significant work regarding whether care relations are theoretically compatible with policing and punishment.[45] In lived experience, however, the care communities in which we all participate are always backed up (and should be backed up) by laws. In a department, seminar, sports team, club, housemate situation, or religious group, when there are incidents of exploitation, disrespect, or tyranny, let alone theft or violence, people can appeal to higher authorities within the institution and to shared rules that govern that institution and that the offender signed on to when they joined the group, and ultimately to the nation's legal system. Such enforcement is often spotty and inadequate, to be sure, but I am not going to argue that it should not exist. Ideally, care and justice should reinforce one another. In an ethics of care, the first action is discourse, and only when dialogue fails to rectify the situation should one move to enforcement protocols.

In my definition of "care," then, the word "meeting" names an ongoing dialogue that must be supported by disciplinary structures, and the word "need" is defined by dialogue on a case-by-case basis. Together they name a fluid, mutually constitutive relation. To understand how that works, we need now to turn to the two entities who will form that relation.

Perhaps the most important word in my definition is the one I have left out. There is no subject in the phrase "meeting another's needs." A definition with room for anyone or anything to do the work of meeting a need allows us to imagine the carer's identity in the broadest possible way. I have also defined the modifier of the object of the verb as generously as possible, simply as "another's." It doesn't matter who the cared-for is; the cared-for could be anyone. The point is that the cared-for is always "an other," who always retains an alterity that must be respected. As we will see, care's "other" may include nonhuman and even nonliving entities, so that we can analyze agents or actors or beings without reference to their particular animate status.

It is important to establish the origins of this emphasis on alterity, because returning to the philosophical roots of this idea can help us in cases where ethics of care falls silent. This concept derives from a lineage in Continental philosophy that is perhaps most relevantly expressed in the work of Martin Buber and Emmanuel Levinas.[46] Levinas insists that one produces one's own being—and indeed, ethics itself—through the experience of acknowledging the other.[47] He imagines the moment of encounter with "the face of the other," for that irreducibly foreign face makes a demand on us, reveals vulnerability, and establishes our responsibility.[48] The encounter with the face of the other lifts us out of the undifferentiated ego and makes ethics possible by establishing another for whom we must care. Similarly, Buber usefully establishes two forms of relation with the other. He claims that we normally conduct transactional, casual I-It relationships, but he exhorts us to aim for an I-Thou relationship, a moment when we fully apprehend the core being of the one with whom we are in dialogue. The I-Thou relation is, in the words of Maurice Friedman, "a relationship of openness, directness, mutuality, and presence. It may be between man and man, but it may also take place with a tree, a cat, a fragment of mica, a work of art—and through all of these with God, the 'eternal Thou' in whom the parallel lines of relations meet."[49] The opposite of care is simply to use the other for our own selfish purposes, forgetting that other's independent being and failing to recognize the other's alterity.[50] As Heidegger explains in his tool-being theory, we tend to take our tools for granted. Only when a tool breaks do we truly see it. At that point we can encounter its fundamental thingness, a kind of relationship that seems closer to the I-Thou.[51]

We can apply three test cases to an ethics of care: first, people very far away; second, the self; and third, objects. Can we see what Levinas called the face of the other when that other is distant from us? Today we live in a media environment that makes it possible to zero in on individual reactions in the midst of a mass event. A cataclysm may occur on the other side of the globe, but in a virtual age, distance and time are altered; it is possible to see the face of the other and interact with that other. Zoom, FaceTime, Skype, and other apps have changed the meaning of "face-to-face." As anyone knows who has loved ones in other nations, it is quite possible to give and receive care from afar in the digital age. It is harder to give care en masse to a large group. Noddings calls this "caring about" and finds it inferior to "caring for," because it fails to be directed to another.[52]

Self-care is a slightly more complicated case. There is no question that we can nurture ourselves or hurt ourselves, and that we should have some kind of ethical guide to help us foster our own best interests, but does that guide need to be an ethics of care? After all, since care discourse is about meeting *another's* needs, meeting one's *own* needs might not qualify.[53] However, it is true that we sometimes conceptualize ourselves as another—speaking to ourselves, scolding ourselves, and rewarding ourselves—and such a case may qualify as a care relation.

For instance, sometimes we address a version of ourselves routed through an external object. Sometimes we must speak on behalf of the silent other, generating a response on their behalf, which is why caregivers often murmur such sentences as "There, that feels better, doesn't it?" when caring for a nonverbal other. Or more profoundly, we must conduct the cared-for's part of the process, imagining, for instance, when the cared-for might tell us to take a break or thank us.

Such projection on behalf of another resembles the way we identify with fictional characters. This is perhaps what we do when we read and feel for a character—which we should not see as a category mistake, but as evidence of a drive to care that is strong enough to vivify and ventriloquize another. Lisa Zunshine has identified our ability to identify with characters as fundamental to fiction-reading. She explains that "the cognitive rewards of reading fiction might thus be aligned with the cognitive rewards of pretend play through a shared capacity to stimulate and develop the imagination. It may mean that our enjoyment of fiction is predicated—at least in part—upon our *awareness* of our 'trying on' mental states *potentially available* to us but at a given moment *differing* from our own."⁵⁴ To be ourselves and others simultaneously, through the act of reading, is a profound mental pleasure, and I would extend it to the experience of regarding oneself as carer *and* cared-for simultaneously.

Another way of producing self-care via a silent other is to project certain qualities onto special objects in the outside world, thereby endowing the inanimate with imagined selfhood. Laurence Hamilton's paraphrase of Hegel usefully speaks to this: "Recognition involves a process of externalising one's powers in the world, having one's powers recognised by another through the medium of the created object, and accepting one's separateness from the other and the material world via the ability willfully to hand over (alienate) the object from oneself."⁵⁵ In other words, we can mediate relationships through externalizing ourselves in objects that we are willing to alienate from ourselves.

Not only can we do this, but we actually must do it in order to achieve healthy maturation. In Donald Winnicott's theory of the transitional object, the child develops an attachment to a particular item, often a blanket or stuffed animal. Neither fully internal nor fully external, the transitional object traverses the space between the child's psyche and the outside world, allowing the child to negotiate the boundaries of the self. We never lose this need for transitional objects. Adults feel the same strain in matching inner reality to outer reality, Winnicott claims, and our immersion in arts, play, creativity, and religion can generate similar psychic relief.⁵⁶ Only certain objects have this special status. A child infuses one blanket with magic but may be indifferent to all other blankets.⁵⁷ Adults, too, ascribe vitality to certain inanimate beings. Not every thing moves us, but one beloved souvenir, one heirloom dish, one special poem, may speak to us with particularly emotional intensity. We may also remember phases in which we were passionately attached to something whose appeal we subsequently outgrew; thinking of the once-loved item can make us feel tenderness toward our former selves.⁵⁸

In these cases, the person has routed a relation with another version of the self—often a fantasy self or a childhood self—through a song, or a cake, or a blanket. It may be felt that this object has a form of presence, inviting a care relationship directly, or it may function as a mechanism for externalizing the self enough to interact with it as if it were an other. The item cannot know it is caring for us, nor can it do the things that are necessary for care, like inquire how we feel under its ministrations. It isn't active or discursive. But through the force of our drive for caring, we imbue the object with these imagined feelings. If we are making an epistemological error, it is a fortunate one: it makes the world full of comfort for us, and it is necessary for healthy development to be able to have care relations with the inanimate, object relations psychologists argue. Thus, to the extent that a particular artifact gives us comfort, we are in a care relationship, though it may be one we have engineered, a marionette show in which we are pulling all the strings.

Steven Jackson objects, however, that it is important to "care for things *as* things, and not for the refracted glow of the human that we perceive in them."[59] Can we love our objects? We already do: that one really good tool, that soft, much-washed piece of clothing, that personalized phone. Such attachments are, in Jackson's words, a profound form of care:

> To care for something (an animal, a child, a sick relative, or a technological system) is to bear and affirm a moral relation to it. For material artifacts, this goes beyond the instrumental or functional relations that usually characterize the attachments between people and things. Care brings the worlds of action and meaning back together, and reconnects the necessary work of maintenance with the forms of attachment that so often (but invisibly, at least to analysts) sustain it. We care because we care.[60]

Our love for the material world enriches our lives and brings us meaning, but other feelings can surface too. In the case of artificial intelligence, including GPS systems and digital assistants, for instance, the human is supposed to engage with the machine as if it were alive, an interaction that can produce a complicated set of feelings that may include frustration, comprehension, delight, identification, and bafflement.

It is crucial to insist on care relations with the inanimate world, because those relations give us a way to circumvent dehumanization. Care is oblivious to the status of the parties to a relationship. Care names a relationship, and that relationship can develop with anyone or anything, including those that a society debars from the status of being fully human because of race, religion, gender, class, or disability, or because it regards such members transactionally and mechanistically as "hands" or invisibilized executors of work from which others benefit. Nothing puts one beyond the reach of care.

However, there is another way to conceptualize our understanding of a living world. In some indigenous cultures, the world is infused with life, and being present in natural relations requires complex enmeshment.[61] While many of us have such relations with household pets, this animist idea moves further into the natural world, positing relationships with insects, rocks, birds, trees. In Graham Harvey's words, the new animism "refers to a concern with knowing how to behave appropriately towards persons, not all of whom are human. It refers to the widespread indigenous and increasingly popular 'alternative' understanding that humans share this world with a wide range of persons, only some of whom are human."[62] It is, in fact, the very act of entering into discourse that makes natural elements into subjects. Nurit Bird-David explains: "We do not personify other entities and then socialize with them but personify them *as, when,* and *because* we socialize with them. Recognizing a 'conversation' with a counter-being—which amounts to accepting it into fellowship rather than recognizing a common essence—makes that being a self in relation with ourselves."[63] Bird-David's formulation rather wonderfully imagines the articulation of a care relation as that which brings the other into being. Similarly, David Abram deplores the Western habit of seeing nature as empty except for resources we can extract from it; he advocates instead for a respectful mutual relationship with the natural world in which all elements are in harmony. This awareness is beginning to change ecological and legal practices in the West. Under the doctrine of "the rights of nature," natural elements are increasingly being accorded personhood and legal rights. Rivers, lakes, rice, and forests have all been legally recognized as persons.[64]

It is also possible to imagine the entire universe as a network of beings. Perhaps the best-known theory of relations with the inanimate is Bruno Latour's actor-network theory, which argues for seeing assemblages of actants, without regard to those actants' animate status. The social simply consists of the momentary interaction of certain actants regardless of motive or meaning. When we turn on a flashlight, the battery and button and finger are all equally important.[65] Similarly, Jane Bennett asks us to think about "vibrant matter"—about the ways in which we are all knotted into a web of shared minerals and chemicals, so that we have kinship with the material elements of the universe.[66] Philosophers of science are exploring the idea of "panpsychism": the notion that everything in the universe has a capacity for selfhood and perhaps a degree of subjective awareness. Most of us, however, need not go as far as the universe. Our care relations might feel something like Jane Eyre taking comfort from the warm rough grasses on the moor: "Nature seemed to me benign and good; I thought she loved me, outcast as I was; and I, who from man could anticipate only mistrust, rejection, insult, clung to her with filial fondness."[67] From the distant stars to the humble grasses, we can care for things outside of ourselves. In thinking this way, we can develop an ethics of the relation with the inanimate.

In the case of such nonhuman participants, it would be absurd to demand that they follow an ethical code. (Moonlight is not going to alter its trajectory because we think it should.) In this case, the ethics in ethics of care shifts: our enjoyment of nonhuman care imposes a certain responsibility on us to maintain them. It is precisely because we have loved these participants and visualized their caring into being that we must maintain this felt relationship. It is, perhaps, precisely *because* they cannot respond that we love them—they do not judge us, they put no pressure on us, they constitute an absence we can fill as we wish.[68] How we act on an ethics of ecological sustenance, or animal rights, or historical preservation is all up to us. For a molecular biologist, it may mean constructing molecule models with care and affection, as the care theorist María Puig de la Bellacasa points out.[69] Someone who feels a care relation with the divine may require a religious protocol. In this respect, we can see the complexity of a care relation, for the relation between an intimately cherished poem and the person who loves it requires that the person do whatever she can to make sure the poem lives on. "Works of art also need our devotion. Their existence depends on their being taken up by readers or viewers," Rita Felski reminds us.[70] The poem does not know it cares for the person; the person does the care work in return. Art "requires our solicitude and active participation," a "critical ethos of attentiveness, respect, and generosity."[71] A scholarly edition, for instance, in which the editors subordinate their own ideas in the service of the text, is an act of care. Editing a collection, in which the editors work to showcase others' writing, is an act of care.

Let me return to the cantilevered bridge, the two arms reaching from opposite shores, rising toward each other to meet at last. The *identity* of each shore matters far less than the *activity* of building the bridge between them. One side might be a person, and the other side might be a forest, or a child, or a temple, or a memory, or a song. Care sees each extend an arm out toward the other, each arm unfurling to meet the other's need, to reach the face of the other, the I and the Thou.

What Is Community?

This cantilevered bridge image matches care that is a relationship between two entities, but what happens when care operates in a group? In that case, the lines might look more like a spiderweb, spinning out in complex constellations, with multiple tensions, knots, gaps, and pathways that are often unaccountable for outsiders.[72] Care in a group can operate rather differently from the carer/cared-for dyad, and these dynamics—care carried to an order of magnitude more complicated—are the ones that we find in fiction and experience in life, the ones that *Communities of Care* explores.

Whereas ethics of care is a well-developed philosophy, the theory analyzing care collectives is much more scattered.[73] Sociologists call such small affiliative groups "personal networks," and political theorists call them "communities," but their research tends to focus on stable, continuous communities and personal networks—small groups of close friends and relations—rather than the kind of ad-hoc, fluid collectives that spring up at moments of need. They also address lived experiences in the modern world, unlike this book, which focuses on fictional ties in the literary record of two centuries ago. Understandably, there are some differences. Modern Western personal networks average about 18.5 people, a network that remains relatively small and stable, although it accommodates minor variations as members die or move away.[74] Fictional networks are, as one might predict, somewhat scaled-down versions; they tend to include perhaps six to ten people, although they are almost always larger than a modern nuclear family and smaller than an institution. Fictional networks are also more fluid, allowing for quarrels and reunions. These differences arise partly because these characters come together for a specific need rather than as lifelong connections, and partly because authors usually prefer not to handle too many characters.[75]

Today, in the digital era, sociologists are beginning to explore virtual communities in which the participants need not share a geographic space.[76] "Postmodern communities are nomadic, highly mobile, emotional and communicative," explains Gerard Delanty.[77] In Ray Pahl's meaningfully entitled article "Are All Communities Communities in the Mind?," he points out that such mental collectives may be more powerful and resilient than on-the-ground communities.[78] Communal loyalties live in imagination, memory, and emotion, carried in our hearts instead of (or as well as) reinforced through constant contact, and so they lend themselves well to imagining our closest connections as characters. In other words, modern networked communities depend upon, and reinforce, the mental skills required to imagine a community of the mind.

Being able to believe in someone who is not physically present may enable us to credit fictional characters. Mary Poovey has made a similar claim about value: the capacity to imagine economic value as an abstract quality, not located in time or space, enabled people to read fiction.[79] I am suggesting a parallel recognition: it is because we can imagine our communities that we can imagine a fictional world. Or perhaps it is the opposite: perhaps it is because we understand fiction that we can maintain a mental space for our social ties. We figure out how to feel passionate interest in fictional characters and how to conduct real relationships with nonreal people. Having learned to believe in the continuity of a character when that character is not present, we can then perform this feat for our own loved ones too.

In this respect, I would date the social network back much further than sociologists like Kenneth C. Bessant and Pahl, who ascribe it to contemporary digital media; I would link it to the development of the novel in the seventeenth and eighteenth centuries. By the eighteenth century, Benedict Anderson famously argues in *Imagined Communities*, social life "led to a conception of community as 'imagined' rather than as a specific form of social interaction. Indeed, the whole point of Anderson's study was to show that community is shaped by cognitive and symbolic structures that are not underpinned by 'lived' spaces and immediate forms of social intimacy."[80] Pahl's supposition that all communities are "communities in the mind" was already noted by Anderson, who asserts that "all communities larger than primordial villages of face-to-face contact (and perhaps even these) are imagined."[81] The nation and the novel both ask us to imagine numbers of people, engaged simultaneously in different activities, yet all members of one society. While we may take Anderson's point that the novel and the nation reinforce one another by training us to imagine people, I would point out that the novel is a space of community (with perhaps a few dozen characters), while the nation is a space of the crowd (with thousands or millions of citizens). Absorption into the vast undifferentiated crowd is, as I have argued, the opposite of participating in the known, egalitarian community. This difference is perhaps why Anderson stresses that the novel/nation assumes an empty, unmarked calendrical time, whereas in the care community time is often felt to be askew, a subjective chronology overpowering ordinary linear measures. The crowd, manageable by bureaucratic systematization, is amenable to organizational schemas, but the community is not; it is regulated by different mechanisms.

If we want to understand how communities function, we could do worse than turn to Jürgen Habermas's *The Structural Transformation of the Public Sphere*.[82] Habermas argues that the early modern period saw the rise of a public sphere, animated by the voice of an informed merchant class that could act as a check on sovereign power. The intimate world of the conjugal family trained these citizens to articulate feelings through private relationships and sentimental fiction, so that when these educated men gathered in coffeehouses, they could read newspapers and exchange ideas. Through their rational exchanges of opinions, people drawn together by the need to trade or to make political decisions learned to form small communities, which, in the aggregate, became powerful enough to control a king. In Habermas's model, members are drawn together by their shared engagement in rational argumentation, not by where they live, making this model a candidate for the origin of the imagined community. While socially embedded, community members can use reason to transcend that origin. Habermas's later work, *The Theory of Communicative Action*, focuses on the discursive actions that constitute that engagement.[83]

In Habermas's story, the private sphere precedes the public one; intimate conjugal life functions to shape the public citizen.[84] But, as Nancy Fraser has pointed out, the public sphere was not nearly as separate from the private sphere as Habermas imagines. Both were shaped by concerns about money, power, labor, skills, exchange, attachments, patronage, commodities, and information.[85] When a diverse, mobile, literate, coffeehouse-based, newspaper-reading male public emerged in the seventeenth and eighteenth centuries, their wives were engaging in the arguably comparable activities of writing letters, teaching children, hiring servants, helping elderly parents, and hosting gatherings.[86] We might ask whether there really is a significantly meaningful difference between public-sphere men drinking coffee with local businessmen in a café and private-sphere women drinking tea with neighbors in the home. Don't both kinds of activity help consolidate communities that confer power on their members?

Habermas rejects this parallel. He tacitly assumes his abstract citizen to be male and considers familial matters to be merely personal rather than universal political interests. For that reason, Habermas did not consider an ethics of care to be part of the political sphere, maintaining that "the kind of [ethics of care] issues raised by Gilligan belong not to the center but to the margins of ethical theory."[87] The result of cordoning off the personal is to "enclave certain matters in specialized discursive arenas and thereby to shield them from broadly based debate and contestation," as Fraser accurately points out; Habermas closes off private issues while regarding public issues as shared.[88] For feminist critics like Fraser, however, women were always already part of the public sphere, where they might have established "subaltern counterpublics."[89] These are "parallel discursive arenas where members of subordinated social groups invent and circulate counterdiscourses to formulate oppositional interpretations of their identities, interests, and needs."[90] Fraser regards these as "parallel" or "oppositional," but what if they join, or overlap?

It is useful to conceptualize the public sphere as a *politically oriented* paradigm and the care community as a *personally oriented* paradigm.

Because the political and the personal thoroughly permeate one another (as feminists know), it is better to conceptualize them not as identities but as orientations that overlap, engage, and ramify. In a politically oriented community, a member primarily acts to shape national policies, but personal effects may accrue along the way. In a personally oriented community, a member primarily acts to help another in need, but those actions may have secondary political effects. For instance, in a politically oriented community, people might debate the best educational policy, and in a personally oriented community, people might teach; ideally, these orientations ought to inform each other, since the debates should be informed by classroom experience, and teachers can benefit from understanding educational policies. Similarly, debates about inheritance laws, medical safeguards, and elder-care legislation, for instance, should involve both communities. Restorative justice is a good example of a joint practice. It offers the care-community experience of small-group discursive engagement, but it is set within the judicial system.

The care community and Habermas's public sphere work in the same ways. Both are imagined communities that operate through discourse. Both must be open to all, which means that their participants have to disregard the status inequalities of the outside world. Members join because of a common concern, and they work out their shared concerns through a discursive process that extends over time.[91] The most fundamental quality shared by the care community and the public sphere is duration. The care community develops over time. Communities fluctuate, and narratives extend over many pages (in Victorian novels, many, many, many pages).

This sense of extension and duration can help us resolve problems in care theory. For instance, care ethicists often disagree over whether caregiving ought to be rooted in authentic feelings or whether one should professionally sideline one's emotions when giving care.[92] Held argues that parents' caregiving should be rooted in genuine caring, and that they should resort to the inferior substitute of a sense of duty only when good feeling occasionally flags.[93] Held is right: surely parents who love their children care for them better, and children who suspect a lack of genuine feeling in their parents can be deeply damaged, no matter how technically flawless the caregiving. On the other hand, Selma Sevenhuisen is also quite right when she cites a point made by a nursing home director: "Carers [must] avoid 'personal feelings' getting in the way of a professional approach."[94] Professional caregivers who take care of strangers have a different responsibility: to suppress their own personal feelings. Psychoanalysts, for instance, learn to watch out for their own countertransference to their clients. An aide who cares too much may not enforce a painful but necessary medical protocol. A teacher who cares too much may be reluctant to give a fair grade. So there is good reason both to express and to suppress feeling—or at least to learn to modulate it.

One way to reconcile this apparent contradiction is to notice that Held's and Sevenhuisen's arguments actually share something in common: both assume a steady-state condition, an institutional setting in Sevenhuisen's case and a parental setting in Held's. Institutions have stable rules, and parents ideally love their children no matter what. But what if we move to a dynamic care situation?

Community life fluctuates; people are constantly joining, circulating, negotiating, and leaving, and the fluctuations of their feelings help determine their role in the group. Like weather, the community is never the same from one hour to the next, and to understand its overall pattern—the climate, if you will—one has to watch it over time. The web is always spinning, snagging, reforming. Thus, the care community lets us understand caring as a longer-term temporal development, not an on-off switch. This sense of an ongoing process is also fundamental to Habermas's public sphere, which instantiates itself through ongoing debate, rather than simply winking into or out of existence. Indeed, as the Seneca Peace Camp shows, a Habermasian consensual debate can extend so long that it makes action almost impossible.[95]

The care community and the public sphere differ in how they imagine people's engagement in the process. Habermas forecloses feelings from the public sphere. He advocates a "rationally grounded consensus" in which "no point of view is excluded or arbitrarily discounted."[96] This is a Kantian model in which people are free from prejudice, intellectually capable of systematically testing propositions, and "fully autonomous, while at the same time maximally respectful of the other participants in dialogue."[97] Habermas himself describes it as an "inclusive and noncoercive rational discourse among free and equal participants" in which "everyone is required to take the perspective of everyone else, and thus project herself into the understandings of self and world of all others; from this interlocking of perspectives there emerges an ideally extended we-perspective from which all can test in common whether they wish to make a controversial norm the basis of their shared practice."[98]

Such an ideal of the absolutely universal and neutral public sphere populated by detached and rational actors is obviously unattainable in reality, as Iris Marion Young has influentially argued.[99] Fraser argues that it is mistaken to imagine "that a public sphere is or can be a space of zero degree culture, so utterly bereft of any specific ethos as to accommodate with perfect neutrality and equal ease interventions expressive of any and every cultural ethos."[100] The very terms of debate privilege certain cultural norms and actors. Women, people of color, people from non-Western cultural traditions, people with experiential or emotional testimony, and people with unconventional gender presentations will be overlooked, ignored, interrupted, contradicted, and misjudged. We will see what Miranda Fricker has named "epistemic injustice": the unfair discounting of certain people's testimony, which is particularly irksome in a place where we expect egalitarian status like the public sphere.[101]

In a care community, on the other hand, arguments from emotion and experience take primacy, but the duration I have described leads to the waxing and waning of those feelings in crucial ways. Traditionally, care has been thought to be precipitated by a profound concern, sympathy, or sentiment, but as I have been arguing, care and feeling run on different tracks, sometimes but not always converging. If the publicly oriented sphere ignores feeling, the personally oriented sphere, the care community, capitalizes on it, but in a complicated way. To understand the care community in relation to the public sphere, we need to explore its central qualities in more detail. If it is a bridge—or a series of spiderweb strands— how does it get built? What materials, what techniques, what mechanisms, can make it extend far enough to connect its members? How can it be pliable yet strong, extensive yet manageable?

The Structural Qualities of the Care Community

Care communities have five major qualities: performativity, discursivity, affiliation, egalitarianism, and temporality. These qualities don't all have equal status. Two of them, performativity and temporality, are descriptive and apply to care, meaning that when care is working well, we'll probably see these effects. Three of them, discursivity, affiliation, and egalitarianism, are prescriptive for good communities, meaning that when we try to build a care community, we *need* these qualities.

I'm going to explain each quality in turn, but—fair warning—my explanation is complicated by two factors: first, it is rhetorically difficult to describe them separately because each depends on the others; and second, it is theoretically difficult to define them owing to the contingent, case-by-case nature of care. These five qualities operate differently in different care communities, and in this book the variation is wider because I am including nineteenth-century and fictional cases. It may help to think of them as ideal characterizations that, in a theoretically perfect care community, would all coexist inviolably and equally, but to remember that lived care operates across a wide spectrum. In the next few pages, I will try to describe each factor in a way that is definitionally clear while also accommodating its entangled, variable reality.

I have mentioned that duration crucially shapes care communities, so it is perhaps no surprise that duration enables the two descriptive qualities, performativity and temporality. Both rely on long-term, fluctuating developments within the care community.

Let's take performativity first. There's no such thing in the public sphere, although Habermas does insist on a "principle of participation": a public sphere can only work if there is widespread political participation.[102] Every individual rationally chooses to step into the town square to share informed views. But care communities are much smaller, and they function instead through durational participation—care repeated over time. Instead of a crowd moving to a place, imagine those people who show up first to get the town square ready. They engage in routinized jobs: sweeping, cleaning up litter, replacing bulbs, checking the mikes, straightening the chairs. They have done this many times, and they are in the town square too, but their motives differ from the rational choices of Habermas's participants. They may have come to feel pride in the condition of the space. They may have come to care about their jobs.

Care is often performative inasmuch as repeating acts of caregiving can produce the feeling of caring.[103] Nannies, nurses, and aides to senior citizens often come to feel genuine love for their charges. In the classroom, as academics know, months of taking care of our students can make us genuinely feel for them by the end of the semester. Building up granular layers of shared experience over time can generate a powerfully nostalgic, shared affection. While care performativity isn't a hard-and-fast rule, it is a strong enough expectation that when it fails, everyone feels distressed. It really is characteristic of good care, and so when it fails, it throws the whole quality of the caregiving into question. When caring never develops—when an aide remains indifferent to a disabled person, or a babysitter persistently feels cold toward a child—the relationship can become irksome on both sides. When initial tenderness is abraded by the constant demands of caregiving, as when a married couple's relationship gives way to a nurse-patient dynamic, everyone suffers.

Fiction recognizes this performative drive. In *Persuasion* (1817), Anne Elliot must express enough "forced cheerfulness" to get her whiny sister Mary moving.[104] Anne's feeling is initially inauthentic, but as Mary brightens, Anne's condition as her sister's companion improves, so she can start feeling truly cheerful. Nursing generates romantic love and friendships in this novel. After all, Louisa's carers agree that they "love [Louisa] the better for having nursed her."[105] Similarly, when Rogue Riderhood nearly drowns in *Our Mutual Friend* (1865), Dickens demonstrates how the attempt to revive him itself generates affection. The community despises Riderhood, but as they work to bring him back to life, the doctor and the rough sailors weep, shake hands, and express intense joy.[106] In *Dombey and Son* (1848), Susan Nipper is aggressively dismissive when employed as Florence's nurse, but the years of caretaking eventually generate affection that manifests after Susan is fired. In these cases, people develop a feeling by enacting it.

Sometimes performativity fails, and that too is important in fiction. Lucy Snowe in Charlotte Brontë's *Villette* (1853) competently performs professional teaching care for students and collegial friendliness for coteachers, even though she intensely despises both groups of people. The mismatch between her acts and her feelings eventually leads to a breakdown. In her case, it is merely performance, not performativity. *The Wings of the Dove* (1902) is a magisterial study of care in which every single factor fails, and one of the most chilling aspects of its failure is Kate's continued coldness toward Milly under all the circumstances that we would normally expect to produce warmth.

There are a lot of advantages, for literary critics, in reading feelings separately from actions. It allows us to assess actions without intuiting deeper motives, especially the actions of characters who are paid caregivers, such as governesses and nurses and companions. It enables us to understand what emotional labor does to a person's development as repeated acts of caregiving lay down deposits that eventually pile up into a feeling. In that respect, it helps us recognize the class privilege in assuming that one has an innate, unique, authentic core that expresses itself through revelatory, voluntary actions. People who are paid to give care may have a very different sense of character, in that, as Lucy Snowe says, "all within me became narrowed to my lot." Identifying wholly with Miss Marchmont, to the point where she no longer feels her own bodily needs, Lucy's self is externally based, built out of years of intimate assuagement of another's needs. The same is true for Esther Summerson, whose lifelong activities are teaching, housekeeping, and companioning, and Little Dorrit, who, since childhood, has been her family's caretaker, seamstress, and homemaker. Instead of assuming that Lucy, Esther, or Little Dorrit has a private inner core, we need to respectfully interrogate the history of their painful external social construction, the ways in which, from the beginning, their subjectivity was negotiated through exchanges of need with others. It's pointless to ask if paid caregiver characters like Miss Wade, Rosa Dartle, Mrs. General, or Mrs. Sparsit are acting in good faith or are hypocritical; of course their acts may not match their inner feelings, but that hardly matters. The real question is whether each person senses the other's need accurately and fulfills it satisfactorily. The feeling doesn't determine the quality of care because, if all goes well, the feeling is bound to change. What's important is action: if you begin to give care, you initiate the performative process, regardless of your private feeling, and when you enact caring enough times, it will (hopefully) come to feel true.

The second principle, temporality, also derives from the duration of caregiving. Care feels temporally askew, and in that sense it differs from the rigid, fearful, forcefully linear chronology that Sedgwick identifies with paranoid reading, or the empty calendrical time that Anderson identifies with the nation, or the consistent, regular, ongoing rhythm of democratic participation that seems apropos for Habermas's public sphere.[107] But care temporality is none of those things. Based in the rhythms of the body, the surges of emotion, and the difficulty of actions, it has nothing to do with abstract hours. Care time is "crip time"—the time it takes someone to button another's shirt, or to get a person to the bathroom. "Crip time is flex time not just expanded but exploded," writes Alison Kafer. As such, it challenges normative temporalities because "it requires reimagining our notions of what can and should happen in time."[108] Kafer is interested in the experience of temporality afforded extraordinary bodies, the way one experiences slowness, delay, bursts, asynchrony. How might the caregiver come to share in that expanded, elongated, or condensed experience of time? Those who have cared for toddlers recognize the truth of the saying that the days are long and the years are short. "Caring involves stepping out of one's own personal frame of reference into the other's. When we care, we consider the other's point of view, his objective needs, and what he expects from us. Our attention, our mental engrossment is on the cared-for, not on ourselves," writes Nel Noddings.[109] Care time, the endless repetition of small tasks, the sudden alarms, the duration of waiting: you are on another bodymind's clock.

However, when such engrossment in the other fails, we often know it because the caregiver is trying to impose conventional timescales. When the caregiver is checking a watch, waiting for a shift to end, it is a sign of being out of sync with the cared-for, and we may well feel upset if the cared-for is subjected to a strict external schedule that pays no attention to real needs. When Mr. Gradgrind demands the definition of a horse from

Sissy Jupe, ignoring her trembling voice, he is forcing her into a lesson plan that violates the rhythm of her feelings. When M. Paul locks Lucy in the attic for the period he thinks it will take her to learn her lines, ignoring her bodily need for food, he is imposing his own periodicity on hers.

Care offers the experience of an unpredictable chronology. Sometimes time feels highly condensed, as in an immediate medical crisis, and sometimes it feels endlessly suspended, as when sitting in a hospital waiting room. One can get stuck in a kind of perpetual present in which past history and future plans fade out in order to deal with the cared-for's urgent needs. A class can seem to drag on forever, or be over in the blink of an eye. Crouching in the dirt with a child, one can enter into a kind of eternal present.

Different members of the care community can feel time's passage differently. As Isabel tells Ralph in *The Portrait of a Lady* (1881), "I don't want to think—I needn't think. I don't care for anything but you, and that's enough for the present. It will last a little yet. Here on my knees, with you dying in my arms, I'm happier than I have been for a long time."[110] Suspension allows members of the care community to act without dealing with longer-term consequences. In *Bleak House*, Esther Summerson recalls that when she was delirious and experienced all the stages of her life concurrently, she was distressed because "divisions of time became confused with one another."[111] Such atemporality might be confusing, disorienting, boring, or frustrating. In *The Wings of the Dove*, Merton Densher finds the days in Venice endless as he waits for Milly's death. Lucy Snowe forgets to eat or exercise, merged as she is into Miss Marchmont's bodily rhythms.

Care's temporal skew is not controllable or predictable, although its rhythms might sometimes be consoling, providing a slower and more personal beat against the onslaught of the merciless clock and calendar time in the industrial, capitalist nineteenth century. Dana Luciano has identified this immersion in deep time as part of the nineteenth-century experience of grieving.[112] At its best, the care community ideally offers a temporal respite as well as a social haven, a space outside of political, productive, or practical needs. In this respect, it has affinities with queer temporality. Theorists of queer temporality have been exploring the political affordances of finding oneself outside of conventional linear (re)productive time—a subject position that might orient one toward suspension, looking backwards, or toward a utopian futurity.[113]

Yet if queer temporality promotes a consistent orientation to past, present, or future, care temporality is a fluctuating network changing over time, one that affords multiple temporal stoppages, suspensions, reanimations, and readjustments of subjective temporal experiences. Karma

Chávez, addressing a concept of "coalitions" that resembles care communities, writes that "coalition connotes tension and precariousness in this sense, but it is not necessarily temporary. It describes the space in which we can engage, but because coalescing cannot be taken for granted, it requires constant work if it is to endure ... it can describe an enduring alliance at the same time that it can help explicate a juncture that happens to be brief."[114] Paradoxically, community or coalition can be both "temporary" and "endur[ing]."

Because caregiving is repeated over a period of time, when we monitor a care relationship we should be watching for these two qualities, performativity and skewed temporality. Their failure indicates a potential problem in a care relationship. In fiction, they can be red flags.

When we move out of an individual care relationship to enter into a larger care community, three other factors come into play: discourse, egalitarianism, and voluntary affiliation. These three qualities also set off alarms when they fail—but unlike those subjective internal states, discourse, egalitarianism, and affiliation are concrete actions that a carer can intentionally perform. As we shall see in the epilogue, carers can consciously adjust their teaching, parenting, and nursing according to these three metrics.

Of these three, discourse is perhaps the most crucial. Community care works best when mediated through discussion, which can be nonverbal (and always is in the case of an infant); a frown, a sigh of relief, a cry, or a shift of posture can communicate how the care is working. As Nodding has argued, "What the cared-for contributes to the relation is a responsiveness that completes the caring."[115] The growth or success of the cared-for indicates that the care has been received. Along the way, carers and cared-fors must work out their shared course of action together, deciding what kinds of care might be working, what might be tried instead, and what might be usefully dispensed with. Without such discourse, care is a tyrannical, one-sided imposition.

While communication is necessary in all care, the care community makes the importance of discussion particularly vivid, since the cared-fors have to explain themselves to multiple carers.[116] In *Dombey and Son*, Mr. Toots has to ask Cap'n Cuttle whether he can accept Mr. Toots's friendship. The indeterminate state of their friendship becomes a frequent topic of conversation. Similarly, in Charlotte Yonge's *The Heir of Redclyffe*, Guy Morville explicitly describes his filial and romantic feelings to his relations as soon as he notices them himself. These are healthy relationships in which people's needs are expressed openly enough that others can consider how best to meet them. However, when discursivity fails, catastrophe ensues. Guy Morville's cousin Philip keeps his feelings secret, even from himself, and his silence and misrepresentation of his real needs have disastrous consequences. In *The Wings of the Dove*, Milly Theale forbids everyone from mentioning her illness, while her carers, Kate and Merton, remain mum about their conspiracy, producing a regime of silence that forecloses real care.

Discourse is important in both the care community and the public sphere, but it plays different roles in each. For Habermas, discourse permits the rational testing of ideas, although he also stresses the necessity of communication for viable social interdependency.[117] But for the care community, discourse has a much more embodied, immediate aim. Through discourse, members mediate relationships, articulate feelings, react to acts, offer help, inquire about needs. Imagine, for instance, a discussion of which treatment relieves pain best, or which lesson is easiest for the student to grasp, or what food would work best for a child's lunch. In both the public sphere and the care community, the risk is that discourse can take the place of action, for everyone's input is solicited as members work toward consensus, a process that can be so prolonged that nothing ever actually gets done (as survivors of many department meetings can testify). But the two forms of discourse, ideally, converge. A public-sphere discussion of a vaccine's efficacy should be supplemented by testimony from people who have taken or administered the vaccine themselves. The abstract and the experiential need to influence each other.

Intimately tied to discursive experience is another principle governing the care community: egalitarian respect. Elizabeth Anderson clarifies:

> To stand as an equal before others in discussion means that one is entitled to participate, that others recognize an obligation to listen respectfully and respond to one's arguments, that no one need bow and scrape before others or represent themselves as inferior to others as a condition of having their claim heard.[118]

Discourse only works if all the members have an equal right to express themselves and to be heard. In the ideal public sphere, status differences must be bracketed so that rational argument can carry the day rather than the identity of the speaker.[119] Obviously inequalities cannot be erased, but members must temporarily suspend them for purposes of the discussion and to ensure that all are regarded as moral agents entitled to attention, no matter how many resources they possess. Epistemic injustice would violate this egalitarian respect.

In Victorian fiction, it is a widely, fervently, if implicitly held belief that every member of a care community matters equally. Differences of status that might obtain in the outer world cease to determine fate within a community of care. In *Dombey and Son*, the fact that Mr. Toots is a wealthy young man and Cap'n Cuttle is an impoverished, elderly ex-sailor—or the fact that Mr. Toots marries an ex-servant—is irrelevant. In both cases it is the lower-class person who appears to be condescending to the heir by accepting his homage. In *Bleak House*, the wealthy Mr. Jarndyce and the indigent, starving Miss Flite care for Esther and each other. In *Persuasion*, Louisa's accident enables Anne Elliot, the daughter of a baronet, to consort with invalids, ex-sailors, nurses, and near-strangers. Anne, like Florence Dombey, has an oppressive biological family with a neglectful, even abusive father, and both Anne and Florence find relief in a community of care featuring a miscellaneous social mix of varied class, age, status, and even species (since Florence's circle includes the dog Diogenes).

Of all the qualities a care community requires, however, egalitarianism is probably the most problematic. It rarely works perfectly in practice. Certain personalities will tend to dominate, and in most organizations, egalitarianism is allowed only in subgroups, not across the board. Indeed, Anderson has argued that postindustrial economic life in the West fundamentally violates egalitarianism.[120] The difficulty of maintaining egalitarianism, however, is no reason not to aim for it, or at least attempt to institute modified versions of it. To develop a functional group, sometimes some members do have to be subordinated to others. In such cases, we usually live with a tacit compromise: we seek egalitarianism in subcategories, not across the board. In a class, students must be treated equally, but so must the TAs, and if the class is co-taught by multiple professors, faculty must be treated equally. In a family, children must have the same status, but then so must the parents. In other words, one group can rank above the other, as long as the members within each group are equal.

Because the care community is *supposed* to be egalitarian, people can complain when that standard is not met. Indeed, the distress of *Dombey and Son* is caused by such a failure: a parent caring for a son and not a daughter. We know that parents ought to love all their children equally; if we didn't, Florence's tragedy would have little purchase. In the little world of Highbury, Emma is the social leader, but when she insults Miss Bates at Box Hill, it is unbearable for the readers, because we share the assumption that everyone deserves equal respect within the community. One reason the Reed household in *Jane Eyre* fails as a care community is that John Reed is so tyrannical and Jane is so despised. The care community cannot erase real status differentials, but it is tacitly understood that every member must be treated as if they were equal—every student, every family member, every patient, should feel equally cared for. In this respect, the care community resembles Habermas's public sphere, in which each person must be able to have a voice, regardless of his status.

In nineteenth-century lived experience, caring was not nearly so equally distributed. Women were overwhelmingly co-opted into caregiving (we may recall Florence Nightingale commenting that "every woman is a nurse"). Fiction, however, allowed people to imagine a different disposition. In many of these novels, mothers are depicted as inept caregivers who are ejected from the sickroom in favor of an elective group of friends, allowing the idealized egalitarian community to replace the problematic biological nuclear family. Mrs. Curtis is incapable of good sickroom behavior in *The Clever Woman of the Family* (1865), Mrs. Touchett is temperamentally unsuited to nurse Ralph in *Portrait of a Lady*, and Esther Summerson has neither an adoptive nor a biological mother available when she falls ill in *Bleak House*. Instead, Rachel's, Ralph's, and Esther's friends gather around, producing a care community.[121]

This is a value I call affiliation: the notion that carers join the care community voluntarily. Voluntarism generates certain expectations. One of the reasons to treat everyone with equal respect is that nobody had to be in the group; since they all chose to be there, they can leave if their needs are not respected. Affiliation also implies that each member has genuinely chosen to participate, and that in itself entitles each member to respect. Affiliation is the idea behind the Victorian dream of ideal women's angelic love of nursing and mistrust of paid nurses (as we shall see in chapter 2), but it is also foundational to the way all care communities work, as well as all political groups, teams, fan organizations, and personal networks. People choose to join, to put in the time and work to be members of the group, and therefore they deserve respect. When people are forced to participate and do so grudgingly, indifferently, or absentmindedly, the care community begins to disintegrate.

Performativity, temporality, discursivity, egalitarianism, and affiliation: these are the qualities that make care, and care communities, work, and they have implications for literary critics. They challenge us to read literary character relationally and externally. The self may not be a core to be found by digging down deep enough, but a construction, built up by act upon act, like a bridge extended through painstakingly riveting a series of plates. People may not be seeking self-fulfillment, but rather a relation in which they lose themselves so wholly in the other that they enter a strange temporality governed by another's rhythms, pulling the silken threads of the web into new tensions. How do characters express their truest feelings? It might not be through a silent inner monologue, but rather via external discourse as they attempt to express their needs (or offer their abilities) to another. In short, I am advocating for a literary criticism that seeks outward-facing character: characters defined by the acts that relate them to others.

The care community and its better-known public sphere analogue share basic values: egalitarian status, discursive regulation, openness, duration, and active participation. The crucial difference is that the care community is personally oriented rather than politically oriented. Its political interests, which are often very much present, are subordinated to and designed to serve the needs of the other. (By contrast, the Habermasian public sphere supposedly relegates private interests to enclaves, although we may well suspect—and Habermas's feminist critics have insisted—that such interests continue to inform the debate in covert, unacknowledged ways). From this difference, other departures flow: the care community wants to meet another's need, while the public sphere wants to figure out the best policy; the care community coalesces with a certain urgency, while the public sphere is ongoing; the care community converses about personal feeling, while the public sphere members debate logical options; and the care community experiences temporal skew, while the public sphere members do not.

My hope is that this chapter will have allowed readers to understand a schematic version of what a care community is, how it works, and what it does. Care is what happens when we try to meet another's needs, whether that other is as near as our own most intimate self or as far away as the other side of the globe, and whether that other is a fellow human or a rock or a poem. Feeling and caregiving run on different tracks, and although feeling can motivate acts of care, acts of care can just as well produce feeling where none existed before, or they may remain wholly separate. But when a group works to meet that need, certain basic qualities become necessary. Members require communication to justify their participation. Members need to feel they have equal status. Members often experience temporal skew.

But none of those factors is guaranteed. They can all go wrong. They do all go wrong. Communal care practiced over time allows us to see the complexities of change. Feelings alter, performances shift, character morphs. Characters and communities in the novel are produced by the same mechanisms that allow people to sustain social networks in their lived reality, but the novel lets us see, in intense miniature, the results of those choices. The dream of a care community in which each person has a right to speak and each person wants to be there is no less precious because of its rarity. And it is perhaps precisely because of its difficulty and its rarity that we rely on fiction to continue giving us the vision of a perfect, inclusive community of care. Nobody yearned for those communities more than Victorian subjects, because they were enduring the great shift away from care communities toward the modern paradigm of an institutional, medical, professional form of care, and the process made them think deeply about what was lost as well as what was gained. In the next chapter, we shall see how a lived practice of ordinary care communities is gradually sublimated into communities of the mind—or, in other words, how care communities become the stuff of fiction.

CHAPTER TWO

Austen, Dickens, and Brontë

BODIES BEFORE THE NORMATE

Going after a Doctor!—Why, what should we do with a Doctor here? It would be only encouraging our Servants and the Poor to fancy themselves ill, if there was a Doctor at hand.—Oh! pray, let us have none of the Tribe at Sanditon. We go on very well as we are.

—LADY DENHAM IN JANE AUSTEN, "SANDITON"

WOULDN'T A CONVALESCENT SEASIDE community want to acquire medical expertise? But in Jane Austen's last (unfinished) novel, "Sanditon" (1817), when the main character tries to hire a surgeon, he is literally as well as figuratively overturned, and the villagers energetically reject the very notion of a resident doctor.[1] Indeed, as we will see, the absence of a doctor becomes the pole around which much of the novel revolves. If we want to understand the Sanditonians' resistance to medical professionals, we will need to understand what forms of care they endorse instead, and why their specifically convalescent population required a different sort of approach. "Sanditon" reveals an older paradigm of care, health, illness, invalidism, and recovery—it is a town predicated on care.

Up to this point, I have been discussing care communities in terms of their theoretical and experiential continuity with our own contemporary life. In the introduction, I argued that we can find communities of care in diverse global and cultural situations, and in chapter 1 I theorized how those communities of care work. Given my insistence on the frequency with which such care communities appear, a reader may well wonder: why ground this analysis in the British nineteenth century particularly, and why focus on fictional rather than actual social formations? Perhaps the real question, however, is not why I focus on the nineteenth-century novel, but rather, what can the nineteenth-century novel do for us? What might this particular cultural construct reveal to us about how care works in communal settings and about the history of care relations?

In the British nineteenth century, home care was not just an occasional incident but a fundamental mode of social life. Care was a *habitus*, to use Pierre Bourdieu's term, a practice so ordinary that people took it for granted without needing to spell out its tenets.[2] People found "the creation of small, select societies around their bedsides one of the greatest advantages of illness," Miriam Bailin explains.[3] Victorian social practices adhered to a communal norm at every class level featuring large families, cohesive neighborhoods, and crowded schools. "Friends did not form isolated dyads but were normally part of highly integrated networks," explains Carroll Smith-Rosenberg. "Women frequently spent their days within the social confines of such extended families. Sisters-in-law visited each other and, in some families, seemed to spend more time with each other than with their husbands. First cousins cared for each other's babies—for weeks or even months in times of sickness or childbirth. Sisters helped each other with housework, shopped and sewed for each other."[4] In her intensive study of correspondence among early-nineteenth-century women, Amanda Vickery confirms those affectionate, sociable, extended kinship ties.[5] Such ties characterized working-class life, Gregory Vargo explains, as groups clubbed together to buy newspapers, whose articles were oriented toward reading aloud to a collective audience.[6]

The Victorian period thus reveals what it might look like to live in a relational, care-based system, for better and for worse; it is a real-life model of the kind of organization that care ethicists often imagine. It is partly because of this lived practice of constant home care that Brigid Lowe calls the Victorian novel "the medium par excellence for an exposition of a sympathetic politics of care, and an effective vehicle for the perpetuation of the conditions for its realization."[7]

Victorian novels constantly depict people forming ad-hoc, flexible, small groups of caregivers, usually composed of voluntary connections and including perhaps three to ten people. Care communities can form around various needs—particularly loss of money or family—but they form most commonly to help someone who falls ill. In *Dombey and Son* (1848), for instance, Florence Dombey's community of care includes two ex-servants, a local shopkeeper, the shopkeeper's best friend, the shopkeeper's nephew, the best friend's friend, her brother's schoolmate, and her dog. Such care communities appear in most nineteenth-century novels. They feature in almost all of the novels of Jane Austen, Charlotte Yonge, and Charles Dickens; in Elizabeth Gaskell's *Ruth* (1853), *Cranford* (1853), and *Wives and Daughters* (1864); in George Eliot's fiction, particularly *Middlemarch* (1871) and *Daniel Deronda* (1876); and in Henry James's novels, especially *The Portrait of a Lady* (1881) and *The Wings of the Dove* (1902). Many characters assume that their primary role is to take care of others. In *Cranford*, for instance, Miss Matty cannot understand a bank circular as anything other than a request for her to offer care, and she wonders aloud whether they need help with their sums. In Anthony Trollope's *Can You Forgive Her?* (1865), John Gray comprehends his rejection as an imperative to give covert financial care to Alice Vavasor. At the end of *Hard Times* (1854), Louisa gives care to Sissy Jupe's children, and at the end of *Little Dorrit* (1857) Clennam and Little Dorrit take care of Fanny's children. Comically or tragically, we nevertheless have a pattern in which Victorian subjects default to care as the norm for intrasubjective relations. While the chapters of *Communities of Care* will address some central examples, in this chapter I will give briefer case studies from Austen, Dickens, and Brontë.

In the Victorian novel, conditions are ideal for the formation of care communities. Living in small groups, characters constantly observe one another's behavior. (As Austen famously explained, fiction ideally addresses three or four families in a country village.[8]) In the middle class and upper class (overwhelmingly the group represented in fiction), half of the population have no gainful employment and therefore have leisure to care for one another; caretaking is profoundly approved of; and nursing occurs within the home, not the institution. In working-class life, clubs for mutual care and self-education serve the same function. Martha Stoddard Holmes confirms that "ensemble plots construct disability as a feature of community life."[9] In Victorian fiction, care really does take a village. And these fictional villages could boast much more diverse carers than in normative practices. In Dickens's novels, the care community consists of teenage apprentices, homeless street urchins, elderly neighbors, local shopkeepers, and convalescent and wounded ex-soldiers.[10]

People expected home care from women because nursing fit the model of the unselfish ministering "angel in the house." Conduct literature writer Sarah Stickney Ellis, for instance, exhorted women to inquire every morning who needed their attentions, advising them to avow daily:

> I will meet the family with the consciousness that, being the least engaged of any member of it, I am consequently the most at liberty to

devote myself to the general good of the whole, by cultivating cheerful conversation, adapting myself to the prevailing tone of feeling, and leading those who are least happy, to think and speak of what will make them more so.[11]

As we have seen, the first generation of ethics of care theory had some affinities with this gendered Victorian notion. Early care ethics writing by Nel Noddings and Carol Gilligan tended to imagine middle-class home care by women, and Noddings even called the selfless joys of caregiving "euphoria."[12]

Care ethics also feels quite Victorian in its endorsement of "motivational displacement" and "engrossment," the sense of sidelining one's own ideas to inhabit another's thoughts. George Eliot famously taught that the other has an "equivalent centre of self, whence the lights and shadows must always fall with a certain difference." This is closely akin to a foundational definition of care: "To be touched, to have aroused in me something that will disturb my own ethical reality, I must see the other's reality as a possibility for my own."[13] Eliot hoped her readers would achieve "a delicate sense of our neighbour's rights, an active participation in the joys and sorrows of our fellowmen, a magnanimous acceptance of privation or suffering for ourselves when it is a condition of good to others, in a word the extension and intensification of our sympathetic nature."[14] Like Noddings, Eliot advocates learning to put oneself aside in order to enter into another's reality, the condition that she regarded as the high ethical aim of fiction. As she wrote, "The consciousness of the moral law, of right, of propriety, of truth itself, is indissolubly connected with my consciousness of another than myself."[15]

The nineteenth century offers thousands of imaginative works that try out different configurations of communal relations, adjusting, challenging, heightening, admiring, and critiquing the work of care. As Wayne Booth once wrote, "the unique value of fiction" is "its relatively cost-free offer of trial runs."[16] Victorian fiction—particularly big mid-Victorian fictions with lots of characters—consists of groups of people in social relation to one another, and although I am focusing on fiction in this book, it is worth remembering that such care relations also suffuse Victorian drama and poetry. "Aurora Leigh," for instance, sustains a long central dispute about whether care ought to be offered through human relationships or institutional professionalism. Literature is therefore a particularly rich place to see how Victorians were thinking about social change, how they depicted changing care relations, how they justified care, how care turned disastrous, and how care saved people. At the same time, we need to remember that literary texts are not just passive, simple examples of a theory that happens elsewhere. Nathan Hensley reminds us that "literature does not recapitulate thought; it is itself thought."[17] A novel is a way of working something through, trying out variations, modeling likely results. Literary texts challenge their readers, confronting us with culturally alien assumptions and unpredictable discursive complications, in ways that can teach us new ideas about the workings of care. Literature of the Victorian period thus provides an exceptionally complex, varied, sensitive barometer of the lived reality and imaginative extension of a care-based system.

Victorian literature particularly offers a dizzying range of examples of care in the three forms we find most commonly adduced in ethics of care: nursing, teaching, and parenting. While later chapters will attend more closely to teaching (in *Daniel Deronda*) and parenting (in *The Heir of Redclyffe*), in this chapter I focus on nursing. I start with nursing because the nineteenth century saw a fundamental shift in medicine that did not occur to the same extent in parental or pedagogical relationships. In the last half of the nineteenth century, the domestic amateur care community—the group of family and friends who voluntarily provided day-to-day care—was increasingly replaced by hired nurses under the guidance of a professional medical expert with no personal relation to the patient. This pragmatic shift toward paid expertise was accompanied by a shift toward a new way of conceptualizing the body: the emergence during the 1850s of the model that disability scholars call the "normate." The nineteenth century thus affords us a particularly valuable opportunity to see what preceded these modern disability-based structures and to witness the troubled transition and eventual instantiation of our current models. In other words, two excellent reasons for focusing on Victorian literature are that it presents examples of care communities, and that it grapples with their absence. This is a literature that centrally thinks, and mourns, about care.

The Mid-Victorian Shift: The Normate and the Professional

One reason that the characters in "Sanditon," in 1817, do not imagine that doctors are necessary is that there was no particular goal to which doctors needed to bring patients. Health was not yet conceptualized as the basic, default state. Rather, doctors tended to conceptualize disease as an abstract, floating, mobile situation, something that might be carried in the air; particularly in miasma theory, the precursor to germ theory, disease was thought of as spontaneously produced by rotting animal or vegetable matter and spread by the wind, to settle onto particularly susceptible people, including people who felt anxious or sad.[18] Early-nineteenth-century medical theories were also still invested in Galen's model, in which disease affected the whole person.[19] Qualities of health had to be restored holistically, so treatment involved assessing the individual patient's experiences and emotions, bodily symptoms, and characteristics like vigor or fluidity.[20] The Romantic-era physician "treated the whole body rather than isolated parts."[21]

This practice changed as doctors increasingly began to see disease as vested in particular organs and to understand humans as basically identical, so that a disease located in one organ would manifest the same way in every person. Disease became a concrete object, visible in a specific location. "The shift, then, was from healing the invalid to finding the disease," Sondra M. Archimedes explains. "Such an epistemological shift was packed with ideological significance: the doctor became a privileged authority, the patient was disenfranchised, and disease assumed a heightened value, justifying the specialized authority of the 'expert' and maintaining the balance of power."[22] In other words, the patient's status declined while the doctor's professional authority rose. The patient became simply a host in which the interesting material, the disease, could be found by a skillful medical practitioner, whose diagnostic gaze penetrated to the body's hidden flaws.[23] Once those flaws were identified, they could be repaired.

The default mode became "normality." Lennard Davis dates "the coming into consciousness in English of an idea of 'the norm' over the period 1840–1860."[24] Specifically, the modern sense of the word "norm" emerged around 1855, with "normality" in 1849 and "normalcy" in 1857.[25] While later research has found some earlier usage, Davis still seems to be right in claiming that the term did not refer to bodily health until the latter half of the nineteenth century, when divergences from the norm became problematic.[26] "When we think of bodies, in a society where the concept of the norm is operative, then people with disabilities will be thought of as deviants," Davis explains.[27] Rosemarie Garland-Thomson clarifies that this is not just an accidental relationship; in fact, the deviant other is absolutely necessary in order to demarcate the limits of the normate.[28]

The normate developed as part of Francis Galton's eugenics movement, which was an attempt to define human beings statistically so as to breed superior specimens of people. When Galton mapped a statistical average and regarded people who did not fall into that average as deviants, he created both an expectation of "progress" toward normality and a strict template of what the body ought to be. The medical model begins here: everyone is, or should be, "normal," and if they fail to be normal, it is a flaw that must be corrected by a medical intervention. As Garland Thomson puts it:

> The meanings attributed to extraordinary bodies reside not in inherent physical flaws, but social relationships in which one group is legitimated by possessing valued physical characteristics and maintains its ascendancy and its self-identity by systematically imposing the role of cultural or corporeal inferiority on others. Representation thus simultaneously buttresses an embodied version of normative identity and shapes a narrative of corporeal difference that excludes those whose bodies or behaviors do not conform.[29]

In other words, disabled people are stigmatized in order to prop up a supposedly universal normate identity. The conceptual opposition between a normate and a deviant other is foundational to modern disability studies. The common tendency today to assume that disability is a physical flaw subject to external correction leaves more invisible impairments like chronic illness and cognitive impairments in a kind of limbo.

Scholars have used the idea of deviance to develop the concept of "enfreakment." The "freak" is someone with a startlingly anomalous embodiment: someone hugely fat or startlingly thin; someone covered with hair, or lacking limbs, or resembling an animal.[30] The freak shows up throughout Victorian fiction, as in Miserrimus Dexter, the legless character in Wilkie Collins's *The Law and the Lady* (1875), or the enormously fat Count Fosco in *The Woman in White* (1860). Dickens created many such characters, from the little person Mrs. Mowcher in *David Copperfield* (1849) to the cognitively impaired Maggy in *Little Dorrit* (1857). The freak is a figure allied with melodrama and stage spectacles. As critics, we have been alert to freaks because they demand explanation. And there is no shortage of Victorian fiction in which people with extraordinary bodies and minds are subjected to public ridicule; in no sense was this a kinder, gentler time to be disabled.

By its very nature, however, the freak remains a rare anomaly. Spectators consider freaks worth looking at only because they are unusual. And although freaks certainly existed before the middle of the nineteenth century, it is no coincidence that the cases I have mentioned from Collins and Dickens all emerged around or after midcentury, as part of the emerging normate/deviant paradigm. While the nineteenth century does have the dynamic of the freak—the stare, the anomalous monstrous body—the point of this chapter is to show how intimately the emerging model coexisted with the continuing experience of an earlier model, a more holistic view of health and disease.

Scholars have spent a good deal of time excavating ideas of disability before the normate. Davis discusses the seventeenth-century notion of the "ideal" body. Only the gods can have an ideal body, so every human is perforce non-ideal; to create an ideal body, one must select perfect elements from a range of real humans (one person's eyes, another's lips).[31] Its opposite is the grotesque, as seen in cathedral gargoyles and the medieval carnivalesque.[32] However, since Davis wrote *Enforcing Normalcy* (1995), scholars have begun to uncover other somatic models in the medieval and early modern periods, bodies that seemed atypical or anomalous according to discourses of monstrosity and saintliness, prodigies and miracles, defects and deformities. Early modern and medieval medical theories and religious beliefs sometimes offered higher status to disabled people, like the concept of the holy fool or the idea that hallucinations could have been divine visions.[33] These ideas were still widely current in the eighteenth century and continued to have some afterlife in the nineteenth. Travis Chi Wing Lau points out that the eighteenth-century pre-normate model could actually offer "more disability adaptation, flourishing, and resistance" than the medical model.[34]

The pre-normate mode that we see in the early nineteenth century is something we could call "ordinary bodies," playing off "extraordinary bodies," Garland Thomson's term for supposedly deviant, non-normate subjects. "Ordinary bodies" means that impairments were commonplace and unremarkable. Before the normate, it was simply true that people had all sorts of bodies and minds, that everyone suffered at some periods, and that decent people tried to help each other endure those pains as well as possible. This idea fit the mobile, floating notion of disease and the holistic understanding of personhood that Michel Foucault posits in *The Birth of the Clinic*. It also included chronic illnesses and cognitive impairments, and it paid attention to ineffable qualities that the emerging medical model largely ignored, such as moods, foods, and feelings. Disabilities were not seen as rare mistakes to be fixed, but simply a condition of life (particularly given the state of hygiene, sanitation, and medical science in the period). In "Sanditon," for instance, the Parker siblings complain of odd feelings: relaxation, nerves, headaches, apathy, sickliness. These intermittent sensations do not prevent them, however, from energetic traveling and intensive socializing. Their somatic condition can accommodate a whole range of states. Fundamentally inclusive and flexible, the "ordinary bodies" mentality already recognized what disability studies has worked so hard to teach us, namely, that we will all be disabled if we live long enough, that at best we are only temporarily able-bodied, and that we need to accommodate variable and fluctuating capacities in bodies and minds.

Such widespread acceptance of ill health makes sense for the nineteenth century. Jasbir Puar, building on Lauren Berlant, has outlined an idea of debility in which certain populations are victimized by global, economic forces, kept in a state of perpetual ill health.[35] Berlant uses the term "slow death" for such an experience: "the physical wearing out of a population and the deterioration of people in that population that is very nearly a defining condition of their experience and historical existence."[36] Zarena Aslami uses the category of debility to address labor in Victorian fiction (we might think of workers like chimney sweeps and match girls here).[37] But it might not be too much to say that virtually all of the Victorian urban population was debilitated by the force of industrial productivity, bearing the brunt of air pollution, poor nutrition, and inadequate sanitation and ventilation. As one doctor wrote in 1882, "almost everyone is filled with the belief that he is debilitated."[38] We could add industrial accidents, war wounds, dirty conditions, adulterated food, alcoholism, neglect and abuse, and frequent pregnancy to the everyday stressors on Victorian bodies. Women were perceived to be particularly vulnerable. "Medically, the female body was constructed as radically 'other' to the male body, weakened by an unstable reproductive system and subject to mental and physical malfunctions," explains Archimedes.[39] Victorians suffered brain-fever, nervous conditions, consumption, spinal complaints, typhoid, alcoholism, gastrointestinal distress, gout, weak eyes, hearing loss, and rheumatism.[40] For the population that Susan Williams dubs "the diseased poor," conditions were particularly atrocious, with filthy water, lack of ventilation, rotting food, intestinal infections, open sewage, tuberculosis, and rampant epidemics.[41] Most of the daily conditions of Victorian life involved suffering. As Ruth Goodman explains, hunger and malnutrition were omnipresent, slow starvation was common, and Victorians were, quite simply, always cold.[42]

We can see this debility operating in the Victorian category of the invalid or convalescent (sometimes called the "incurable").[43] The invalid or convalescent lived a life in the fluctuating space between health and illness, experiencing attacks and remissions, recoveries and declines, and living what Harriet Martineau memorably called a *Life in the Sickroom* (1844). The invalid's life took on a different rhythm, one not susceptible to "a medical model of symptom, diagnosis, treatment, and response."[44] The focus was on living with a condition rather than seeking medical interventions and, particularly in Christian narratives, on achieving a spiritual attitude of profiting from suffering. The invalid's situation could include both illness and disability. These terms were not necessarily dissociated as they are now, for it was not always possible to tell what particular disturbance caused a person's suffering; indeed, one kind of ill health might morph into another.

The friends and family who supported the "incurable" provided personalized attention, amelioration, and distraction. They gave the reparative, restorationist care I addressed in the introduction. Given the absence of a medical model, what convalescents had was a social network, a care community—social support that ideally made daily life easier.[45] During convalescents' extended periods of boredom, rehabilitation, or irritation, Victorians engaged in "personalized caregiving practices" such as paying them social visits, bringing them interesting novels to read, and preparing pleasant meals for them.[46] The treatment for ordinary suffering, in other words, was leading a nicer ordinary life. Care might involve tender, nonsexual touch, appreciation, communication—forms of alleviation outside the medical care model. In *Romance's Rival*, I argue that the ability to move to such caring touch was one of the main attractions of disabled suitors in the Victorian novels. We might say that this was a preindustrial form of care, one that expressed the carer's personal idiosyncrasies and the cared-for's personal preferences. It was homemade, inefficient, individualized, and unreproducible. This kind of care assumes that the sufferer has an individual history, emotions, and daily experiences that form part of the condition. Such a care community contrasts with the generic rows of beds in the industrial-era hospital, a form of mass care that speaks to the notion that bodies are essentially identical, each manifesting the same organs in the same order, to be treated in the same ways.[47] The community is very different from the crowd.

Victorian invalidism and convalescence were considered intermittent and ambiguous states, with reparative treatments. Erika Wright argues for seeing Victorian health in terms of a continual labor of watchfulness about diet, anxious prevention of risks, evasion of environmental triggers, and management of energies.[48] Convalescence was, Hosanna Krienke writes, "a condition of ongoing recovery and extended uncertainty," in which, as one physician explained, people were "in an intermediate state—neither ill, nor yet quite well."[49] There were attempts to institutionalize care-community treatment through the mechanisms of the medical club and the convalescent home. The convalescent home, which was designed to provide the domestic comforts of middle-class life—because this environment was understood to be the ideal atmosphere for recovering from illness—formed an important alternative to the hospital.[50] Similarly, medical clubs, benefit clubs, and friendly societies emerged in the 1830s as a way of hiring doctors for working-class members. These small collectives, where members pooled their resources to ensure care for all, formally replicated the cultural ideal of the care community.[51] Sanditon, an early seaside resort, is such a structure, a permanently constructed care community awaiting visitors.

The Parker family in "Sanditon" demonstrates this invalid pattern of intermittent swinging between health and illness, with constant "Disorders and Recoveries" that derive from a "natural delicacy of Constitution in fact, with an unfortunate turn for Medecine [which] had given them an early tendency at various times, to various Disorders;—the rest of their sufferings was from Fancy."[52] One moment Diana Parker is declaring that the sea air of Sanditon would be fatal to her, and the next she is journeying to Sanditon. Diana and her siblings Susan and Arthur maintain their precarious health by being constantly alert to risks from air, noise, and food. Diana is both sick and healthy at once, like Schroedinger's cat, and is neither wholly dismissed as a hypochondriac nor pitied as a genuine sufferer. The truth-value of her complaint is less important than the way her apparent somatic needs drive her to initiate or withdraw from social relations. Bodily care, in the prenormate fictional world, is primarily an occasion for moving people around into different communal configurations—a prospect literalized in the town of Sanditon, which was established for the purpose of housing invalids. "Ordinary bodies" signifies a *social* situation, not a medical one; it is, perhaps, the original social model.[53]

This ongoing, residential management of one's daily intakes feels different from the decisive act of calling in a doctor. Diana declares that "we have consulted Physician after Physician in vain, till we are quite convinced that they can do nothing for us and that we must trust to our own knowledge of our own wretched Constitutions for any relief."[54] The Parkers prioritize the experiential felt knowledge of their own bodies, not the diagnostic expertise of the hired professional.[55] The Parkers imagine duration, an ongoing engagement with wretched constitutions. But the medical model has quite a different temporal rhythm, composed of successive sharp climaxes: a disabling event happens, a diagnostic moment occurs, a treatment is administered, the body's fortunes turn toward the cure.

"Sanditon" plays with this prospect when Mr. Parker, hastily misreading an ad for a surgeon, drives his carriage onto bad roads to reach the house that he assumes belongs to the medical man. However, Mr. Parker soon finds that there is no surgeon in the village, and when his carriage overturns, he sprains his ankle. Instead of a decisive medical fix, Mr. Parker must stay at the home of Mr. Heywood, whose wife and daughters care for him for a fortnight, a prolonged home visit that allows the two families to become friends and prompts the Parkers to invite Charlotte Heywood to Sanditon. In other words, the plot is set in motion, and the characters' relationship produced, by the absence of medical intervention, for had the surgeon been present, the Heywood-Parker relationship would not have developed. The story literally goes astray as the imaginary doctor is replaced by the real care community. These opening pages show how an acute crisis is converted into a long-term social relationship.

Medical professionalism differed from care relations in other ways as well, most obviously because it involved a trained man replacing an amateur woman. Disturbing as the "angel in the house" idea is to modern readers, at least it allowed women some mastery in the sickroom. The male professional made that impossible. Professionalism created "skilled service occupations" filled by men who had attained "a professional training in specialist knowledge to be applied in the service of others," in the words of Penelope J. Corfield.[56] Corfield's phrase "in the service of others" is important.[57] From the spiritual ministration of the clergy to the somatic attention of the doctor, to the pedagogical instruction of the educator, the men were being trained to do service work. These were jobs previously done at home, for free, by women. As Monica Cohen has shown, professional service and domestic life had a close resemblance in the nineteenth century, for both were motivated by care for another and both demanded special skills.[58] The sedentary, silent labor performed by lawyers, authors, scholars, and clergymen looked more like female middle-class leisure than masculine work, as Victorians understood it.[59] To give your best labor to help others—to write up rules, or soothe suffering, or teach youths, or compose poetry, or judge art, or offer moral homilies—seemed so feminizing that professional rituals developed in part to consolidate the male professional's difference.[60] The professional's competence, John Kucich concludes, "appropriates, in the process, the psychological and emotional authority of the feminized private sphere."[61] Moreover, the rise of the male professional inculcated a hierarchical system of authority in which a stranger's expertise overruled ordinary people's lived knowledge of each other's needs.[62]

The medical man's ascendancy in the public sphere began slowly, with a small clause in the New Poor Law Act of 1834 that authorized magistrates to call in doctors if the poor became ill. The New Poor Law attempted to replace local parish relief, a system first codified in 1601, with a rationalized, centralized governmental structure that aimed to discourage dependence of any kind.[63] As Lauren Goodlad remarks, "the Old Poor Law had presumed a society of stable communities and face-to-face relationships," while the new system introduced fixed disciplinary rules for civic institutions.[64] People who were accustomed to relief offered through charitable personal bonds "recoiled from the depersonalizing regimentation of institutional life: from workhouse diets, workhouse uniforms, enforced silence, and enervating monotony. Thus, the idea of the workhouse as a corrupt, disorderly, and barbaric place was in many respects indistinct from the equally repellent idea of it as a hyperrational, impersonal, efficient instrument of social discipline."[65] Some tried to push the new regime back toward a system that resembled care communities. Clergyman Thomas Chalmers, who wrote the influential book *The Christian and Civic Community of Towns* (1821), fought to make the new system more community-based by creating parishes and parish schools that were small enough to foster relationships among parishioners, neighbors, clergy, and teachers. In his model of organized charity, "Chalmers envisioned society as an extended family—seamlessly coherent so long as voluntary pastoral relations were dutifully maintained."[66] The care community remained as an ideal for many reformers, charitable organizations, and fiction, even as it was ebbing in reality.

Meanwhile, the medical profession modernized in a messy fashion, requiring decades of legislative and experiential experimentation.[67] The Medical Act of 1858 defined medical qualifications and unified the institutional structure of the profession, creating standard procedures for licensing, training, and registering medical professionals, whether apothecaries or surgeons or physicians.[68] The act itself was more of a symbolic framework than a foundational alteration—many previous practices continued—but it marks a turn toward a vision of medicine as a form of expertise that required training and state supervision, and it insisted on a system of public health. Louise Penner and Tabitha Sparks explain: "Medical authority in Victorian England was fully embedded in social and political infrastructure. We see this in the growth of medical offices in parishes, unions, factories, and prisons, in the advent of public health vaccinations, health inspectors and coroners, as well as in legal measures like the Contagious Diseases Act."[69]

State oversight—controversial, unpopular, and spotty as it was—eventually became a boon for public health. In spite of the New Poor Law's punitive nature, Ruth Hodgkinson credits it with "the evolution of the medical services out of piecemeal rules, regulations, and experiences into a comprehensive system." Because the law required a doctor to be attached to each workhouse, "the National Health Service has its direct roots in the medical services of the Poor Law."[70] The sense that the state would be liable for its citizens' health, that neglect of the poor and dispossessed would be a criminal act, and that doctors had to demonstrate a fundamental level of competence was a major step toward a situation in which everyone would be guaranteed a basic level of health care regardless of their economic status, as opposed to haphazard, amateur nursing in disparate home environments. My interest here, however, is in thinking about the conceptual shift involved in this institutionalization of public health. Medical care turned toward the public and away from the private, became reconfigured as a male job rather than a female duty, began to focus on physical repair rather than holistic well-being, and became a specialized task rather than part of ordinary life.

During this transition, which lasted from the 1830s through at least the 1860s, the doctor retained an ambiguous status: uncomfortably positioned in a residually close social relation with the patient while also shifting toward the role of a paid consultant. Maria Frawley explains that doctors began to regard patients less as suffering humans who required relief and more as "cases," or even "cell complexes"—generators of interesting medical data for diagnostic use.[71] Moreover, "the focal point of a career in medical innovation shifted away from the network of primary relationships with the sick toward a network of secondary relationships with other clinicians."[72] If patients were becoming the stuff one analyzed with one's clinical peers, clearly social relations were shifting. The awkward conflation of economic and personal relationships in the doctor's life resembled the ambiguous situation of clergy, lawyers, and publishers, whose clients expected a neighborly rapport but whose professional status required a measure of detachment.[73]

Victorian fiction registers ambivalence about the move to paid expertise. In Miriam Bailin's words, the doctor's interest in "material considerations of profit, reputation, or the assertion of professional authority" often felt to patients like a "contaminating" influence.[74] In many mid-Victorian novels, good doctors tend to be enmeshed in the social networks of the town as friends and neighbors—for example, Trollope's Dr. Thorne, Oliphant's Dr. Marjoribanks, and Gaskell's Mr. Gibson. Their medical treatment is administered within a rich relationship that involves hospitality, their children's friendships, courtships, family ties, and social calls over the course of years. In *Middlemarch*, set in the 1830s, Lydgate ignores and even despises the community's need for neighborliness.⁷⁵ Focused on his own skills, the young doctor neglects local social ties, and the townspeople's hostility eventually makes it impossible for him to continue his medical work in the town. Similarly, Martineau's Edward Hope in *Deerbrook* (1838) struggles to treat the town when public feeling turns against him. People mistrusted doctors not only for their interest in money but also for their tendency toward medical interventions, which felt dangerous to people accustomed to a kind of steady-state monitoring. Mrs. Taft, a minor character in *Middlemarch*, complains about doctors' "dreadful trifling with people's constitutions." She condemns "Mr. Cheshire, with his irons, trying to make people straight when the Almighty had made them crooked."⁷⁶ In Wilkie Collins's *Poor Miss Finch* (1872), a blind woman is induced to have an operation that restores her sight, with disastrous consequences, and on the other side of the Channel, Gustave Flaubert's *Madame Bovary* (1856) describes an even more catastrophic operation on a clubfoot. These fictions record alarms about medical interventionism.

By contrast, fiction generally depicted amateur nursing as idyllic. "Nursing the sick was, for both men and women, as sanctified an act as suffering itself. As long as it was not for hire, nursing was repeatedly invoked to verify in a way no other activity apparently could the genuineness of one's affections, the essential goodness of one's character."⁷⁷ The nurse not only demonstrated her good character but also directed that virtue into a good relationship.⁷⁸ Bailin explains that in fiction, "the relations between nurse and patient . . . are portrayed as tender, reciprocal, and mutually constitutive."⁷⁹ Familiar examples from Dickens include Joe's kind care for the delirious Pip, Little Dorrit's nursing of the feverish Arthur Clennam, and Aunt Betsy's watchfulness over David Copperfield. It would be hard to find a more dramatic case of mistrust of state care than *Oliver Twist*, for Oliver's experience of bad care at the workhouse contrasts with his paradisal convalescence when nursed at home by Rose Maylie. Oliver would agree with Noddings that caregiving can induce a state of "euphoria."⁸⁰ In reality, of course, nursing could easily render family members impatient, repulsed, inept, and exhausted, but Victorian fiction worked to depict an idealized care community, not the realistic stresses of the situation.⁸¹

By contrast, the hired nurse was often depicted as a bleary, greedy, drunken figure, such as Sairey Gamp or Grace Poole, and accorded little subjectivity. At midcentury, the professional nurse was credited with neither the medical expertise of the doctor nor the loving attention of the carer: she was reduced to nothing more than appetite. This began to change in the 1850s, when Nightingale's reforms and Gaskell's nursing novel, *Ruth*, promulgated a new vision of nursing reform that made paid nursing respectable. By the fin de siècle, we begin to see brisk, efficient, professional nurses in fiction, particularly in the "New Women" novels that explore nursing as a career.[82]

Looking back at the nineteenth century now, we can see an overall, if messy, trend toward centralization, oversight, and governmental control of health and education. The citizens' well-being from birth to death, both physically and mentally, was becoming cast as a public responsibility. This shift to governmental policy, however, in no way reduced people's affinity for a relational, personal, affective form of care—if anything, the shift made it into the subject of intense nostalgic yearning. Domestic care became rarer and more cherished as its role was taken over by paid experts. What we see is the difficult, slow, partial emergence of professional medical expertise, but with a strong continuing cultural preference for amateur domestic caregiving, and that preference was expressed in the stories that Victorians told about themselves. If anything, Victorian writers became even more attached to nostalgia for the enmeshed community once germ theory was developed, writing fictions that resisted the new imperative to isolate, sterilize, and sanitize.[83] We can sense these shifts by exploring texts written before, during, and after the transition to the normate-professional mode, as the ordinary bodies–care–community model begins to move out of ordinary lived experience and into fiction, becoming a community in the mind.

Persuasion *and the Pre-normate*

Before working on "Sanditon," Jane Austen produced a novel about ill health, *Persuasion* (published 1817), whose famously pallid, drooping heroine, Anne Elliot, has lost her bloom. Bodily debility, Puar writes, is "the debilitating ongoingness of structural inequality and suffering," a somatic expression of hopeless economic ordinary life.[84] The theory works in a historical sense as well. After all, rooting somatic decline in economic disempowerment, "the physical wearing out of a population," makes perfect sense for describing dependent single women in the early nineteenth century.[85] Mary Favret links "the repeated bouts of vertigo and dislocation Anne suffers in Wentworth's presence" to the ongoing suffering, chaos, and disorientation of the Napoleonic wars.[86] Whatever pain Anne feels within, to others she is nondescript, a pale, silent semi-presence. Anne's body is literally enacting the invisibilized passivity that characterizes her economic status.

But what is different about debility in 1817 is that it is not regarded as an especially bad plight, nor as something caused by a bodily flaw, and no particular agent is held responsible. It is simply how people live, and it can fluctuate. Anne gets her bloom back periodically. Virtually everyone in this novel has some experience of being impaired by a condition: debility, injury, nervousness, depression, broken collarbone, brain damage, obesity, rheumatic fever. Most of these conditions need to be alleviated over time, and in the most extreme disabling cases, Louisa's and Mrs. Smith's, all that can be hoped for is gradual improvement rather than a cure.

There is one exception. Interestingly, having a handsome body and functional mind often seems to be associated with emotional coldness, as in the cases of Sir Walter Elliot, Elizabeth Elliot, Mr. Elliot, and Mrs. Clay. As John Wiltshire points out, "Sir Walter thinks he and his like are immune from time," whereas the novel actually emphasizes "the changes and vicissitudes wrought by time" and presents "the human body as an object besieged by its onslaughts."[87] The two handsome and lonely Elliots lead an utterly stagnant life. Sir Walter, "at fifty-four, was still a very fine man," while Elizabeth, stuck for thirteen years in the same round of balls and visits, was "still the same handsome Miss Elliot that she had begun to be thirteen years ago."[88] If there are extraordinary bodies in this text, it is Sir Walter's and Elizabeth Elliot's: in a Regency context, the bodies that we would see as normal today seem simply monstrous in their cold and perpetual preservation. These characters have exiled themselves from the ongoing history that has weathered the Crofts, faded Anne, depressed Benwick, irritated Mary, immobilized Mrs. Smith, grieved Mrs. Musgrove, and taught Wentworth tenderness for the weak. Only when one admits the possibility of bodies changing—aging, weakening, hurting—and loving the person through those changes can one admit the idea of historical change, which is perhaps *Persuasion*'s great subject, as Deidre Lynch has argued.[89] Sailors become weather-beaten; women lose their bloom. "It is a period, indeed! Eight years and a half is a period!" exclaims Wentworth.[90]

Care communities punctuate *Persuasion*, becoming successively larger and more powerful. The first and smallest such community begins when Anne visits her querulous sister Mary, who demands that Anne "come to Uppercross Cottage and bear her company as long as she should want her."[91] Mary's request allows Anne to travel to a place where she will be appreciated. *Persuasion* insists on caregiving as the provision of better ordinary life—amusement and companionship—although Mary's care community is so small, limited to her in-laws, that it has internal tensions. The second care community works more harmoniously, for its membership is determined by affinity rather than familial relations. Captain Benwick lives with the kindly Harvilles, siblings of his deceased fiancée, who in turn have befriended Captain Wentworth because he cared for Benwick through news of her death. The Wentworth-Harville-Benwick community deeply attracts Anne, accustomed as she is to the Elliot family's formality. She yearns hopelessly to be part of the group, musing wistfully, "These would have been all my friends."[92]

Louisa's accident both incorporates Anne into the community she yearns to join and extends it. The third care community is the largest yet. Louisa's carers are quite diverse: they include her family (parents, brother, sister) and her siblings' connections (Charles Hayter, Anne, Mary), plus Captain Wentworth; the virtual strangers Captain Benwick and the Harvilles, with the Crofts as concerned but not directly involved connections; and working-class subjects, including the Musgroves' old nursery-maid Sarah and the unnamed workmen who carry Henrietta to the house. Contrast this heterogeneous group with Sir Walter Elliot's chosen community in Bath, a rigidly hierarchical organization of affiliates chosen solely for status. These divergent social worlds disorient Anne, who decidedly prefers the care community to the status-based social scene.[93]

This community operates according to tacit rules quite unlike those in the *Baronetage*. First, its members care for each other, not just for their patient. "Mrs. Musgrove had got Mrs. Harville's children away as much as she could, every possible supply from Uppercross had been furnished, to lighten the inconvenience to the Harvilles, while the Harvilles had been wanting them to come to dinner every day; and in short, it seemed to have been only a struggle on each side as to which should be most disinterested and hospitable."[94] Second, unlike an upper-class hierarchy preserved in the published pages of the *Baronetage*, this community is a fluid group: members move in and out of the circle, negotiating, for instance, whether Mary or Anne should stay.[95] Third, whereas the Elliot family judges by etiquette, this care community valorizes tender feeling, as expressed through both hospitality and poetry. Whereas the Elliot family identifies people through a lineage, the care community emphasizes synchronicity, the mutual exchange of assistance. Within the alternative social vision of the care community is space for relationships not possible elsewhere, such as the nurturing of same-sex ties (Captain Benwick's and Captain Wentworth's mutual devotion), or an unmarried woman's sudden value ("no one so proper, so capable as Anne!"[96]).

Note, too, that the care community takes the place of paid medical professional authority. Only one member is presumably paid, the old nurse, but her affiliation is explicitly presented as motivated by affection. The apothecary is called in for Anne's nephew, and the surgeon for Louisa, but their judgments are paraphrased briefly and then these characters disappear from the narrative. The fullest narrative attention goes to the caregiving that enables social relations to form around the sufferers, generating the plot while producing an alternative to the stratified, formal social hierarchy in which Anne has been immersed from birth.

Anne remembers this care function when she is exiled to Bath, where she rebels against her father's and sister's rules by seeking out Mrs. Smith. The social circle of Anne's friend is even more radically fluid, egalitarian, and decentralized than Louisa's. While "the nobility of England and Ireland" occupy strictly delineated social space, the laborers, nurses, and sick people with whom Mrs. Smith communicates compose an alternative, interconnected, networked version of Bath.[97] It is a vision that horrifies Sir Walter, who sputters: "a mere Mrs. Smith, an every day Mrs. Smith, of all people and all names in the world, to be the chosen friend of Miss Anne Elliot, and to be preferred by her, to her own family connections among the nobility of England and Ireland! Mrs. Smith, such a name!"[98] Sir Walter's disgust is an early indication of the limits of care communities, the moments when the poor, the disabled, and the marginalized are forced to live their debility alone. It also shows that Sir Walter's perspective promotes disindividuation. Anne's friend is not a unique person to Sir Walter, but "a mere Mrs. Smith, an every day Mrs. Smith." She is a type, just as the "nobility" is a type.

Mrs. Smith's fluid community contrasts not only with Sir Walter's strictly hierarchical and already archaic social stratification but also with the individualist model of the self-interested, entrepreneurial *Homo economicus* represented by Mr. William Elliot. Mr. Elliot refuses his moral and legal responsibility to take care of Mrs. Smith, insisting instead on following his own pleasures. Captain Wentworth endorses a comparable type of autonomous self-reliance when he begs Louisa to be as impervious to outside influence as a glossy hazelnut.[99] However, Wentworth's attempt to assume an impenetrable persona does not last, for his real sympathies are with suffering, as shown by the way he is drawn to Anne's weariness. Moreover, through Louisa's trauma and recovery, Austen demonstrates that the self is not like a closed, autonomous monad, but rather is tremblingly permeable, dependent, interrelated. As Adela Pinch puts it: "Louisa is now the opposite of the hazelnut Wentworth held up to her as an image of firmness of mind. She has no 'baked crust of consciousness to parry sensations from the outside world.'"[100] Louisa learns the hard lesson that when you jump, you must make sure someone is there to catch you—perhaps the most elemental example of interrelationality.

Bodily decline makes history visible. If Elizabeth has remained unchanged for thirteen years, Anne and Mrs. Smith have a different somatic reality: "Twelve years were gone since they had parted, and each presented a somewhat different person from what the other had imagined." Two strong, glowing, healthy teenagers have become a pale lady and "a poor infirm, helpless widow."[101] Significantly, Mrs. Smith is not cured. The improvement in her health at the end of the novel is simply due to a better ordinary life, a more varied diet and interests. Nurse Rooke is most useful to Mrs. Smith as a friend and confidante, not as a medical assistant. Nobody ever seems to think of calling a doctor for Mrs. Smith. Pleasant social relations are the way people get through their suffering, and when Anne indulges herself in imagining scenarios of dramatic mortal illness and heroic interventions in the sickroom, Mrs. Smith immediately punctures her illusions.[102] Rather, we have a regime of ordinary bodies: everyone gets tired, feels distressed, experiences pain. That is why everyone needs help with the children, an invitation to dinner, a fellow driver to help pull the reins, a sympathetic listener regarding the in-laws' disrespect. *Persuasion* recognizes that we live in a relational world where "we love her the better for having nursed her," in which both tender friendships and marital pairings flower out of care relations.[103] This caregiving opposes both Mr. Elliot's world of cutthroat capitalism and Sir Walter's regime of hierarchical birth, not to mention the "slow death" of structural inequality (as Berlant names it) to which so many nineteenth-century people were consigned, the single women in *Persuasion*, as well as colonial subjects and the poor. For Austen, writing before "normality," suffering was simply what happened over time, and indeed, how one knew that time had happened.

"A Christmas Carol" and the Fight for Care Communities

Persuasion is fully invested in the "ordinary bodies" model, but this paradigm starts to come under some stress at midcentury, as we can see in "A Christmas Carol," published in 1843. "A Christmas Carol" is one of our most famous disability stories, although Tiny Tim appears in only a few paragraphs and says almost nothing. Yet I want to suggest that Tiny Tim's lack of specific character is not a bug but a feature—not a failure to imagine the interiority of a disabled child, but rather an effort on Dickens's part to affiliate Tiny Tim with the rest of the population of this novel. For this is a novel in which almost everyone is disabled and disindividuated. Dickens needs to pull Scrooge out of his reliance on state management and the crowd, out of his faith in individual self-interest, institutional relief, and the isolated self, and instead lure him into the world of care communities. Dickens achieves this by generating a third type of personhood, between the mass and the monad: the type.

In this novella, the suffering of widespread "ordinary bodies" functions as a way to consolidate different persons into types. In the opening chapter, before the ghosts arrive, we already have multiple figures who are not very different from each other. Scrooge and Marley "had been two kindred spirits," virtually identical.[104] The charity visitors are simply "gentlemen" and "a few of us." Scrooge's nephew has no name yet, and Cratchit is simply "the clerk."[105] Characters seem less like particular figures than representatives of crowds: the misers, the gentlemen, the family, the workers, the poor.

Scrooge reacts to these undifferentiated types by calling them "the surplus population"; he refers the charity visitors to the institutional care of the workhouse and the prison and demands "to be left alone."[106] Like Mr. Elliot, or Captain Wentworth in his hazelnut speech, Scrooge defines himself as an autonomous monad devoted to maximizing his self-interest. He understands himself as an economic agent whose relations are purely financial (supporting public institutions, minding his own business) rather than sympathetic. He is the modern man, a supporter of the New Poor Laws who applauds the new state management of the indigent.

This is the mistake that Scrooge's ghosts need to correct by instilling a horror of isolation and a yearning for communal feeling. First, when Marley visits, the ghosts who forfeited their own chance in life weep for their uselessness, desperate to help those who are still living.[107] Then the Ghost of Christmas Past reminds Scrooge of how sad it was when he was "a solitary child, neglected by his friends."[108] He contrasts this misery with the ecstatic holiday dance at Fezziwig's warehouse, in which Fezziwig includes his apprentices, workers, servants, wife, daughters, local shopkeepers, and neighbors. The beaming, congratulatory employer, caring for the community under his control, teaches Scrooge a lesson: an employer ought to think of himself as a carer. As Scrooge notes, "He has the power to render us happy or unhappy; to make our service light or burdensome."[109] Through the lessons of Christmas Past, Scrooge learns to value a well-regulated community in which each individual tries to secure the pleasure and well-being of the others, and to recast an economic organization as a social collective that embodies both meanings of "company."

The Ghost of Christmas Yet to Come perpetuates this lesson by showing Scrooge a dreadful vision in which he dies alone. The unattended deathbed—or in Scrooge's case, the deathbed where hired attendants literally steal the clothes and bedding off the corpse—is the nightmare of a culture accustomed to communal nursing. The Ghost of Christmas Yet to Come foresees a world of indifferent hired aides, of prisons and workhouses, in lieu of a community of care. Dickens determines our perspective by placing us in the social world Scrooge has rejected and allowing him to overhear comments in the urban crowd.[110] From his isolated childhood to his neglected old age, Scrooge lives outside communal care. His isolation is the central problem of his life as depicted in "A Christmas Carol"—both because his existence is impoverished and because he is reneging on the pleasant duty of helping others.

Currently, disability readings of "A Christmas Carol" focus on Tiny Tim, but that is because we are reading a modern idea of a visible anomaly back onto a pre-normate world. In fact, Tiny Tim has an "active little crutch" along with a prosthetic frame, a specially adapted chair, and mobility assistance from his family members, so he moves about easily.[111] We don't even know what Tiny Tim's limbs look like, because this story dates from a period when, as we have seen, there was relatively little interest in diagnosis or anomaly. Modern readers often invoke Tiny Tim as shorthand for a saintly, sentimentalized icon, but as Julia Miele Rodas points out, the character himself is more complicated. Tiny Tim demonstrates agency, defiance, and smarminess in his refusal to toast Scrooge and his self-praise as inspirational to churchgoers.[112] Is Tiny Tim insufferable or ideal? The normate model does not help us much in achieving an interesting reading of "A Christmas Carol." It is true that Tiny Tim has a visible disability, but the text is not very interested in diagnosing it or curing it or using it to provide an interesting insight into his subjectivity or its effect on others, so that his character remains minimal.

But if we turn to a model of ordinary bodies, we see a much more widespread experience of debility. The story opens in a frozen, bleak, starving London. For Scrooge, "the cold within him froze his old features, nipped his pointed nose, shrivelled his cheek, stiffened his gait; made his eyes red, his thin lips blue; and spoke out shrewdly in his grating voice."[113] And although we remember this story for its feasting, in fact the feasts occur against a backdrop of starvation and suffering. Bob Cratchit is freezing, since he has an inadequate fire and does not own a coat, and the Cratchit family habitually goes hungry; the boy who tries to sing a carol to Scrooge has a "scant young nose, gnawed and mumbled by the hungry cold as bones are gnawed by dogs."[114] The charity gentlemen warn Scrooge that this is a season "when Want is keenly felt."[115] Christmas Present puts on a goodly show, but beneath his cloak are Want and Ignorance, who are "yellow, meagre, ragged, scowling, wolfish" children, with shriveled hands and pinched bodies.[116] Dickens's novella is just like Christmas Present: apparently bluff, feasting, and generous, but in reality hiding the bodies of starving children.

The wizened, half-starved, shivering, and grimy bodies of Dickensian urchins in all the novels are disabled, but we do not see them that way because they are, well, ordinary, and we are accustomed to conceptualizing disability as a marked, unusual condition. "Ordinary bodies" readings allow us to notice widespread debility, impugning an entire social failure by making it particularly and painfully visible in the bodies of children. Perhaps, wherever an indigent child enters a narrative, Dickens is pulling in the ordinary bodies model.[117] In this respect, the debilitated, worn-down, surplus population represented by Mrs. Smith in *Persuasion* as a marginal figure becomes the main subject of "A Christmas Carol." If Tiny Tim dies, it will be because as a small, weak child, he is particularly vulnerable to the brutal forces of cold and hunger—not because of his leg. Nor is there a prospect of a cure. In the regime of ordinary bodies, the emphasis falls on endurance, accommodation, treatment, and support.

What if disability in "A Christmas Carol" is about malnutrition and exposure rather than a single saintly character? In that case, the real resolution is Scrooge's provision of fire and food. This makes sense inasmuch as Scrooge's original crime is signaled by his refusal to provide "meat, and drink, and means of warmth" to the poor.[118] Once he has been taught by the Ghosts, Scrooge eagerly joins his nephew's community and befriends needy neighbors. His very first act upon awakening is to send a giant turkey to the Cratchit household, and when Bob Cratchit comes to work, Scrooge tells him, "Make up the fires, and buy another coal-scuttle before you dot another i, Bob Cratchit!"[119] As a result of this largesse, "Tiny Tim ... did NOT die."[120] His personalized care, becoming "a second father" to Tiny Tim, keeps the boy alive.[121]

Thus, when Tiny Tim says, "God bless Us, Every One," perhaps we are supposed to notice not the identity of the speaker but the final words, *every one*, and respond to the multiple, inclusive social ideal that we have seen in the unnamed speakers—women, men, gentlemen, poor.[122] The point is not to save Tiny Tim per se, but to save the crowds that Tiny Tim represents, to save "every one." This is the lesson Mary-Catherine Harrison takes from "A Christmas Carol": that Tiny Tim must be read as a type so that our sympathy for him can extend to all disabled children.[123] Readers may be as disindividuated as characters. We are all expected to be moved by the same stimuli, to act in concert. That is why the narrator can wish that we *all* keep Christmas: "may that be truly said of us, and all of us!"[124] The novel is not about an individual fully developing a unique psychology, but about an isolated person like Scrooge coming into fellowship to become, as it were, a corporate being, to achieve "all of us" and "every one" and the joy of feeling our own isolation dissolve in the fellowship of other readers. It is a different model of character: achieving satisfying growth via external charitable acts, instead of fulfilling the particular psychological needs of a unique inner self.

This is a way of reading "A Christmas Carol" that makes sense of elements we normally overlook. In this "ordinary bodies" reading, the elements of hunger, cold, deprivation, and isolation are not merely a scenic background but in fact the whole point of this story, and Tiny Tim merely functions as a local embodiment of those larger forces. Scrooge's conversion is only symbolically about saving Tiny Tim. It is in fact a recognition of the need to participate in the lifesaving work of warming and feeding and sustaining those in need, and to do so as part of a larger community of care. It enlists the readers in the work of this social collective. It imagines character as formed through repeated actions over time, meeting the needs of others in an affiliative group characterized by mutual respect and communication. As in so many of Dickens's novels, the lonely, isolated figure—David Copperfield, Oliver Twist, Mr. Dombey, Esther Summerson, Arthur Clennam, Ebenezer Scrooge—finally finds a sustaining, supportive community of care. Dickens's novels orient toward blissful social enmeshment.

What the novella does not do, however, is engage in medical expertise. If "A Christmas Carol" had been written a decade or two later, Scrooge might have shown his beneficence by calling in a doctor. For novels of the 1840s may have been the last ones to unproblematically assume that ordinary bodies required care communities. Subsequent fiction often explores the effect of the new medical professionalism, registering the stress of the move to a model in which disability or disease requires an intervention to make the person "normal."

Charlotte Brontë and the Transition to Professionalism

Charlotte Brontë began writing *Jane Eyre* in 1846, a few years after "A Christmas Carol" was published, and in that novel the ordinary bodies-care-community model is still dominant. It continues through *Shirley*, written in 1849, where care is offered by neighbors and friends rather than by doctors. But only a few years later, when she began *Villette* in 1851,

Brontë found herself tracing the transition to the medical model.[125] *Jane Eyre* and *Villette* land on opposite sides of the medical shift.

Jane Eyre showcases two extravagantly disabled figures, the mentally ill Bertha and the blind amputee Rochester. Analyses of disability in this novel, then, usually address these characters' extraordinary bodies and minds, reading Bertha and arguably Rochester in terms of enfreakment.[126]

Like "A Christmas Carol," *Persuasion*, and "Sanditon," however, *Jane Eyre* has many characters with ordinary deficits. Jane and her circle suffer chronic nervous illness, debilitating trauma, mental disability, nervous impairments, consumption, addiction, obesity, malnutrition, and frostbite. Julia Miele Rodas finds autism in multiple characters.[127] Children experience typhoid and consumption; an aunt has a stroke; a caretaker is alcoholic; a cousin is bilious. Most of the characters at Lowood constitute what Scrooge called "the surplus population": they are orphaned, impoverished girls. From its famous opening paragraphs, concerned with "nipped fingers and toes" and a humbling consciousness of "physical inferiority," to its ending lines prophesying St. John Rivers's imminent death, his "last hour," this is a novel in which ordinary people suffer, and in which a significant measure of someone's moral virtue is how well that person works to alleviate that suffering in others.[128]

Jane Eyre records mistrust of paid medical aides. When Rochester is blinded, he sneers about the "hireling" who serves him.[129] Paid caregivers are depicted as hasty and neglectful, like the apothecary treating Jane after the red room, the busy doctor at Lowood during the typhoid epidemic, the hired nurse at Mrs. Reed's deathbed, and of course Grace Poole, Bertha's caretaker. The only decent care comes from personal social relationships.[130] Jane crawls into bed with Helen Burns, travels to Gateshead to sit with Mrs. Reed after her stroke, and pities Bertha. When Jane becomes the cared-for in turn, it is the Rivers siblings who nurse her, laying the basis for lifelong bonds. *Jane Eyre* thus promulgates a vision of affectionate family or friends offering tender care to those they love, with paid service work visible only as an occasional, unsatisfactory alternative. In the era of ordinary bodies, ordinary people take care of each other in communities of care.

In fact, it is because she is enmeshed in relations of loving care throughout the novel that Jane can learn to become what she describes as "your neighbour, your nurse, your housekeeper . . . your companion—to read to you, to walk with you, to sit with you, to wait on you, to be eyes and hands to you."[131] Such care may include provoking and teasing along with alleviation of suffering; care names a living, complicated relation between people, an ongoing imaginative projection into the life of the other. Jane's marriage is not an escape from care but a perfect care relation. When Rochester refers to his "deficiencies," Jane answers that she loves him all the more. Rochester answers by depicting marriage as a kind of caregiving, contrasting Jane's ministrations to those of hired aides: "Henceforth I have hated to be helped—to be led: henceforth, I feel, I shall hate it no more. I did not like to put my hand into a hireling's, but it is pleasant to feel it circled by Jane's little fingers. I preferred utter loneliness to the constant attendance of servants; but Jane's soft ministry will be a perpetual joy."[132] A voluntary, non-economic care relation can save someone whose vulnerable body might otherwise have led her to become a fallen woman or to starve to death. But Bertha's body, meanwhile, even more marginalized, gets no such care community, and that appalling failure of the private home nursing sphere indicates the need for something like state supervision and medical attendance.

Six years later, Brontë's last novel, *Villette* (1853), offers a devastatingly revised version of caring as it looks ahead to the new conditions of medicalization and the normate-deviant split. In the bleak world of *Villette*, domestic caregiving has disintegrated. Hired nursing is now the rule, as we shall see in more detail in chapter 3. The only voluntary familial care occurs when Mrs. Bretton nurses Lucy after her illness. Lucy finds its restorative pleasure excruciating, however, because she knows it must end, her agonized yearning vividly demonstrating how the midcentury shift to the normate might have felt.[133] Significantly, where Jane loves a convalescent, Lucy loves a doctor, at least through much of the novel. But she is bothered that Dr. John's amiability is available for hire and consequently cannot be trusted as authentic, that his cordiality has nothing to do with real social relations.[134] The doctor is constantly called in to tend to patients, making a strong contrast with the momentary appearances of the apothecary and surgeon in *Persuasion* and the absence of any doctor in "A Christmas Carol." In *Villette*, what we have is a realm of "hirelings," led by someone implicated in the new medical science. While paid medical attention seems unproblematic to modern readers, it clearly distresses Lucy Snowe, who regards such professionalization as a sign of inauthenticity. Along with medicalization, Brontë also depicts suspicious, skeptical diagnostic attention, as when everyone recognizes that the child Désirée is faking her sickness.[135] The characters in this novel are either vigorously healthy people or monstrous, deviant beings like the ancient, witchlike Madame Walravens, or the nonverbal, profoundly cognitively impaired Marie Broc. The old regime of widespread ordinary debility seems to have vanished. The change from *Jane Eyre* to *Villette*, then, reveals the ways in which Victorian fiction registers the immense shift to the normate, including its emotional costs.

Conclusion: Sanditon's Future

Grounding this study of care communities in nineteenth-century Britain has allowed us to explore a pre-normate, pre-medical situation: ordinary bodies cared for through communal participation, with repeated holistic caring, aiming for long-term social amelioration. Whether in Anne Elliot's Bath, Scrooge's London, or Jane's Marsh End, characters find sustenance by joining affiliative, egalitarian small groups. Such visions would become increasingly rare by the fin de siècle and almost impossible in the twentieth century as World War I precipitated the development of institutional care on a vast scale. Moreover, Victorian medical discoveries ranging from anesthesia to antibiotics would make the medical model of intervention a viable mode, certainly much more so than the rather hapless early Victorian doctor with his unprovable pet theories and personal social ties.

Eventually, the surgeon will come to Sanditon. Austen already foresees medical modernity. The Heywood family forms the foundation of an ideal care community, for as Mr. Heywood assures Mr. Parker, we "are always well stocked . . . with all the common remedies for Sprains and Bruises—and I will answer for the pleasure it will give my Wife and daughters to be of service."[136] Generous, voluntary, affectionate home care is what early Victorians wanted. But the novel also depicts poor care: Mrs. Parker is helpless, "terrified and anxious, neither able to do or suggest anything," while Parker's siblings advocate extreme, dangerous measures: teeth-pulling, leeches, deprivation of food.[137] The fantasy of the sustaining care community coexisted with the reality of dangerously inept amateurs.

Meanwhile, to return to this chapter's epigraph, Lady Denham's rejection of a Sanditon physician derives partly from a rather chilling refusal to acknowledge that "Servants and the Poor" might be ill, and partly from a reluctance to pay fees to a doctor.[138] This lack of medical care serves her own economic self-interest, for Lady Denham sells her asses' milk as a sovereign remedy instead of "physic." Her complaint reveals just how necessary state-sponsored medical offices were for parish workhouses and prisons, for how else would "Servants and the Poor" get help? Dickens depicted a glorious provision of voluntary care for this debilitated population in "A Christmas Carol," but both Austen and Brontë were far more skeptical regarding such an extension of private feeling to public needs.

The first half of the nineteenth century, then, seems to be the last time that care communities could constitute the main way of caring for the sick. This is not to say that such communities disappeared; indeed, it is the work of this book to assert that they remain very much with us. But the first half of the nineteenth century is the last time they are visible as the default way of dealing with sickness. And they are depicted in texts whose fine emotional detail, social observation, and variation make them extraordinarily rich studies of such social dynamics. Moreover, a recognition of the ordinary bodies–care–community dynamic gives us, as literary critics, a significant way to read work from this period: a way that invites our attention to modes of subjectivity constituted by relational enmeshment achieved through repeated acts of care.

As the century moved further into professionalization, institutionalization, uniformity, and state-sponsored caregiving, fiction remembered these loving groups, re-created them, and, in so doing, showed how such groups might work. The Sanditons of the nineteenth century became communities of the mind. "We go on very well as we are," cried Lady Denham, somewhat anxiously, perhaps because she suspected that they would not go on that way for long.

CHAPTER THREE

Global Migrant Care and Emotional Labor in *Villette*

IN THE PREVIOUS CHAPTER, I argued that *Villette* (1853) marks Brontë's transition into the new era of professional medicine, hired care, and state-sponsored institutional care. *Villette* firmly places fond personal care communities into the nostalgic past and exemplifies the dismay many Victorians experienced regarding the emergence of paid care, but it does more as well: it reflects on the forms of labor on which this new regime was built. Lucy Snowe is an early example of a modern migrant global caregiver in British fiction. In writing about this kind of personhood, Brontë challenges our assumptions about character, subjectivity, and feeling, producing narrative structures that continue to reverberate in literatures of migration to the present day.

Although Brontë's focus on the migrant caregiver was fairly new for nineteenth-century British fiction, she was not the only one who wrote this way.[1] *Villette* relates to other mid-Victorian novels with companions and governesses, particularly to nineteenth-century fictions of migration like *Clara Morison* (1854), the early Australian novel by Catherine Helen Spence.[2] *Villette* also boasts an eminent descendant, Jamaica Kincaid's *Lucy*: particular experiences of Lucy Snowe's become definitive markers of migration when Kincaid rewrites them for her own Lucy character, Lucy Potter, a century and a half later. Additionally, Lucy Snowe's experience trains us into patterns of reading that might structure modern nonfictional accounts of service workers and caregivers. Once we notice, for instance, Lucy's descriptions of the caregiver as a piece of furniture, we can begin to register how often this metaphor appears in modern sociological literature.

In this chapter, I draw on recent sociological studies to show that Lucy's psychological state actually conforms to well-known conditions among this vulnerable population. Lucy Snowe, fascinatingly, invites both sociological and literary readings to the extent that she manages to be both a unique figure and a prototypical example, both a fictional figure and a generic case, another example of the binocular doubleness I have been addressing throughout this book. In Lucy Snowe, however, these two poles do not coexist. Lucy cannot occupy both spaces at once, and that is precisely the problem; as I mentioned in the introduction, when someone gets locked exclusively into the carer or caregiver role, it unbalances the sense of self. Lucy's peculiar personality is at odds with the enforced requirements of her generic job: the conditions of her employment corrode her personhood. Forced to conform to a slot that denies her inner feelings, she engages in an internal war that is no less violent for being brutally private.

This vocational crisis of subjectivity means that we cannot read Lucy the way we would assess a middle-class Victorian female character who has leisure to explore her own private feelings and wishes. Attempts to deduce the true story of Lucy Snowe's psychological trauma have rarely worked. As Sandra Gilbert and Susan Gubar wrote a generation ago in what remains one of the most influential readings of this novel, "It is amazing, however, how mysterious Lucy's complaint remains. Indeed, unless one interprets backwards from the breakdown, it is almost incomprehensible."[3] Lucy's frenemy Ginevra speaks for many readers when she frets, "As if one *could* let you alone, when you are so peculiar and so mysterious! . . . But *are* you anybody?"[4] Gilbert and Gubar have ascribed Lucy's breakdown to sexual repression, and Amanda Anderson thinks she is mourning for a lost maternal ideal, but neither of those factors change at the end of *Villette* when Lucy has recovered, so neither can be the full cause.[5] Instead of looking for Lucy's feelings by asking *whom she cares about* (Graham, M. Paul, her lost family), perhaps we should be looking for Lucy's actions by asking *whom she cares for* (Mrs. Marchmont, Madame Beck's children, the students). After all, when Ginevra asks Lucy who she is, Lucy answers: "I am a rising character: once an old lady's companion, then a nursery-governess, now a school-teacher" (342). Her work gives the truth of her self.

Lucy's caregiving jobs—companion, nursery-governess, and schoolteacher—have defined her subjectivity at a fundamental level. But if Lucy is in many ways typical of the paid caregiver, she is not just one among many such subjects. What makes her special is that she is a fictional construct developing her own narrative, and that position allows us to recognize just how the interiority so fundamental to the novel form depends on class privilege.⁶ (Even the near-contemporary *Clara Morison* is not a first-person account but an omniscient third-person.) A subject who experiences her emotions as exploited for money, altered by migration, alienated by language, publicly erased, categorized in racist statements, or privately fetishized cannot offer those feelings as unproblematic truths. Lucy is a sociological case study who explains herself, even if the Ginevras of the world cannot comprehend her answer. What does it mean to be "a rising character" instead of a deep character, a major character, a rounded character? What does it mean to define oneself by economic promotions rather than inner traits?

As literary critics, we are used to probing an archaeology of knowledge, sensing a political unconscious, digging into a text, unpacking it. Those spatial metaphors imply that the answer lies within and our skillful delving can root out the prizes. But a care-based subject is more like someone laying down layer upon layer of clay coils, building up a solid structure over time. The clay compacts into a hard carapace. The question isn't what treasures lie within, but rather, how and why that clay mounts up. We are used to drilling down. What do we do with a character who builds her self up?

Emotional Labor and Sociological Readings

Service work was first defined as an economic category in 1853, coincidentally the same year *Villette* was published.⁷ However, service work has a longer history. Christine Kotchemidova claims that emotional labor begins with late-eighteenth-century urbanization. In a traditional village where there was only one blacksmith or miller, that person did not need to try to attract customers by projecting good humor, but once multiple small businesses came into competition, the most pleasant person attracted more customers.⁸ By the mid-nineteenth century, emotional labor was widespread, particularly among women, whose financial survival could depend on how well they pretended to care for those over whom they were hired to watch. Service work in the form of paid care was an enormous employment category for Victorian women.⁹

Victorian fiction is full of governesses, companions, and nurses. These people give care for money without necessarily caring much at all, like Miss Briggs in Thackeray's *Vanity Fair*, Miss Macnulty in Trollope's *The Eustace Diamonds*, and Mrs. Sparsit in *Hard Times*; and governesses like Mrs. General in *Little Dorrit*, wives like Edith Dombey in *Dombey and Son*, and nurses to the elderly like Mary Garth in *Middlemarch*. Lauren Hoffer explains:

As the paid friends of other women, companions were expected to enact the private virtues supposed to be organic to relationships between women in exchange for money or alternative forms of compensation ... but this economic aspect of the relationship was problematic. A sympathy that is in essence purchased like a commodity immediately loses its sense of being an altruistic emotional interaction.[10]

As we have seen with nursing, hiring out one's capacity for friendship was worrisome. Women were caught in a double bind: they were supposed to behave in acceptably feminine ways, but selling that behavior suggested it could be artificially drummed up, thereby undermining its reality. In Hoffer's words, generating "a manipulative, performed sympathy" corrupted any sense of genuine sympathy.[11] Caregiving was supposed to be a voluntary, private, amateur activity, so that selling one's care made Victorians suspicious. Yet middle-class women, debarred from selling their bodies or labor, had little else to market except their capacity to care. As Mrs. General remarks, "I cannot, therefore, put a price upon services which it is a pleasure to me to render if I can render them spontaneously, but which I could not render in mere return for any consideration."[12] This delicacy, however, cannot be taken at face value; it serves to set a salary without allowing negotiation by her employer.

Victorian companions, nurses, and teachers experienced a dynamic that Arlie Russell Hochschild has famously designated "emotional labor"—consigning aspects of one's affective life to commercial uses, creating a crisis of authenticity. Emotional labor "requires one to induce or suppress feeling in order to sustain the outward countenance that produces the proper state of mind in others." Because such labor commodifies "a source of self that we honor as deep and integral to our individuality," the worker can become "estranged or alienated from" her core self.[13] After all, as we have seen, caregiving, an economic necessity, is not necessarily aligned with caring, an emotional reaction. It is quite possible to give care without feeling caring at all.

In simplest form, we can say that Lucy—like Mrs. General or Miss Briggs—does not really care for the objects of her caregiving. In Lucy's case, this dissonance causes intense stress, but she also, paradoxically, cherishes it as a guarantor of psychological liberation, so that she does not combat it until it is nearly too late. While men and women alike can perform emotional labor, the fact that women enact the most intimate feelings produces a particularly devastating gap between truth and performance. Thus, minor characters in Dickens, Trollope, and Thackeray may be experiencing an emotional split. Their flattery of their employers, utterances that readers are inclined to condemn as hypocritical, may actually constitute a difficult negotiation between private feeling and public exigency. As Jill Rappoport and Lana Dalley remind us, "Writing the history of nineteenth-century Economic Woman requires new modes of conceptualization that take into account her carefully circumscribed socioeconomic position and the behavior it elicited; she cannot simply be modeled on Economic Man."[14] A prime example of that new mode of conceptualization would be the need to manage emotional labor, the fundamental condition of women's service work.

What does emotional labor do to our reading of the nineteenth-century novel?[15] We need to read paid caregivers as people whose inner truths and outer behavior have ceased to correlate. Characters like Mary Garth and Miss Macnulty must flatter employers whom they have good reason to mistrust, Mr. Featherstone and Lizzie Eustace. Perhaps the frequent characterization of the companion as "stupid," as in the case of Miss Briggs, actually evokes the kind of self-imposed stupefaction required for someone to retain self-respect while performing false friendship. No form of feeling is acceptable, because all self-expression is liable to the suspicion of being faked for monetary gain. Payment taints everything. Miss Briggs gurgles and sobs in front of Becky Sharp; Miss Macnulty does not express sympathy in front of Lizzie Eustace. Both the excess and the deficit of feeling irritate the employers, for both seem inauthentic. This is the kind of bind (literally) that Dickens depicts in Rosa Dartle's face. Rosa bears a scar, "or I should rather call it, seam," that traverses her lips, as if her mouth is violently sutured together to prevent the truth escaping.[16] The seam speaks for her, becoming "a dull, lead-coloured streak, lengthening out to its full extent, like a mark in invisible ink brought to the fire."[17] A form of writing, but devoid of signification, it is a smear or mark, at the very edge of intelligibility. Like a strip of duct tape across a protester's mouth, the seam calls attention to the desperate need and the simultaneous impossibility of self-expression.

Another coping technique might be to undertake ritualized activities that displace the actions they really want to do. We might rethink Mrs. Sparsit's stirruped foot as a way of keeping herself from striding out of the room, or Mrs. General's nonsensical reiterations (papa, potatoes, poultry, prunes, and prisms) as a displacement of what she might really want to say. Clara Morison, forced to act as servant-companion to a succession of problematic women, retreats into deferential, depressed silence. Her only outlet is in writing, but that proves risky and she curbs herself there too.

We need to read these characters' acts not as markers of their personal honesty, but as methods of coping with self-alienation. Thus, attending to emotional labor may require us to develop reading protocols that see surface behavior not as an indicator of inner feeling but rather as an attempt to baffle, deter, and deny that inner feeling. Characters' actions erect those clay walls, protecting, hiding, and belying whatever is within the vessel.

While Victorian fiction has plenty of these minor figures, Lucy Snowe has an unusual status as the main character and the narrator of *Villette*: as a sufferer from emotional labor who writes her own story, she is a rarity in Victorian fiction.[18] Initially, she equates readers with the employers from whom she must hide her deepest feelings, so she evades and baffles us. The materials she hides from the reader are her most sacred personal memories (the fate of her parents, her recognition of Graham, her discovery that it was M. Paul who helped her when she disembarked in Labassecour), which she refuses to transform into material for inauthentic performances for an employer. But the story of *Villette* is, in part, the story of Lucy gradually managing to imagine a different type of reader, someone with whom she can be in a genuine, nonmonetized care relation that allows some self-expression that feels authentic.

Charlotte Brontë herself knew the stress of emotional labor, for she drew on her own teaching experience in imagining Lucy Snowe's struggles. During her years as a governess, Brontë found the lack of privacy stifling. As she wrote to Emily in 1839, "I see now more clearly than I have ever done before that a private governess has no existence, is not considered as a living and rational being except as connected with the wearisome duties she has to fulfil. While she is teaching the children, working for them, amusing them, it is all right. If she steals a moment for herself she is a nuisance."[19] But showing exhaustion or depression was not permitted. When Brontë seemed downcast, her employer scolded her.[20] To avoid such criticism, Brontë eventually learned to mask her feelings, but this performance was itself tiresome. She confided in her friend Ellen Nussey that "if teaching only—were requisite it would be smooth & easy—but it is the living in other people's houses—the estrangement from one's real character the adoption of a cold frigid—apathetic exterior that is painful."[21] She yearned for "mental liberty" and freedom from "this weight of restraint."[22]

In the novels she wrote after this governessing experience, Brontë represented how it felt to be a middle-class woman forced to work in education. *Jane Eyre* foregrounds Jane's advertising, salary negotiations, and frequent recourse to a language of professional labor to deflect Rochester's advances. The novel represents paid nursing as indifferent at best, via

Grace Poole, the apothecary, and the hired nurse at Mrs. Reed's bedside, while regarding voluntary caregiving as valuable. One sign of Jane's goodness is that she freely chooses to become Rochester's nurse and Adéle's teacher, turning paid caregiving into genuine caring.

As we saw in chapter 2, however, *Villette* limns a world of paid care. All the companionship, teaching, and nursing are more or less unpleasant salaried services in this story, from Lucy's first job taking care of Miss Marchmont to Dr. John's ministrations, to Lucy's management of "the crétin," Marie Broc. These services never get represented as delightful private nurturing relationships. When Lucy watches Marie Broc over the long vacation, she feels hopelessly degraded. Lucy has the experiences of a professional nurse but the feelings of a private individual. Paul Marchbanks reminds us that Victorian professional attendants presumably became inured to their charges' possibly messy intimate bodily functions, but such habituation would not necessarily have occurred in the private sphere; Lucy never does get used to Marie Broc's body (66).[23] Marie Broc and Madame Walravens are depicted as monstrous, part of the shift to the extraordinary bodies model. It was perhaps the trauma of private nursing that turned Brontë toward thinking about paid care, for she wrote *Villette* after the horrific experience of nursing three dying siblings (Branwell, Emily, and Anne, who all died within eight months), as well as an elderly father, aunt, and servant, all with serious health issues.[24] Paul Marchbanks identifies "the tension visible between Charlotte's loud support of dependent care and her admission of bitterness concerning such care's practice."[25]

In the introduction, I mentioned that people engaged too much in caregiving may spend so long a time engrossed in the cared-for, suppressing their own needs, that they can lose touch with their own individuality. (People who get stuck as cared-fors have the opposite problem: their unique needs are so highlighted that they can forget they are types.) *Villette*, told through someone experiencing this problem, facilitates type-based reading. And given readers' usual emphasis on individual character, this tendency to typify adds to the eeriness of the novel's effect.

Lucy is a prototypical migrant service provider. The Labassecourienne students are all examples of the "continental 'female,'": they all have a more or less identically plump body, smooth hair, and a demeanor of amiable, phlegmatic calm (87, 235). Lucy calls them a "swinish multitude" (91). The city itself is generically named Villette, or "little city," and in an earlier draft Brontë gave it an even more typifying term, Choseville ("thing-city").[26] In *The Powers of Distance: Cosmopolitanism and the Cultivation of Detachment*, Amanda Anderson notes *Villette*'s tendency to "impersonality, what Lucy calls a 'disindividualizing' manner."[27] This cultivation of a flat, impersonal persona, the product of a cruel pathology generated by work conditions, can become deeply problematic.

Along with disindividuation, *Villette* rethinks narrative form. Instead of telling us about the formative events of her life—her family disasters—Lucy itemizes her employer's daily microaggressions and her struggles to respond (which often involve suppressing her feelings). It is a different vision of narrative as a story based on quotidian daily events instead of catastrophic crises—a kind of narrative suited to people wearily spending their lives in repeated small, demoralizing, emotionally false care acts, far from home.[28] So too in *Clara Morison*: much of that novel charts a life of wearily requesting and keeping jobs, learning how to perform household tasks, figuring out how to cope with employers. *Villette* has an intermittent, desultory rhythm. If Lucy's daily life requires repeated fake care acts to keep her employers happy, so too, for much of the novel, her writing requires constant falsifications pitched to keep the reader contented. Writing, infected by emotional labor, becomes bad-faith care. Brontë worried about this herself. In a letter to her publisher in 1852, Brontë confessed, "I seem to dread the advertisements—the large lettered 'Currer Bell's New Novel' or 'New Work by the Author of 'Jane Eyre.'"[29] As Ewa Badowska notes, Brontë resented "the way commodity culture invaded the preserves of her privacy."[30] For Victorian subjects like Brontë, payment rendered feelings inauthentic, yet her feelings were what she had to sell. Brontë searched for a way to rectify what she saw as the slippage of human relations into degrading, debased transactionality, including relations to the reader.

Victorian Migrations

It is important to remember that Lucy is a fictional representative of a real global economic shift in the mid-nineteenth century. In Brontë's time, paid caregiving was provided by people who were often migrants: Irish servants, French chefs, German governesses. This population had some similarity to today's home health workers, nannies, housekeepers, day care providers, house cleaners, cooks, and senior citizen center aides, who have often migrated from other nations and who also find that their work conditions are profoundly shaped by their capacity to function in an alien language and different culture. In the United States today, those caregivers are overwhelmingly people of color, and because of the nature of their jobs, they have also been disproportionately vulnerable to the Covid-19 pandemic raging throughout 2020 and 2021. In the mid-nineteenth century, race was understood differently, but the same dynamics of disorientation and vulnerability obtained.

In *The Figure of the Migrant*, Thomas Nail argues that migration is one of the definitive experiences of modernity. As societies fluctuate, power dynamics expel certain populations and filter others, and the migrant becomes, in his words, "a socially constitutive power."[31] Nail argues that we need to stop reading the migrant in relation to states, but rather adopt a paradigm of mobility in which the circulation of populations matters more than where they start or end. Such circulation governs *Villette*, from its beginning in Lucy's emigration, through its middle in the mobility of the Bretton and Home families, to its end in M. Paul's failed return.

Brontë wrote *Villette* as a global migrant caregiving population was beginning to emerge.[32] In England, imperial shipping routes, travel outfitters, emigration manuals, colonialist initiatives, and patriotic rhetoric about making a British home in the wilderness all converged to make emigration popular in the latter half of the nineteenth century, particularly for unmarried women who were perceived as "superfluous" at home.[33] Today many states have well-funded governmental programs encouraging citizens to find work abroad, including the Philippine Overseas Employment Administration and similar programs in Bangladesh, Sri Lanka, and Thailand.[34] Anne Longmuir points out that Lucy heeds the emigrationist rhetoric of her own period, which Brontë may have encountered particularly through her friend Mary Taylor, who moved to New Zealand and strongly advocated for emigration.[35]

I have mentioned two innovations in Brontë's writing in the age of global migrant caregiving: a narrative largely composed of a rhythm of daily microaggressions and responses instead of major climaxes, and a model of character that is typified instead of deeply individualist. But Brontë also develops particular markers for the migrant's journey. While contemporary migration narratives express diverse experiences, reading *Villette* as an early articulation of the global migrant experience in the Anglophone tradition suggests some foundational formal qualities for this emerging literature. And because migration narratives are so often assumed to be a postmodernist, postcolonial, twentieth- and twenty-first-century genre, it is particularly useful to notice how it emerges earlier.

First, it is crucial to note how traumatic Lucy's journey is, both the physical crossing to Labassecour and the longer journey in which she develops a kind of hybrid identity in the transition between nations and homes. The "dangerous crossing" trope may have originated in accounts of the slave trade, the most enormous and traumatic experience of global migration imaginable. But it rapidly became a convention in fictions of migration, as Rita Kranidis points out, for the time spent on ship was seen as morally and physically risky.[36] In *Clara Morison*, Clara is debased by continual contact with vulgar personalities during the voyage, and the landing is terrifying, as she finds herself in physical and sexual danger among aggressive men at a boardinghouse. In *Villette*, alone on the dark waterfront, Lucy is cheated by a boatman, abused by the stewardess, and sickened by the voyage, and when she finally reaches the port, disoriented by the different language and monetary system and harassed by strange men, she gets dangerously lost in a strange city. The coachman leaves her trunk behind, and because she has no French, she "could say nothing whatever" (68). *Villette* establishes the "dangerous crossing" as more important than one's parents or childhood, since Lucy describes the former in detail while neglecting the latter—or more precisely, framing the latter *as* a dangerous crossing:

> Picture me then idle, basking, plump, and happy, stretched on a cushioned deck, warmed with constant sunshine, rocked by breezes indolently soft. However, it cannot be concealed that, in that case, I must somehow have fallen overboard, or that there must have been wreck at last. I too well remember a time—a long time—of cold, of danger, of contention. To this hour, when I have the nightmare, it repeats the rush and saltness of briny waves in my throat, and their icy pressure on my lungs. I even know there was a storm, and that not of one hour nor one day. For many days and nights neither sun nor stars appeared; we cast with our own hands the tackling out of the ship; a heavy tempest lay on us; all hope that we should be saved was taken away. In fine, the ship was lost, the crew perished. (39)

Note that by using weather as a metaphor, Lucy takes the event out of the realm of individual motives and personal choice, making it an indifferent, inhuman event, signalized by a physical pressure that changes the body. This is what the service economy feels like. As a result of this paradigmatic dangerous crossing, she experiences what John Hughes calls "the sense of life lived in isolation, transit, and subjection."[37]

Similarly, Kincaid's *Lucy* opens as the Antiguan au pair, Lucy Potter, arrives in Britain, disoriented and dismayed by the unfamiliar spectacle. Lucy Potter's journey feels as upsetting as Lucy Snowe's, even though it is not literally dangerous, as if this constitutive emotion must be recorded even when the narrative conditions have changed. Kincaid's Lucy, like Brontë's Lucy, refers to her childhood home only occasionally and parenthetically, and this replacement of one story of origin (parents) with another (crossing) can be read as one of the new narrative forms ushered in through stories of migration. *Villette*, of course, ends with the ultimate "dangerous crossing," the shipwreck and loss of M. Paul en route from Guadeloupe. Lucy Potter symbolically completes M. Paul's journey, moving from the West Indies to the Anglo-American world at last.

Global migrants' job conditions themselves tend to conform to certain kinds of conditions, thereby imposing shared experiences on different women's lives. Whether one is a Lucy Snowe or a Lucy Potter, a mid-Victorian British teacher or a twentieth-century Antiguan au pair, one will probably struggle with cultural disorientation, loss of privacy, loss of autonomy, sneering cultural dismissals, odd friendships, unexpectedly intimate interactions with a female employer, and the necessity of performing a certain kind of professionalism that may not match one's own real feeling.

Lucy's work experiences are typical of this group, as are Clara Morison's. Most modern migrants must be "enterprising and adventurous enough to resist the social pressures to stay home and accept their lot in life."[38] Similarly, as Lucy Snowe begins to entertain the possibility of emigrating, she applauds herself as vigorous, energetic, strong-minded, and bold (49). Women often get the idea of migrating from meeting others who have traveled, and Lucy decides to emigrate after meeting a wealthy school friend who went abroad (51).[39]

This initial strength of mind may help the migrant accept her difficult lot. Both Clara and Lucy overcome their middle-class origins in turning to low-status manual labor, including servants' jobs. Lucy pleads with Madame Beck: "I was ready to turn my hand to any useful thing, provided it was not wrong or degrading: how I would be a child's-nurse or a lady's-maid, and would not refuse even housework adapted to my strength" (72). Moving abroad for unskilled labor gives global migrants what Rhacel Salazar Parreñas calls a decrease in social status and an increase in financial status simultaneously.[40] Like Lucy, recent arrivals today often take live-in work because they "need a place to live as desperately as they need income," although live-in jobs are notoriously difficult and most women escape them as soon as they can.[41]

Modern activists have pointed to the unregulated nature of the domestic realm in which home health care workers, nannies, and aides labor, but even in its dangerously unsecured condition, the modern home is still safer than the mid-nineteenth-century home. Lucy's experience of the pensionnat includes behavior that would be both scandalous and legally actionable today: inappropriate intimacy, verbal abuse, bribery, classes held on spontaneously chosen subjects or canceled on a whim; teachers asked to perform household and child-care labor; teachers hired and fired for private motives, including religious biases; espionage and theft; and constant invasive surveillance. The legal protections afforded employees today, insufficient as they are, do not exist at all in *Villette*'s world. There are no regulations against sexual harassment. There are no contracts. There are no federally mandated minimum wages or maximum hours. There are no legal remedies for job actions undertaken for personal motives. Thus, the Pensionnat des Damoiselles can be read as a nightmare version of what many workers deal with today—an intensive depiction of the dangers of working in an unregulated space.

Lucy starts as a home health care aide to Miss Marchmont, then becomes a maid to Madame Beck and a nanny to Madame Beck's children, but her employer suddenly promotes her, on a whim, to become the English teacher of the first class. Today's global migrants are less likely to experience such rapid alterations. A caregiver today might similarly shift roles, say from home health worker to nanny-babysitter to personal aide; these are all jobs that require individual attention to one person, a carer/cared-for dyad. But today that person would be unlikely to be suddenly forced to teach a class of sixty teenage girls. Even if an au pair like Lucy Potter wanted to become a teacher, she would be required to undergo years of training, and even in an overcrowded school she would be responsible for a class with half the number of Lucy Snowe's students at most. Lucy operates in a world without teaching licenses or educational degrees, so that, scandalously, just about anyone could declare herself a teacher. We experience Lucy's transition from intensive, individualized care to a pedagogical performance before a large crowd as a profoundly shocking shift. She moves from care work, here defined as intimate relations with another person or a small community, into service work, performing for a larger public from a professional distance.[42] A classroom ought to be a care community, but Lucy's is not: it is instead a theater of specular and disciplinary performances.

Lucy's disindividuation—one of the most disorienting elements of her narrative style—is nowhere clearer than in the novel's racial language, which presents her as nothing more or less than the generic Englishwoman. Lucy experiences the rampant national stereotyping that Susan Bayley has described as defining the lives of nineteenth-century governesses abroad. Bayley limns the dominant conventions: the cold, hardy, practical English; the flighty, vain French; the drunken poor Irish;

and the honest but humorless and unattractive Germans, all of whom are represented among the personnel of the Pensionnat des Demoiselles.[43] "As a result [of mutual stereotyping], governesses were depersonalised and dehumanised, impugned for the purported misdeeds of their home countries, and pressured to deny or suppress their national and religious identities," she explains.[44]

Lucy's "depersonalised and dehumanised" experience, however, also derives from the period's theories of race. *Villette* appeared in the midst of a ferment about racial characterization that included Robert Knox's *The Races of Man* (1850), Arthur de Gobineau's *The Inequality of Human Races* (1853–1855), and J. C. Nott and George R. Gliddon's *Types of Mankind* (1854). Irene Tucker explains that the early nineteenth century saw the development of an anatomical model positing a standardized view of human bodies in which people were organized by the visual marker of race into a static, unchangeable hierarchy.[45] But Victorian racial thinkers had difficulty using race as a metric to sort out populations in any consistent ways. While Victorian ethnographers believed that people belonging to a nation constituted a race, they also argued that some races, like the Caucasian, covered several nations (Scandinavia, Germany, England), and that some nations included members of different races (England had Celts as well as Saxons; Canada had Native Americans alongside European settlers). Belgium, interestingly, was an uncertain case, possibly related to the Welsh.[46] To be English—or, in the new ethnological terms, to be Caucasian, Scandinavian, or Germanic—now meant to be part of a specifically defined race. By the 1850s, the body was turning into an identical, generic item, to be classified by race and to be fixed when it deviated.[47] Such standardization matches the kind of industrial iterability of modern institutions and the diagnostic, interventionist mentality of the medical model; we can see a consistent theory of bodies emerging at midcentury.

Like Kincaid's Lucy Potter, who starts to see her own skin as black once she lives among white employers, Brontë's Lucy Snowe begins to regard herself as English when she moves to Labassecour. Paul White points out that "many migrants may not have held a particularly strong view of their own ethnicity prior to movement, but . . . they may find themselves in situations where they are confronted by an alternative ethnic awareness that labels them and confines them to a stereotyped 'otherness' from which there appears little chance of escape."[48] Each Lucy experiences her own ethnic difference as both somatically visible and uncomfortably tied to fundamental aspects of her personality as employers reference her blackness or Englishness to explain her. Lucy Snowe, as a middle-class white

English woman, expects to domineer over others. Thus, when she herself becomes a racially marked subject of others' colonizing campaigns, her outrage is palpable, and we experience the shock along with her.

Lucy's Englishness appears to be written on the body. M. Paul notes Englishwomen's "tall stature, their long necks, their thin arms" (378). By contrast, Lucy notes "the full, firm comeliness of Labassecourien contours" (144). Their national difference extends to personality and mind. M. Paul itemizes the Englishwomen's pedantic, skeptical, proud character and "pretentious virtue," and Lucy believes that the Labassecouriennes are lazy, stupid, insincere, and vain (378; 90–92). In such a case, one cannot change one's nationality—it permanently forms one's deepest identity, from one's lips to one's moral character. In this respect, *Villette* seems to concur with the nineteenth-century consensus about the hierarchical races of man, in which bodily characteristics like one's forehead or nose corresponded to basic attributes. Knox insisted that "race is everything in human history; that the races of men are not the result of accident; that they are not convertible into each other by any contrivance whatever."[49] Race was deterministic and unchangeable.

On the other hand, the plot of *Villette* enacts a cosmopolitan understanding in which nationality is not an essential racial identity, but a culture that can be adopted, rejected, or mixed with elements taken from other cultures. After all, as Lucy notes, "Villette is a cosmopolitan city, and in this school were girls of almost every European nation, and likewise of very varied rank in life" (90). Indeed, by the end of the novel, when she speaks French fluently, runs a business, and settles down as a permanent resident of the city, Lucy has essentially become a hybrid English/Labassecourian subject.[50] No longer consigned to typical Englishwomanhood, Lucy becomes a person who can choose which cultural elements compose her identity.

Cosmopolitan theorists explore how far Victorians might have embraced a fluid and flexible international persona, rather than always working to export Englishness abroad. Such cosmopolitanism, according to Anderson, can be defined as "the capacious inclusion of multiple forms of affiliation, disaffiliation, and reaffiliation, simultaneously insisting on the need for informing principles of self-reflexivity, critique, and common humanity."[51] This more multicultural view speaks of national origin as a personal choice, not a somatic core.[52] Some critics have argued that Lucy softens to embrace elements of Continental culture.[53]

Thus, *Villette* seems to endorse both racial and cosmopolitan views of ethnic identity, sometimes simultaneously. Lucy asserts that she is essentially English—but her life story is one of progressive Labassecourianizing. Migration narratives are famously marked by hybridity, ambivalence, reversions, and complexly shifting self-understandings.[54] *Villette* is no exception. Indeed, Tamara Silvia Wagner has argued that Victorian migration narratives use the migrant's isolation to problematize the role of the cosmopolitan.[55] But perhaps we could say that Lucy resists the cosmopolitan story Brontë is writing for her. Perhaps Lucy's Anglophilia is a psychological mechanism to cope with migration, a defensive, retroactive construction of Englishness precisely because her English identity seems to be getting diluted. Perhaps it is because her constitutive migrant experience is one of mobility and circulation (as Nail argues) that Lucy feels the need to insist that she is really rooted in a nation.

It seems like it would be difficult for an English person to be victimized by racist or colonialist campaigns, given the assurance gained by identifying oneself with a global superpower. After all, this was a nation whose members fervently argued for their own moral superiority to the rest of the world, and who represented women as the privileged carriers of that ideology. Armored by utter faith in her own predominance, Lucy asserts her Englishness by insisting on the inferiority of her interlocutors and seeming scornfully impervious to their anti-English diatribes. Helen Cooper points out that "Lucy's identification of her Catholic pupils as 'mutineers,' 'a stiff-necked tribe,' 'swinish,' lazy, incapable of sustained mental effort, lacking in self-respect and in need of English discipline echoes familiar tropes in the literature of imperialism," reminiscent of missionary discourse.[56] James Buzard agrees that Lucy regards "the Francophone Catholics among whom she lives in Villette as uncivilized savages."[57] On the other hand, Englishness did not confer some kind of magical potency protecting the carrier from colonialist anxieties. National privilege may be performed out of desperation or defensiveness rather than conviction, and it coexists intersectionally, of course, with other forms of identity that complicate it; in the nineteenth century, pride in being English may not have compensated for the sense of degradation in being of the wrong class, gender, region, or sexual orientation. Charlotte Brontë, who often identified women with slaves, had a low-status Irish heritage, grew up in a remote province, starved at a dismal charity school, and experienced poverty and the death of much of her family, certainly does not seem like someone who would regard Englishness as a magically potent state that wards off all vulnerability.[58]

We should not read Lucy's imperialist tropes as transparent revelations of her deep beliefs, but rather as defensive mechanisms against her employers' campaign to Labassecourianize her. After all, as we saw in the introduction, service work perpetuates an externalized selfhood in which one often works to conceal rather than reveal one's deeper feelings. Madame Beck and M. Paul are trying to infiltrate her mind, to alter her affiliations. They want to indoctrinate her into their own culture, and they do so partly by giving her propaganda (pamphlets slid into her desk, for instance) and partly by publicly denouncing her culture. No wonder that she takes refuge in a counterdiscourse to build up those walls against the invasive employer.

Lucy has to endure the mortifying experience of her employers interpreting her every action in aggravatingly racial ways. She cannot just be herself; she represents all Englishwomen. The governess "was identified primarily with her nationality rather than her personality," writes Bayley.[59] When she gazes at a painting, she is exhibiting the strangeness of Englishwomen; when she receives letters, she is revealing Englishwomen's odd notions of friendship (225, 325). When she decides whether or not to act in the play, she is exemplifying the characteristics of Englishwomen (148). When she aggravates M. Paul, he tells her entire class that Englishwomen are unattractive. He "spared nothing—neither their minds, morals, manners, nor personal appearance. I specially remember his abuse of their tall stature, their long necks, their impious scepticism (!), their insufferable pride, their pretentious virtue" (378). Although Bayley characterizes this as a "teasing denunciation," in a racialized context it is far worse than that—imagine how M. Paul's diatribe would sound if directed at a West Indian employee.[60] His racism is more outspoken than the covert, cowardly judgments that Kincaid's Lucy Potter endures in the United States two centuries later.

Lucy Snowe expresses a typical global-migrant anxiety when she explores whether her employers can work through their presuppositions about her national/racial identification in order to continue employing her, and when she has to balance between passionate defense of her home country and strategic silence so as not to offend those with power over her. Thus, Lucy's utterances about race do not simply emanate from her internal character but are also profoundly determined by her vocational situation.

If a character's very sense of her internal self is a defensive reaction against her employers—and if the narrator's statements seem at odds with the author's plot—readers get destabilized; racial identity and cultural residence no longer represent fundamental truths but rather strategic, temporary, shifting strategies. Brontë is perpetuating a new kind of narrative form in which ongoing, involuntary employment conditions shape someone's character. Victorian readers might have been used to a *Bildungsroman*, in which a young person grows to discover ideal work, but in much migrant literature, starting with *Villette*, the work comes first: uninteresting labor painfully, inexorably, remakes a person.

Villette's "most compelling phobia is that of not belonging, of having no place, of the state of being 'placeless,'" note Kate Lawson and Lynn Shakinovsky. "To be 'placeless' is to be unemployed, but for Lucy this position has larger reverberations as she is haunted from the outset by deprivation and dispossession."[61] By insisting on her Englishness and Protestantism, then, Lucy articulates her resistance to Labassecour, naming a core self at odds with her environment. Without language, possessions, or rank, Lucy no longer knows exactly who she is. Her growing assertion of Englishness is not necessarily a preexisting truth but rather an urgently self-justifying move, a self-invention. Her self is not essential but fluctuating, changing in response to external stimuli. Like Bhabha's postcolonial agent, there is no "subject prior to the social," only an "interactive and contingent" dialogic self characterized by negation and interrogation.[62] Inventing herself as English does not root her, but rather makes her self morph in ways that might bewilder a reader accustomed to a more stable idea of character.

From Care to Service

Lucy's first caregiving job is serving as companion to Miss Marchmont. Initially, Lucy dreads ministering to an invalid, but she softens when she learns how to treat an attack, finding that "by the time she was relieved, a sort of intimacy was already formed between us" (41). The act of care introduces the feeling of caring, "a growing sense of attachment" (42). But in the care dyad, Lucy effectively loses her own self. "Two hot, close rooms thus became my world; and a crippled old woman, my mistress, my friend, my all. Her service was my duty—her pain, my suffering—her relief, my hope—her anger, my punishment—her regard, my reward" (42). Lucy overidentifies with her cared-for, adapting to the sedentary, undernourished life of an invalid, becoming herself "thin, haggard, and hollow-eyed" (48). In this dangerously intimate care dyad, "all within me became narrowed to my lot" (42). Similarly, Clara Morison, taking care of a terminally ill woman, nearly dies in her sympathetic service. The dyad can deplete the carer to an unsafe degree.

In her second job, at Madame Beck's pensionnat, Lucy continues to practice care work that is characterized by deep absorption, or, to use care theorist Nel Nodding's term, "engrossment."[63] Lucy carries and caresses little Georgette, the youngest child, whom she adores (341). Lucy tells us that Georgette's "clasp and the nestling action with which she pressed her cheek to mine, made me almost cry with a tender pain . . . this pure little drop [of feeling] from a pure little source was too sweet: it penetrated deep, and subdued the heart, and sent a gush to the eyes" (134). As "the tender pain" indicates, this kind of love is "too sweet": it reminds Lucy of the risk of merging herself in another. Like Lucy, modern nannies and caregivers often pour intense passion into their relation with their charges.[64] This is a relationship Kincaid retained in her rewriting of *Villette*, giving Lucy Potter a special passion for her youngest charge, as if the relationship with a particular child becomes a necessary marker for care narratives, a sign that the caregiver can really care.

This engrossment is complicated, however, by the fact that Lucy is responsible for all three Beck girls—Fifine and Désirée as well as Georgette. Fifine is likable enough, but Désirée is "a vicious child" whose mother fails to control her, as Lucy tartly notes (102–3).[65] In caring for three children, the intense melding that Lucy had previously experienced with Miss Marchmont is no longer possible—her economic responsibility no longer aligns with her emotional loyalties. Georgette's mother sends her away, a real loss for Lucy, who remarks rather poignantly: "I was sorry; I loved the child, and her loss made me poorer than before" (139). Now she has two cared-fors for whom she cares very little. This transitional state prepares us for her next situation, when Lucy moves from care into something like a service economy, in which she must cater to a larger public or customer base. In a move very typical of employers, Madame Beck increases her workload without paying her market rates for her new job. "Madame raised my salary; but she got thrice the work out of me she had extracted from Mr. Wilson, at half the expense," notes Lucy shrewdly (89).

When Madame Beck forces her to become the English teacher, Lucy steps into a classroom with sixty students who are "more numerous, more turbulent, and more unmanageable" than any other class, as well as only a few years younger than she is (84). Individual relations are impossible; she has to cope with a whole crowd. The hostile students revolt against their instructor, and Lucy feels fundamentally disempowered by her hesitant French. Lucy must quickly develop a new method, and she decides to act, substituting dramatic, violent visual tableaux for words. Ripping up a student's exercise, pushing a student into a closet and locking the door on her, Lucy achieves mastery over the girls (88–89). She learns to perform a kind of persona that keeps the girls disciplined and attentive. At first, Lucy is intellectually enlivened by this new challenge. She rejoices that "it was pleasant. I felt I was getting on; not lying the stagnant prey of mould and rust, but polishing my faculties" (90). At night she lies awake "thinking what plan I had best adopt to get a reliable hold on these mutineers" (91–92).

In this respect, Lucy's pedagogy is the opposite of her previous one-on-one care experiences. In nursing, she passionately identified with her cared-for, but in teaching she deliberately distances from the students in her charge. Whereas she previously offered intimately physical loving care, she now expresses hostility, even sadism, from her separate stance on the *estrade*. John Kucich notes that "Lucy Snowe's carefully orchestrated displays of anger against her students" are not authentic feelings but deliberate performances, much like her "calculated displays of contempt" for Ginevra Fanshawe (917–18).[66] As in her development of a defensive racial essentialism just when she is becoming most cosmopolitan, Lucy can recalibrate her identity in response to cultural pressures.

Assuming a deliberately inauthentic performative self allows her to maintain a space of freedom, keeping a division between "the life of thought, and that of reality" (85). Lucy can feel pride in her "keen relish for dramatic expression" (156). The famous scene where Lucy acts in the vaudeville reveals, to her own surprise, just how skillful an actor she is, making her resolve to curtail her acting in the future (156). Acting can never become a pleasure in itself; it must be merely instrumental, a cover for something else. Behind this performance, she can retain her private self, guaranteed inaccessible in part because it operates in a language and according to cultural and religious norms that are not shared by school personnel. This is how Lucy develops what Sally Shuttleworth calls "the precarious division between the rigidly-defined social self, and the inner impulses which can never be articulated or even acknowledged."[67] Lucy learns to fetishize what Leila May calls "a 'deep self' unavailable to political and economic forces of materiality."[68] Indeed, it is possible that Lucy invents such a deep self through the act of protecting it. To return to the clay metaphor, building the pot itself shapes and defines the space within—but that does not mean there is anything in that secret void.

In fact, Lucy comes to prize that secret self so much that she refuses a much better paying job as companion to her friend Paulina, who might discover her private feelings. She declares, rather startlingly, given her previous two jobs:

> To be either a private governess or a companion was unnatural to me. Rather than fill the former post in any great house, I would deliberately

have taken a housemaid's place, bought a strong pair of gloves, swept bedrooms and staircases, and cleaned stoves and locks, in peace and independence. Rather than be a companion, I would have made shirts, and starved. (330)

Lucy determines that she will never risk engrossment again. By contrast, she exults, Madame Beck "left me free: she tied me to nothing—not to herself—not even to her interests," having given her the gift of her "liberty" (331). Liberty, for Lucy, becomes associated with a secret world that is increasingly necessary as her external self is increasingly consumed. She cannot risk Paulina invading it—perhaps to discover how empty it really is.

As a teacher, then, Lucy has been conscripted into emotional labor. Hochschild argues that by commodifying human responsiveness, emotional labor pushes workers to fetishize a secret inner self, "an inner jewel that remains our unique possession no matter whose billboard is on our back or whose smile is on our face. We push this 'real self' further inside, making it more inaccessible."[69] Lucy is required to show a smoothly agreeable front to Madame Beck and a carefully orchestrated disciplinary anger to her students, so both these aspects of herself come to seem tainted. Such self-management is exhausting for modern as well as Victorian caregivers, so people often find it easier to make themselves feel the emotion authentically than to keep up the charade. This is one reason performativity is such a big part of care. But until care performativity begins its work of reconciling inner and outer, it is hard to keep two incompatible feelings going. Lynn May Rivas notes that today caregivers' "obligation to manage their emotions emerged as the most oppressive aspect of the job. Ironically, this emotional labor is not recognized as work. Rather, it is invisible."[70] By emphasizing this invisibility for the main character in a novel—a person who, structurally, ought to be the most visible—Brontë creates a disorienting mismatch between readerly expectations and economic realities.

Such economic realities also govern moods. Today some service workers inflate their emotions to try to match the tone they have to project in order to make themselves feel authentic. Flight attendants try to generate internal joy to match their enforced smiling, as Hochschild shows. Other workers, however, resemble Lucy in taking a grim pleasure in making the split as wide as possible. Edward Frame, a waiter, explains that "you experience a special rush when your job is to project an aura of warmth and hospitality while maintaining an almost clinical emotional distance. It's the thrill of the con."[71] Like Frame, Lucy takes a bitter joy in intensifying her internal split, and one can imagine *Little Dorrit*'s Mrs. General doing so as well. Lucy identifies her authentic self with spontaneity, irritability, and perverseness, because such feelings are not "useful" and cannot be commodified; in fact, they work against her continued employment and thus offer the momentary pleasure of private rebellion.

The economic pressures of competition are very much in evidence in Lucy's life, for at any moment she can be replaced by another teacher, and the pensionnat itself could fail if parents decide to take their children elsewhere. In one crisis, the school seems about to collapse—"a dozen rival educational houses were ready" to push the school into ruin, and it is only saved by Madame Beck's capacity to hide her anxiety, performing instead a careful "good-humoured, easy grace," complete with "chuckling and rubbing [her hands] joyously" (110–11). The labor of performing pleasantries pays off. The parents are convinced, and the school is more popular than ever. Such a lesson is not lost on Lucy, although she performs a different, much pricklier role than her smooth employer.

Lucy's hunger for real feeling perhaps accounts for her attraction to the most natural, spontaneous person she knows, M. Paul. She is entranced by his utterly transparent emotional life, including his ebullitions of anger, his childish jealousies, and his sudden rapprochements. As Hochschild remarks, once our culture has had to "develop an instrumental stance toward feeling," "we treat spontaneous feeling . . . as if it were scarce and precious; we raise it up as a virtue. It may not be too much to suggest that we are witnessing a call for the conservation of 'inner resources,' a call to save another wilderness from corporate use and keep it 'forever wild.'"[72] Lucy may feel something like this for M. Paul—his emotional wildness represents an ideal vision of liberation for her, the opposite of her built-up artifact of selfhood. However, "if the authentic self is a product of emotion work, in what sense can we say that managed emotions are less authentic?" asks Amy Wharton.[73] M. Paul's emotional wildness is a product of social forces too. His self-expression is possible because he enjoys privileged status as a male, an intellectual, and a cousin of Madame Beck's. He cannot be fired as Lucy can be; he has a liberty she is structurally prevented from reaching. Moreover, as a lifelong Labassecourian, he can have a naive, unproblematic faith in the obvious value of his own culture that is very different from Lucy's fluid and hybrid identity. The reader can only wonder what M. Paul's journey to Guadeloupe might have done to his sense of self, for he disappears on the way back, as if he literally can never come home again.

The person who really shares Lucy's mobility is Graham, another migrant. But Graham has perhaps succeeded too well: he acts so flawlessly that he can no longer access uncomfortable truths. Lucy calls him "faithless-looking" because he is so universally pleasing, and she mistrusts his diffuse amiability, for to her it does not reflect any particular feeling (19, 402). Graham correlates to Lucy's specious performative cover, while M. Paul's passion matches her own fiery, secret core self.

Once she has set up a fetishized authentic secret self, however, Lucy is frustrated by her inability to inhabit it. She is forced to maintain her false persona morning, noon, and night, so that the acting in which she once found delight becomes a source of unutterable weariness. Lucy's private space is also her public workplace; she can never let down her guard or commune alone with her secret feelings. Tellingly, Lucy continues to act when narrating to us. She yearns, "Oh!—to speak truth, and drop that tone of a false calm which long to sustain, outweighs nature's endurance" (297). Such a statement makes us ask why Lucy does not "speak truth," and why the implied addressee requires a "false calm." At this point, Lucy seems to be conceptualizing her relation to her readers as another employer-employee relationship that requires emotional labor—but she also recognizes readers' potential for a different role, as shown by the fact that she pleads for the chance to tell us the "truth."

Madame Beck herself embodies the disorienting collusion of a private space designed for public visibility. Anderson notes that "just as her home is continuous with the institution of the school that she directs, so too her maternal activities are indistinguishable from her pedagogical ones: both are marked by secrecy, surveillance, and absence of affect" (50). Madame Beck treats her children like her employees, with cool distance, while students and teachers jostle in inappropriately intimate proximity. "For a lowly service worker, work is nearly indistinguishable from life," remarks Joshua Gooch.[74]

While surveillance is a problem for modern caregivers, it was far more acute in the nineteenth century, when household management books explicitly told the mistress of the house that it was her moral duty to make servants adhere to certain behavioral codes. Madame Beck and M. Paul constantly invade Lucy's private spaces. They participate in the power dynamic of "maternalism" that we addressed in chapter 1, in which the employer manages the employee's intimate life under the guise of friendship.[75] Pierrette Hondagneu-Sotelo writes that such personal relations are "a key mechanism of oppression and labor control. According to this line of thinking, the employer's maternalism mandates the employee's rituals of deference, which reinforce inequality and hierarchy."[76] In a Victorian context in which "deference and hierarchy" were seen as the natural, even divinely ordained order, maternalism would have been even more difficult to contest.

Lucy's situation may seem a result of her particularly friendless, traumatized personal history, but we can also read it as a structural norm: these conditions go with the job, no matter what her original history might have been. After all, Lucy Potter, who left behind a loving social world in Antigua, feels just as isolated as Lucy Snowe. The caregiving plot is characterized by a sense of loneliness amid multitudes. "I might have had companions, and I chose solitude," Lucy says (139). Hondagneu-Sotelo describes modern live-in work in a similar way:

> The boundaries that we might normally take for granted disappear in live-in jobs. They have, as Evelyn Nakano Glenn has noted, "no clear line between work and non-work time," and the line between job space and private space is similarly blurred. Live-in nanny/housekeepers are at once socially isolated and surrounded by other people's territory; during the hours they remain on the employers' premises, their space, like their time, belongs to another. The sensation of being among others while remaining invisible, unknown and apart, of never being able to leave the margins, makes many live-in employees sad, lonely, and depressed. Melancholy sets in and doesn't necessarily lift on the weekends.[77]

Other caregivers in Victorian fiction similarly suffer from isolation and invisibility.[78] Clara Morison feels acutely alone as a servant, while living next door to a sympathetic family she feels she cannot befriend. Miss Wade rebuffs her schoolmates; Agnes Grey feels alone in her employer's family; Mary Garth feels isolated when caring for Featherstone. In a Victorian world in which characters survive through social enmeshment, solitude is often a marker of tragedy.

By the end of *Villette*, Lucy suffers extreme self-estrangement, having donned the self-protectively drab camouflage of a ghost, or a nun, or a shadow, while feeling her own core self to be vividly enraged and alert. She carefully cultivates what Anderson calls the "nondescript cover" of her behavior.[79] Caregivers can sometimes take a perverse pride in managing to make others overlook them, like Lucy. One modern caregiver explains: "You're almost nonexistent and yet you're there.... [It's] like you're there, but you're not there ... [when they can do something] without even realizing that they're doing it because you're there, that's quality work."[80] Lucy, too, enjoys tricking others into overlooking her: "In quarters where we can never be rightly known, we take pleasure, I think, in being consummately ignored" (109). Yet Lucy's "pleasure" derives, perversely, from controlling her own degradation. Rivas notes that "invisibility is the most extreme form of alienation—the ultimate manifestation of self-estrangement."[81] Lucy certainly feels invisible. She even uses the same metaphor used by modern workers: an article of household furniture. Hondagneu-Sotelo records a housekeeper's complaint that her boss would "act as if I was a chair, a table," just as Lucy notes that Graham treats her like one of the "unobtrusive articles of furniture, chairs of ordinary joiner's work" (108).[82] This seems to have been a common trope, for Rosa Dartle is also described as furniture, and a German article advises prospective governesses to prepare to be treated like furniture.[83]

However, Lucy also uses her own, very Victorian metaphor for alienated emotional labor, and this metaphor takes on (quite literally) a life of its own. Lucy announces that she has "a staid manner of my own which ere now had been as good to me as cloak and hood of hodden gray; since under its favour I had been enabled to achieve with impunity, and even approbation, deeds that if attempted with an excited and unsettled air, would in some minds have stamped me as a dreamer and zealot" (49). It is crucial for Lucy that she conceptualize her external manner as merely a "cloak," beneath which she can actually be a "zealot."

The two factors are linked, and each of her love interests perceives a different side. Because Lucy sees Graham as aligned with her colorless cover story, it is not surprising that this, in turn, is all Graham sees in her. When Graham casually calls her merely "quiet Lucy Snowe," an "inoffensive shadow," she is dismayed by this evidence that she has performed her masquerade too well (351). But Lucy is charmed when M. Paul, the votary of intense interior feeling, errs on the other extreme, calling her an ambitious, flaming, ardent being (170–71). Whereas Graham credits her self-presentation as a shadow, M. Paul consistently identifies her with light—flames, rays—a language that reaffirms her most fundamental selfhood.[84] After all, although her last name is the famously cold Snowe, her first name is Lucy, which means "light."[85]

If one were to design a costume for a person who imagines herself as shadow and flame, it might well be a "a figure all black or white; the skirts straight, narrow, black; the head bandaged, veiled, white" (273). Since Gilbert and Gubar's formative reading, critics have tended to see the nun as a symbol of sexual repression or disembodiment.[86] While the image of a nun conveys a constrained, repressed life, it is important to recall that the real person wearing the nun's habit is Alfred de Hamal, a man enjoying an illicit romantic escapade. On the outside there is a full outfit that gives one impression (virginal, female, selfless, silent), and on the inside there is the opposite (sexually adventurous, male, pleasure-seeking, love-letter-writing). On the outside there is a "dark, usurping shape, supine, long, and strange? . . . It looks very black, I think it looks—not human"; on the inside there is a shining light, for when de Hamal kindles a cigar in the attic, he produces "a solemn light, like a star, but broader" (284). Both a shadowy self and a frightening flame, the nun represents a horrifying embodiment of Lucy's pathologically split sense of self.

The nun makes Lucy's descriptions of herself—invisible, inoffensive, shadowy—all too vivid. "She had no face—no features: all below her brow was masked with a white cloth" (329). To be a nun is to become faceless, silenced, shrouded, a generic inhabitant of the pensionnat, a terrifying vision of what Lucy might become if she continues her emotional labor. This nightmarish vision represents Lucy's terror of dwindling into her surface self, subsiding into nothing more than the grimly fake performance she maintains at the pensionnat.

The problem is that Lucy sees no way out. Lucy's employment status is too insecure to directly confront her boss. Her anxiety about her ability to get a job with equally good conditions leads her to vow to tolerate the surveillance (131). Such a tacit armed truce is typical of put-upon care workers and their overdirecting employers.[87] But with such intimate proximity of carer and employer, resentment over extra work—and cultural and personal disagreements—can build up until an explosion occurs. Sometimes "a conflict begins over a mundane issue: a seemingly misspent hour, a seemingly sharp word. Quickly, the confrontation flares, exploding into a screaming match."[88] In Lucy's case, the conflict begins when Madame Beck tells Lucy that she should go to bed (the "misspent hour"), and Lucy responds by shouting that Madame Beck needs to stay out of her life. However, their fight changes nothing and is never referred to again (494–95). Madame Beck's denial is typical, since the employer often engages in evasive shifts to cover up the breakdown of the relationship.[89] In this case, although Madame Beck refuses to fire Lucy, Lucy can simply walk out because—fulfilling the immigrant dream—she has been able to start her own business.

It is certainly possible to see Lucy's situation at the end of the novel as nearly surreal, spangled with the hallucinatory experience of the nighttime extravaganza and the fairy-tale witch, with a uniquely stifling personality in Madame Beck and a particularly stressful relation to Graham Bretton—and of course, with a famously dismayingly ambiguous ending. But *Villette* also has another side, one of entirely predictably scripted behavior. Lucy's decision to emigrate, her difficult crossing, her desperation for live-in work, her exploitation and surveillance by her employer, and her own psychological disintegration under these conditions are nothing if not realist, and in those actions she speaks for thousands of others. Indeed, Hondagneu-Sotelo might be thinking of this novel when she writes: "Live-in housekeepers leave their jobs for various reasons—lack of privacy and respect, low wages, long hours, social isolation, disputes, and sexual harassment or the threat of it."[90] What Lucy experiences is, in other ways, all too drearily common, even 150 years later. We may want to read it as an anomalous, imaginative fairy tale of one woman's peculiar psychology—but we also have the right to read it as a representative story of the life experiences of a particular population and a serious investigation of the conditions of service work, care work, and global migration in the modern economy that was emerging in Brontë's lifetime.

From Caregiving to Caring

The pathologically split Lucy I have been describing is not someone who would (or could) narrate her own life. Torn between a devastatingly false surface and a violently furious private self, this Lucy has no language for her story. Refusing to speak preserves her cover of invisibility, but it also acts as passive-aggressive resistance to a reader she imagines as yet another exploitative employer. Instead of marveling at the novel's strange gaps, we should be impressed that it manages coherence; instead of asking why Lucy the character is so often silent, we should be asking why Lucy the narrator becomes able to speak at all. In other words, knowing what we know about the conditions of migrant service labor, *Villette*'s narrative difficulties seem entirely predictable, and what is perhaps remarkable is the fact that the story gets written in the first place. How does Lucy cobble together a self that allows her to tell her story?

What happens is that Lucy develops a relationship with a person who will listen to her. She enters into a care relation outside economic exchange. It is true that her relation with M. Paul is tenuous, imperiled, and problematic and often includes what we would today identify as sexual harassment and verbal abuse. But bad care is better than no care. The fact that someone is trying to meet her needs—even bumblingly and dangerously—is profoundly meaningful for Lucy. It gives her a template she can use to trace another care relation, this one with a reader. Given the deep mistrust of paid care we saw in chapter 2, the key factor in this relationship is its voluntary, unpaid relationality.

On a pragmatic level, Lucy recovers mainly because M. Paul makes it possible for her to leave a bad job. Lucy loses her lover, but she gets her school, and (to her own surprise) she finds that running her own business gives her the happiest three years of her life.[91] Lucy's mental health improves when she founds a new business and acclimates to Labassecourian culture. Helen Davis argues that *Villette*'s narrative difficulties derive from its effort to present the socially unacceptable story of a successful, ambitious businesswoman who remains outside the marriage plot.[92] Lucy's complaint is situational, based in an unbearably stressful care environment, so she recovers when she leaves it.

More profoundly, in M. Paul she acquires someone who wants to hear her story. She finally ceases to be invisible.[93] Through the novel's forty-four direct addresses to the reader—more than in any of her previous novels, Davis points out—we can begin to intuit the character of the narratee.[94] This person is sometimes sympathetic, but on the whole seems rather judgmental: apt to chide Lucy, get the wrong idea, issue religious diatribes, and overlook details.[95] Lucy's imagined reader does not want to hear her "impressions" (51, 240) and, famously, needs to be given reassuring fictions catering to naive beliefs about happy women's lives (39, 546). Who might this censorious, fussy, impatient, conventional figure remind us of but M. Paul? The narratee may not exactly be M. Paul, but seems to be modeled on him in important respects that allow us to read all of *Villette* as a long thank-you letter to Paul and a full explanation of what Lucy owes him, not just for his love but for the life he gave her—the career that allowed her to escape the pensionnat.

The companion figure seems fundamental to the caregiver's survival. Jamaica Kincaid, too, provides her Lucy with an intimate friend, as if the invisible caregiver cannot bring her own story to speech unless she can invoke a person to hear it. This interlocutor need not be a romantic partner, just a person who sees past the caregiver's invisibility. The companion need not be particularly sympathetic, or even real. For example, Sairey Gamp invokes a probably fictional friend, Mrs. Harris, to create enough alterity to allow her to make her feelings heard. Miss Wade needs a companion, even a mistreated orphaned girl, for Tattycoram's passionate, complex antagonism guarantees that Miss Wade feels seen. Like Lucy, Jane Eyre and Clara Morison find their sympathetic others in a male love interest who functions initially to confirm that she still has the cultural, imaginative, and intellectual credentials for communication beyond her sphere. In chapter 1, I pointed out that self-care often requires projecting part of the self into an "other"—often a transitional object—so as to achieve the alterity required for a care relation. These novels show the process at work as despised governesses, nurses, and companions affirm their selfhood through invoking an other.

Two other aspects of M. Paul's character give Lucy the emotional health to write her story. First, when he exits Labassecour, he cedes his space to Lucy, who literally steps into his place to make it her home. M. Paul never returns home, and for all we know, the three years he spends in the West Indies may have profoundly troubled his faith in Labassecourian ways. Or perhaps, if he had come back, he would have continued to call out Lucy's foreign ways. But his disappearance from the narrative gives her a chance to develop a relation to Labassecourianism that is all her own. Second, because he is absent, she can write to him, fully realizing herself in words, a pleasure that need not end simply because he vanishes. M. Paul has taught her how to write "in full-handed, full-hearted plenitude," for, as she remarks wonderingly, "there was no sham and no cheat, and no hollow unreal in him" (544). This is a new idea of authentic writing that she can emulate.

It is perfectly true that, as John Hughes concludes, "the narrator follows bewildering, perverse, or obscure antinarrative principles that raise the shock and intensity of narrative alienation or disappointment to a new level."[96] But if Lucy is "bewildering, perverse, or obscure" as a narrator, perhaps that is because we have not accounted for the persistent effect of emotional labor on the development of narrative. We must see the subjectivity of service workers and global migrant caregivers as central to the history of the novel, and we must credit the narrative innovations required by their situation: typified characters whose actions conceal rather than reveal their feelings; life led as a sequence of small events; narrative landmarks that include the difficult crossing, the beloved child, the invisible protagonist, and the companion; the intimate incursions in the live-in situation (sexual harassment, surveillance, indoctrination); and in best-case scenarios, the mode of escaping from the insupportable service situation.

It is perhaps worth noting that Miss Wade's story in *Little Dorrit* features many of the same narrative conventions: a crossing (she traverses between France and England), an unhappy teaching experience, love for a child (her adoration for the girl at her school), invisibility (she insists on her own unimportance relative to her employers), and an intimate friend (Tattycoram). After an initial passionate attachment to a child, both Miss Wade and Lucy Snowe insist on a stony detachment from their charges, resisting the performative imperative to care for the subjects of one's caregiving. The major difference is that whereas Lucy Snowe insists on the falsity of her performances, Miss Wade aggressively proclaims her truthfulness—two different ways of coping with the felt inauthenticity of emotional labor.

Villette demonstrates the truth of Eva Feder Kittay's claim that care work is "a costly morality."[97] In an era in which care was lauded as the ultimate proof of feminine self-abnegation, love, and service to others, and in an economic bracket in which women had to enact love for their students, employers, spouses, and relations to survive, *Villette* shows just how corrosive that felt. Brontë insists—correctly—that care work was becoming overwhelmingly a paid activity, relegated to exploited, underpaid migrant women. It offered either dangerous overidentification or sickeningly inauthentic performance. It generated frighteningly mobile, fluid identities in which race became a defensive posture and rage could corrode the self. *Villette* fearlessly reveals the devastating results of learning to care without caring, turning one's emotions into a form of labor in order to make a living, building a carapace of self out of repeated acts of caregiving that bear no relation to one's inner feelings. To notice the devastating work of emotional labor is to remember that care performativity does not always work, to acknowledge that people do not necessarily come to care about those they care for, and, above all, to assert that anti-sentimental stories of labor are worth telling too. To read Lucy as a type is, paradoxically, to uphold the validity of this sort of character. We readers are required to play the role of the intimate companion, the addressee whose presence—intuited, fictional, absent, and unsympathetic as it might be—makes it possible to tell these stories.

In that respect, *Villette* actually helps shape two traditions normally associated with postmodernism—not only migration narratives but also texts that interpolate their readers and writers. In lieu of being an archaeologist of knowledge, digging down, I have tried in this chapter to be more like an art historian who sympathetically observes a potter's technique in the context of the history of similar productions. If we have been seeking buried treasure, Lucy Snowe is baffling; if we are seeking a living tradition of people making the best they can with the clay they are granted, Lucy Snowe is exemplary.

In this chapter, I have used this metaphor because the act of placing layer after layer of clay coils reminds me of the repetitive acts of care that constitute Lucy's life, the constant daily service work. Yet external actions by paid caregivers constitute only one part of the world of care. In most Victorian fiction, as we have seen, paid care is relegated to minor characters and the central event is the unpaid, voluntary, affiliative care of loving friends in a community of care and the web of complex feelings that results. In the next chapter, we explore what seems like the opposite of poor Lucy Snowe: the world of richly vested sympathies.

CHAPTER FOUR

Beyond Sympathy

THE STATE OF CARE IN *DANIEL DERONDA*

True, generous feeling is made small account of by some, but here were two natures rendered, the one intolerably acrid, the other despicably savourless for the want of it. Feeling without judgment is a washy draught indeed; but judgment untempered by feeling is too bitter and husky a morsel for human deglutition.

—CHARLOTTE BRONTË, *JANE EYRE*[1]

CHARLOTTE BRONTË DESCRIBED paid caregiving that does not generate caring, but it is the nineteenth century's premier theorist of sympathy, George Eliot, who showed the other side: inner feelings of caring that do not produce action. To paraphrase Jane Eyre's remarks: action untempered by feeling is bitter, but feeling without action is a washy draught indeed. As we have seen, feeling and action work on separate tracks, but when those tracks do not converge, subjects often feel distress. Certainly the mechanistic, unmotivated repetition of caregiving without caring can lead to a corrosive sense of inauthenticity, but interestingly, it is just as miserable to feel for someone without being able to act, for that experience makes one feel despairingly powerless. Both extremes— the invisibilized paid caregiver and the sentimentally sobbing "angel in the house"—are associated with female roles (understandably, given women's overwhelming association with caregiving), and both are toxic. This chapter explores the pathology of feeling without acting, and by vesting it in Eliot's last novel, *Daniel Deronda* (1876), we will also be able to think about the ways in which sympathy, sentiment, and care work on a geopolitical scale.

This critique of feeling constituted a major shift for Eliot, for she strongly endorsed sympathy in her earlier work. In 1856, in "The Natural History of German Life," Eliot imagined subjectivity rooted in tradition and landscape, and she famously asserted:

> The greatest benefit we owe to the artist is the expansion of our sympathies. Appeals founded on generalizations and statistics require a sympathy ready-made, a moral sentiment already in activity; but a picture of human life such as a great artist can give, surprises even the trivial and the selfish into that attention to what is apart from themselves, which may be called the raw material of moral sentiment.[2]

Art, she believed, could produce new moral sentiments through expanding the reader's sympathies. Yet twenty years later, Eliot was not so sure she wanted this result. Late novels often revisit care and suffering. Just as Charlotte Brontë had a more somber assessment of care dynamics by the time she wrote *Villette*, so too did Eliot, by the time she tackled her last novel, "[bring] the ultimate value of sympathy into serious question," in the words of Rosemarie Bodenheimer.[3] Most Eliot critics try to resolve this problem by arguing that, in *Daniel Deronda*, Eliot advocates supplementing or altering sympathy in some fundamental way. In this chapter, I argue instead that Eliot is actually moving away from sympathy toward a paradigm more like an ethics of care—an action-based, performative set of deeds—and that Eliot's embrace of care has important political and critical ramifications. Daniel's move from helpless universal sympathy to targeted activity in this novel is a turn toward care that reveals a major shift in Eliot's thinking.

Comparing sympathy to care allows us to think about the differences between these states, instead of assuming they are part of a larger continuum. In this chapter, I argue that sympathy is a feeling generated by passive specularity and centered on the self as a way to confirm one's own moral sensitivity, a very different state from caregiving, a performative activity geared to the other's needs. I also address a third term, "sentiment," which I argue expresses the sensation of failed caregiving, not—as most critics assume—the intensification of sympathetic identification. People can live quite comfortably in the sensation of sympathy, or in the activity of care. What is intolerable is to be stuck between them—to be launched in the direction of action (or feeling) yet be unable to keep up that momentum. Sentiment is the flip side of emotional labor: both sentiment and emotional labor name the excruciating experience of failing to join your caregiving to your feelings, which suggests the profound and intimate failure of either being incapable of acting (passive, helpless) or being impervious to feeling (inauthentic, invisible).

Daniel Deronda is also useful for care theory inasmuch as it imagines care in a political sense. In chapter 1, I argued for a personal network intertwined with the Habermasian political sphere. But in *Daniel Deronda*, the personal network scales up to the real work of building a nation; the personal network becomes the state itself, and the care community entirely swallows the public sphere. I read this novel's nation-building vision in the context of both ethics of care political philosophy and communitarian thought in order to assess its claims about the role that care communities ought to take in the state.

Daniel Deronda, then, offers us two important interventions for thinking about care: a political exploration of the role of care in the state, and a personal exploration of the pathology of feeling. These two functions are not unrelated. (After all, Eliot treated both in "The Natural History of German Life.") Deronda's turn away from sympathy and toward care is so successful that he wants to project it onto a larger field, but the novel breaks down in the attempt to imagine a care-based polity, both formally and ideologically. *Daniel Deronda* literally takes care as far as it will go, beyond the horizon of the novel, beyond the temporality of the present, to a time and space that the novel itself cannot glimpse. *Daniel Deronda* moves beyond sympathy, but it also moves beyond landscape, to a completely alternative future.

The History of Sympathy

The philosophy of sympathy (essentially synonymous with what we call "empathy" today) was formulated in the eighteenth century, most influentially by David Hume and Adam Smith. Hume argued for sympathy as an involuntary contagion of feeling, while Smith regarded it as a deliberate act of imaginative identification, or, in Rae Greiner's words, an epistemological recognition, a "cognitive process," "a way for minds to conceive other people and situations and make judgments about their conditions."[4] However, both Smith and Hume thought that sympathy was crucial for maintaining social bonds. They "confidently adduce sympathy as the self-evident ground of social virtues, the affective root of 'fellow feeling,' 'benevolence,' and 'humanity.'"[5] Like care ethics, sympathy offered an alternative to the rational *Homo Economicus*, "a way to foster the sensitivity, generosity, and compassion increasingly regarded as incompatible with the rational self-interest required in their professional lives."[6]

Eighteenth-century sympathy theory undergirded two popular styles of fiction, sentiment and sensibility. "Sympathy" refers to the theory by which one understands or feels another's feeling, but "sensibility" shows characters animated by strong feeling for others, while "sentiment" attempts to elicit such feelings in the readers. Both the novel of sensibility and sentimental fiction used emotional interdependence to encourage future benevolent action.[7] The idea was that someone who emotionally identified with suffering would be inspired to alleviate it.[8] Virtuous action therefore comes from intensive personal connection. Sympathy could permit identification based on spontaneously shared feeling rather than identification based on class, birth, or wealth.[9] Ann Wierda Rowland points out that sympathy undergirded both abolitionist and pro-slavery rhetoric, as writers either mobilized descriptions of suffering slaves torn from families or penned accounts of virtuous slave-owners with grateful slaves.[10] In the eighteenth century, then, writers employed sympathy as a powerful rhetorical tool to move readers toward certain political actions.[11] Lynn Festa sums up: "Sentimental novels are also seen to possess political agency, inasmuch as they move their readers not only to tears but also to right action."[12]

In the Romantic period, however, sympathy began to feel both intensely necessary and somewhat problematic. Adela Pinch argues that in the early nineteenth century Romanticism was in a complex relationship with the language of sensibility.[13] The issue was that sympathy relied on a worrisome idea of feeling. Sympathy views "feelings as transpersonal, as autonomous entities that do not always belong to individuals but rather wander extravagantly from one person to another," Pinch explains, but in the Romantic period "people increasingly learned to claim their emotions as the guarantors of their individuality, buried in their breasts," so that in Romanticism's famous inward turn, feeling proved one's private, unique subjectivity, quite the opposite of a contagiously spread responsiveness.[14] Nancy Yousef points out that it might be more helpful to think of Romantic feeling as "intimacy," not as "sympathy." The oblique or missed connections made possible by physical proximity allow for different possibilities of subjectivity than a fully transparent, egalitarian, widespread, contagious sympathy.[15]

Victorians therefore did not inherit an unproblematic direct transmission from Smith and Hume; their ideas of sympathy had already been critiqued and reworked by Romantic writers, and the concept continued to change throughout the nineteenth century.[16] Sentimental feeling might offer private pleasure or moral self-approbation, but its link to social action had become ambiguous. Victorian authors could no longer necessarily assume that sentiment would rouse readers to demand change. Dickens's early work, for instance, shows a quasi-Romantic certainty that readers induced to sob over suffering children would fight for reforms, with sentimental urging that Oliver Twist, David Copperfield, Smike, Tiny Tim, or Little Nell might be saved if only the reader cared enough. By the time Dickens wrote his late novels, however, he had developed a more despairing sense of the diffusion of abusive conditions throughout the system. In *Bleak House*, for instance, Jo is not salvageable, nor is he idealized as an endangered innocent. Moreover, like Romantics, Victorians believed in a deeply buried unique individuality, but increasingly they ascribed this to psychological complexity rather than affective intensity. They began to ascribe the desire to help people to biological explanations of instinct and evolutionary accounts of the benefits of cooperation, not necessarily to ineffable moral feeling. Eliot participated in this materialist reconsideration, strongly influenced by George Henry Lewes's empiricist account of how organisms express a moral calculus as she revised and rewrote his work after his death in 1878.[17]

Nineteenth-century thinkers troubled the eighteenth-century idea of sympathy as the sense of feeling fellowship with another. Audrey Jaffe claims that in the Victorian period sympathy in fact became a *refusal* of shared feeling. Instead of feeling for the sufferer, Victorians regarded suffering as a spectacle they wished to disavow. By gazing in revulsion at the degraded figure—the impoverished man or the fallen woman—they reassured themselves of their own security regarding their own middle-class respectability. Thus, while sympathy continued to be important in the Victorian period, its meaning had drifted quite far from the eighteenth-century theorizing with which it began. Sympathy was still a crucial way to understand how much someone knew or felt for another, but those recognitions might be private or actually hostile. They might inhibit, not produce, moral acts. Pinch sums up the dwindling influence of sensibility/sympathy:

> Though we can think of Sensibility as having a continuous presence throughout the Romantic era and beyond, its most comprehensive beliefs and forms did eventually die out in the nineteenth century. The word itself ceased to denote a whole set of beliefs about emotion, morality, and art. Under the growing influence of more modern psychological and materialist understandings of the emotions, "sensibility" came to be defined, for example, in *Chambers Encyclopaedia* of 1862, merely as the physiological capacity to feel.[18]

The great charge of emotional effect had become material feeling.

Instead, Victorians often sought ethical guides in a shared social nexus: Christian teachings, conventional duty, institutional acts.[19] They followed Carlyle, who famously wrote, "Indeed Conviction, were it never so excellent, is worthless till it convert itself into Conduct."[20] Miriam Bailin explains that nursing itself expressed this Victorian preference for action. "In a characteristically Victorian adaptation of the moral assumptions underlying the previous century's cult of sensibility, the shedding of tears over human distress was not in itself sufficient to attest to one's benevolence but required instead the practical demonstration of compassion that nursing affords."[21] From the 1830s onwards, through the Evangelical movement, with its associated development of Sunday schools and Bible readings, and the development of a large civil service bureaucracy and an expectation of governmental intervention against abuses, a version of ethics that stressed action rather than feeling used legislation, inspections, and documentation to do the work previously relegated to individual acts of personal benevolence. As we saw in chapter 2, the shift to a state practice of medical oversight, starting with the New Poor Laws, bears witness to this emphasis on structural guidelines rather than individual feeling. After all, sympathy might be evoked by charismatic members of the "deserving poor," but a state is supposed to take care of everyone in need regardless of the personal feeling they may generate.

Active, pragmatic, inclusive reading experiences were common in nineteenth-century culture. Victorian readers would comment along the way as they read aloud to each other, wrote reviews that urged characters to behave differently, and attended dramatic versions of beloved sentimental stories like *East Lynne*, *A Christmas Carol*, and *Uncle Tom's Cabin*. These readers did not naively believe that the characters in these stories were real and could somehow benefit from their advice; rather, they saw no particular reason to discontinue the habit of active intervention just because the characters were fictional. Victorian middle-class women, engaged in this interactive reading style, would have had a strong reaction to accounts of dying children, starving waifs, or suffering animals and might have wanted to act on behalf of particular characters. Trained into habits of helpfulness, Victorians exercised that skill on texts as well as people.

It is no coincidence that the most popular dramatizations drew on the most famously sentimental tales. Sentiment provoked an especially urgent desire to insert oneself into the story. Most critics see sentiment and sympathy merging with one another, in a kind of murky bath of ardent soggy feelings.²² But this mapping is altered when we bring care into the mix, for we now have a spectrum running from the passive specularity of sympathy at one end all the way to the active performance of care at the other extreme. It is my contention that sentiment belongs much further along toward the care point on this continuum. Sentiment is what happens when someone gets stuck on the way to care. Conversely, for modern critics, sentiment can be annoying because it jolts us into wanting to give care, or, as Emma Mason argues, because it interrupts the calmly analytical stance to which we are committed as critics.²³ Sentiment names the irritating feeling of wanting to act when one cannot—a sensation that must have been particularly aggravating for Victorian female readers, who were trained to practical philanthropy. Those Victorians who enjoyed sentimental tears might have seen them as testimony to their anxiety to give care and confirmation of their moral virtue, while Victorians who disliked sentimental tears may have resented the text that manipulated them into frustration. As Austen's Emma remarks briskly: "If we feel for the wretched, enough to do all we can for them, the rest is empty sympathy, only distressing to ourselves."²⁴ The sensation of "empty sympathy" is sentiment—the distressing experience of encountering suffering we cannot alleviate, the irritation at spoiled care. By contrast, sympathetic tears are tears of sorrow at the state of the world or shared mourning for memorials of loss.

A few examples will demonstrate the difference. Sentimental scenes provoke a desire in the reader to act to save the character. Often the reader wants to speak up on behalf of a character who suffers through being forced to stay silent. For instance, in Tennyson's "Enoch Arden," a sailor assumed to have been lost at sea returns to discover that his wife has remarried, but he nobly refuses to reveal himself. Enoch Arden therefore makes a choice, and it is one in which it is eminently possible for someone to interfere. The innkeeper Miriam Lane expresses this urge for the readers, yearning "incessantly / To rush abroad all round the little haven. / Proclaiming Enoch Arden and his woes."²⁵ Enoch, sternly forbidding Miriam Lane to speak, forbids us as well, an interference with action that we might find exquisitely painful. Similarly, in Felicia Heman's "Casabianca," the boy is standing on the burning deck because he's waiting for permission to leave, but his dying father cannot give the word. Again, the reader wants to speak and save the boy, but cannot. In "A Christmas Carol," Scrooge begs to speak during the ghostly scenes, to no avail. It is agonizing to become an invisible, inaudible voyeur of his own life, unable to say the necessary word. Care depends on discourse, but these characters are barred from saying the words that might save them, and so are we.

Sympathy, by contrast, happens when we watch someone else's suffering passively, with a kind of melancholic self-congratulation. It often calls on the reader to think, not to speak. Thus, sympathy is often evoked in the pensive space of the internal monologue, as in Tennyson's "Tears, Idle Tears":

> Tears, idle tears, I know not what they mean,
> Tears from the depth of some divine despair
> Rise in the heart, and gather to the eyes,
> In looking on the happy Autumn-fields,
> And thinking of the days that are no more.[26]

Communing with private memories, mourning the lost, is an emotional experience with which we can identify, and we do not generally want to save the thinker from remembering. Rather, our relation to this scene is a specular one: watching someone saddened by memories, we may share the feeling. To return to the earlier examples, we feel *sentiment* for the doomed children in "Casabianca" and *A Christmas Carol*, but we feel *sympathy* for their fathers. We might sorrow to see the dying father and Bob Cratchit's suffering, but it doesn't really occur to us that we can transform their experience. With the boy and Tiny Tim, however, we feel we could intervene.

These two states can overlap, however, depending on the reader. When two people see something sad, one may be driven to try to fix it, while the other just watches mournfully. The move into the specular passivity of sympathy can easily happen when we regard tragedies happening on the other side of the globe. Noddings calls this "caring-about"—we might care *about* the victims of a famine or typhoon, but does that mean we care *for* them in the sense of actively trying to help them?[27] The modern category called disaster porn, the viral horror scenes that viewers consume, may be said to be motivated by sympathy. Such passivity can be produced not only by our geographic distance from the scene but also by historical change: how could we now help, say, Victorian street urchins? Unlike homeless children living in our own cities, who can produce immediate and intolerable feelings that lead to activity rather than contemplation, Victorian street urchins are likely to be seen by modern readers as merely sad spectacles.

In much nineteenth-century fiction, gloating over one's own feeling became proof of selfishness, the opposite of its earlier function as evidence of capacity to reach out to others. This trend arguably begins with Mr. Woodhouse in *Emma*, whom Claudia Johnson has argued is Austen's critique of a 1790s "man of feeling" in whom sensibility has become timidity and delicacy and selfishness. Austen replaces this figure with the new model of English masculinity, the laconic, strong, pragmatic man of action, Mr. Knightley.[28] By midcentury, the sentimental man is often a villain. Perhaps the most startling example is Count Fosco, a master criminal who identifies himself as a "Man of Sentiment."[29] Other men of sentiment are helpless, foolish, or selfish beings. There's Harold Skimpole in *Bleak House*, an icon of selfish self-absorption; Eliot's Tito Melema is governed by self-indulgent sentiment; and Gaskell depicts the fatally weak Osborne Hamley in *Wives and Daughters*, who cannot resist a disastrous secret marriage. In these cases, the sentimental man's failures have to be redressed by sturdier, stronger partners, a Mr. Jarndyce, a Romola, or a Roger Hamley. Jarndyce flees to the Growlery to escape precisely the gushing scenes of gratitude that had been the centerpiece of sentimental fiction, so that we register his virtue by his resistance to sentiment, not his immersion in it.

One uneasy issue is whom we sympathize with, and whom we reject, as readers. The problem with sympathy, Anna Lindhé writes, is that to sympathize with one character often requires us to dislike a different character, so that when readers are trained into empathetic identification with, say, David Copperfield, they are equally trained into irrational bias against Uriah Heep.[30] Lindhé's critique echoes Paul Bloom's argument in *Against Empathy*, where Bloom notes that sympathetic reading often has us identifying with awful people (as in Westerns, for instance). Bloom asserts that empathy is a bad guide to moral actions. We tend to favor people who are like us (so it can be allied with racism and biases), while empathy tempts us to make emotional, irrational choices, like pursuing short-term gains instead of long-term improvements, or favoring particular individuals instead of working for the good of the many.[31]

Eliot was uncomfortably aware of our tendency to sympathize with likable figures and worked hard to redirect us to less attractive characters, most famously when asking, "But why always Dorothea? Was her point of view the only possible one with regard to this marriage? I protest against all our interest, all our effort at understanding being given to the young skins that look blooming ... [for] in spite of the blinking eyes and white moles ... Mr. Casaubon had an intense consciousness within him, and was spiritually a-hungered like the rest of us."[32] In its efforts to teach us the feelings of the awful men Mr. Casaubon and Mr. Bulstrode, *Middlemarch* goes as far as any novel could in heroically pushing readers to the limits of sympathetic identification. However, Eliot could do less about another problem that plagued sympathetic reading. As Ann

Cvetkovich has argued, such texts actually retrain readers into merely personal expressions of feeling, foreclosing actual political action.[33] We can train ourselves to understand Bulstrode's emotions, but we cannot work through him to rectify his injustices. Stuck in the world of personal feeling, one could not necessarily step across into activity. It is this final critique that Eliot grapples with in *Daniel Deronda*.

To understand Eliot's critique of sympathetic passivity, however, we have to be aware of where her ideas of sympathy began. Although most theorists of sympathy start with Hume and Smith, Eliot was deeply influenced by her immersion in Spinoza, Strauss, and Feuerbach. By translating these Continental philosophers, the two latter of whom derived their own ethical ideas from Hegel, Eliot was immersed in a more embodied, socially oriented idea of responsiveness to the other.[34] Eliot translates Feuerbach thus: "The other is my *thou*,—the relation being reciprocal,— my *alter ego*, man objective to me, the revelation of my own nature, the eye seeing itself. In another I first have the consciousness of humanity; through him I first learn, I first feel, that I am a man: in my love for him it is first clear to me that he belongs to me and I to him, that we too cannot be without each other, that only community constitutes humanity."[35]

This sense of the importance of the other lies behind Eliot's mature philosophy, as summarized by Suzy Anger:

> Eliot's fundamental moral principle is that the capacity for sympathy is a necessary condition for a moral agent, since morality grows from the ability to imagine another's state of mind. Her presiding moral position is clearly expressed in an often-quoted passage from her letters: "My own experience and development deepen every day my conviction that our moral progress may be measured by the degree in which we sympathize with individual suffering and individual joy" (*GEL*, II:403). Morality grows from our ability to imagine and understand another's state of mind (hence the enormous importance of art and fiction), and the information needed to make correct moral judgments must come from sympathy, the only condition through which one can learn the effects of one's actions on others.[36]

Reading teaches us how to enter sympathetically into other human experiences, and such sympathetic engrossment in others' feelings, Eliot believed, is the germ of morality.[37]

Eliot's appreciation of the profoundly formative relations with "another," this insistence that "the relation [be] reciprocal," could come from any contemporary ethics of care argument.[38] Eliot espouses exactly what Nel

Noddings recommends in *Caring*: motivational displacement, the decentering of self to enter fully into another's experience. Indeed, ever since Carol Gilligan drew on examples from *The Mill on the Floss* when inventing ethics of care, the theory has leaned on George Eliot.[39] Care ethicists today write in the world that Eliot helped shape, and we readers can appreciate ethics of care because Eliot has primed us for it. We have all inherited Eliot's metaphor of the web, her interest in interdependent consciousnesses, her belief in the intricate ways one person can affect others, and even her multiplot narration from multiple perspectives, a form that helps readers recognize the validity of each person's point of view.[40]

However, in writing a novel about a political movement, Eliot ran up against a problem: sympathy not only does not guarantee good acts but may not generate action at all. In *Daniel Deronda*, she dealt with the fact that learning to see from another's perspective, though perhaps a personal moral triumph, may not go further. Sympathy is not necessarily useful. Care, on the other hand, is so geared toward deeds that it can easily slide into political action, whereas sentiment is that political action thwarted and baffled. This tripartite division helps make sense of *Daniel Deronda*. Indeed, it may constitute a political theory of its own.

From Sympathy to Care

Daniel Deronda probes exactly that crevice between sympathy and care. Daniel's early universal sympathy has the effect of paralyzing him into passivity. He experiences what Leona Toker calls "the reduction, cancellation, suppression, surrender of one's own self under the sway of sympathy."[41] Daniel is stuck in counterproductive sympathy because he does not know how to move toward active care, a problem the narrator describes as he floats down the river:

> His early-wakened sensibility and reflectiveness had developed into a many-sided sympathy, which threatened to hinder any persistent course of action.... His imagination had so wrought itself to the habit of seeing things as they probably appeared to others, that a strong partisanship, unless it were against an immediate oppression, had become an insincerity for him. His plenteous, flexible sympathy had ended by falling into one current with that reflective analysis which tends to neutralize sympathy.[42]

This insincerity, this neutralizing, oppressive, passive sympathy, is reminiscent of Jane Eyre's critique of Georgiana as "savourless" and "washy."

This passage's critique of sympathetic advocacy has engaged many Eliot scholars' attention. Rosemarie Bodenheimer sees the rejection of sympathy as marking the end of the realist novel for Eliot. Audrey Jaffe argues that *Daniel Deronda* replaces one form of sympathy with another ("passionate feeling"). Thomas Albrecht and Amanda Anderson both argue that generic sympathy needs to be replaced by a deliberate act of selecting particular objects of sympathy. Rachel Ablow thinks that Eliot argues for supplementing sympathy with remorse or gratitude, but she confesses that this is a "not entirely satisfying" solution. Lisbeth During argues for a racial component. Jaffe notes that *Daniel Deronda* "characterizes sympathy as a currency whose random expenditure engenders emotional paralysis and inhibits action."[43]

This passage makes more sense, however, if we see it as the moment when Eliot installs care in lieu of sympathy. For Daniel's utter passivity is the fundamental problem. As George Levine points out, what is "missing from this ideal intellectual prostration, this visionary embodiment of objectivity, is the impetus to act at all," and perhaps that is the point—to goad the reader into demanding action.[44] As the reader's impatience mounts, Daniel suddenly does manage to do something: in a scene that, as Neil Hertz remarks, is "rendered precisely as the movement of a neutral consciousness drawn into action," he rushes to save Mirah.[45] This is the scene where Daniel moves out of passive, specular sympathy into performative, active care, initiating a new mode in Eliot's moral imagination. The scene problematizes sympathy and then explicitly offers care as the answer.

To understand just what kind of care Daniel develops, we need to review his history of care relationships. The crucial relationships of his life are characterized by poor care—care relations that specifically fail to be reciprocal or to acknowledge his real needs—and by a response of passive, helpless acquiescence.

First, Daniel's filial relationships are fundamentally problematic. His mother abandoned him as a toddler, and she introduces herself to her adult son by stating, "I am your mother. But you can have no love for me" (536). Daniel continually tries to assure the Princess Halm-Eberstein that he sympathizes with her imaginatively, insisting that, "though my own experience has been quite different, I enter into the painfulness of your struggle. I can imagine the hardship of an enforced renunciation." This is the kind of cognitive recognition that Adam Smith defined as sympathetic. However, his mother rejects this model, insisting on the experiential uniqueness of her own experience: "No . . . You are not a woman. You may try—but you can never imagine what it is to have a man's force of genius in you, and yet to suffer the slavery of being a girl" (531). Herself victimized by a tyrannical father, she sees no alternative to the two alternatives of liberty and slavery; she has no model of communal, mutual relations.

Sir Hugo's care mistake is the opposite of the Princess Halm-Eberstein's. His comes not out of loveless rejection but out of selfish affection, not out of unnecessarily cruel renunciation but out of excessively careless inclusion.

> The mistakes in his behaviour to Deronda were due to that dullness towards what may be going on in other minds, especially the minds of children, which is among the commonest deficiencies even in good-natured men like him, when life has been generally easy to themselves, and their energies have been quietly spent in feeling gratified. No one was better aware than he that Daniel was generally suspected to be his own son. But he was pleased with that suspicion; and his imagination had never once been troubled with the way in which the boy himself might be affected, either then or in the future, by the enigmatic aspect of his circumstances. He was as fond of him as could be and meant the best by him. (145–46)

This is a failure of sympathy: Sir Hugo has never once tried to imagine how Daniel feels. And it is not adequate care unless one can imagine the other's needs. Sir Hugo is using Daniel transactionally, like a mirror reflecting greater glory upon himself.

A failure to establish relations with the other also characterizes Gwendolen's relationships. The problem is that Gwendolen imagines herself as a liberal subject who can triumph over anything. "Other people allowed themselves to be made slaves of," thinks Gwendolen exultingly, but "it was not to be so with her" (31). She "felt ready to manage her own destiny" (32), unaware that others' actions might constrain or reshape her own life, or even that other people might have legitimate needs of their own. Of course, her life proves that power-seeking, pleasure-seeking autonomous individualism is naive at best, self-destructive at worst. Gwendolen's inability to imagine others' personhood makes her catastrophically incapable of perceiving Grandcourt's real personality.

Gwendolen demands care from everyone, her mother, her servants, and Daniel, without any idea of reciprocity. "From start to finish she finds it impossible to imagine how other people radically different from herself and independent of her can even exist," Lisbeth During sums up.[46] She expresses her needs as demands: "I will bear any penance. I will lead any life you tell me. But you must not forsake me. You must be near. If you had been near me—if I could have said everything to you, I should have been different. You will not forsake me?" (590). This is more of a show of groveling submission to a dominant male than a relation of affectionate care. The narrator discusses it in terms of who experiences more "coercion" (363). She never sees Daniel except as "a priest"—and, as he remarks tetchily, he "was not a priest" (363, 580–81). For Daniel to marry Gwendolen would be to cement himself into a pathological relation in which he would constantly be giving care, without any reciprocal attention from Gwendolen. To be stuck in one role, as carer or cared-for, is very unhealthy. Not until the very end of the novel does Gwendolen finally manage to see Daniel as another person, "for the first time feeling the pressure of a vast mysterious movement, for the first time being dislodged from her supremacy in her own world" (677). Only in their final scene, when she begs, "Don't let me be harm to *you*," does Gwendolen succeed in extending care to another by genuinely trying to think about another's needs (680).

Nor is Daniel's friend any better than his potential love interest. Hans "seemed to take Daniel as an Olympian who needed nothing—an egotism in friendship which is common enough with mercurial, expansive natures" (153). Caring for Hans costs Daniel his own chance at a scholarship. Since Daniel is constantly catering to people who demand care, his social life consists of "acts of considerateness that struck his companions as moral eccentricity" (149). In Daniel's social world, in which everyone is pursuing self-aggrandizement, devoting oneself to others is a "moral eccentricity" at best, an inexplicable self-sacrifice at worst. Hans belatedly rectifies this imbalance at the end when he informs Daniel of Mirah's love. Like Gwendolen, Hans grows toward seeing Daniel as a subject requiring care.

The agent of change in Daniel's life is a disabled man, Mordecai. In Victorian fiction, the disabled subject is often the one who can retrain those damaged by bad care relationships, because the disabled character has survived by learning to manage a care community successfully, organizing servants, friends, and family members into a group that helps the subject function.[47] Mordecai's community of care is the Ezra Cohen family. As is typical of communities of care, these are affiliative, voluntary relations. The Cohen family is not related to Mordecai, but as Ezra remarks, they take care of him from "charity" and also because even though "he's an encumbrance," "he brings a blessing down, and he teaches the boy. Besides, he does the repairing at the watches and jewellery" (336). Although Daniel privately smiles at what he considers a comic mix of "kindliness" and "calculation," what he misses is that the Cohen family and Mordecai have balanced their responsibilities, engaging in mutual service, reciprocally caring for one another so that each feels valued and useful. Mordecai's teaching and repairing ensure his dignity as a valued member of the group, rather than purely an object of charity, as Daniel himself is to Sir Hugo. Because Mordecai and the Cohens fluidly shift between the roles of carers and cared-fors, the community maintains an egalitarian balance, and this experience teaches Mordecai how to achieve a healthy care relation with Daniel.

Daniel's relation to Mordecai looks at first like yet another example of bad care, a lopsided power dynamic in which a teacher coercively projects onto a student instead of sensing the student's own need. "Cast in the roles of pupil and disciple, Deronda experiences the immense and sometimes overwhelming power of Mordecai," Michael Ragussis notes, characterizing Mordecai's influence as "a kind of coercive conversion."[48] By contrast, in an ethics of care, a good teacher "accepts *his* [the student's] motives, reaches towards what *he* intends, so long as these motives and intentions do not force an abandonment of her own ethic."[49] Mordecai seems to have little interest in "the student's feeling toward the subject matter," instead imperiously informing Daniel how he must already feel. In this respect, Daniel's teacher resembles Daniel's biological mother, adoptive father, love interest, and best friend, in that they all project onto Daniel what they need him to be, without seeing who Daniel really is. This is bad care inasmuch as they are not engrossing themselves in the other.

Daniel's experience with Mordecai, however, differs crucially from his other relationships in one respect: this relationship has reciprocity. Daniel learns from Mordecai, but he returns the favor by providing Mordecai with a home, furniture, clothing, and medical care. Surely Daniel's disposition of Mordecai's body is as coercive as Mordecai's direction of Daniel's soul, but as long as each man is equally bossy in his own sphere, Daniel can feel that the obligations are balanced, instead of always feeling like the one conferring the obligation. This reciprocity, however, is more important for Daniel than for Mordecai, for Mordecai is quite indifferent to his own terminal illness, absolute poverty, and total dependence. By regarding himself, with absolute conviction, as the person conferring care, Mordecai allows Daniel to see himself, for the first time, as the object of someone else's caring and therefore a person of value, a person who merits others' care and concern. Mordecai is the only one of Daniel's cared-fors who offers care in return instead of making demands of him, projecting onto him, groveling before him, or exploiting him.

It is not necessarily what modern readers would regard as a healthy relationship, but it is good enough to retrain Daniel. As we have seen in the case of M. Paul and Lucy, people can flourish in a mutual care relationship even when it is notably imperfect. The men move from the unbalanced initial state of Mordecai's overriding insistence and Daniel's abashed, uncertain response toward a mutually sustaining care that culminates in the kind of merged sensibilities depicted by care ethicists. Mordecai announces, "You must be not only a hand to me, but a soul—believing my beliefs—being moved by my reasons—hoping my hopes—seeing the vision I point to—beholding a glory where I behold it! . . . You will be my life: it will be planted afresh; it will grow" (422–23). This relationship closely resembles Noddings's depiction of a pedagogical care dyad: "In 'inclusion,' the teacher receives the student and becomes in effect a duality. This sounds mystical, but it is not. The teacher receives and accepts the student's feeling toward the subject matter; she looks at it and listens to it through his eyes and ears."[50] This euphoric mutuality is what Daniel calls "the blent transmission" that the two men achieve (632).

In the nineteenth century, it might have been easier to imagine such a successful mutuality in a teaching relationship than in the rapidly professionalizing medical arena. In *Villette*, of course, teaching is corrosive, an exhaustingly relentless falsification of Lucy's feelings. She enacts a spectacle of violence as the teacher, cowing the girls into submission because she does not have the language to communicate. But *Daniel Deronda* showcases a better pedagogical relationship, one that moves from a tyrannical imposition to a joint project as teacher and student learn to communicate.

Daniel's racial identification, like Lucy Snowe's, is both chosen and innate, both cosmopolitan and biological. Lucy's Englishness is written on the body, but she can overcome it through a chosen Labassecourienne identity. Daniel's Jewishness is also written on the body: as Cynthia Chase famously points out, the plot only works if he never looks at his own circumcised body.[51] Although Daniel's mother tried to override his legacy with a cosmopolitan secular upbringing, Daniel must choose to be the Jew that he always already was. The reader feels "that it is because Deronda has developed a strong affinity for Judaism that he turns out to be of Jewish parentage," in a temporally upside-down world in which causes and effects chase one another.[52] Race here is simultaneously both innate and chosen.

Mordecai and Daniel's relationship reveals one of the most interesting qualities of care dyads: the way a care relationship overrides conventional gender, sexual, and biological identifications. The relationship between a carer and a cared-for may fluctuate among erotic passion, friendly affection, family feeling, deep loyalty, pure duty, and mutual irritation.[53] We need to resist our temptation to assume that eroticism is always the underlying truth and our job is to find it and name it. In a care relation, what matters is the enactment of care, not the underlying feelings, which may fluctuate along a range that includes everything from passion to distaste.

In this relationship, care explicitly transcends the body. Mordecai's death actually consolidates his and Daniel's conjoined mind. "Death is coming to me as the divine kiss which is both parting and reunion—which takes me from your bodily eyes and gives me full presence in your soul," exults Mordecai (683). Slipping into Daniel's very soul, the teacher lives on: "Where thou goest, Daniel, I shall go" (683). Each carries on his care to the end as Daniel gives his dying teacher physical comfort and Mordecai explains his soul to his student. The novel ends by insisting that "nothing is here for tears" in Mordecai's quiet death.[54] These final words explicitly forbid sentiment, but there is no reason for sentimentality, because care has been duly and fully administered. Sentiment is generated by the reader's discomfort with something undone, something unsaid. Mordecai's death, by contrast, marks the completion and fulfillment of the relationship.

Mordecai's example sets the path for Mirah. Just as Mordecai's previous care community is the Ezra Cohen household, Mirah receives care from the Meyrick family. In Mirah's case, her father's exploitation kept her unnaturally acquiescent. Retrained by the Meyricks, she finds it possible to express both gratitude and dissent, to be emotionally honest in a way that was impossible with her father, and she continues this self-assertion when she moves in with Mordecai. Crucially, she feels empowered to reprove Mrs. Meyrick, causing that matron to apologize and retract (315). Mirah continues to speak out when she corrects Mordecai's parable of the Jewish maiden, asserting her point of view in a way her father never permitted (618). In return, Mirah offers the kind of acknowledgment that Noddings regards as crucial: "What the cared-for contributes to the relation is a responsiveness that completes the caring. This responsiveness need not take the form of gratitude or even of direct acknowledgement. Rather, the cared-for shows either in direct response to the one-caring or in spontaneous delight and happy growth before her eyes that the caring has been received."[55] This growing cheerfulness, this flourishing, is precisely the way that both Mordecai and Mirah respond to Daniel—and it is how Daniel responds to Mordecai's teaching as well.

A care reading can help stress the fact that Mirah and Daniel are both survivors of parental loss who have settled into damaging passivity and who have had to relearn viable social relations through Mordecai. It is the disabled man who has the most to teach them. Moreover, because both Mirah and Daniel have lost their foundational Jewish community by losing their mothers, choosing each other via Mordecai restores that primordial loss.[56] Denied mothering themselves, they establish what Virginia Held has called a "mothering relationship" (which, she stresses, anyone can participate in, not just mothers); victimized by their fathers' unthinking projections of their own needs, they become careful to see the other fully. Daniel and Mirah end the novel aiming to found a new state, using something like the maternalist model: their state will be a kind of parent to its members, who will be "bound together" (in Held's words) "by relations of concern and caring and empathy and trust."[57]

The State of Care

Care offers us a useful way to read the controversial ending of *Daniel Deronda*. Readings of Daniel's turn to Zionism rarely pay much attention to the work he actually plans to do, perhaps because Eliot leaves those details somewhat unresolved. As Irene Tucker points out, Eliot asks us to imagine a "novelistic afterward" that she has "not yet written."[58] However, this vagueness is not a failure of imagination, but a way of reorienting the citizen toward a more relational form of political belonging that Eliot could not describe because it did not exist in the world, and perhaps could not exist. At the Philosophers' Club, Mordecai asks, "Can a fresh-made garment of citizenship weave itself straightway into the flesh and change the slow deposit of eighteen centuries? What is the citizenship of him who walks among a people he has no hearty kindred and fellowship with, and has lost the sense of brotherhood with his own race?" (445) In other words, how can hereditary kinship relate to political citizenship? In a maternalist model, how do you extrapolate parental relations into national identity?

The nation, in Eliot's view, had to be based on "filial sentiment," which would extend toward kin and then "the extended family of the nation."[59] Like a care community, this model relies not on biological ties but on affiliation—the "filial sentiment" that extrapolates from kin to extend to others. As a result, Daniel imagines a nation not as a government validated by citizens but as a human collectivity united through affection. His aim is "to identify myself, as far as possible, with my hereditary people" and to "bind our race together" by "giving them a national centre" (557, 632, 677). This is not a political calling but a social mission. He is trying to form a nation solely through the personally oriented network, ignoring the politically oriented network with which it normally coexists.

Deronda's decision to found an organic community is a very Victorian aspiration. In his *History of the Protestant Reformation* (1824–1826), the radical reformer and journalist William Cobbett depicted Catholicism "as a kind of welfare state, a reservoir of communitarian values, and a lost utopic sphere."[60] Cobbett's position chimed in with other proponents of the medieval revival in the 1820s and 1830s, from A.W.N. Pugin to Thomas Carlyle, who yearned for preindustrial comradely fellowship, a yearning later taken up by William Morris and John Ruskin. This sort of approach resonated for Victorians, who regarded liberal "individualism" as "a serious evil undermining the political and social order of their times."[61] The drive to compete, the relentless focus on gaining profit regardless of others, the vision of oneself as an independent agent fighting for a place in the market, suggested "anomie, isolation, and egotism."[62] Instead, Victorian thinkers turned to a nostalgic fantasy of preindustrial community, perhaps most famously articulated by Ferdinand Tönnies, whose theory of *Gemeinschaft und Gesellschaft* (1887) contrasted *Gemeinschaft* (a traditional community rooted in the land and the family) with *Gesellschaft* (a modern, urban, heterogeneous, industrial society).[63] The widespread cultural fantasy of *Gemeinschaft* is profoundly important to Eliot's fiction, most of which she sets in the last decades of the eighteenth century and the first of the nineteenth, the period when Victorians believed traditional community was slipping away, and it forms the model for what Deronda wants to found in the East.[64] In Bernard Semmel's description:

> Eliot viewed the national tradition as a frame of life that connected past, present, and future, making it possible to recognize duties of parents to children and children to parents. These links to past and future would enable men and women to overcome their natural egoism and to extend their sympathy, first to the individual beings with whom they had a tie of blood and responsibility, and then to the wider group with whom they shared a common heritage of language, culture, and history.[65]

Eliot's advocacy of a sympathetic, historical communal life predicts modern communitarian theory. Communitarianism argues that humans are already enmeshed in social relations, with inherited customs, rules, and connections, rather than the wholly free agents imagined by classic liberalism. "Community" is usually associated with a past golden age of harmonious, organic local life, and communitarians advocate returning to those deep traditions.[66] They prioritize three forms of community, according to Daniel Bell: communities of place, based on geographical location (the village); communities of memory, based on shared significant experiences (the nation, the ethnic group); and psychological communities, based on meaningful face-to-face interactions (school, family, work).[67]

The philosopher Charles Taylor resembles his Victorianist forebears when he insists that "the free individual of the West is only what he is by virtue of the whole society and civilization which brought him to be and which nourishes him; that our families can only form us up to this capacity and these aspirations because they are set in this civilization."[68] As this statement reveals, communitarianism can be deeply retrospective. Laurence Hamilton critiques the movement for assuming that a person's needs "are embedded in the cement of her own culture," as if it were not possible to move beyond one's formative influences.[69] Communitarianism can seem worrisomely conservative, endorsing religious conformism, and its gender politics can enshrine female dependency.[70]

Daniel Deronda speaks to contemporary care ethicists as well as communitarians. While communitarians dream about a return to organic community, care ethicists have been working to make ethics of care into a meaningful basis for real-world political reforms. Peta Bowden and Daniel Engster, for instance, both advocate understanding the state and the citizen as participants in a care relation, so that the state does not just exist in order to guarantee personal liberty to its citizens but also to offer the best care to all its residents, to guarantee their safety, health, and happiness.[71] Another form of communal care-based governance is proposed by Eva Feder Kittay, who wants the state to have "*social responsibility* (derived from political justice realized in social cooperation) for enabling dependency relations satisfactory to dependency worker and dependent alike," along with "social institutions that foster an attitude of caring and a respect for care by enabling caregivers to do the job of caretaking without becoming disadvantaged in the competition for the benefits of social cooperation."[72] Kittay calls this principle *doulia*, the name she gives to voluntary collectives of reciprocal caregiving. A principle of *doulia* might inspire a government to pay people for providing child care or elder care to members of their own families, to offer such caregivers training, and to allow for vacations and sick leave. In care ethics, then, the state is by no means outside the work of care, but instead fundamentally involved in caring for its citizens.

Yet it is interesting that in the last scenes of *Daniel Deronda*, Eliot does not try to depict the political or economic outline of the new state, but rather, reverts to something more familiar: a local, affiliative community of care. It is as if the future nation felt so far beyond the bounds of possibility as to be unwritable, and she compensated by giving us a smaller social group to conceptualize in its place, the reliably, familiarly manageable community standing in for the new nation.

This is the group forming in the last pages of the novel as the Cohens, Meyricks, Mallingers, and Klesmers unite to support Daniel and Mirah's wedding. It is a classic care community: affiliative (none of the guests, except Mordecai, is actually kin to Daniel or Mirah), egalitarian (Eliot stresses the willing coexistence of the respectable Meyricks and the humble Cohens), and discursive (Eliot describes it through a succession of speeches and interjections). The participants have all been carers. The Meyricks recognize that the caregiving binding them to Mirah "would always make a sweet memory to them. For which of them, mother or girls, had not had a generous part in it—giving their best in feeling and in act to her who needed?" (681). The Cohens, too, are present because Mordecai could not "have borne that those friends of his adversity should have been shut out from rejoicing in common with him" (681). Even Gwendolen has finally become capable of recognizing Daniel's care for her and writes a letter giving him back care in turn. I have pointed out that both Mirah and Daniel initially experience toxic parenting and friendship, and when we see this novel in terms of care relations, we can recognize that the whole narrative works toward the slow and difficult formation of relations of care in a society that is generally governed by self-aggrandizement, as signalized by the gradual self-reformation of people like Hans and Gwendolen.

This nuptial care community is what I have been calling a personally oriented community: people motivated by the desire to meet others' needs, which may have secondary political effects, like a parenting group that may end up advocating for state-supported child care. Here the characters' personal care for Daniel and Mirah has led to a political investment in the future of the Middle East. But Eliot presents no countervailing politically oriented community, no Habermasian public sphere. She offers no sense of an organization trying to figure out what the new nation's land use, legislation, constitutional protections, economic policy, or international relations might look like, although Eliot had access to at least two ways of writing political Zionism that would have incorporated such issues.

First, Eliot might well have set *Deronda* amid British parliamentary politics, an approach that would have been accessible for the author of *Felix Holt* (1866). In this genre, Eliot could have modeled her treatment of the Zionist question on her contemporary Anthony Trollope's treatment of the Irish question in *Phineas Finn* and *Phineas Redux*, published just a few years earlier (1867–1868 and 1873, respectively): Trollope's hero has a personal and sometimes professionally inconvenient investment in this political dispute. Eliot was also already influenced by Trollope in *Daniel Deronda*, as Nancy Henry argues, for the Gwendolen plot was informed by Trollope's depiction of a cynical, soulless, financially materialistic society in *The Way We Live Now* (1874–1875), which Eliot was reading while composing *Daniel Deronda*, as well as by *The Prime Minister*, published the same year as *Deronda* (1876).[73] Even if Eliot did not imitate Trollope, she might have tied Daniel's choices to the political issues in the news. Daniel and Mirah emigrate in October 1866, just before 1867's Second Reform Bill. Daniel's act of repatriation is a profoundly meaningful one, for the nation was debating what might justify the participation of working people in governance and asking whether property or personal qualities still needed to be part of citizenship.[74]

However, Eliot has her character explicitly reject this mode of political work. Daniel refuses to go into Parliament, declaring, "I don't want to make a living out of opinions." Sir Hugo points out that "the business of the country" cannot be done "if everybody looked at politics as if they were prophecy, and demanded an inspired vocation" (322). Of course, the novel does end with an "inspired vocation" and "prophecy." Daniel assumes his leadership in the East in spite of the fact that he owns no property and pays no rates there; he is neither a citizen nor an elected political leader. Nor does he form political opinions in the way Habermas imagines, by reading newspapers and engaging in rational discourse with other men who also feel a stake in national affairs. There is no public sphere here, no discourse of rights or liberty. Daniel's end is more of an alternative to the liberal political realm than an extension of it.

Second, Eliot might have imitated her peers in writing a political novel that employs sentiment as a way to ignite the reader's desire for change. Eliot corresponded with Harriet Beecher Stowe and knew *Uncle Tom's Cabin* well. Sentiment was a major technique in the novels of the early nineteenth century, particularly in the genres of the industrial novel, the anti-slavery novel, and the anti–Poor Law novel. For example, Frances Trollope's *Michael Armstrong, Factory Boy*, Stowe's *Uncle Tom's Cabin*, and Dickens's "A Christmas Carol" all mobilize readers through making us chafe over children's mistreatment. But as I have noted, sentiment had become a problematic way to generate political action by the mid-nineteenth century, and Eliot's avoidance of this mechanism indicates some skepticism about it. In *Daniel Deronda*, no Jewish child or elder suffers unnecessarily (we are explicitly assured that the Cohen children enjoyed the wedding mightily), although the mistreatment of innocent Jewish children could have produced a powerful argument for the need for a homeland. In *Daniel Deronda*, care has been received and acknowledged, and there is no uncomfortable residue left to spur the reader.

For this is the point about *Daniel Deronda*: it makes the move from sympathy to care so thoroughly, so overwhelmingly, that nothing is left over. I have pointed out how Daniel and Mirah and Mordecai are all retrained through care, and as evidenced by their contributions to the nuptial care community, care ends up suffusing and altering everyone: the Meyricks, the Klesmers, the Mallingers, and Gwendolen herself. As the community goes, so goes the nation: can the nuptial community be embedded in the foundation of a state? Modern observers would regard this ideal of the nation as a close social group as dangerously homogenizing at worst, daffily idealistic at best, but that is why we have case studies in novels. My point is not to endorse the idea that a new nation ought to be built on the basis of care relations, nor to point out the now-inescapable irony that such a nation overlooks any possibility of care relations with those already living there. Rather, I want to say that, if most readers find the ending of *Daniel Deronda* unsatisfactory, the difficulty and ambition of formulating such a vision might be precisely why. In other words, the sketchiness of this vision is the sign of an attempt to imagine something new: care citizenship. Just as *Villette* predicts a world of global migrant caregiving, *Deronda* imagines a future in which a nation could be a community of care. Beyond the horizon of the novel, beyond the borders of the known characters and their world, *Daniel Deronda* tries to imagine care community on an international scale.[75]

If *Villette* foresaw a bleak world devoid of personal caregiving, *Daniel Deronda* prophesies an ecstatic world filled to the brim with care, with no room for any other concerns. Neither extreme is healthy or viable. If *Villette* recognizes the corrosive, dehumanizing effect of emotional labor exerted to give care without caring, *Daniel Deronda* imagines an idealistic future in which caring solves all problems. If Lucy Snowe becomes self-alienated through her emotional labor, Daniel Deronda is passive and exploited through his too-ready sympathy. To paraphrase my epigraph: Lucy's action without feeling is bitter, but Daniel, feeling without action, is savorless and washy. In reality, personally oriented communities need to work with politically oriented groups, amateur care communities need to work with state-sponsored medical services, and care needs to be accompanied by justice. Writing in the stress of the midcentury transition to a modern world, Brontë and Eliot made different predictions, but in each case, choosing one side only shows all the more stringently the need for a cooperative future.

CHAPTER FIVE

Care Meets the Silent Treatment in *The Wings of the Dove*

DISCOURSE IS THE CORE OF A CARE relationship. When the carer and the cared-for can communicate, in any form (written, verbal, visual, nonverbal), they can adjust behavior to match the other's needs better in a mutual attunement that can prevent carers from becoming tyrannical and cared-fors from feeling disempowered. When we scale up to the level of a care community, we find that discourse regulates the members' social ties. Habermas believed that a system of communicative action among egalitarian participants characterized the political sphere, where "the best rational argument and not the identity of the speaker was supposed to carry the day."[1] While a care community does not need rational discourse, it does require everyone to attend to each other, regardless of members' status. Members need to hear other members justify their inclusion, explain their attachments, and articulate when and why they want to leave. Without such discourse, everyone will be hurt and baffled by the others' actions. In both political and personal networks, the idea is to achieve a communal consensus based on shared ideas, rather than imposing authority vested in particular individuals. So it is no surprise that in fiction we find that viable care communities constantly discuss their participants' relationships, whereas problematic communities of care are dogged by dysfunctional silence.

Henry James's late novel *The Wings of the Dove* (1902) explores what happens to the novel form when it is shaped by silence, not discourse. In reading *The Wings of the Dove*, we see how a move into modernist style is provoked by the overriding imperative toward discourse. Like an onrushing stream blocked by a wall of rocks, it carves a new network of channels, and it's my contention that James erects such a barrier in order to diffuse and disseminate discourse into a different kind of topography, a channel that opens between the reader and the text. The wall I have been describing is the fourth wall, and James figures out how to break it by making discourse trickle through its chinks or crash over its top, reaching us beyond the novel. In other words, *The Wings of the Dove* does not ask us to watch characters forming a care community, but rather incorporates us into the work of caring for a fragile text. Instead of the activist leap we have seen in sentimental texts, the reader becomes an analyst or a conservationist. Instead of a Victorian reader's intervention in a realist narrative, we must learn to act as carers for a rarified text pockmarked with dangerous spaces of silence, stretches where our particular tendance is especially needed.

We have seen that Victorians often leapt into sentimental readings because they desperately wanted to help doomed young people: the suicidal Mirah, Tiny Tim, Little Nell, or the boy on the burning deck. Inasmuch as *The Wings of the Dove* centers on a dying youth, it seems to invite such sentiment. However, this novel does not allow the fantasy of a heroic readerly intervention. Milly cannot be saved. Instead, we stew in the failures of care at every level, including our own. In reading this novel, we do not do the sentimental work of fighting the helplessness engendered by reading, but rather steep ourselves in the bittersweet pleasures of that silent marginalization from the work of the story. *Wings* makes us inhabit a twentieth-century idea of reading that is silent, private, passive, and voyeuristic rather than active and sociable like nineteenth-century reading, and it forces us to grapple with what care could possibly mean in such a practice. *Wings* trains us to participate in discourse rather than identify with characters.

Thus, *Wings* marks a turn in the uses of care—and a turn in this book—from intradiegetic character relations to an abstract metalevel in which reader and writer use a care framework to reconsider speech, writing, authority, and authorship. In the first three chapters, we have seen how characters like Ebenezer Scrooge, Anne Elliot, Jane Eyre, Lucy Snowe, and Daniel Deronda are transformed as they learn to enter truly mutual care relations with others. We stayed on the intradiegetic level and we looked at character formation in a relational mode, seeing these figures as members of collectives who defined themselves against others, rather than as isolated individuals. But in these last three chapters, we will be using a more formalist perspective, thinking about how care might function as a paradigm that structures forms of reading, writing, and academic practice. We will explore how a reader can be co-opted into the role of carer (as in James's *Wings of the Dove*), how an author might present her writerly influences as a care community (Yonge's *Heir of Redclyffe*), and how we ourselves, as academics, can deliberately invoke the structures of communities of care in our research, teaching, and service. In the extradiegetic turn of these last chapters, we can think about textuality itself as a scene of caregiving.

A novel centered on the death of a person and the burning of a text, *Wings* concentrates on absence, silence, and destruction and in that respect rouses our desire to take care of it. Its language is fragile—its information must be teased out carefully, like the thinnest filaments. What I am saying here is that the famous difficulty of late James style requires a form of reading that we might well call care. Instead of trying to care for Milly Theale, we care for her story—a readerly role reinvented for the twentieth century. Late James style thus sublimates, disseminates, and abstracts the work of care.[2]

The Jamesian Care Community

Henry James grew up in a family deeply concerned with caregiving. Jean Strouse writes that, "in [the James] family, the concern elicited by illness passed for love—and doctors were the scientifically sanctioned personification of solicitude and care."[3] Virtually every member of the family experienced sustained periods of invalidism, with Henry James Sr. and all the James children (especially Alice) enduring debilitating illnesses that particularly affected their backs, eyes, digestion, and nerves.[4] Psychosomatic illnesses often served as the Jameses' expression of distress over roles they were being pressured to adopt, and family members also shared recommendations for treatments as a way of demonstrating affection. The James clan could counteract the effects of geographic distance, maintaining their emotional closeness by sharing intimate somatic information and affectionate medical advice. They maintained their care community through their shared ill health. Thus, it is perhaps no surprise that a character's sickness and death form the central events of two of James's major novels, *The Portrait of a Lady* (1881) and *The Wings of the Dove*. Both assume that we know ordinary Victorian care practices and can tell how its characters deviate from them, and both attempt to work out how feelings and communications form under the stress of illness.

James began working on *Portrait* in 1877. He was responding to *Daniel Deronda*, published the previous year, by building up the unhappy marriage plot associated with Gwendolen while eschewing the Jewish plot connected to Daniel.⁵ Perhaps James imagined this revision as a way of caring for Eliot's novel by overhauling and improving it, turning the thorny contemporary political Zionism of Eliot's last work into a smoothly cosmopolitan narrative, with settings in Scotland and Rome repurposed as scenic backgrounds rather than sites of regional self-assertion in ongoing struggles for independence or unification. James depoliticized his politically charged source text, transforming it into an account of prosperous, attractive people's private feelings.⁶ But *Portrait* also revises its predecessor through language. James complained that *Daniel Deronda* was characterized by "something that one may call a want of tact. The epigraphs in verse are a want of tact; they are sometimes, I think, a trifle more pretentious than really pregnant; the importunity of the moral reflections is a want of tact; the very diffuseness is a want of tact."⁷ Speaking too much—making one's beliefs too obvious—is dangerous in *Portrait*, where feelings need to be conveyed obliquely, in hints and subtle shifts, in a man's failure to stand in front of a woman, and in which an entire chapter can be devoted to an internal realization that is never spoken aloud.

In revising *Daniel Deronda*, James replaces Daniel's nuptial care community with Ralph's deathbed care community, as if in a neat demonstration of the difference between comedy and tragedy. Ralph's long dying process derives additional emotional power from the way it makes rivals, parents, friends of friends, and cousins merge into a mutually harmonious community. As James recollected in the preface to *Wings*, Ralph's "deplorable state of health was not only no drawback; I had clearly been right in counting it, for any happy effect he should produce, a positive good mark, a direct aid to pleasantness and vividness."⁸ James's relish may remind us of Miriam Bailin's observation that, to Victorians, "the creation of small, select societies around their bedsides [was] one of the greatest advantages of illness."⁹

Twenty years later, *The Wings of the Dove* seems to be heading toward exactly such a "happy effect," such a "greatest advantage," as it too moves toward the young person's deathbed. In both *Portrait* and *Wings*, James replays the traumatic death of his beloved cousin Minny Temple in 1870 by making a wonderfully promising young person aware of being doomed to die of something like consumption, with catastrophic emotional effects on the remaining characters. In both *Portrait* and *Wings*, a woman schemes to get her lover married to a wealthy American ingenue in order to get her money. The plot succeeds, but the threesome ends up miserable, the victim discovers her best friend's culpability, and the schemer is no longer allowed a happy ending.

However, in *Wings* James deeply revises his earlier work. No longer is the care community the central ameliorating force. *The Wings of the Dove* is a study of living without care—perhaps even explicitly rejecting care. The dying youth remains alone and silent; the woman targeted by the couple has nobody else to turn to and there is nothing she can say. The care-community structure—widely understood, prominently invoked in the previous novel, foundational to James's own familial ties—is deliberately blocked here, and the novel becomes a study of what happens when the care community that the characters and readers alike expect cannot form. In the introduction, I pointed out that authors' late novels often give the most interesting version of care, as they strive to cope with the displacement of domestic care by professional medical men and the euphoric sickbed unions depicted in youthful writing give way to more sober and skeptical accounts of difficult relationships strained by ongoing suffering. Just as Brontë's joyous care mutuality in *Jane Eyre* is superseded by the transactional, unhappy paid care of *Villette*, so too the cathartic death in *Portrait* turns into the much more ambivalent death in *Wings*.

The Isolation of Wings

Milly is a paradigmatic Victorian consumptive invalid: a pale, spiritually sublime lady who suffers from too much passion but redeems others through her prolonged dying. Milly's physical symptoms and voyage to the recuperative climate of Italy indicate consumption, even though James never explicitly names her disease. Nicola Ivy Spunt stresses that Milly's actual diagnosis may not matter:

> The heroine remains the victim of consumption even if she does not decidedly have the disease. She is vulnerable to the ravages of commodification, of being used and finally wasted by virtue of her desire for Densher. Consumption emerges as a relational mode in *Wings*, and pathological commodification constitutes the ethical and ontological predicament in which all three protagonists find themselves enmeshed.[10]

Given that Milly's illness resembles consumption so much, readers might reasonably expect the consumptive heroine's typical end: a graceful decline surrounded by loved ones, with deeper feelings developing as Densher nurses her to the end.[11] But in *The Wings of the Dove*, the reader's expectation of tender nursing is profoundly thwarted. On her deathbed, Milly has chosen to surround herself with hired servants and medical consultants in lieu of friends. The reader does not see her final moments, and although her death arguably redeems Densher, it also destroys him, not to mention Kate.

At first, Milly does acquire a care community. Stephanie Byttebier has traced Milly's attraction to other people, pointing out that Milly wants at first to treat her disease by becoming more social.[12] Milly's doctor, Sir Luke Strett, actively tries to set up a care community. He is incredulous at the extent of Milly's isolation: she has absolutely "nobody whatever," "no relations at all," no parents, siblings, or cousins, since her family has died.[13] Instead, Milly depends on her paid companion, Susie Stringham (194, 195). Through Susie, Millie develops a voluntary affiliative care community, or as she calls it, "my entourage" (335): Mrs. Lowder, Kate Croy, Lord Mark, Merton Densher, Susan Stringham, Sir Luke Strett, and their pleasant British friends (178–81). Milly is aware that these friends want to care for her. She senses Lord Mark's offer ("do let a fellow who isn't a fool take care of you a little"), and she realizes that Mrs. Lowder "too wished to take care of her—and wasn't it, *à peu près*, what all the people with the kind eyes were wishing?" (182). But this is a novel written after care communities had given way to professional medicine, and Milly's actual care will come from hired medical experts. Even in the moment of feeling the pleasure of pleasant people wishing to care for her, Milly becomes nostalgic and retrospective, crying tearfully that "I shall never be better than this" because, as she explains, "I mean that everything this afternoon has been too beautiful, and that perhaps everything together will never be so right again" (183).[14] The care community exists only in a fortuitous group in a shared moment that is over before it begins.

Nor is the care community quite as unselfish as it seems; closer attention to its members gives us some cause for concern. Sir Luke Strett and Susan Stringham are paid for their care; in a nineteenth-century framework, that makes their motives suspicious. Meanwhile, Kate, Densher, Lord Mark, and Mrs. Lowder are pursuing Milly's money. In *Portrait*, Isabel's fortune attracts a spouse who values her money rather than Isabel herself, and in *Wings*, Milly, with a vastly larger fortune, ends up with relationships that have a transactional quality. Only some characters do emotional labor in Arlie Russell Hochschild's sense, performing fake feelings for renumeration, but all the members of this community of care have their feelings mediated through a financial nexus.

Money produces divergence from care norms. First, Milly's wealth allows her to enforce total denial of her illness. Friends are harder to control, but hired carers can be instructed to keep silent. Second, Milly's wealth is what Kate and Densher covet when they pretend to love Milly herself. Her fortune becomes a kind of idealized self—imperishable, sustaining, enviable—as her real body deteriorates. Susan notes "the mass of money so piled on the girl's back" and observes that money essentially replaces her (99).

Villette critiqued the new world of paid care from the point of view of the carers who are paid to sideline their own feelings, but *The Wings of the Dove* shows how toxic paid care can also be for the employers, who can demand, and receive, care that actually harms them. If paid caregivers have to perform false emotions for money, then paying cared-fors are at liberty to indulge their own feelings, even when doing so is disastrous. Money short-circuits the usual discursive negotiation, replacing a discussion of mutual judgments and feelings with a commodified exchange.

Milly rejects care, whether genuinely felt or offered as a paid service. She fears that "the vain sympathy, the mere helpless gaping inference of others," might kill her (343). Byttebier points out that it is precisely because Milly vests so much power in other people's reactions that she believes their responses could kill or cure her.[15] She sees isolation as "a great boon," a limitless freedom (198). "No one in the world could have sufficiently entered into her state; no tie would have been close enough to enable a companion to walk beside her without some disparity." She wants to move in a mass of strangers, coveting the urban anonymity afforded by a crowd—an experience that, as we have seen, is very different from the small community of care.

Merton Densher knows what his role is supposed to be. Densher is desperate to validate care relations. Like other practitioners of emotional labor, he works up his own feelings to match the way he acts. Until he manages to produce the emotion to validate his acts, he finds his pretended care relation so shameful that it cannot be spoken. Unable to bear the idea that he has pretended to court a dying girl to get her money, he decides that he is truly in love with her and that, by refusing her money, he can retroactively purify his caregiving.

Care haunts this novel throughout: the shadowy form of Milly's "entourage" that never quite works, the feeling that Densher musters as a retroactive explanation, the strangled emotions that Susan cannot speak. Shoved out of the intradiegetic mode, pushed out of character experience, care diffuses into style. The language of the novel, as we shall see, is, in some ways, a care-based mode of speech. Its difficulty derives from all the qualities inherent in care relations: contagiousness, particularity, fluctuation, relationality. *The Wings of the Dove* is written in the strange voice of care itself, or perhaps it would be more accurate to say that it is written out of care, in all senses.

In viewing *Wings* as written out of care, as diffusing care into style instead of localizing it in characters, we might consider James's comments about the way this novel evolved. The characters disappointed their author, James notes, by failing to manifest enough. "Every one, in short, was to have enjoyed so much better a chance that, like stars of the theatre condescending to oblige, they have had to take small parts, to content themselves with minor identities, in order to come on at all."[16] Alex Woloch sees this passage as testifying "to the pathos and the *disappointment* of minorness," but it is significant that James acknowledges that "every one" of his characters is underdeveloped, including the major characters Kate, Densher, and Milly. The real problem is that characters' "small parts" could not play out the dynamic at the scale he envisioned, not even when he reconfigures them as "registers or 'reflectors.'"[17] Perhaps his dissatisfaction lay in the nature of characters itself, not these particular characters. This situation created a crisis for him. As Mark Seltzer explains, James expresses "a vigilance of care" for his characters; what, then, happens when the characters fail to materialize?[18]

The characters fail, and that releases their thoughts into the environment, floating like spores. By eschewing direct communication, the characters blow discourse into more obscure, vague, problematic currents. Everything becomes contagious in *The Wings of the Dove*. Sharon Cameron points out that in *Wings*, "thinking is not private and it is not internal . . . it appears to emanate from others."[19] David Kurnick agrees that the novel features what he calls "stylistic infectiousness," marked by shared metaphors and pervasive feelings.[20] In an uncomfortable situation, we have been reading along silently only to find ourselves co-opted into this making of thoughts, our very passivity as readers becoming part of the dynamic into which this novel compels us. The characters' failures produce our shared reading experience.

Style as Care

Can literary style produce a care community? We saw in chapter 1 that a care community has social relations that are egalitarian, voluntarily affiliative, and performative and members who regulate their relations through discourse and experience skewed temporality. A care community is fluid, networked, decentralized, and it operates on a case-by-case basis. In *The Wings of the Dove*, each of these qualities characterizes the language of the novel.

Egalitarian collectivism is a hallmark of James's style. The writing, Kurnick explains, "intimates an alternative realm where, as Sly and the

Family Stone would have it, everybody is a star."[21] There are no Woloch-style minor characters in *The Wings of the Dove*, but a swarm of comparable characters participating en masse, for "Jamesian style—harbors a radically collectivist ethical imagination only tangentially related to the differentiating moralism of his plots."[22] Part of this disorienting egalitarianism is that there are no minor characters who are marked by class or occupation as disposable figures. The characters who in other novels would occupy the liminal space of the paid caregiver are full members of the crew by virtue of their financial standing. Companion Susan Stringham, aunt Maud Lowder, and doctor Luke Strett are already financially independent, so they are not performing emotional labor for pay, but rather out of uncomfortably opaque private motives that make them subject to the same searching analysis as all the other figures.

Performativity is key to *The Wings of the Dove* as well. Leo Bersani argues that in this novel James regards truth as a naive crudity that only hobbles the imaginative flights through which characters develop. After all, James himself asserted that "to 'put' things is very exactly and responsibly and interminably to do them."[23] It is thrilling for readers to participate in such performances, with characters inventing themselves as they go along, but this precludes us from imagining those characters as preexisting beings moving through a preset world well or badly, beings who can set moral examples or offer us salutary warnings, in the ethical model of high-Victorian realist fiction.[24] In this respect, James alters the way that care is understood. In George Eliot's novels, Omri Moses argues,

> the desires of characters are themselves structured by and mirrored in a tissue of already fashioned communities. If characters change, it is because they come up against this matrix of preexisting relationships and find themselves needing to adjust. James, on the other hand, wishes to show not only how characters change but—since reality itself is only the sum of the improvised and unprepared connections to it—how the social sphere remains open to transformation as individual agents access and modify it.[25]

Daniel Deronda adheres to a realist understanding in which we are supposed to credit characters enough to develop feelings about them, but *The Wings of the Dove* operates on a textual level in which no such interventionist or specular reading attitude is possible, because we are actually building the characters as we go. In other words, in *Wings* we cannot gaze at characters hopelessly (sympathy) and we cannot dream of saving them (sentiment), for instead we participate in their performative development, reading to comprehend and thus realize their selfhood.

These characters' constant shifting connects intimately, once again, to the community of care. As Bowden puts it, "Our identities and self-understandings are in continuous flux, in virtue of the way we are embedded in a dynamic and changing context of relations."[26] In James's narrative form, too, identity is entirely determined by relationality. Moses explains: "Each of his characters is so profoundly relational that she or he cannot be bound to any independent—which is to say, preestablished and recurring—form of being."[27] Wholly dependent on each particular case, adapting as the situation alters, and intimately interrelating with others who themselves are adapting to her, the Jamesian character is the ultimate interdependent subject imagined by ethics of care, living in and through a communal social network.

If characters constitute themselves through stylistic interactivity, then the worst thing one can do to a character might be to silence her. Silence means the disintegration of the self that had formed in language. In *The Wings of the Dove*, perhaps this is what happens to Milly: a thick silence gradually buries her, silting her in place. Rita Charon has written eloquently about the need for carers to pay attention to the cared-for and offer a response, but this becomes impossible if the cared-for refuses to share.[28] Silence stops the story as well as the self. Bersani claims that for James, "the 'I' itself has become merely the neutral territory occupied by language," but what happens to that nascent "I" if there is no language in the territory at all?[29]

To present characters who form through an intimate, collective, fluctuating relationality—and then to introduce silence—is to betray them profoundly. In *The Wings of the Dove*, money enables the cared-for to repress all discussion of her condition, and the carers to suppress the rationale for their caregiving. In each case, silence fills the mold left by the thing that should have been there. These silences come to resemble illness. They are chronic, recurrent, contagious, disabling attacks. But silences also bear a grotesque affinity to care communities, for they generate social relationships and unify disparate individuals, creating a complex social relation. In *The Wings of the Dove*, silence becomes the unholy twin to both sickness and care, replacing each. It will be helpful to look first at the silence of Kate and Densher's conspiracy, a poisonous silence that seeps into everything else, before moving on to the silence produced by Milly's demand that nobody acknowledge her illness.

Conspiracy of Silence

Let us start with the way that Kate and Merton's plan develops in, and depends upon, silence. It is Kate who initiates the "conspiracy of silence" in this novel (456).[30] Milly experiences Kate's first attack when Kate's very presence strikes a disturbingly aggressive, alien note, "something that was perversely *there*" (186). What is "perversely there" is the visible record of Kate's relation with Densher. Thus, when the tone alters, "she knew it afterwards to have been by the subtle operation of Kate" (185). Kate changes the atmosphere strongly enough to force Milly into trying "to escape from something else": her first recognition that Kate is suppressing a certain name. Kate's failure to mention Densher is a notable, repeated silence that "altered all proportions, had an effect on all values" (158). Milly feels it as a shiver, "a clear cold wave," as if she is figuratively infected by Kate's duplicity. Day after day, the omission metastasizes: "with the lapse of hours and days, the chances themselves that made for his being named continued so oddly to fail. There were twenty, there were fifty, but none of them turned up," creating days "practically all stamped with avoidance" (191).

Linked to this silence is Kate's violence of expression. When Milly confides that she is going to see Sir Luke Strett, Kate asks bluntly, "'What in the world is the matter with you?' It had inevitably a sound of impatience, as if it had been a challenge really to produce something" (187). Kate is not in tune with the cared-for. She is speaking from her own mysterious and unsympathetic motives. Milly does not know exactly why Kate resents her, but she intuits enough. In the first flush of mutual adoration, the narrator tells us, Kate had "no suspicion of a rift within the lute"—a comment that of course reveals that the rift is already there (149). Like the rift within the lute, like the crack in the golden bowl, Kate's withholding of Densher's name breaks the relationship past repair as it spreads.

The second attack occurs when Milly returns from visiting Sir Luke Strett. Once again, Kate breezes in with an alien sensibility that Milly suddenly realizes "was the fine freedom she showed Mr. Densher. Just so was how she looked to him, and just so was how Milly was held by her— held as by the strange sense of seeing through that distant person's eyes. It lasted, as usual, the strange sense, but fifty seconds; yet in so lasting it produced an effect," a revulsion against Kate's falsehood, and a wish to baffle her (208). Thus, Milly commences her own great lie, "answering beautifully, with no consciousness of fraud," about her illness (209). Like Kate, she speaks literal truth but keeps silent on the central point around which everything else revolves. This lie keeps Kate at arm's length, for

Kate cannot join a community of care when the patient insists that she requires no care.

Kate and Densher develop a silence that also harms their own communication. At first, Densher relishes their connection: "It was constantly Densher's view that, as between himself and Kate, things were understood without saying, so that he could catch in her, as she but too freely could in him, innumerable signs of it, the whole soft breath of consciousness meeting and promoting consciousness" (370). Yet Kate is so pleased that Milly wants to visit Densher that she fails to pick up on his tone. She was "sufficiently gratified and blinded by it not to know, from the false quality of his response, from his tone and his very look, that he had answered inevitably, almost shamelessly, in a mere time-gaining sense" (371). She experiences a "failure of perception" (371).

Kate and Densher's silence is toxic because what they want is not Milly's well-being but Milly's money; money is the real, if unacknowledged, object of their care acts. In this respect, they violate what Noddings posits as a basic rule: carers should "wish to please [the cared-for] for his sake and not for the promise of his grateful response to our generosity."[31] Similarly, Charon imagines the ideal carer as being able "to attend gravely and silently, absorbing diastolically that which the other says, connotes, displays, performs . . . thereby getting to glimpse the sufferer's needs and desires, as it were, from the inside."[32] But, *The Wings of the Dove* asks, what if the sufferer is lying about her "needs and desires"? What if the carer does not really want to know? What if the person who "absorbs diastolically" is in fact the wrong one? What if that person is the sufferer, counter-transferentially picking up her attendant's subtle cues, to their mutual dismay?

Kate's two attacks in London at the start of Milly's illness find counterparts in two attacks of Densher's in Venice at its end. Like Kate, Densher falls into awkward silence accompanied by aggressive tonal mishandling. The first episode occurs when Milly asks why Densher is staying in Venice. Densher finds himself speechless, stuck in a "horrible" and "odious" silence, because he cannot confess that Kate has made him stay (414–16). He thus resentfully reacts to Milly by asking whether it will be "safe" for her to leave the house (420). Like Kate earlier, he has broken their tacit silence with an excessively blunt query about her state of health. This confrontation is literally hurtful, for both of them. He accidentally touches Milly's "supersensitive nerve" and "winces" in response (418). This is not an erotic metaphor but the opposite, for they shudder away from painful contact.

The second attack occurs when Milly excludes Densher from the palace. Densher's cautious, indecisive vigil in a gloomy, grimy Venice, waiting for Milly to die, makes him feel "abject" and "sordid" and "odious," as well as profoundly uncertain what to do (434). He exemplifies the very opposite of Noddings's claim that "when I receive the other, I am totally with the other . . . and I do not ask myself whether what I am feeling is correct in some way."[33] Densher, instead, constantly asks himself whether his feelings are correct. He is utterly demoralized by having to perform a false position vis-à-vis two women for days on end, with everything depending on his capacity to keep the balance going in impossible conditions. He comes to realize that he is speaking "another kind of lie, the lie of the uncandid profession of a motive. He was staying so little 'for' Milly that he was staying positively against her" (421–22). In this attack, Densher's mere mute presence, neither trying to approach Milly nor trying to leave, offers a kind of final affront, a disquieting insufficiency, an irritant just when she needed it least. He has imposed emotional labor on himself, engaged in expressing a false feeling for money.

Summoned to one final meeting with Milly, Densher has some kind of climactic exchange, whose content remains hidden from us. As John Auchard accurately states, "What transpires between Milly and Densher—forceful as wordlessness or as unreported words—provides one of the major structural silences of the novel."[34] Through this meeting whose content we can never know, Densher's personal guilty silence swells into a silence that affects the reader.

The Silent Treatment

While Kate and Densher have occasional attacks of hostile omissions, Milly arranges a different form of silence—an ongoing, continual stillness that seems like a chronic, debilitating condition. Milly's silence is an objective correlative or textual representation of the disease that is never clarified for us. The ambiguity of her disease—which is just like, but never quite established as, consumption—allows it to float free of literal meaning. Her diagnosis consists of unspoken words, and her nursing proceeds in the same way. Like the incurables or invalids of nineteenth-century experience, Milly's experience is one of intermittent and ongoing situations, but she refuses the social ameliorations that normally manage the condition. And although she turns to professional medical attendance, we do not hear the diagnostic interventions that would explain her prognosis.

Milly's embrace of the silent treatment begins with her choice of nurses. She chooses her primary caregiver because "she had had from the first hour the conviction of her being precisely the person in the world least possibly a trumpeter" (182). Selected for her reticence, Susan Stringham's first intimation that something is seriously wrong is presented as a form of oddly suppressed communication, "an explanation that remained a muffled and intangible form" (106). Milly insists on confronting her own mortality in soundless isolation, seated on a cliff in the Alps. Meanwhile, "Mrs. Stringham stood as motionless as if a sound, a syllable, must have produced the start that would be fatal," and she subsequently decides not to speak of the scene at all (112, 114). At every key moment between Milly and Susan Stringham, silence replaces more conventional caregiving. Susan is qualified as companion by having no significant life or feelings of her own, and she willingly surrenders her life to enter Milly's. But Milly does not want Susan to share her feelings. The pair enter a dreadful mutual guilt trip. What is the purpose of a companion who is forbidden to offer companionship? "Each held and clasped the other as if to console her for this unnamed woe, the woe for Mrs. Stringham of learning the torment of helplessness, the woe for Milly of having *her*, at such a time, to think of" (315). The carer's desire to help the cared-for cannot be enacted, so it becomes another burden for the cared-for to carry.

Similarly, Milly's doctor, Sir Luke Strett, occupies a strangely indeterminate role. Like mid-Victorian doctors, he is both a social connection and a hired expert. Strett is "the greatest of medical lights," yet what he offers is not medical advice so much as "Sir Luke's friendship," a sociable interest that Milly appreciates as distinct from "mere professional heartiness, mere bedside manner" (186, 189, 193). Strett advises Milly to live a full and happy life, particularly by marrying Densher, the man she loves—as Susan and Mrs. Lowder determine in a confused conversation in which Mrs. Lowder is trying to fit this romantic advocacy into the conventional categories of diagnosis, intervention, and cure (320–22). Strett socializes with Milly and her circle in Venice, making medical supervision indistinguishable from personal friendship. Strett and Susan are both wealthy enough to disregard Milly's payments to them, and both assert that their caregiving derives from personal feeling for Milly, yet the fact of that pay, whether needed or not, gives Milly the right to determine what they will do (331–32). She is ultimately in charge of how they execute their caregiving.

Milly forces her carers to administer silence. In some ways, this decision is justified; Lord Mark's words can indeed be said to kill her. On the other hand, by humoring her demands for denial, her carers are abetting a dangerous fantasy that precludes real medical interventions. Densher regards his "stillness" as "a policy or a remedy" (436). Yet the fact that the self-interested Kate and Densher are content with the silent treatment may give us pause. *The Wings of the Dove* presents a topsy-turvy world where one shows sympathy by refusing to show sympathy, gives care by sedulously avoiding any appearance of caregiving.

All the people in Milly's community of care learn to deliver the silent treatment. Her doctors, her servants, and her friends are not allowed to speak. Neither Sir Luke Strett nor his Italian counterpart, Dr. Tacchini, will reveal her diagnosis (314, 443, 441). Milly's appearance is notable for its absence of medical information; Densher reminds us that Milly vowed "that she wouldn't smell of drugs, that she wouldn't taste of medicine. Well, she didn't" (478). The servants in Milly's palazzo feel "the force of the veto laid ... on any mention, any cognition, of the liabilities of its mistress. The state of her health was never confessed to there as a reason" (427). Susan Stringham is not permitted to comfort her. Teahan sums it up: Milly's illness "is not only unrepresented, but apparently unrepresentable as such, approachable only in a series of infinitely decreasing increments."[35] Silence takes the place of sickness. This silence models treatment. It mimics care inasmuch as it is shared among members of her community of care, it expresses their respect for the cared-for's wishes, and it depletes the carers. Just as regular care increases in medical crises, so too does Milly's silent treatment (as one might call it) intensify at her worst stage.

The silent treatment climaxes, of course, at Milly's deathbed, when she most absolutely refuses speech. Lord Mark has left. She will not speak to Susan. Densher can learn nothing except that "something had happened—he didn't know what" (428). Moreover, "nothing had passed about his coming back and the air had made itself felt as a non-conductor of messages" (429). And so, very much unlike Ralph Touchett, Milly dies alone and still. "She doesn't speak at all? I don't mean not of me," Densher asks Susan. "Of nothing—of no one," Susan replies. "She's more than quiet. She's grim" and "she'll never tell" (439, 440). As Milly's condition heightens, so does her silence, the gloomy twin of her illness, the strange shadow of her care. By the climax, her death, even people far away from her are infected, and the imperative to be silent spreads over multiple subjects, not just her health. As Densher sums up: "I can't talk to any one about her" (443). Neither Densher nor Milly mentions Kate for six weeks (449–50). Meanwhile, Kate and Densher have also ceased to communicate. Kate's "law of silence" forbids correspondence—their betrayal of Milly is unspeakable, but it would be absurd to speak of anything else (435).

Silence makes it impossible for readers to have a typically active nineteenth-century relation to the characters, forcing us to interact with the language instead. I noted earlier that Jamesian characters, who develop through language, would regard silence as a death sentence. To some extent, this is true. When Milly goes forever silent, the novel ends. But silence is also the mechanism generating *The Wings of the Dove*, because the injunction on direct speech is precisely what produces the Jamesian stylistic efflorescences that constitute the book in the first place. If the characters could communicate directly, this novel would not exist. *The Wings of the Dove* becomes a silent central artifact for which we are taxed with the baffling, enticing, worrisome problem of caregiving. Charon's description of a clinical relationship is also a wonderful account of good reading practice:

> To attend gravely and silently, absorbing diastolically that which the other says, connotes, displays, performs, and means is required of effective diagnostic and therapeutic work. By emptying the self and by accepting the patient's perspectives and stance, the clinician can allow himself or herself to be filled with the patient's own particular suffering, thereby getting to glimpse the sufferer's needs and desires, as it were, from the inside.[36]

For "clinician" take "reader"; for "patient" take *The Wings of the Dove*. And this becomes a twentieth-century idea of reading, in which the very passivity, fragility, and textual immersion of the reading experience is no longer something to fight but actually the basis of a care relation to the text. To be permeated by the other, to absorb its suffering, seems very different from simply wanting to save Tiny Tim, and yet they have something in common: the reader's job is to care for a frail other.

Killing Silences

Much of *The Wings of the Dove* constitutes a standoff between two women in which each privately gloats over the central fact of her existence—her lover, her illness—refusing to entrust it to her supposed best friend. But neither woman is fooled. Kate's very silence, by showing Milly the real importance of Densher, renders Milly fascinated, even obsessed, by this unspoken truth. At the same time, Kate recognizes that Milly is ill, but as she remarks, "It's a matter in which I don't want knowledge. She moreover herself doesn't want one to want it" (280). Ironically, it is their moments of apparent candor that are the most constrained: "It was when they called each other's attention to their ceasing to pretend, it was then that what they were keeping back was most in the air" (342). It is an exchange of denials, not information.

The two great silences merge to permit a kind of ghastly version of a marriage plot to be played out in conditions that ought to have precluded it. Because of Kate's silence about her engagement, Densher seems free to woo Milly; because of Milly's silence about her illness, she can seem to respond to his courtship. Every aspect of this plot is unspeakable and impossible, and it can only function if nobody articulates it. This silent emotional snarl could not be further from Habermas's communicative rationality.

If the two great lies had succeeded, Milly would have married. Because they fail—the conspiracy and the treatment collide—Milly dies. But the economy of silence must be sustained. A third silence emerges, one that by its very nature can never be filled in. Kate burns Milly's final letter.

Kate's destruction mutes Milly's words forever. And her act of burning Milly's letter sets up a new regime of silence between the surviving conspirators. Milly becomes an unspeakable subject, carried with an "intensity with which it mutely expressed its absence" (521). Densher and Kate rarely meet, and when they do, their talks are "more remarkable for what they didn't say than for what they did" (523). The avoidance governs their conversation. "Not to talk of what they *might* have talked of drove them to other ground; it was as if they used a perverse insistence to make up what they ignored" (525). If Milly's death is the central silence of the narrative, Milly's letter's holocaust is the causal omission of its style. In both cases, there is a final silence that can never be repaired. But the attempt is what makes this novel exist. Perhaps *The Wings of the Dove* is one long attempt to reconstruct the sacred lost words. Auchard regards Milly's death as the climax of a history of self-erasures, seeing the novel as resting on the "foundations of vacancies, silences, negations—as distinguished energies—speechless moments, secrets, hidden disease, undiscovered sources of wealth, sin, or perception, broken sentences, unheard words, unseen letters, unexplained crimes."[37]

Conclusion: The Art of Reading

In *Wings*, we are not in a somatically oriented world; there a woman would have an actual disease like consumption and be cared for by people who do real things like giving sponge-baths, culminating in the sentimental convention of a deathbed farewell to one's fiancé. Rather, we are in a stylistic world in which a woman is affected by something like consumption—but also something like hurt feelings due to unexpectedly aggressive concealments. She is treated with something like care—but it is composed of negations. The result is death—but we never see the bodily death, just the burning of the letter. In other words, the whole dynamic of illness-care-death occurs here, but transposed via silence onto the level of language. If style could get sick, it would be something like *The Wings of the Dove*.

In lieu of *Portrait*'s cathartic deathbed care-community scene, James offers us the whole novel as an intensive, interrelated communion. Frederic Jameson says that James's writing

> stakes out the space for unique interpersonal feelings that have no name in the first place—a space of apposition and anaphora, the enigmatic references to an "it" the writer has not identified but which we are supposed to recognize and to remember. At any rate, it is this virtual discovery and revelation of a whole layer of human relations that are not unconscious but which the literary apparatus had hitherto been too primitive to register, that is, to my mind, James's most enduring claim to greatness.[38]

Jameson imagines us reading *The Wings of the Dove* much the way Charon cautions us to be alert to connotations and tones. These subtleties of interpersonal relations become a signal strong enough for the literary sentence to pick up, a sub-audible vibration, only when nestled in silence, and only when we care enough to listen closely.

In the introduction, I wrote about the Heideggerian concept of "tool-being": when tools break, we become aware of their being, their qualities and materials. If the novel is a tool, silence breaks it down. Instead of seeing fictional language as a kind of transparent liquid medium in which realistic characters swim, we have to see the language as if it were rocks, solid stuff that gets built into the characters, cracked and chipped at the corners to let the water through. Its brokenness is why it needs us to enter into a care relation with it, for our reading can help restore the imperiled meaning.

We work to make this novel function by parsing difficult sentences and piecing together clues. Martha Nussbaum explains that as we participate in the lives of James's characters, "we actively care for their particularity, and we strain to be people on whom none of their subtleties are lost, in intellect and feeling."[39] Each individual act of reading painstakingly reconstructs the lost, silenced, secret meanings. Cumulatively, too, we readers form a community of care, our acts of care taking the form of reading and writing annotations, explanations, editions, teaching aids, scholarly articles, special issues—all the material that works to help this novel flourish, restoring its discourse for other readers' needs.

Milly and Densher model our relation to the novel. Like Milly, the novel is an unreachably silent, lovely, elusive object. Like Densher, we read this book by remaining, irritable, uncertain, and full of false starts, outside "an impenetrable ring fence, within which there reigned a kind of expensive vagueness made up of smiles and silences and beautiful fictions and priceless arrangements" (456). Densher's difficulty in treating prickly Milly is rather like our struggle with late James. Like Densher, we need to move toward a different attitude, one of admiration of the "beautiful fiction." We, like Densher, may come wanting to obtain something straightforwardly valuable, whether money or meaning, but the gift we receive may be something other than we could have imagined: a form of communication that changes the way we think of narrative, a hush that makes a discourse happen. In that sense, Milly's last letter takes care of us as well, and precisely because it has gone forever silent. Like Densher, we may well retroactively decide that we loved it all along.

The Wings of the Dove takes the community of care as far as it can be taken after George Eliot, introducing us to the silence that lies on the other side of the roar. Silence lies behind Densher and Kate's conspiracy, behind Milly's denialism, behind Milly and Densher's quasi-engagement and Milly and Kate's quasi-friendship. Silence characterizes relations with Susan Stringham, with Sir Luke Strett, with Maud Lowder. Silence replaces illness, love, and friendship, and it eventually insinuates itself into the very language of the novel. As Samuel Cross sums up, "calculated reticence structures the novel."[40]

In this book I have argued for appreciating the particular forms of communication precipitated by emotional labor—the tics, repetitions, and divergences required by carers who cannot directly express their feelings. Perhaps what *Wings* does is to show us the artistic potential in that blockage of ordinary communication. When you can't say what you mean, perhaps what you produce is art. Perhaps Mrs. Sparsit's lace-making, or Lucy Snowe's netting, those intricate crafts that turn in on themselves, are ways of generating something in lieu of the speech that is blocked. Even Rosa Dartle has a seam across her lip, and a seam is not just a scar but also a form of craft. *Wings*, an entire novel produced out of thwarted and blocked discourse, is a climactic example: a novel in which people turn their love and their friendship into an elaborately restrained form of style.

In the nineteenth century, care developed from a shared social practice to a professional, paid act, and depictions of illness, care, and medical attention changed after midcentury. But in this twentieth-century novel, written when care had shifted almost entirely to professional and institutional venues, perhaps the care community has become even more private, moving within the individual mind, communing with a text. Or, at least, that is what *The Wings of the Dove* conveys: the care community has become an intertextual, intangible, discursive negotiation, abstracted from the social real.

But I do not want to end this story in the clichéd and dubious mode of the triumphant modernist apotheosis. For high modernism was not the inevitable end of the care community dynamic. Half a century before James, Charlotte Yonge imagined writing as a collective activity, a form of authorship that was robustly social and mutually supportive. This novel had its tradition too, and it also perpetuated the care community dynamic into the twentieth century, although in the forms of genre fiction and popular novels rather than high modernism. The extradiegetic appeal to care did not necessarily produce only rarified modernist apotheosis but also the robustly popular mid-Victorian domestic novels. In the next chapter, we will see what happens when an author imagines writing itself as a communal act. James conscripted readers, but Yonge invokes fellow writers, generating a cheerful, chatty, sociable community of authorial multiplicity that, in a sense, is the opposite of the high modernist priest of language. To follow the metaphor I have been using in this chapter—if James artfully builds a wall of rocks, Yonge brings in a whole construction crew.

CHAPTER SIX

Composite Fiction and the Care Community in *The Heir of Redclyffe*

What new terminology might be needed to describe a close reading that is also a critical reading but that also does not do violence to the text or feel it necessary to pretend that the author is always already dead, that the text writes itself, or that it is necessary to erase the human in human relations because of a threat of anthropocentrism?

—AMY J. ELIAS, "CONTEXT ROCKS!"[1]

IN 1853, AT the height of the midcentury transition to the medical model, two Charlottes published influential novels that placed different bets on the future of care. One was Charlotte Brontë's *Villette*, which records the emotional costs of the emergence of paid caregiving. The other was Charlotte Yonge's *The Heir of Redclyffe*, which celebrates the power of care communities. To a greater extent than perhaps any other Victorian novelist, Yonge perceived a successful life as a fundamentally relational one, and her novels are both thematically and formally structured by communities of care. In this chapter, I argue that Yonge, like James, made care the basis of a particular kind of literary style. She used the structure to rethink authorship itself as a communal activity. *Heir* enacts complex relations with its literary peers in ways that go far beyond our current models of influence and that deserve our attention just as much as the high modernist shift. Like *Wings of the Dove*, *Heir* has an extradiegetic mode that breaks the fourth wall, but whereas James uses silences to bring in the reader, Yonge draws connections to fellow writers, producing a thick web of textual connections so that the novel emerges not from a single genius but rather from a thoroughly well-populated social world, synthesized from the joint efforts of an imagined community.

In the introduction, I discussed the way a well-balanced character partakes of both the type and the individual; in *Heir*, these two versions of character are vested in two different families, the biological and adoptive families of the main character, Guy Morville. The Morvilles incorporate him into a type, for they produce a lineage into which each subject gets slotted. In each generation, the Morvilles produce one man destined to the same kind of sinful career. But when Guy's grandfather dies and he is adopted by the Edmonstones, he learns that a complex community can afford a different sort of personhood in which one can explicitly adopt lateral influences from peers—a voluntary, affiliative, discursive relationship, as opposed to the inborn and essential descent of the Morvilles.

Guy's fate, then, can help us think about these two sorts of characterizations, since he is explicitly aligned with both, and it can afford us insight into what makes a communally produced character different from a crowd-affiliated type. It is the characteristic duration of the care community that allows this double self, for duration lets relations and identifications change over time, and the community itself has a fluid disposition that resists stable, permanent forms. In the novel's present, Guy is an individual, an ordinary teenager living with the middle-class suburban Edmonstones, but his past and his future belong to the allegorical ancient identity of the lord of Redclyffe, and this identity is reinforced on his visits home. He floats between both forms of character.

Because *The Heir of Redclyffe* is exceptionally attentive to these issues of temporal fluctuation, it invites us to explore how the care community uses chronology and, perhaps more importantly, to see how a care community might introduce us to a radically nonlinear form of time. In this chapter, I look at how *Heir* understands historicity in the context of a larger theoretical question: how do we read relationships among texts? The problem of how Guy relates to his families is congruent to the issue of how *Heir* relates to its literary predecessors. Those intimate relationships accommodate rebellion, disidentification, and estrangement, but they are also characterized by identification, adoption, revision, and incorporation. In both the intradiegetic families and the extradiegetic intertexts, we float in a disorientingly ahistorical logic where an orderly, chronological lineage turns back on itself, allowing us to occupy multiple temporal registers simultaneously. Both Guy and his novel, *Heir*, are specific mid-Victorian subjects and yet also participants enmeshed in larger relationships that cross time and space. Exploring this dual register will help us figure out whether we can read other texts, or even textuality itself, this way.

Skewed temporality is associated with queer, feminist, and disability theorizing, as I discussed in chapter 1. Queer temporality offers nonreproductive alternatives to linearity, including utopian futurity and alternative histories, while crip temporality is characterized by subjective bursts and stasis, chronic lingering, lulls, and attacks. In each case, one may experience subjectively diverse, multiple, creative experiences of time rather than conventional chronology or the strictly repetitive temporality of sameness that Eve Kosofsky Sedgwick associates with paranoid reading.[2] Susan Stanford Friedman defines twenty-first-century feminism as drawing "on juxtaposition and collage, associational positing of networks and linkages across continents and through time."[3] This communal, associative, reparative networking is a different mode from the agonistic male models fighting for mastery, Woloch's minor-major battles, and Bloom's Oedipal wrestling with fathers. As we shall see, communal forms of relationship governed many publishing genres that were female-dominated in the nineteenth century, particularly the novel and the periodical, and they have metacritical implications for ourselves, both in our work as editors of others' work and as editors of our own writing. Today we too occupy an alternative chronology: in the digital era, we envision ourselves not as strenuously excavating the disintegrating last relics of the past but rather as choosing among multiple, simultaneous virtual texts floating above markers of time or space. This chapter, then, explores the way *Heir* is shaped by skewed time. Its temporal fluidity facilitates alliances across eras, resulting in a kind of communal writing, an alternative model of authorship, that has implications for ourselves as well.

Theories of Textual Interrelationality

There are three main theories on which we currently draw to conceptualize an author's relation to others: influence, plagiarism, and intertextuality. As we shall see, each has useful qualities, but none suffices on its own. Each frames the problem in ways that foreclose certain kinds of critique that we may want to pursue, and each neglects important information.

Influence is the oldest of these theories. Virginia Woolf claimed that women think back through their mothers; F. R. Leavis argued that Austen led to George Eliot, who led to Henry James; Harold Bloom imagined sons swerving away from their progenitors. These writers viewed influence diachronically, with predecessors enabling subsequent authors. The major achievement of a single great individual created a legacy affecting people in the next generation, who either expressed grateful indebtedness or fought for their own individuality. As Bloom wrote, this is a "historicism that deliberately reduces to the interplay of personalities": person A responds to person B without regard to their cultural milieu.[4] This stress on personal reactions may be useful for biographical work and canon-building, but it neglects authors' horizontal relations, tending as it does to reach for ancestry rather than peers, and it utterly disregards the structural and material conditions—and even the genre expectations—that determine what is written, published, and praised. It now seems like naive neoliberalism to soar blithely over the ways that race and gender and access to publishing networks condition what gets written and how it gets read.[5]

Moreover, influence stresses historical order to an extent that we may want to problematize. Knowing that Yonge's novel was published in 1853, we feel certain about who could and could not have influenced her, and which historical events are likely to be relevant or irrelevant. This is the dynamic that Wai Chee Dimock calls "synchronic historicism": "phenomena are stuck fast to neighboring phenomena in the same slice of time."[6] We are the custodians of an inherently chronological tale, and we aim to fit a forgotten text into an empty space, sequentially: Whom do we slot in between the death of George Eliot and the first publications of Virginia Woolf? Who predated Jane Austen? This is not an inherently problematic way of organizing literary experience, but it is limiting, for if we are always trying to fill in gaps in a linear historical record, then we may not be noticing alternative modes of organization, nor the kinds of possibilities, texts, and feminisms that an atemporal, nonlinear arrangement might support.

A second model of textual relationships, plagiarism, uses an economic model to regard texts as an artifact with a certain value, a thing that can be claimed or stolen. Brian Connolly calls this the "proprietary claim to knowledge."[7] In this case, the text is an inert product whose content and creator's identity are irrelevant to its status as intellectual property. We are in a marketplace of ideas, and someone has swiped the goods off the counter. Wayne Booth describes this theory as "an unthinking individualism: what's mine is mine and what's yours is yours, and I fill my responsibility to you if I resist the impulse to steal from you."[8] While useful for expressing the kind of damage that intellectual theft can wreak, the plagiarism idea offers only a single, suspicious account of influence that does not allow for inspiration, allusions, borrowings, homages, or pastiches. It does not fit the culture of collective authorship that flourished in the eighteenth and much of the nineteenth century, before copyright laws. Rather, it presents a dire either-or situation in which the only possible relation to another's work is either theft or no theft. And while it does institute a code of behavior, that code is punitive rather than ethical: writers are taught to avoid danger rather than to aspire to good principles, and decent citation is regarded as a safeguard, not a positive ethical good in itself.

The third model is intertextuality, a more theoretically sophisticated postmodernist idea than influence or plagiarism. Intertextuality imagines texts in fluid linguistic intermingling without human intention; in Julia Kristeva's words, "The notion of intertextuality replaces that of intersubjectivity."[9] Kristeva coined the term "intertextuality" while explicating Bakhtin's theories, and the idea was further developed by such theorists as Riffaterre, Genette, and Barthes. Like weather systems, language moves in complex, chaotic eddies. In lieu of the generational model of influence, intertextuality requires a perpetual present, as if all texts coexist and interact constantly. Intertextuality frees us from the confines of authorial intentionality and the limits of authorial agency, as Roland Barthes explains in "The Death of the Author," and it is particularly liberating for critics who can enjoy what Nancy Miller calls "the (new) monolith of anonymous textuality, or, in Foucault's phrase, 'transcendental anonymity.'"[10] Barthes explains that writing becomes "that neutral, composite, oblique space where our subject slips away, the negative where all identity is lost, starting with the very identity of the body writing."[11]

However, intertextuality's disregard for personal authorial input and cultural formations presents a problem for modern critics. In intertextuality, all texts are alike, products of linguistic interplay, regardless of who wrote them, when, and where. This kind of radical disconnection seems to violate what we know about how writing is actually produced. It is particularly worrisome that intertextuality ignores the much more difficult conditions under which people of color, women, and other marginalized voices might generate their work and experience its reception. Erasing authorial agency is not a good idea for people who struggle to have that agency recognized in the first place. Intertextuality is so committed to a radically egalitarian, postmodernist, and fluid vision of culture as a "communications network," Mary Orr points out, that it often dismisses the idea of inheritance as an elitist remnant, thereby undermining the traditions that empower authors who feel otherwise marginalized.[12]

Orr's idea of "positive influence" aims to redress the balance. Insisting on a "positive influence" in the case of African-American and women writers shows how newcomers become able to "empower their various heritages" and make a tradition retroactively visible inasmuch as it necessarily led up to the achievements of the present.[13] Whereas intertextuality inhabits what I have called a perpetual present, "positive influence" invites a creative, playful sense of chronological duration, permitting future renewal and reuse while reanimating the past.[14] Advocating for intertextuality as the basic principle, however, while allowing for tradition in certain selective cases seems to muddy both systems; moreover, although it does help us read the work of women and people of color, intertextuality also may inadvertently support the assumption that white male writers are the default mode—the colorless norm to which no particular styles, forerunners, or traditions apply.

I suggest that seeing texts as participants in a care community can provide a useful alternative to the problematic modes of tagging authors as influencers, originators, or pure textuality. The care community partakes of the best of influence and intertextuality theory, but also adds new features. Because the community consists of personal relationships, it features the kind of histories, friendships, rivalries, loves, and mentorships traditionally enshrined in influence studies—but the literary care community is also a decentered, fluid, intertextual network, constantly shifting as relationships change over time and carers become cared-fors and vice versa. Thus, while the care community grounds influence studies in the author's personal connections, it also, by following out the social dynamics of those relationships, imagines connections according to the fluid nature of intertextual exchangeability. For instance, Henry James viewed George Eliot as an older personal connection, but he also acknowledged, expanded, critiqued, and reworked Eliot's materials in his own writing, and viewing Eliot and James as members of a care community allows us to accommodate both sets of relations.

The care community, however, is not just a mode of reconciling influence and intertextuality, for in its characteristic focus on duration (change over time) and temporality (nonlinear felt chronology) it introduces new components into the way we think about relationships among texts. This chapter, then, not only looks at care communities in *The Heir of Redclyffe* but also thinks about what *Heir*'s instantiation of care communities can teach us about textual connections outside of time.

Charlotte Yonge's Care Communities

Yonge was deeply immersed in caregiving in both her personal life and her professional work. Rosemary Mitchell has traced Yonge's belief in conservative ideal communities, which she envisioned as a harmonious relation between a caring gentry and clergy and their grateful, deferential social inferiors.[15] Her yearning for an idealized traditional community aligns her with the communitarians addressed in chapter 4, and certainly her lifelong writing of historical fiction allowed her to promulgate Victorian medieval nostalgia as she imagined communities in a preindustrial, pious past.

However, it is also important to notice the active care work that characterized her own life. Because Yonge never married, she had no maternal care-work duties, but she more than compensated in her voluntary caregiving. She championed a group of younger female friends and relations whom she nicknamed "the Goslings" (herself being Mother Goose) and with whom she produced coauthored stories.[16] Yonge nursed her closest friend, Marianne Dyson, who could not walk and suffered from severe headaches.[17] Additionally, she witnessed her mentor, Keble, caring for his invalid sister Elisabeth.[18] Living her entire life in the village of Otterbourne, and devoted to the church that her father helped to build, Yonge was deeply involved in local issues. By the time Yonge was seventy, she had taught Sunday school for an astonishing sixty-four years and claimed this as her real profession, asserting that "any claim she had to recognition [was] that of a veteran Sunday-school teacher" rather than an author.[19]

However, Yonge's extended family and publication work pushed her care networks past Otterbourne. As Susan Walton explains, "Instead of visualizing [Yonge's] territory as within a small, restrictive, rural, family unit, we should think of her enveloped in a large, vibrant community of families ranging over the counties of Hampshire, Oxfordshire and Devonshire, with links out across the world."[20] Connected to the Coleridges and other prominent families, Yonge participated in extensive networks of family, editorship, and mentorship, which segued into her periodical labors. Yonge began editing *The Monthly Packet* as she started writing *Heir* and remained its editor for thirty-nine years, making her "the longest-serving novelist-editor of the nineteenth century," in Beth Palmer's words.[21] She also edited a private amateur magazine called "The Barnacle," and the journal of the Mothers' Union, *Mothers in Council*.[22] In these journals, she published the work of her connections, and the readers who accessed this work helped her form new ties beyond her home village.

Yonge's participation in periodical culture immersed her in a synchronic space in which disparate worlds coexisted, impinging on one another through spatial juxtaposition and coincidental echoes rather than in a linear, chronologically logical progression. Linda Hughes thinks of print culture as a kind of city, "defined by multiple centers," with different neighborhoods, movements, and temporal rhythms, all of it an "interactive mix of disorder and order."[23] Journalism involved a fluid idea of textuality, since the author pitched the original piece to a particular journal's style, the editor altered it, the author recorrected it, and the author might well change it again if that author republished it later.[24] In a periodical context, then, writing is contingent and flexible and emerges from a social organization. This was especially true of "The Barnacle," which contained coauthored work produced by Yonge's own circle. Her writing experience, by the time she came to write *Heir*, was of jostling, miscellaneous community whose writing she had the power to alter, and of herself as a person who mentored younger writers by correcting their work.

This was not an outlier position. In thinking of herself as a community participant, Yonge was enacting an idea of authorship that was particularly common among women and that dated back to at least the eighteenth century. Hilary Havens argues that "eighteenth-century authorship should be conceived of as a fluid group" whose members continually enter and exit.[25] Literary coteries worked to contribute and revise and extend authors' writing. As Paula McDowell notes, eighteenth-century female polemicists advanced a model of personhood that did not feature "an autonomous or absolute or even gendered individual but a unified, collective, and 'fluidly sexed' body—a dispersed, connected, and fundamentally political being."[26] Similarly, eighteenth-century audiences regarded fictional characters as fluid beings whose further adventures could be imagined outside the source text. Characters were "simultaneously everywhere and nowhere, in the hands of countless strangers and yet never wholly reducible to any particular manifestation," David Brewer explains.[27]

This idea of fluid, enmeshed literary subjectivity persisted into the nineteenth century. Kimberly Stern has argued that nineteenth-century female critics adopted a fundamentally collectivist mentality, which could range from informal social networks to formal assemblies like the salon.[28] "The work of aspiring female critics thus depended upon more than the material conditions and connections afforded by actual literary networks: it depended upon imagined and, perhaps more crucially, upon reimagined communities of writers," Stern notes.[29] Women's literary networking not only helped them professionally but seemed fundamental to their vision of themselves as authors. Linda Peterson explains that reconstructing the conditions under which Victorian women writers functioned requires us to "emphasize supportive or enabling aspects of their relations. . . . What Oliphant labeled a 'coterie,' [others] treat as a 'network'—a group of writers tightly or loosely linked by region, religion, politics, or shared interests."

Such networks "were crucial to women's success."[30] They undergirded one of the first works of feminist criticism, *Women Novelists of Queen Victoria's Reign*, a book coauthored by nine women who wrote about their friends, mentors, and rivals. Women corresponded, revised each other's work, reviewed one another, and established associational organizations to parallel the men's clubs and coffeehouses.

What more natural than to use such networking as a mode of conceptualizing writing itself? "Many critics have observed that, in a sense, women writers 'collaborate' with the historical and literary figures they seek as precursors and revise," Jill Ehnenn comments in her study of coauthored Victorian women's writing.[31] It would be hard to find a better example than Christabel Coleridge's 1903 biography of her close friend Yonge, which mingles extracts from Yonge's personal writings with Coleridge's commentary; in Sharon Marcus's apt description, "its dialogic form mimics the structure of a social relationship conducted through conversation and correspondence."[32] Although Yonge had died in 1901, she is essentially a coauthor of her own biography. In *Women Novelists of Queen Victoria's Reign*, living authors work through complex relationships of critique, reassessment, and homage with their posthumous subjects.

In Victorian literary culture, cooperative writing was actually more common than the modern idea of the single author of genius, which Ehnenn identifies as an economic innovation, a way of selling a product while denying the actual practices of the nineteenth-century publishing industry.[33] Such cooperative writing made no distinction between past and present. Linda Peterson explains that "if Victorians did not literally repeat their predecessors' texts, they often repeated the conventional forms of self-interpretation and countered them with different conclusions. Or they countered with alternative hermeneutic systems."[34] In other words, Victorian writers engaged with others' texts without, apparently, much regard to whether their interlocutors were precursors or contemporaries, living or dead, ancient or modern.

Yonge demonstrated this collaborative attitude not just in her periodical editing but also in the poetry and fiction she wrote. Elisabeth Jay has pointed out that Yonge tended to chime in with other poets rather than aiming for an original voice of her own. In writing her novels, Yonge famously subjected all her drafts to review by her father and Keble, and when writing *Heir*, she leaned heavily on her group of prepublication readers, deleting and changing scenes according to their advice.[35]

Yonge's productivity rivaled that of her famous contemporaries Anthony Trollope and Margaret Oliphant, for Yonge wrote over a hundred novels, many of which are enormous (*The Pillars of the House* is well over a thousand pages), in addition to her prolific production of nonfiction books: schoolbooks, biographies, history, and reference works. She sometimes published four books per year. Her "linked novels"—twenty-two novels written over fifty-four years—constitute a vast saga depicting relationships among several large families over several generations. Maia McAleavey has written about the excess of Yonge: the vast novels, the enormous families, the plenitude of events, while Kelly Hager and Karen Bourrier note that Yonge's fictional families feature unusual numbers of substantive sibling characters.[36] Yonge's famous family chronicles follow an impressive number of characters, over decades, and through multiple independent and simultaneous subplots.[37]

This vast sprawl aligns *Heir* with the capacities of a digital era, databases that can keep track of variant sources and elements. After all, in the digital realm we perform decentralized networking, perpetuating and rewriting others' memes and tweets and posts. We too operate in a web, a world of information that circulates collaboratively within a virtual community, each of us using others' writing in an intimate play of appropriation and revision and amplification.

As befits this expansive fictional network, Yonge uses a fictional structure that focuses on the dynamics of communities rather than the psychological depth of particular individuals. Kylee-Anne Hingston points out that, in her family chronicles, "Yonge uses a community based, multiple-focus narrative structure," seamlessly shifting narrative perspectives among multiple characters in the same scene. "These frequent shifts of perspective thus in effect emphasize the interdependency of each character and each plot in the narrative."[38] Yonge was so committed to her ensemble cast of characters that in the family chronicles it is impossible to identify any single main character, and even characters given less attention in one novel will later become the focus of a subsequent linked novel; for instance, Tom May is a minor younger sibling in *The Daisy Chain* but the protagonist of *The Trial*. Yonge ensures that her characters have a fundamentally egalitarian status, stressing lateral familial ties rather than Woloch's industrial hierarchy.

Yet Yonge's embrace of multiplicity has a significant limit: her typological belief in a fundamental truth. Typology, reading modern incidents as expressions of foundational biblical revelations, was a particularly important tradition for Yonge, as Gavin Budge has shown.[39] As the basis of a fictional practice, however, typology creates tensions, for, in Peterson's words, it "asked writers to interpret within established conventions and yet produce fully individual lives."[40] The writer must depict a character both as a unique individual and as an example of a larger truth, both as a realist self and as an allegorical example of a scriptural original.

One way Yonge accomplishes this dual characterization is to depict the realistic modern character as errant, as requiring the difficult sloughing off of extraneous individual traits in order to expose the pure core spiritual self, even if (perhaps especially if) that process of stripping down the self requires the modern subject's pain or death. Yonge depicts this as a durational process, for the passage of time is required to break down the exterior self to its original inner being. In *Novel Craft*, I point out that Yonge tends to use botanical metaphors for stripping down the self, as she imagines the individual self to require pruning in order to find its spiritual core.[41] Flattened, stripped, glued down, the self finds its truth in its complete abjection to the divine. *The Daisy Chain* is patterned according to such metaphors: living plants, including the eponymous daisy chain, must be transformed into scriptural representations. In *Heir*, Yonge employs a similar botanical metaphor when Guy's adopted sibling-cousins participate in grafting a wild rose from Guy's home, Redclyffe, into a domestic tree in the Edmonstones' garden. Like that small slip, Guy will now grow by taking his nutrients from his adopted family.

Yonge's typological belief is also visible in another of her interests, ecclesiastical restoration. In Simon Goldhill's account, restorationists aimed for something that was not literally the original but *should have been* the original.[42] They would alter actual historical forms in order to make the church look like their historic ideal. "Restoration removed centuries of fabric as disfiguring interpolations, as if they were wrongly added lines in a text which could be cut out by an editor."[43] Yonge's long history in periodicals adapted her well to imagine buildings as items that could use pruning, as she strongly advocated removing historical additions to reveal a church's supposedly true shape.[44] In this perspective, the past is never past. It is always here, available for reworking, and a gifted editor-restorationist can fearlessly reconstruct what it ought to have been all along.

From her fiction to her editing, then, Yonge considered writing a composite process; working on multiple texts simultaneously, collaborating with different readers, and cross-cutting among multiple points of view within each text, she used a fundamentally interrelational style. Yonge regarded everything from architectural history to gardening from this collaborative perspective. The fact that her interlocutors could not respond may not have mattered much. If an editor does not hear back from a contributor, or a collaborator falls silent, the other's unreachability does not erase one's duty to keep working. But it is one thing to imagine Yonge getting writing advice from her friend Keble; it is quite another to imagine Shakespeare, Scott, or Manzoni as Yonge's interlocutors. This idea of atemporal collaborative work is disorienting for a reader who has been trained to "always historicize." How do we read the synchronicity of a text in which everything is always happening at once? What can the communities of *Heir* teach us about time?

Guy's Two Families

Heir is structured as a feud between Philip Morville, a rational, modern, skeptical man, and his cousin Guy Morville, a chivalric martyr figure. Philip represents the modern man, the rational, efficient, secular individual pursuing his own self-interest (rather like Scrooge, as we saw in chapter 2).[45] Guy grows up in the gloomy Morville castle, while Philip rules over their mutual cousins, the Edmonstones, a modern suburban family with three daughters, Laura, Amy, and Charlotte, and a disabled son, Charlie. Eventually Guy marries Amy Edmonstone, while Philip marries her elder sister Laura. But Philip's calmly arrogant reliance on his own rational ability to act causes him to infect Guy with the illness that kills Guy on his honeymoon—a tragedy that traumatizes Philip. Like Scrooge, Philip needs a hard lesson to teach him to devote himself to others.

The Edmonstones' community of care matches the criteria I laid out in chapter 1: affiliative, egalitarian, performative, discursive, temporally askew. It is female-associated, since the family consists of three daughters, a mother, a grandmother, an Irish female cousin, and a baby girl, while its main male members, Charlie, Philip, and Guy, require the most care. Care relations override medical interests; the Edmonstones do use a doctor, but he is a long-standing family friend whose advice is significantly directed by his affection for the family members. Nursing care for Charlie, Philip, and Amy, the most chronic sufferers, consists of the sort of everyday alleviation we saw in chapter 2: the ordinary bodies model of trying to distract and amuse invalids in order to ameliorate their daily lives.

The Edmonstones are such a paradigmatic care community that a review of their lifestyle can help us understand the pros and cons of this kind of organization. The family is highly permeable and inclusive, folding in neighbors, wards, cousins, family friends, and connections. Charlie's father is "so fond of inviting, that his wife never knew in the morning how many would assemble at her table in the evening. . . . The change was good for Charles, and thus it did very well, and there were few houses in the neighborhood more popular than Hollywell."[46] Spatially speaking, Charlie lives in a parlor next to his mother's room. People are always having important transactions in this space, a room that is both a secluded retreat and a public thoroughfare, so that he is always in the middle of the action (15). Sociality and digressiveness characterize this community, although the narrative also invites us to query whether those are uniformly positive traits, as we imagine the wife's difficulty catering nightly to an unknown number of guests and preserving a sense of privacy as her personal space becomes her son's parlor. Social relations within the care community require active interventions. When Guy asks Mrs. Edmonstone about his mother, she worries "whether she might be about to make disclosures for which he was unprepared" (76). How, she wonders, can she say something nice about his mother without criticizing the grandfather who hated and destroyed her? Mrs. Edmonstone finally finds a letter that praises how affectionately Guy's mother played with the family's babies and toddlers (77). The tenor of this letter shows a voluntary, affiliative, comfortable relationship, a lovingly expanded family, while Mrs. Edmonstone's response demonstrates her sensitivity to Guy's emotional needs.

As this letter shows, the extended clan must constantly negotiate their relationships via discourse as individuals explicitly inquire whether others are willing to enter the kinds of relationships they want and as they show a capacity to sense unspoken needs in others. Guy asks Mrs. Edmonstone to act like his mother, and he proposes to Amy literally across her mother's lap, including the family in the marital arrangement in a way that Clare Walker Gore argues is characteristic of Yonge's fiction. Gore points out that Yonge depicts characters forming "alternative family units" with siblings who have unconventional gender roles, and "when Yonge does center a novel on a marriage plot, she redefines marriage as familial, condemns relationships that are seen as exclusionary, and uses the integration and inclusion of disabled (and thus celibate) characters as an indication of worth."[47] Guy and Amy's marriage expands almost immediately to include the desperately ill Philip, while Philip and Laura's later marriage incorporates Amy and her daughter.

The central event in the book is not the marriage, however, but rather the crisis, requiring intensive care, when the rival cousins both fall ill in Italy. On Guy and Amy's honeymoon, they end up having to nurse Philip, who is also touring and has come down with a debilitating fever. Guy is an ideal carer: "His whole soul was engrossed: he never appeared to think of himself, or to be sensible of fatigue; but was only absorbed in the one thought of his patient's comfort" (414). "Never was there such a nurse as he," Philip exclaims (434). But Guy contracts the illness, and Amy, who is pregnant, must nurse both men in a strange country, a stress sustained only by the characteristic atemporality of care. Amy finds that she is so "fully occupied" that she "never opened her mind to the future" (458). The illness acts as a kind of reset button, erasing previous dissatisfactions and starting relationships afresh, as when Guy's fatal illness fundamentally alters Philip's lifelong suspicions of him, and when Philip's ghastly appearance, in turn, reconciles Charlie to him at last. When Guy dies, Amy is sustained only by the need to care for Philip. "It will be worse for him than for you," Guy had cautioned. "Take care of him" (469). Caregiving literally keeps her alive as she spends the first day of her widowhood helping Philip in the classic ordinary bodies mode: "She talked to him, read to him, tried to set him the example of taking food, took thought for him as if he was the chief sufferer . . . working . . . for him who had been [Guy's] chief object of care" (472). Although Philip survives, he is traumatized by Guy's death, disabled by the residual effects of the illness, and devastated by guilt for the rest of his life.

Because Yonge is so centrally interested in care, she is astute about its emotional dynamics and complex negotiations. When the Edmonstones go to Ireland to visit their increasingly infirm grandmother, they leave behind two vulnerable members of the care community who cannot travel, disabled Charlie and his sister Amy, the melancholic widow and new mother. But the trip benefits Charlie and Amy by prodding them out of their cared-for roles, giving them the new pleasure of caring for others. Amy "was glad to be of some use, by enabling her mother to leave Charles" (555–56). Charlie feels "full of eagerness and pleasure at the very notion of being of service to [Amy], if only by being good for nothing but to be waited on" (556). Allowing Amy and Charles to become carers instead of cared-fors feels so empowering that the fragile siblings bravely decide to travel to take care of the ailing Philip, because they enjoy "the pleasure of being of use" (561). Within the community of care, roles must remain fluid; nobody is stuck as perpetual cared-for or caregiver, but everyone helps everyone else in turn, a value vividly illustrated when Charlie and Philip, each too weak to walk, take a carriage, "each anxious for the comfort of the other." In this perfect example of mutual care, they are both carers and cared-fors, harmonizing in shared appreciation for the other's needs (574).

The Edmonstones' community of care has advantages (closeness, mutual care) but also disadvantages (nosiness, mutual interference, chaos). One issue is that all of the Edmonstones' care relations are initially directed inward, toward one recipient, Charlie, a concentration of attention that destabilizes the family. Charlie resents their concern and passive-aggressively resists it, while the eldest daughter, lacking parental attention, falls into a problematic romantic entanglement without her parents noticing, and the youngest daughter's education is ignored. Care here falls into a pattern of obsessive daily upkeep alternating with neglect, a situation that is not good for anyone.

Another problem is that Philip dominates the Edmonstones with a model drawn not from care but from military organization. As a military man, Philip is accustomed to a chain of command, and he takes control of his own family in the same way. The care-community-minded Edmonstones, however, resent and resist this form of organization. As I pointed out in the introduction, there are many ways to organize a small group besides care communities, including a military-style hierarchy, and Philip's idea of group dynamics clashes with the Edmonstones'.[48] Communication requires a fundamental respect for the other, the ability to imagine that the other deserves to be heard. In Philip's condescending assumption that he already knows how everyone else will react, we see his lack of respect for others' alterity. For instance, Philip hoists and hauls the disabled Charlie as if he were an inert object, infuriating Charlie (39, 239). This treatment contributes to Charlie despairingly considering himself doomed to be "a helpless log," "chained down" for the rest of his life (91, 92). Through most of the novel, Philip's form of care is to calmly override his cared-fors' feelings and insist on substituting his own perceptions—an example of the kind of projection that Noddings warns carers to avoid.

The Edmonstone care community has serious problems in working out what the proper relation of members ought to be to one another. Because relations are voluntary, they must constantly be assessed, and sometimes they remain murky, as in the case of teenage Charlotte, who overhears her cousin Eveleen's elopement plans and has to decide whether to tell her parents, or Laura, whose fiancé commands secrecy when her parents expect openness. Each person fumbles around trying to figure out the right course, exhibiting a fluidity and adaptability so extreme as to create near-constant crises. Moreover, the community of care is so porous that it is easily destabilized. One person's judgment can be corrupted by another's; one person's plans can be derailed by a change in the group's needs. For much of the novel, Guy is banished because his cousin Philip accuses him of gambling and manipulates Mr. Edmonstone into believing it. After all, a permeable community can exile people as well as welcome them. In other words, in a community of care so many people's feelings are at stake, and there are so many issues of status, respect, and sensitivity, that bad decisions are easy to make and discussions can go on interminably.[49]

Inasmuch as the Edmonstone ménage focuses on the culture of everyday life, they find it hard to prioritize amid their constant chatter about clothing, flowers, recent novels, news, and social events. When Charlie first meets his cousin Guy, the importance of this encounter gets lost in the local noise of Charlie's irritation at being seen in a garish dressing gown, eagerness to see a puppy, resentment of his father's obvious attempt to amuse him, sympathy at his elder sister's embarrassment, and mischievousness given a chance to tease his little sister (17–18). In a realist novel, a teenager's shame about his unfashionable outfit can easily occlude issues of greater moment.

The way Guy reforms this family is to help them redirect their discursive distractions toward spiritual self-discipline. Guy sets them an example of intense focus and a symbolically meaningful life. When Guy dies, we watch Philip, Laura, Amy, and Charlie, having learned to follow his example, try to achieve their best selves in a world without Guy. Guy has bequeathed them a way of understanding themselves on the satisfyingly deeper scale of scriptural ultimate truths, beyond the pettily expostulating hyperlocalism of domestic realism.

The last two hundred pages of *Heir*, after Guy's death, depict the Edmonstones working to balance the needs of a physically disabled youth, an unhappy widow, a sister suffering from depression, a cousin intermittently delirious from malarial fever, an elderly grandmother, an exhausted mother, a rebellious cousin, and a baby. Everyone consults with doctors, travels to nurse each other, and checks that the carers left behind are not getting depleted. Nobody is more important than anyone else; they want to help all members equally, having achieved a family that functions as a paradigmatically fluid, inclusive, female-associated community of care.

Guy is able to reform the Edmonstones partly because he comes from a very different organization. Guy's biological family, the Morvilles, offer a strictly patrilineal descent marked by strong forms of status differentiation. Family for the Morvilles means a traditional ancestry, and that lineage is male, singular, silent, sequential, and guilty. The grimly inescapable Redclyffe lineage designates one man in each generation who will be the heir of Redclyffe and who seems to live in isolation, hardwired to repeat his ancestors' mistake. (Each Morville man commits violent crimes.) After all, Redclyffe is entailed and "has always gone in the male line" (529). The all-male Morvilles are entirely historically oriented and inhabit an ancient castle amid a population that is "a primitive race, almost all related to each other, rough and ignorant, and with a very strong feudal feeling for 'Sir Guy'" (285). As we shall see, this family is deeply indebted to Scott's *Guy Mannering*, and the Redclyffe village population is based on that novel's lawless Scots, who are reckless sailors, smugglers, gypsies, thieves, and poachers. According to Lynn Shakinovsky,

> The very concepts of lineage and inheritance contain within themselves the idea of replication, of passing on what is received down through history. The tightly woven domestic model into which Guy and Philip are interpolated appears to function as a fate that is predetermined and inescapable; it is through this claustrophobic and stultifying destiny that Yonge investigates the infinitely destructive potential of sameness, of repetition as it is played out through the generations.[50]

The Morvilles refuse discourse. The grandfather tells Guy nothing of his history until he decides the time is right. When he does tell Guy, "the boy sat the whole time without a word," speechless with horror, which, significantly, the grandfather does not notice (79). Because Guy's despair is internal, unspoken, it cannot be rebutted. The discursive framework of this lineage model—one important man, by himself, in relation to nobody—is nondialogic: there is no need to speak because nobody else's opinion matters, and if he does speak, he does not expect a reply. Their gloominess extends to the physical space: Redclyffe, situated on a rugged northern cliff, has a forbidding interior with a "large, gloomy room, where the light of the lamp seemed absorbed in the darkness of the distant corners," that is inhabited only by the memory of "the moment when [Guy] found his grandfather senseless in that very chair" (283).

Daniel Stout explains that the manor or the estate produces "a set of preestablished, noncontractual obligations into which persons (including the lord, who is himself 'held of' the manor) are slotted. Within this structure, individuals appear . . . as entities who either will or will not meet the scripted, predetermined requirements."[51] Anyone, in other words, can be the heir to Redclyffe, and once there he will be scripted into its role, regardless of his individual history, personality, desires, or aims. This substitutability is true of Redclyffe, and it has larger complications. Because the Redclyffe world is based on a single heir, it does not recognize any principle of social reciprocity, egalitarian respect, or communal responsibility. Thus, the villages under its control deteriorate. The only kind of social relation it can muster is that of an old retainer's feudal fidelity, a loyalty that is itself historical, inherited from generation to generation. Markham, the loyal retainer, has also served Guy's father and grandfather.

He seems to be based on Rolf in Friedrich de la Motte Fouqué's *Sintram* (a strong influence on *Heir*), the comrade who stays with Sintram throughout his life and helps him work through his ancestral curse.

To modern eyes, Redclyffe vividly illustrates what it would feel like to live Bloom's theory of influence. To remain hyperaware of one's inheritance, to feel the threat of repeating one's forebears, is to be caught in a nightmarishly diachronic imperative, where the best one can hope for is a swerve away from inherited determinism. In this case, the novel is either reiterating the work of its powerful forebears or experiencing a violent, wrenching turn away from them. The Morvilles' insistent historicism is so strong that under its gloomy influence Guy calls Goldsmith's, Richardson's, and Sir Walter Scott's novels "ancient books," even though they are the same novels that the Edmonstones enjoy as part of their wide-ranging literary explorations (30). In the irresistible predetermination of the Morville regime, these novels become hoary progenitors; in the inclusive modernity of the Edmonstone ménage, they become cheerful elements of daily discussion.

The issue in *Heir* is whether Guy can achieve what Bloom calls "poetic misprision"—repetition with a crucial difference. Guy agonizes that he is "heir to the curse of Sir Hugh, and fated to run the same career, and as he knew full well, with the tendency to the family character strong within him, the germs of these hateful passions ready to take root downwards and bear fruit upwards, with the very countenance of Sir Hugh" (80). Being introduced to de la Motte Fouqué's *Sintram* by the Edmonstone coterie, however, enables Guy to imagine a fictional predecessor rather than a real ancestor, giving him a new intertextual possibility. As Amy reminds Guy, "Sintram conquered his doom" (71). Amy's comment teaches Guy that he can alter his fate by choosing to leap laterally into someone else's story. That realization prompts him to a new idea: Is it possible to be Sintram rather than a grandfather? Rather than a literally inborn fate, can one elect literary, symbolic, atemporal affiliations, reading actively so as to, in effect, choose one's own adventure? The fact that it is Amy who suggests *Sintram* indicates that in *Heir* this form of flexible relationality, unlike a grimly all-male lineage, is female-associated.

In *Heir*, the main character is both a "guy," in the sense of being a generic, typical person, and Guy Morville, a particular character. Growing up, he is an unruly teenager who does not study enough for tests and is impatient with elders at local tea parties, but he is also a Christian involved in an allegorical journey toward redemption. Guy is the *Heir*—the person already born into a lineage of original sin, already, like all humans, inheriting the fallen world. Gavin Budge has identified Guy as a Christ figure. His major spiritual breakthroughs occur at Easter and Christmas, and he experiences his own version of Jesus's temptation in the wilderness.[52] He finally sacrifices himself to save his cousin. Similarly, Susan Colón argues that the novel retells the parable of the Pharisee and the publican in Luke 18, with Philip as the Pharisee.[53] Guy's typological story has him sinning, being sacrificed, and achieving redemption. Budge and Colón are certainly right to identify the biblical origins of Yonge's story. But we should note that it is not the least remarkable aspect of this novel that a young woman in a country village—a young woman who at that point was virtually unknown as an author—would have the idea of turning Christ into an impatient local teenager.

For it is a more modern literature that allows for a different kind of selfhood, with the lateral influence of Sintram replacing the linear determination of ancestors. After all, instead of the gloomy and haunted Gothic castle, the Edmonstones' comfortable suburban home offers a good setting for domestic realism: "The drawing-room of Hollywell House was one of the favoured apartments, where a peculiar air of home seems to reside [with] its bright fire and stands of fragrant green-house plants. There were two persons in the room—a young lady, who sat drawing at the round table, and a youth, lying on a couch near the fire, surrounded with books and newspapers, and a pair of crutches near him" (3).[54] Instead of the silent ghost of the dead grandfather in the gloomy corner, we have Charlie, the boy on the couch, who is literally "walled up" in modern periodicals and publications. This is the space that introduces Guy to a wider world of relationships with multiple people and texts (30).

Elisabeth Jay accurately notes that *Heir* "functions as a model reading club, where characters, and, by implication, readers, are taught to 'read aright' through being variously exposed to contending principles, exemplary readings, and recent and contemporary poetry upon which to try out their newly acquired reading skills."[55] Crucially, *Heir*'s characters imagine reading as a selective activity. Reading becomes an active mode of editing that suppresses or avoids undesirable elements. The cousins argue about strategic forms of reading so as to maximize the affective and didactic qualities of texts. They debate whether it is acceptable to enjoy Byron's descriptions of scenery while avoiding "his perversions of human passions" and powerful, brooding heroes, and wonder whether it is safe to read Dickens's work (30–31, 87, 399–400). Is selective reading possible? Can one judge an author whose works one has not read? They discuss *The Vicar of Wakefield*, *Sir Charles Grandison*, *Le Morte d'Arthur*, *Dombey and*

Son, Scott's "The Lady of the Lake," and Southey's *Thalaba the Destroyer* (30–31, 44, 87, 150). The cousins concur that "men with minds in the right direction" include Shakespeare, Spenser, Scott, Wordsworth, and possibly Milton, but they rule other authors out of bounds (400). (They concede that Milton was religious, even though his religion "was not quite the right sort.") At Hollywell, reading is an interactive mode that must be debated among members of a group.

Writing, too, demands multiple actors. Guy has to decode the authorship of a joint letter from Philip and Mr. Edmonstone; Charlie has to deduce the origin of the ghostly traces of poetic lines on the blotting pad in his room; Philip notices that a song transcribed for piano has both Guy's and Laura's handwriting; Mrs. Edmonstone tacitly edits a letter in the act of reading it aloud; Philip spontaneously translates Manzoni; in a party game the characters must guess who wrote each list (a challenging job since Charlie mischievously writes in another's voice). At the end of the novel, Charlie finally finds a way to use these skills by becoming Philip's parliamentary ghostwriter. Charlie will spend his adult life putting words in Philip's mouth. Whereas Philip used to override and ignore Charlie's feelings, now, in a perfectly fitting reversal, Philip must spend his career parroting Charlie's statements. The two cousins will flourish via what we might call composite texts, writing and speaking each other's words, producing materials to be reported in the periodicals behind which Charlie was ensconced at the beginning of the novel.

Synchronous Influence and Composite Fiction

Composite textuality also defines the metalevel of this novel. *The Heir of Redclyffe* operates by virtue of a number of intertextual influencers who appear to hover omnipresently, interfusing this novel without regard to their temporal origin. (Today we might see this as "cloud-based.") Besides the scriptural exemplars, Dickens is equally important to *Heir*. The characters argue about *Dombey and Son*—published just a few years before *Heir*—and when they discuss the death of little Paul Dombey, they are unaware that it is a template for their own future. Guy himself will replicate Paul's tragedy, and Amy, who cries heartily over little Paul's death, will be forever shaped by Guy's. In both stories, the dead boy's beloved dog consoles the miserable surviving sisters. Philip, who despises Dickens as part of the pile of "cheap rubbish" that is, at best, harmless because "their principles are negative," turns the group's attention to Alessandro Manzoni's *I Promessi Sposi* (1821–1827; republished 1840) instead (30–31).

I Promessi is one of the three most important Romantic texts undergirding Guy's story, the other two being Scott's *Guy Mannering* (1815) and de la Motte Fouqué's *Sintram* (1815, published in English translation 1841).[56] Yonge admired Manzoni so much that she translated *I Promessi* so that her father could enjoy it.[57] Yonge's characters explicitly invoke the figures in *Sintram* as models for their own behavior, and Guy's child is even named after Sintram's mother.[58] De la Motte Fouqué and Scott describe the doomed heir of a sinning race who occupies a craggy northern castle on a sheer cliff, a man struggling toward moral salvation—precisely the situation of the Morvilles at Redclyffe. Yonge borrowed some of Scott's characters' names (Guy, Wellwood), personality types (inept tutors, brooding patriarchs), and specific episodes (duels, shipwrecks). It is hardly surprising that Scott was a formative influence on the work of someone born in 1823. Yonge was allowed to read one chapter a day of the Waverley novels throughout her childhood.[59] She wrote that "I may respect, admire, rely on other authors more, but my prime literary affection must ever be for Sir Walter!"[60]

However, as much as she loved Scott, Yonge was also deeply influenced by Austen and saw herself as Austen's successor, especially since she too grew up in Hampshire among Austen's connections, and many of her novels rework Austen's.[61] The Edmonstone family evokes *Sense and Sensibility*, and in fact Yonge originally named the Edmonstones the Dashwoods.[62] Like Austen's family, the Edmonstones include a coolly reasonable eldest sister whose love affair with an enigmatic, reserved man remains secret, a more emotional younger sister, and an immature third sister. While Guy is no Willoughby, Amy, like Marianne, ends up mourning for her lost love.

It is certainly possible to read Guy's two families as replaying the divide between Scott and Austen that is traditionally credited with undergirding Victorian literary forms. This one novel, indeed this one character, embodies the relation between a big national story of the movement of historical forces and a small domestic marriage plot. It is also possible to read *Heir* as a creative revision of a possibility inherent in *Guy Mannering*. In Scott's novel, the heir, Harry Bertram, is adopted by a middle-class family, the Vanbeest merchant clan in Holland, but we learn almost nothing about his upbringing there. Yonge revises this plot to reverse its polarities; in *Heir* we learn all about Guy's adoptive middle-class milieu and very little about his ancestral locale.

But the influences don't divide quite that neatly, as this novel's intertextual references exceed Guy's two families. Guy's story, the tale of the self-sacrificing good man, also invokes Malory's *Morte d'Arthur* (1485),

Southey's *Thalaba the Destroyer* (1801), Byron's "The Giaour" (1813) and "Childe Harold's Pilgrimage" (1812–1818), Kenelm Digby's *The Broadstone of Honor* (1822), Spenser's "The Faerie Queen" (1596), Keble's "Lectures on Poetry" (1832–1841), and Richardson's *The History of Sir Charles Grandison* (1753). *The Heir of Redclyffe* is a kind of community of its own, a chorus of half-recognizable voices chiming in together. Perhaps Yonge was taking Keble's famous advice, "don't be original."[63] For *Heir* does not read as the work of an insecure novice writer shoring up her work with references to the greats. *Heir* does not feel derivative or plagiarized, and it is no pastiche of its source texts. Rather, it is a novel whose emotional effect is amplified because it harmonizes with so many other stories. This is a textual community of care. *Heir* treats everything from the story of Christ to *Dombey and Son* as if they occupy the same no-time of literature: a kind of egalitarian, intimate crowd in which one can swap stories with, say, Malory or Sir Walter Scott. Yonge reuses her sources but also changes them freely, showing no interest in the sanctity of a text written by someone else in the past. *Heir* often feels as if Yonge is coauthoring with colleagues who simply happen not to be aware of their collaboration.

Reading *Heir* as a communal form invites us to assess Yonge's interactions with her intertexts in terms of care theory. If Yonge is their carer, is she treating her cared-fors appropriately? One concern in care relations is that the carer can project an inauthentic need onto the cared-for. Real care demands "motivational displacement": helping the cared-for do what he or she wants.[64] Noddings warns us to avoid "the projection of one's own personality into the personality of another."[65] When Yonge rewrites her sources, is she respecting their own personalities or projecting hers onto them?

Sometimes she domineers, giving bad care. When Yonge conflates Scott, Manzoni, and Fouqué in *Heir*, she makes them into convergent allegorical accounts of the same dynamic of a sinning, erring, repentant boy in a wild landscape, not independent narratives by people from different national and linguistic traditions who are writing in different genres (myth and historical fiction). Some of these losses are profound. Where *Guy Mannering* addresses the painful process of land enclosure, dispossession, and the rise of a monied middle class that pushes out the older landed lairds, *Heir* simply has attractive, scenic crags.[66] Whereas Scott's work addresses the nostalgic recovery of an imagined national past, Yonge's novel envisions moving into a modern world that provides up-to-date ethical and spiritual guidance for self-improvement. Similarly, Yonge ignores the fact that Renzo, the young man in Manzoni's *I Promessi Sposi*, is a peasant embroiled in class struggle against the massive legal, military, financial, and sexual power wielded by the nobility. Guy has little to do with class differences, for he lives in a pleasantly homogenous, middle-class, suburban England.[67] Thus, Yonge smoothly eradicates her predecessors' more radical national and class critiques, overriding cared-fors who cannot speak back.

However, Yonge may have thought she was taking care of her writerly colleagues, editing away their bad elements so as to allow the pure core spiritual narrative to shine through. In this respect, she may have felt that she was giving good care to her mid-Victorian readership, "meeting another's need" (to use my definition of care) by trimming away these texts' problems. For not only does Yonge erase the regional and class politics of her forebears, but she also alters these source texts in ways that her own audience would have preferred, muting the aristocratic violence and illicit sexual obsessions of her Romantic sources. In *I Promessi Sposi*, Don Roderigo is trying to abduct and rape another man's fiancée. Sintram is passionately in love with a married woman. Guy Mannering fights a duel with a man he suspects of trying to seduce his wife. These powerful illicit desires motivate the sins from which the good characters must recover by slow repentance and good deeds. In *Heir*, however, the story of sexual obsession survives only in a harmless if embarrassing teenage crush mix-up. Similarly, the Edmonstones' cousin Eveleen is a cleaned-up version of Edith Dombey, for Eveleen runs off to marry her true love, not to engage in a vengeful affair with her husband's clerk. In these revisions, Yonge is aiming to care for her readers by giving them what she perceives as the best possible version of the story, retroactively improving Scott and the others according to a typological model in which, as in ecclesiastical restoration and botanical preservation, one brought out the inner truth by eradicating the individual particularities that obscured it.

Yonge's attitude toward her sources parallels Guy's attitude toward his families. At various points, both are alienated from their origins, misunderstandings flourish, texts are misread, and half-truths are adopted and believed. The Edmonstones' care is not always good, and neither is Yonge's, for the same reason: a failure to respect alterity. Yonge overwrites her sources just as Philip commandeers over his own family. When Philip dictates a letter to his uncle, it is not so different from Yonge rewriting *Guy Mannering* into her own story. In both cases, this writer ignores the differences, insisting that the author knows best.

We have seen that silence poisons the care community in *The Wings of the Dove*. In *The Heir of Redclyffe*, this iconic novel of communal care, similarly catastrophic failures of discourse punctuate the story. When members of the Edmonstone community cease to communicate, their ties fray badly. Laura and Philip contract a secret engagement; Guy is honor-bound not to reveal how he spends his money. In both cases, misunderstandings and resentments and suspicions flourish in those silences. Guy is banished, and Laura falls into depression. However, these silences have a silver lining. When the characters become alienated from their communities' exhausting "constant solicitude," they sometimes discover spaces within which they can find themselves (556). Discovering one's separateness, one's individuality, can be painful in a nineteenth-century novel devoted to communal norms, but from a modern perspective, we can see its advantages. Guy's isolation allows him to grow up as his own man, and *Heir* comes into its own in its differences from its sources.

Reading Together

It seems like *Heir* sets up a vivid contrast: an archaic, masculine, aristocratic, violent Gothic lineage of Morvilles against a modern, female-dominated, middle-class, comfortable household community of care with the Edmonstones. But Yonge complicates this opposition. True to the care community model, she wants to figure out how to produce a composite world of the two families from which Guy comes so that the novel will enfold them both. Part of this project is overriding time—the "ancient books" of Redclyffe mingle with and turn out to be the same as the modern "cheap rubbish" of Hollywell, just as the widowed Amy lives with her mother and brother as if her marriage had never occurred, yet she knows that she "can't turn into a young lady again" (593). In a disorienting mélange, the past and the present merge, like two transparencies sliding over one another to form one image. In an impossible no-time, our binocular vision brings something into focus that is both current and ancient, both present and future.

Influence theory often invokes the family. But family relations are more complex than "thinking through our mothers," as Woolf said, or Bloom's swerve from the fathers. Perhaps it takes a full novel, a long Victorian domestic-realist account, to do justice to the fluctuations of those feelings within the family, to include cousins and siblings so as to enable lateral movement. It might be fairer to see influence as a relation full of all the complex, minute, nuanced emotional movements of a care community: disavowal, repudiation, readmission, embrace, acceptance. Guy finds it difficult to think through his mothers, who are dead or absent. Yet Guy is also unsure if he can swerve from his fathers, one of whom is criminal while the other is a "weak fool" (223). Progenitors may be elected, and their usefulness fluctuates.

In fact, the most deeply meaningful sources may not come from the past but the future—from the children. When Guy is disavowed by the Edmonstones and banished to Redclyffe, he is saved from despair mainly by befriending the clergyman's boys (299). He is also sustained by the adoration of his little niece Marianne Dixon, whose first name is perhaps a memento of the novel's grounding in *Sense and Sensibility*. Philip's grief for Guy is assuaged by his gentle, kind reverence for Guy's daughter (594). That daughter is herself named after a mother in *Sintram*, another generational reversal. In a dangerous midnight shipwreck scene, Guy tells certain sailors that they cannot join the rescuers because they have to live for the sake of their elderly parents. The children give care to the adults. Perhaps, as readers, we are cared for best by those who come after us.

Yonge depicts this reversal in the scene I mentioned earlier, when the Edmonstones graft a wild rose from Redclyffe onto the domestic bushes of Hollywell. Gérard Genette's theory of "transtextuality," which describes a later text being "grafted" upon an earlier one, makes it easy for us to read Yonge's scene as a representation of textual layering.[68] The new composite plant represents the novel itself, with its Romantic seed, its Sintram/Scott Redclyffe myth, growing beneath its ordinary mid-Victorian domestic garden bark. Meanwhile, the image of the Edmonstones' healthy tree and cooperative community nurturing a small wild slip from elsewhere is an apt image of Guy, transplanted to Hollywell.

It is, however, a strange image. Grafted trees are weak at the point where the new plant was inserted, and because the original rootstock continues to flourish, the tree reverts to its original nature and the grafted addition may die out. Thus, this image prefigures Guy's early death. Moreover, the symbolism is backwards, in terms of both status and chronology. We would have expected the modern, middle-class Edmonstones to be grafted onto the Morville lineage, which is after all the parent stock, the old aristocratic family. But Yonge's metaphor offers the opposite. Here the fundamental rootstock is the Victorian one, and the wild Romantic rose is added later, pulling its nutrients from its Victorian base. The rose is a fundamentally composite item whose elements coexist according to an alternative, nonlinear logic.

The unsuccessful graft, the uncertainty about which sustains the other, occurs in the family as well. After all, the Edmonstones and the Morvilles are cousins, and some vestiges of the other's system infect each family. Hollywell proves worryingly susceptible to male tyranny, particularly by cousin Philip, and one may say that the aim of this novel is to punish and curb Philip's desire for power. Charlie also domineers. "His mother had always been his most devoted and indefatigable nurse.... His father attended to his least caprice, and his sisters were, of course, his slaves; so that he was the undisputed sovereign of the whole family" (14). Being an "undisputed sovereign," however, makes Charlie a peevish, irritable petty tyrant. It is only when Guy challenges and even conquers him that Charlie begins to wake up to a sense of respect, learning, in Charlie's own words, "what it is to live with his match" (63, 86). Similarly, Guy must learn not just to patronize an impecunious relation, but to accept help from him as well. It is psychologically healthy to experience both carer and cared-for roles.

Similarly, Redclyffe must be reformed along Edmonstone lines; Guy returns to improve Coombe Prior, enjoy the maternal affection of the kind innkeeper, and mentor the sons of the local clergyman. But his greatest hope lies in importing an Edmonstone. As Guy declares, "he never would make things comfortable [at Redclyffe] without Amy" (369). Yet it is not clear that the dark lineage of Redclyffe really can be fixed. In looking at "that grim old castle," with its crumbling walls and bleak, empty rooms, Guy wonders whether it is a space that could "ever be a home for a creature like Amy, with the bright innocent mirth that seemed too soft and sweet ever to be overshadowed by gloom and sorrow" (372). Guy dies before he can bring Amy back, but, significantly, he has conceived a daughter who will be brought up at Hollywell, interrupting the direct transmission of patrilineage. Philip, whose tyrannical, proud mindset correlates with Redclyffe, fittingly becomes the new heir of Redclyffe—although, ironically, having been won over to Guy's side, he now regards it as a punishment. The heir is a type, but one's personal history, the novel shows, can alter the meaning of that type.

What does it mean to be a person in this novel? Is it a type (the heir of Redclyffe) or an individual? Let me offer a third option: a vision of subjectivity that is distributed, multiple, and non-coterminous. Charlotte Mary Yonge shows up throughout her own novel. Charlotte is the name of the sharp-tongued, precocious, alert girl of eleven (5). Mary is the vicar's daughter, Mary Ross, the helpful, unmarried, active, twenty-five-year-old woman who adores her father and works hard in the parish (38). Both are clearly self-representations of Yonge herself at different ages. When Amy asks Mary Ross to be one of her daughter's godmothers, we get another Mary, Mary Verena Morville (524). We have here another case of binocular vision, in which the childish version of Yonge can interact with the young-woman version of Yonge, in the perpetual present of the novel, mingled with a third, infantile version of Yonge that is laced with fictional paternity. For Mary Verena Morville shares one name with her author and another with a character in *Sintram*. Forget looking back through your mothers. Think about your daughters.

Or, to be more precise, think about your goddaughters. Mary Verena is the biological daughter of Amy and Guy, but the goddaughter of Mary Ross, Laura, and Philip. She is born into an elective community, a constellation of affiliative carers, in a relation that is irresistibly reminiscent of the avunculate in queer theory. In her celebrated reading of *The Importance of Being Earnest*, Eve Kosofsky Sedgwick counsels us to think of uncles and aunts instead of fathers, of lateral kin, alternative lineages, an elective family.[69] And what works for Mary Verena Morville might also work for Charlotte Mary Yonge. Yonge wrote for a conservative religious audience in the mid-nineteenth century, but we can claim her as part of our own family, reading her retroactively, reconfiguring the mother through our own daughterly needs.

With her two-part name, her Edmonstone curls, and her Morville eyes, Mary Verena Morville is brought up by the Edmonstones while living part of the time in the castle at Redclyffe, in a new community formed around her and her needs and incorporating members of both families. She constitutes a living merger of the mythic and the domestic, and perhaps that is how Yonge wanted her own authorship to work. *Heir* does not end with the death of the male heir, nor with the succession of the new male heir, but with Mary Verena, heir in a different sense—not the heir of Redclyffe, but the inheritor of relationships, histories, and caregiving experiences that override the dark castle with another social meaning: the elective community. This idea might not be the heritage that Yonge intended to convey, nor what she hoped to influence us to think, but it might be the idea we take from her in the end.

Composite Writing, Temporality, and Community Criticism

What if we take the communal world of Charlotte Yonge seriously as the basis for fiction? What would it mean to emphasize community as the condition for writing, to seek a kind of writing that synthesizes multiple voices and creatively reworks many texts?

One result would be a change in how we measure value—specifically, we would downgrade originality in favor of composite writing. Genre fiction—often condemned as formulaic—might instead be judged as composite writing. We might benefit from reading fantasy, science fiction, romance, and horror novels, which predictably follow the conventions of multiple other texts, not as failed bids for singular originality, but rather, as the expression of an interestingly communal, capacious sense of textuality. For instance, J. K. Rowling's Harry Potter series is frequently critiqued as derivative, but a care reading would turn those multiple voices into a feature, not a bug.[70] We could also use this perspective for fictions that revise earlier work, like Jean Rhys's *Wide Sargasso Sea*, which Caroline Rody reads as a "radically participatory literary universe" that works "to value inclusion, not individualism, to honor difference and multiplicity."[71] My point is that a care-community reading can help us read popular writing (often but not always by women) by focusing on its achievement of complex relationality, instead of judging whether it achieves the status of a unique utterance.

My larger argument, however, is that all texts are composite texts. As Virginia Woolf explained, works never have "single and solitary births" but rather express "the experience of the mass."[72] All texts are produced by people who internalize others' work as they send out drafts to different people and work with editors and readers and collaborators who shape the product. Every text carries the traces of its development in a social nexus. Every writer draws on a coterie. In academic writing, the marks of other readings are on the very page, in our quotations and citations and footnotes. A page of literary criticism—any page of this book, for instance—constitutes a record of the composite work of writing. Does it matter that I am citing people who wrote in different periods? They can be made to speak to each other, suspended in the space of argumentation, floating atemporally in the perpetual present of writing.

Intertextuality is true: language is fluidly interactive. Influence is true: writers are thinking about other writers. But reading the text as communal labor makes it clear how those two factors converge. Composite writing has been here for a long time. It is visible in the work of female polemicists and coteries in the eighteenth century, it governed the lives of women writers in the nineteenth century, and it characterized minor character retellings, popular fiction, fan fiction, and genre fiction in the twentieth century. And now, in the digital era, composite writing has become the mode of online circulation and academic criticism. Like any other care relation, it can be done well or badly. Yonge did it well when her revision brought out elements in her source text we might not otherwise have seen, and badly when her version obscured or overrode elements of the source text of which she disapproved. As I pointed out in chapter 1, we can have care relations with the inanimate, but that places a special burden on us to be careful and tender of its needs, because it cannot speak back to us. We need to decide whose needs we are meeting: those of our own readers, or of the authors of the texts we study, or, if possible, the needs of both. In neither case, however, can we hear the voice telling us what to do, and we need to imagine that voice on behalf of the silent other.

Just as Yonge synthesized and edited her sources for the benefit of her readers, so too I hope to have translated Yonge's complex, composite novel into a theoretical model that might meet my readers' needs. We are, of course, doing it rather differently. Yonge tried to meet her readers' needs by providing a prettified, sexually purified version of her source texts. Meanwhile, I have been trying to reconstruct her work retroactively to meet our own needs for a composite, fluid, temporally askew model of interrelations. Sometimes one can give good care without knowing it; one can meet the needs of generations yet unborn. Sometimes one can model what a selective, interactive reading looks like. Yonge identified herself as a Sunday school teacher rather than a novelist, and as Mother Goose mentoring her Goslings rather than a mother. She herself stepped out of the direct lineage. So we can elect her as our teacher or our Mother Goose or our godmother, the ancestor we choose and with whom we continue to struggle, selectively reading and editing and rewriting her work, practicing the kind of communal care that she modeled for us nearly two centuries ago.

EPILOGUE

Critical Care

> *How might the university, both internally and externally, become a caring community?*
> —KATHLEEN FITZPATRICK, *GENEROUS THINKING*[1]

IN *COMMUNITIES OF CARE: THE SOCIAL ETHICS OF VICTORIAN FICTION*, I have been examining communities of care in three ways: first, by looking at the relationships of characters in nineteenth-century novels; second, by exploring the formal innovations in theories of reading and writing that the care-community structure facilitates; and third, by analyzing the larger dynamics of communities in lived political and personal experience. I am interested in the moments when readers are motivated to leap in and save the characters, or when readers are forced to assess their own role as co-makers of meaning. I have tried to attune this book to the ways in which nineteenth-century subjects' comfort with care communities might have informed period texts, while their experience of emotional labor in an emerging service economy might have shaped a sense of character. Throughout this work I have tried to address both the lived experience of care and the textual elements of care, for it feels important to become aware of the ways in which literary and lived experiences inform each other. Here at the end of the book, I return to the metaphor of the cantilevered bridge that I used in chapter 1, as I want to think of ways that our lived experience of communal relationships can be a plank thrown out toward literature, a solid ground to stand on as we reach toward alien fictional worlds. And when we are immersed in literature, intimately feeling the characters' mutual reliance, that too makes a solid platform from which we can stand and gaze back at our own lives, viewing ourselves differently from that other standpoint.

The two arms of a cantilevered bridge can be connected with a pin or with a light truss bridge or, really, with anything. If those two arms reach across strongly enough, some creative play is possible in the middle, taking multiple forms of connection, even doing fanciful work. I want to stand in that midpoint now, in a place where reading and acting meet each other. For me, and I imagine for many of my readers, that place is in academic work. In this epilogue I want to leave readers with a sense of how academia might fit into the realm of the care community, asking whether the department, the classroom, the institution, can or should operate like one of those care collectives, other-mothers, fictive kin, or queer families of choice we saw in the introduction. I have entitled this epilogue "Critical Care" for three reasons: critique is an act of care (in teaching and service); our scholarly criticism can be seen as care as well, particularly in our use of citations (in our research); and the need to bring care to academia (as an institution) is a critical one. I write these words during a pandemic in which those returning to the university are traumatized. The need for care is urgent; it is critical.

In order to bring our gaze to bear on the university, it will be helpful to review, briefly, some of the ways in which this book has implemented the idea of care communities. First, a theory of the novel has arced across this book. Traditionally, historians of the novel have regarded the nineteenth-century novel as achieving a sense of characters as unique individuals with psychological depth. More recently, critics have elaborated a view of the nineteenth-century novel as the story of the crowd, the anonymous urban traveler amid a mass of strangers. But I am interested in a formation that moves at a midrange scale, the community, which asks us to think of nineteenth-century characters as socially enmeshed figures who derive meaning from their relation to others. The relational, communal self is hard to maintain; it requires a kind of binocular vision, a toggling between individual and type (between unique self and crowd). When people get stuck as cared-fors, they can become tyrannical, imposing their individual preferences on others (as Milly Theale and Charlie Edmonstone do), but when people get relegated to the carer role, they can be reduced to invisibilized, generic servers (like Lucy Snowe and Daniel Deronda). Entering a viable care community relation can jolt people out of those preset roles, shaking them into a healthier sense of self, because the care community requires constant fluctuation as all the members reach out to others and receive others' consideration in turn. Individualists become happier when they can join the community, as in *Persuasion*, *A Christmas Carol*, or *The Heir of Redclyffe*.

In reading fiction, however, we need to be aware of the pathologies of care when such communal enmeshment has not been achieved. We need to recognize how a character might subside into a type: the migrant, the gentleman, the housekeeper, the governess. Characters paid to offer service are forced to perform inauthentic feeling for money. Emotional labor might give us a new perspective on the paid caregiver character, as someone whose utterances and actions are meant to conceal rather than express the self, or whose self takes shape through the performative repetition of caregiving, producing certain emotional resonances. In literature, the paid caregiver's life has different milestones (the best friend, the difficult crossing) from the conventional main character's, as we saw in the case of Miss Wade and Lucy Snowe. It is crucial to recognize that minor characters have their own interesting life and are not just failed major characters. They need to be read in terms of the particular forms of subjectivity that service work produces, and their stories need to form part of the long history of the migrant global caregiver.

We also need to read characters in the fiction of the first half of the nineteenth century in terms of the paradigm of "ordinary bodies." Up through the 1850s, Victorian subjects regarded suffering as widespread, natural, and inevitable, and they assumed that other people should be trying to alleviate and distract patients. This culture did not have much faith in medical cures. The ordinary bodies idea accommodated chronic illness, intermittent attacks, and all the injury and aging and disease included in the long span of a life. Through midcentury, people were expected to provide amateur caregiving in social collectives—the care communities that are recorded in so much Victorian fiction.

Most of the care depicted in Victorian fiction is actually fairly bad, but the care dynamic can work even with inadequate caregiving. Care is robust and capacious, accommodating the oversolicitude of Mrs. Edmonstone in *Heir*, the tyranny of M. Paul in *Villette*, the projection of Mordecai in *Daniel Deronda*, and the corresponding faults of their cared-fors: the selfishness of Charlie, the inauthenticity of Lucy, the indecisiveness of Daniel. Care does not require genuine feeling or skilled nursing; it can fail in both the intention and in the execution, and in Victorian fiction it quite frequently does. When we assess these care dynamics among characters, we can ask a few key questions: Do they express egalitarian mutual respect? Do they work out issues discursively? Are they actively performing care? But even if the care community demonstrates favoritism, fails to communicate properly, and reverts to passivity, it seems that as long as the carer is genuinely trying to meet a need, cared-fors can muddle through the carers' inept methods to achieve some version of a real relationship. That first rough approximation of a decent care relation strengthens members enough to reform so that they can institute more permanent, more functional care relations afterwards. Mordecai and Daniel figure it out; so do M. Paul and Lucy. Good-enough care allows people to survive emotionally. And a care community has a better chance of giving good-enough care than a single carer, because when one member is depleted or aggravated, another can step in. Mrs. Edmonstone can be replaced by Guy, who has a better way to deal with Charlie, and when Guy dies, Amy can take over, newly informed by her nursing experience. The point is that nineteenth-century characters are basically always trying to get into care relations with one another, and so it is crucial that we have a way to read laterally for social relations, instead of solely drilling down into the secret motives of each individual character.

We can also read those social relations extradiegetically when we explore authorship as a kind of networked community instead of a linear model. Charlotte Yonge seems to have imagined herself as just such a socially enmeshed subject, part of a jostling, shifting batch of colleagues, floating free of conventional chronology. The communal model is particularly useful for women writers, writers of popular fiction, and writers who come out of journalistic experience. We need not always assume that authors reach for a purely original idea while struggling to throw off others' influences, but can acknowledge that authors are, rather, those who cheerfully adapt, edit, revise, domesticate, rewrite, and evoke each other. It made sense for authors to synthesize, recombine, and alter each other's work in a nineteenth-century care-community context, but it may also makes sense in a digitally networked writing experience today.

However, in Victorian British experience the care-community norm began disappearing after midcentury and was gradually replaced by a new model: extraordinary bodies, medical cure, and paid professional expertise. The community of care became the locus of nostalgic yearning rather than the ordinary reality. In the new dispensation, the care community felt like an ideal that had floated out of reach. When invoked, it was an impossible dream. It is the tacit model for Daniel Deronda's Zionism, and as such it defies any sort of pragmatic planning or probability. It is what ought to mediate Milly Theale's decline, but because it does not, we are able to measure the catastrophic betrayals of her actual death. For many late Victorian readers, the local amateur care community became a kind of fantasy community of the mind, pushed beyond the horizon of the fictional world.

This historical shift helps us understand one more area where enmeshed subjectivity matters: the reader's role. Victorian readers, particularly early Victorian readers, carried their daily life as active caregivers into the reading experience. Eager to help those in need, even if they were merely fictional characters, Victorian readers felt frustrated when the fictionality of those suffering denied them the chance to intervene, and they experienced that balked care as sentimentality. But twentieth-century modernist readers developed a different idea of intervention, as we saw in *The Wings of the Dove*. James forecloses a sentimental reading of *The Wings of the Dove*—there is no possibility of leaping in to save Milly—and instead, by foregrounding the character's slippages, silences, and mystifications, makes us aware of our own power to supply the language that has vanished. By the end of the nineteenth century, the concrete potential of care communities with their person-to-person contact has become sublimated into an internalized communion with a textual other. In *A Christmas Carol* we want to see food and warmth for Tiny Tim. In *The Wings of the Dove*, we want to see Milly's missing words. In each case, we want to meet a need, to fill a gap. But the need we are meeting has changed profoundly over the century's course.

The type of care we are interested in can change the way we imagine narrative structure. What does the story of a migrant caregiver look like? It might be punctuated by disorientation, narrated by racial discourses, characterized by multiple microaggressions, and shaped by struggle to find an interlocutor—a shape that looks nothing like the conventional *Bildungsroman* or marriage plot. What does dying look like when you have too much money? It might mean sinking into a transactional, financially mediated dystopia in which events are marked by their failures to be spoken. The novels I have addressed here take on such narrative challenges as the need to found a new nation, the shape of mourning, the experience of having two families, the challenge of alienating work, and the struggle with emerging state management of poverty and illness. These are the kinds of stories for which care is central. These are the kinds of stories for which care is still central today.

I am hoping that readers can use the fictions I have addressed in this book, from Austen to James, to extend the philosophy of ethics of care. It seems important to me to evaluate how care works at the midrange scale, between the private dyad and the public institution—a model that is suggested by immersion in a historical era that did not yet boast large-scale state care. The community, perhaps a dozen people, does not need to be together in a physical place; it can exist in the mind, in the digital realm, in the nowhere land of a story, in the virtual space of a Zoom screen. But that community will work well only if it demonstrates commitments to egalitarianism, performativity, affiliation, and discursive involvement. Habermas's public sphere manifests most of these qualities, although his politically oriented networks need to work alongside care communities' personally oriented ones. Just as importantly, the experience of lived reality in care communities today must help sustain our sense of how such coalitions work. I have discussed the way these social formations have helped people survive in the African American community, in queer families of choice, in self-fashioned crip collectives, on teams, and in schools and clubs and neighborhoods. In *Communities of Care*, I have started not with a top-down theory but rather with care communities in both lived reality and fiction, and from there I have built a theory that can account for how these communities work based on those experiential case studies.

Reader, whatever your need—whether it is in narrative theory, historical research, disability theory, or ethics of care—*Communities of Care* is trying to meet it by beginning to outline ways of thinking made possible by a communal model. Throughout this book I have used the metaphors of a cantilevered bridge, a lens, and a web. These metaphors don't mesh together, because each describes a different dimension of care community theory. A care relation is like a bridge, the carer and the cared-for reaching out toward each other until their arms can meet. Reading with care theory is like looking through a lens that pulls into focus the minor characters and silences that are normally at the edge of our perception. Finally, participating in a care community is like interacting with a web, a complex, fluctuating assemblage of skeins with multiple connections, vibrating to the lightest pressure, swinging out and ripping away and reconstituting itself as its anchor points change. I want now to think about what it might mean to build that web in real time and space.

Teaching Care-fully

At the beginning of this book I wrote: "Reader, I want to warn you from the start: although this book has a title featuring the word 'care,' it is not going to be pleading for us all to care more about each other, nor will it be praising Victorian characters for truly caring. Forget the pleasant platitudes of care. Think of care as a practice—a difficult, often unpleasant, almost always underpaid, sometimes ineffective practice." At the end of this book, I want to focus on one of the most difficult and unpleasant of care acts: critical care, the hard work of critiquing others that care sometimes demands of us.

Care can go badly for many reasons. Money complicates care, for instance. People dislike pure transactionality, as when someone makes a purchase while completely ignoring the person ringing up the sale. But people also dislike false empathy, like friendliness that turns out to be a ploy to make a sale, and they are wary of real emotion, like a customer who shares too much intense personal information. We seem to expect just enough feeling to smooth over the economic exchange, but not enough to override it. We want a babysitter who is neither absolutely businesslike nor effusively attached to our child. We want a Goldilocks amount of caring—"just right" care somewhere in the middle between these extremes. This concern derives from a long history of anxiety about paying for what has been coded as a voluntary, heartfelt, spontaneous female offering since at least the seventeenth century. We aren't comfortable with coldly buying care outright, but neither do we want to dive into a messier realm of feeling with a stranger. Yet of course the home has always been the site of paid labor, and for centuries caregivers have been paid service workers; to feel that paid care is a betrayal is to perpetuate a dangerous cultural myth.[2]

Care ethics emphasizes that all of us are interdependent, enmeshed in thousands of microcaring exchanges through a constant flow of mutual acknowledgments, help, and courtesy. Care goes badly if that flow stops, as can happen if the carer cannot adopt the cared-for's perspective, if the cared-for neglects to acknowledge receipt of the care, and, especially, if the members of the care relationship get stuck in their respective roles. Carer and cared-for must express mutual respect. They must discuss their actions so as to adjust them better to the other's needs. They must keep their roles fluid, so that the carer can sometimes be rejuvenated by receiving care and the cared-for can take on the more powerful role of carer. But how can members of a relationship enforce such ineffable qualities as fluidity and respect and communication?

Often we rely on emotions to make a relationship work, hoping that if we feel genuine caring for the other, then the qualities of respect and discourse and mutuality will naturally follow. But care does not mean trying to inspire people to purify away all distressing dross in order to be our best selves. *Communities of Care* began in sync with the postcritical work of scholars like Lisa Ruddick and Rita Felski, who advocate a more positive, joyful form of literary criticism, reading (in Felski's words) "to strengthen rather than diminish its object—less in a spirit of reverence than in one of generosity and unabashed curiosity," as opposed to the current critical practices that Ruddick describes as "intellectual sadism."³ Similarly, Kathleen Fitzpatrick's injunction to think generously has profoundly shaped this project. However, my book has ended up committed to a different methodology. In this epilogue, I advocate for pragmatic guidelines rather than appeal for good feelings. I want to assess what critics do rather than judge them for who they are. In my view, the vocabulary of care can articulate more precisely what has gone wrong than simply complaining about bad manners, and it is a better guide to good behavior than a general injunction to be kind.

This is true of daily life as well as critical writing. If you want to hold the elevator door, help get the suitcase down, or chat with the stranger seated next to you, I hope this theory helps you remember to figure out the other's need first. Sometimes the person doesn't want to rush for the elevator; sometimes the traveler prefers to be the one to handle a fragile item; sometimes the stranger wants quiet time. Apparently kind acts can backfire; just ask visually impaired people who get hauled across the street by sighted people thinking they are doing a good deed.⁴ It is more useful to pay real attention to the other than to focus on being your own best self.

We build a social network not through imposing unwanted acts of kindness on others, but by respecting others' wishes, and we do so by communicating in order to fine-tune the relationship. I am not advocating sympathy (feeling), but care (action). And care works through discussion. Whether you are cared-for or carer in a particular transaction, explain your rationale for inviting, rejecting, or modifying the intervention and listen to the other's response. Register their facial expressions, their silences, their voices.⁵ If the person extending care is doing the wrong thing, tell them so. If the person you are trying to care for refuses the offer, hear it.

I want to stress that these acts of mutual care are not neutral. In a neoliberal, financially driven world, care for its own sake is itself a radical act. Leah Lakshmi Piepzna-Samarasinha describes how exhilarating it is for disabled people to form a care collective, to empower themselves to help one another.⁶ Likewise, Karma Chávez records the possibilities of coalition among queer women of color, regarding their very fluidity, precarity, and adaptability as advantages.⁷ In a culture that privileges straight white male able bodies, those who might not otherwise survive—people of color, women, disabled people, queer people—learn to band together. For instance, the Crunk Feminist Collective builds an online network of mutual support among Black women, drawing on the history of African American communal structures. "We actively refuse to do anything alone, so we collectivize every part of our existence and find new applications for the communal self-care of our mothers," they write.[8] Communal work means meeting others' needs for deeper reasons that resist managerial and monetized structures. And that in itself is an act of resistance.

Such quietly radical care-community work might fit the undercommons, Stefano Harney and Fred Moten's celebrated concept of the academic positionality that they identify as not-quite professionals, people who are "in but not of" the academy, members who trouble its privatized and professional norms.[9] After all, recognizing the collectivity of our academic lives rebuts academic emphasis on individual achievements. Sarah Burton and Vikki Turbine explain an important truth about care:

> Care and kindness is [sic] not simply a particular attitude of geniality or occasionally "brightening someone's day." Instead, we need to comprehend it as both radical dispositions and radical acts: speaking truth to power, refusing damaging hierarchies, rejecting restrictive and exclusionary interpretations of "professionalism." Care is both remembering to take new colleagues for lunch *and* challenging harmful and marginalising policies; it is recognitions of, and robust responses to, university policy and rules failing to understand us as human *and* checking in on the welfare of colleagues. Care is, most of all, *a constant vigilance as to your power and how you wield this*.[10]

Turbine enacts her radical kindness by maintaining a "virtual collective," an online space for playfulness and creativity and support in navigating academic systems.

In this epilogue, I explore what our academic lives look like when we prioritize care. I am not trying to come up with new ideas, but rather, to use the care-community structure to bundle multiple preexisting resources and recommendations into a single idea. After all, academic care is not new at all; it is foundational to teaching, service, and research, as I will be arguing. But to name it is to tease out a side of our work that is often obscured by institutional politics and professional reward structures. I'll be addressing our care work by foregrounding the admonition "meet another's need" and by testing social structures against the four requisite qualities of a viable community: performativity, affiliation, discursivity, and egalitarianism. If I am right that we are all already doing care work in academia, then readers should expect to recognize lived realities in the following pages rather than discover brand-new ideas, for we will be seeing our lives through another lens. Care work is vital for everyone in an academic community: undergraduate and graduate students, tenure-track and contingent instructors, staff and administrators. All are involved in academic configurations that we can choose to conceptualize as communities of care.

Let's start with one of the three canonical examples of care: teaching. Can we use care-community theory to improve dynamics in the community-scale group found in a small class—and should we?

The first question to ask is whether a class ought to be configured as a care community, which is a different question than whether to give care. Let's resist the temptation to assume that care communities are always the aim. After all, a care community is only one of several possible ways of organizing a group, and it will not necessarily be the right choice if the aim is to transfer information efficiently, inculcate skills, execute a strategy, mobilize many people, or achieve a concrete goal. Could an Introduction to Biology lecture course of 150 students really become a care community, and if so, would that be the best model? Remember that a care community consists of perhaps fifteen to eighteen people at most and does not scale up easily, and that care communities function through dialogue, which may be impossible at that course scale. Remember also that care communities are prone to disorganization, slowness, diffused decision-making, endless discussion, fluidity, permeability, changeableness, like the chaos we saw in the Edmonstone family. One can give care (meeting the needs of others) in many different social organizational forms; the specific model of the care community is not required.

Thus, to consciously choose to make our classes emulate a care community model is to aim for specific goals, not just vaguely advocate for warm feelings. We are saying that we want the people in this class to meet each other's needs. We are choosing to conceptualize the classroom as a space where everyone feels seen and valued, where discussions, dialogues, produce a mutual understanding. However, a class is not just a way of generating shared satisfaction—after all, students could do that much more easily in student-centered social spaces like parties or dorm rooms—but is, above all, devoted to learning something. A class has a mission beyond mere sociality. That imperative generally produces some structures of authority and regulation that are inimical to the care community. So when we are thinking about how to make a class into a care community, we need to balance its goals by deciding when we are willing to suspend efficiency and authority in order to produce the emotionally meaningful resonance of disparate people functioning together for shared benefit, and, conversely, when we need to break out of the care-community mode to ensure that everyone is learning. How might a class realize egalitarianism, affiliation, discursivity, and performativity?

Egalitarianism presents a particular problem. If everyone is on the same level, how can one member discipline or grade the others? The easiest solution is for teachers to suppress their unique status by demoting themselves and becoming just one member of the group as far as possible. Ideally, instead of a class with authoritative pronouncements emanating from above and silent, obedient acolytes gazing up at a sage on a stage (or mutinous Labassecouriennes quelled by Lucy Snowe's cruelty on the estrade), we can enjoy an interactive, egalitarian, vocal classroom. The student-centered classroom encourages students to take the initiative in their own education, making learning into an active mode guided by the student's own needs. Student-centered classroom techniques speak to values like creativity and self-discovery and social negotiation, which may well be just as important as the values prioritized by our educational system, if not more so.

Yet the student-centered classroom can also have real problems. In the classroom, we all know who is really in charge, and to pretend otherwise can feel uncomfortably like bad faith. To coerce students into pretending they have the power is an elaborate charade that ignores their real needs, and that can become intolerable for everyone if the students misrepresent or misbehave and nobody is empowered to rectify the situation. Many students are, at best, only mildly interested and not particularly informed about the class topic; after all, they are taking the class in order to learn about it. To put such students in charge of the class is to force them to perform a kind of expertise and capability they may not yet have, and to expect them to step up to do the unpleasant work of disciplining a peer seems deeply unfair to both parties. Moreover, if we assert that a person who has never studied the topic before can teach the class, we downgrade the expertise of faculty and play into the hands of those who regard us as dismissable, interchangeable cogs—the very attitude that has led to the adjunctification of the academy. It takes us decades of intensive, specialized study and years of practice to be qualified to teach a course. What message does it send to stand aside and insist that total novices can self-teach instead? What message, in particular, does it send when those who struggle to gain respect in the classroom—people of color, women, younger instructors, instructors for whom English is not a first language—then are told to suspend the authority they have won with such effort?

Real care requires us to inhabit our roles with attentiveness, care, and forethought—and real care is hard and sometimes unpleasant, especially when it requires us to criticize other people. Providing critical care in academia—critiquing as an act of care—meets the other's need to improve and learn. Yes, we should empower student-driven learning, and yes, we should do presentations and group work and think-pair-share exercises, but teachers must retain their authority. Teachers are the ones who can and should correct students' errors, redirect discourse when it is heading in a problematic direction, and make sure the quiet ones are included too. Foundational care ethicist Nel Noddings was a professor of education and stressed that teaching is a caring relation that must be affirmed on both sides. A healthy pedagogical care relationship is one in which each side feels the other's interests, needs, and pleasures, and the teacher can enter enough into the student's perspective to help guide that student.[11] But such guidance is possible only if the teacher retains the capacity to critique and the student is willing to hear that critique—if, in other words, they retain their respective roles as teacher and student.

A better way to introduce egalitarianism into the classroom is not to put the teacher on the same level with the students, but rather, to ensure that within each level members have equal status. In, say, a large lecture class, all undergraduates can be treated equally but are ranked below the TAs, who should themselves be treated equally; if the class is team-taught, the faculty should also be given equal rank. The faculty form their own care community, the TAs form theirs (sustained by regular meetings), and the students form a third (fostered by student breakout sessions). In this case, the course holds multiple smaller communities, and each community is egalitarian in itself but hierarchically related to the other communities. This organization allows for authority, efficiency, and oversight.

Affiliation presents another challenge for a class. Instructors might not be able to do much about the fact that some students did not freely choose to be present but signed up only to fulfill a requirement. Nevertheless, they might verbally recognize the students' reluctance and work with them to craft a version of the course that they *would* voluntarily buy into; this exercise would recognize the students' interests as important and hopefully produce willing affiliation. This is also an exercise that students can do on their own by finding ways to choose what they had to do ("Well, I didn't want to take this whole course, but I *did* want to read that text or learn that information, so that's what I choose to do"). The reality may be that it's a required class for some students, but since affiliation is performative, like other care relations, acting as if one wants to be there can make it feel true. Anyone who feels disaffected needs to figure out how to convince themselves they want to be present.

Participants might ask themselves: is there real discursive interaction? If the students are stubbornly silent, or if there are only a few speakers who talk all the time, instructors might design exercises that prompt everyone to speak (like think-pair-share, or going around the room, or doing group work) to get them into the habit of discursive intervention. But it is also useful to remember that communication can be nonverbal, and that people can participate in the discursive work of the class in other ways.

It can be comforting to keep the principle of performativity in mind, because it makes it feel more acceptable when students or instructors are not already invested in the class. After all, as the student performs respectful behavior over the duration of the class, that repetition will eventually produce what feels like authentic interest in the class. As the instructor performs enthusiasm for the material over the semester, that repetition may eventually generate the feeling, but if the feeling never develops, that is acceptable too, so long as the action continues. Care consists of acts, not feelings. Teachers perform concern for students from the first day of the semester, and students perform respect for teachers, although they are strangers to each other. But week after week of enacting these feelings can make teacher and student genuinely care for one another, often making those pedagogical relations some of the most meaningful of our lives.

On a larger scale, instructors should remember that we are trying to meet another's need, and it may be helpful to think about who that other is in a small class, and what the need might be. For the instructor, the other is the student, and the need is to get that student capable of performing certain skills or acquiring a certain type of knowledge. But the students may not identify this as their true need. Students may perceive their real need as getting a good grade, satisfying a requirement, accumulating credits, or impressing a professor who can help them later. The mismatch between those aims produces dissatisfaction. Everyone needs to communicate about how to make the course serve their needs if members wish to produce the sense of voluntary affiliation that a good community requires.

Too often, this discussion gets replaced by assessments. The biases of student course evaluations are widely acknowledged, but a care lens reveals other problems. The student course evaluation violates the foundational elements of care (reciprocity, egalitarianism, discourse), since it is a one-way document issued after the course has already ended, it is not acknowledged by its recipient, it is anonymously generated, and it is not part of the ongoing mutual discursive regulation of caregiving. Instead, we need a constant conversation in which instructors and students keep discussing what works, adjusting their behavior accordingly. Instead of student evaluations, we need student interventions, and we need them throughout the semester. Grades suffer from the same problem—they must become ongoing learning experiences rather than a single moment of assessment. Grading with critical care means entering into the students' minds as much as possible and helping them produce the best arguments for their positions. It means writing comments on essays that derive from motivational displacement: rather than acting like a judge who assesses a finished product, instructors should engross ourselves in students' point of view and work with them to express that view in an ongoing process.

I have argued that the strongest care is the kind that satisfies the most needs simultaneously. Merely meeting physical needs is adequate, but if you can meet emotional, intellectual, and aesthetic needs at the same time, the care will be much richer. In the classroom, the immediate need is for intellectual growth or mastery of material, but participants' physical comfort and emotional consideration and even aesthetic pleasure should be met as much as possible too. The strongest care occurs when the room is comfortable, the surroundings are pleasant, and the tone is satisfying. If a seminar is not working, it may be not because the care is bad but because it is too weak, trickling through only one tube instead of cascading through multiple channels. As I write these words during a pandemic in which teaching has gone online, I also know that many communities are "communities of the mind"; community is just as possible in a Zoom meeting as it is face to face in a classroom, because what matters is not whether the meeting is virtual but whether the participants feel comfortable. If home is unsafe, if a classroom is broken down, it will impede care-community formation, no matter whether that community is virtual or not.

Teaching as an act of care can itself be an important political act, a form of resistance against institutional, corporate, financial logics, as bell hooks reminds us:

> Teachers who care, who serve their students, are usually at odds with the environments wherein we teach. More often than not, we work in institutions where knowledge has been structured to reinforce dominator culture. Service as a form of political resistance is vital because it is a practice of giving that eschews the notion of reward. The satisfaction is in the act of giving itself, of creating the context where students can learn freely. When as teachers we commit ourselves to service, we are able to resist participation in forms of domination that reinforce autocratic rule. The teacher who serves continually affirms by his or her practice that educating students is really the primary agenda, not self-aggrandizement or assertion of personal power.[12]

To care for students is to create a personal relation based in trying to help the other. As Bill Readings writes, "The condition of pedagogical practice is, in Blanchot's words, 'an infinite attention to the other' (161). This infinite attention is an ethical obligation that cannot be discharged, and an obligation whose infinitude is created in no small part by our being-in-community."[13] What hooks and Readings teach us is that the scene of teaching is an ethical obligation, an affirming and attentive relation to the other. This is true for teacher and student alike. And as Mordecai and Daniel's relationship showed us, as long as the student and the teacher feel that the other is genuinely trying, it is possible to make their rapport work. We push the arms of the bridge across toward each other, day after day, hour after hour, and the other registers the outreach with gratitude, even when those arms might not be perfectly constructed or flawlessly finished.

In the Service of Care

One of the best results of bringing ethics of care to academia is that it gives us a strong tool for validating service labor. If care is the basis of social organization and human relations, then we need to fully appreciate the crucial activities of mentoring, advising, administrating, and organizing. Like Eva Feder Kittay, I imagine that in a care-based society we would honor "those who were valiant in their care of others, as well as those who showed us the dignity of all lives, no matter the extent of the dependency."[14] What if we regarded service as a valuable activity, not a grudgingly performed chore, with particularly noteworthy service work eagerly studied by those who wish to emulate it? Certainly a fuller appreciation of service would allow for enhanced recognition of the work done by academic administrative and support staff. As Fitzpatrick asks, "What kinds of new discussions, new relationships, new projects might be possible if our critical thinking practices eschewed competition and were instead grounded in generosity?"[15] What kinds of honors would we give those who best fostered interdependency? What kinds of careers would we make if service was our goal rather than research—or if we conceptualized research as a form of service in itself?

At the same time, I want to push back against the assumption that service is always beneficial and that we all ought to take on more of it. Carers need to be able to say no, and that is particularly crucial for people of color, who disproportionately perform the labor of sustaining academic community, as they are constantly asked to do the diversity work for their institutions plus the additional work of representing and educating, as Roopika

Risam points out.[16] Perhaps instead of just lifting the burden of service work, we can reconfigure that service so that it helps the person doing it. Mentoring, like every care relationship, needs to be mutual. Jean Ferguson Carr explains that "mentoring is necessarily a reciprocal act: it means paying attention to each other, checking in on each other to see about progress or signs of distress," while Nancy Miller urges us to see mentoring as a relationship of collaboration.[17] If mentoring means giving up one's own time to help another, it may feel burdensome, but if mentoring constitutes a close relationship in which both parties feel cared for, it ought to be mutually enriching. The drive for mutuality is powerful. Recognizing that we are wired to want reciprocity, we should recalibrate academic mentoring to facilitate it. If a university has set up official mentoring structures, it might direct the mentee to return care to the mentor, perhaps by giving copyediting, technology, or research assistance, or taking the mentor out for a meal on the institution's dime. Such a relationship would encourage more senior faculty to be mentors, and it would empower mentees instead of fixing them in the perpetually subsidiary role of the grateful supplicant.

It may be helpful to remember that caring is not about reaching out to everyone all the time, but specifically about "meeting another's need." Thus, if asked to attend an event, you can ask, first, if the event is meeting the needs of a person you care about. Second, is the event meeting that need adequately, and if not, can you change the event in order to do that? If both answers are negative—if the event is not meeting the need of a person you care about, and it is not possible to change it to do so—then give yourself permission to say no. Similarly, when asked to do some task as a favor, you can take advantage of the way care allows us to alienate ourselves and treat yourself for a moment like the other, asking whether this work is going to meet a need of your own. Will it expand your expertise, develop new institutional knowledge, teach you new skills, make a difference for people you care about, or build good relations with the people who asked the favor? If not, tell yourself that there is no reason to take it on and save your labor capacity for more rewarding forms of care.

My point is that asking questions about what "meets another's need" and what does not can help promote healthy care dynamics. Concrete queries produce clear answers, pulling the problem out of the morass of worrying about how other people will feel if you say no. Care is a set of practical actions that may or may not correlate with feelings. In this respect it differs from something like Fitzpatrick's "generous thinking," "a mode of engagement that emphasizes listening over speaking, community over individualism, collaboration over competition, and lingering with the ideas that are in front of us rather than continually pressing forward to where we want to go."[18] Whereas Fitzpatrick posits generosity as a universal principle, care emphasizes case-by-case variability. After all, more generosity is not always a good idea. I am certain that everyone reading this book can think of colleagues who have been given the benefit of the doubt for far too long.[19] Calls for generosity can worsen the situation of those who already give up too much, particularly female faculty and faculty of color performing disproportionately the work of mentoring. The imperative to be generous might even inadvertently perpetuate what the philosopher Kate Manne calls "himpathy": the sympathy that is disproportionately granted to white, privileged men and usually accompanied by anger against the women who dare to accuse them of transgression.[20]

If readers want to improve departmental morale, care-community principles might work better than a general injunction to practice generosity. After all, a department is ideally a paradigmatic care community, a small collective of largely equal members voicing their opinions while working for a common good, and if a department fails to meet that standard, then one might start by scrutinizing the levels of affiliation, performativity, discursivity, and egalitarianism in the group. Affiliation may, in fact, be the most crucial, for although one would assume that members of a department wish to be employed at the institution, if that is not the case, if, say, one member is impatient or despondent at the conditions of employment, that can demoralize the faculty. Members then need to figure out how to reperform affiliation, which may mean figuring out what conditions an institution should provide to make them genuinely want to belong and fighting for those conditions. In other words, if voluntary affiliation fails, the answer is *not* to talk yourselves into being happy members regardless, a hollow pretense that is not going to last if the conditions that have disturbed affiliation continue. Rather, the answer is to figure out what reforms of pay, workload, and conditions would make you happy to be faculty members and then fight for that.

Discursive involvement and egalitarianism can also be problems in a department, since the most vocal members may domineer, allowing no space for other members' interests. If the chair knows that the problem is inequity demonstrated by spotty discursive involvement, the chair could consider moving to other forms of discourse, perhaps written or online, that might be more comfortable for quieter members or that require input from everyone for major decisions (such as a vote or a written comment). Articulating an expectation of egalitarian status can itself do some good—by drawing attention, for instance, to disproportionate advising burdens carried by some colleagues.

If a department is going to treat adjunct and graduate student faculty as full members of the faculty, their input must be welcomed and invited as much as anyone else's, but getting their discursive involvement may particularly be an issue. If full inclusion does not feel appropriate for the institution, then graduate students and contingent faculty must form communities of their own (online groups, listservs, meetings) where they can formulate their own statements, which can be communicated to the rest of the department. As with teaching, in governance each of these communities must be egalitarian within itself, although they may be hierarchical in relation to others: the graduate student group may rank below the faculty, but within the group all graduate students must feel equally valued. As we have seen, forming such collectives can be an act of radical justice. This is not just a feel-good attempt to bond, but rather the installation of a strong collective that empowers its members to fight and to survive. And the decision about whether to have everyone in one egalitarian community or to divide into three or four smaller communities in hierarchical relation can help make a department's needs and vision of itself clearer.

Finally, a chair might also think about how the department serves the other's need, asking first: Who is the other? The students? The faculty? Other departments and programs? The rest of the institution? The larger profession? The public? The needs of the other will vary drastically depending on whose needs we are addressing. Mapping this out can help a department form policies keyed to specific cared-fors and assess moments when those multiple care relationships come into conflict—for instance, when decent pay for adjunct colleagues requires higher student fees or cutbacks in tenure-track faculty perks. In such cases, honesty about each group's needs may help a department in weighing different agendas.

Digital humanities has been demonstrating how to foreground a discourse of ethics of care. In 2015, Bethany Nowviskie posted an influential blog, "On Capacity and Care," in which she called for digital humanities to foster restorative time, collaborative structures, and professional development. The aim was to produce a community based on "sustainability, resilience, and repair" instead of "the Silicon Valley logics of disruption, innovation, and endless churn."[21] While Nowviskie's idea of care is somewhat different from mine, it shares the same emphasis on egalitarian respect and mutual assistance, and it is perhaps no surprise that Fitzpatrick's *Generous Thinking* comes out of this field. In the specific case of digital humanities, articulating these values prods scholars to respect the heretofore underappreciated librarians and data-entry workers (many of whom are female and people of color) as much as the predominantly white male computer programmers.[22] Digital humanities scholars following Nowviskie have also identified themselves with the proud tradition of communities of color; Kate Dohe, for instance, identifies an "explicitly Afrocentric centering of *community* [that] broadens its scope beyond coders and managers, and instead encompasses the communal ways of knowing and doing work in this space."[23] Indeed, scholars of color have testified to finding a welcoming alternative academic community online.[24] For all its faults, Twitter has provided a platform on which people of color, trans scholars, graduate students, contingent faculty, junior scholars, and senior people can converse in spontaneous, flexible, interest-based temporary collectives outside of the usual hierarchical structures. No paywalls, no titles, no institutional spaces separate them. These groups qualify as Ray Pahl's "communities in the mind," and as such, they have become exemplary communal spaces.

In this epilogue, as you may have noticed, I have been working up in scale, moving from individual pedagogical encounters to the seminar, the department, and now, the university itself. Fitzpatrick hopes that universities might relate to one another and to their communities by prioritizing community and cooperation rather than competition.[25] The university, she insists, does not exist to serve itself. It must not hoard knowledge or wealth or resources for its own empowerment. To use the terms I offer in this book, the university must meet the needs of others.

What specific changes might happen if universities took on this challenge, consciously turning themselves toward others' needs? First, we would have to ask who the other is: do universities exist to serve students, parents, trustees, their endowments, their employees, faculty, employers, the state, the general public, the cause of knowledge? In each case, what is the need that the university might be able to meet? A university might work differently if it conceived itself as primarily serving its students (as is generally true of community colleges), or the cause of knowledge (the aim of many research universities), or the workforce requirements of employers (this is the case for vocational and training programs), or the needs of residents (as for most state schools).[26] Those needs will inevitably conflict as well as overlap. Sometimes serving the cause of knowledge requires spending time in a lab or archive, away from students. Sometimes serving students entails teaching them concepts that the state might find dangerous. Sometimes caring for students, faculty, and staff must first tackle the harder care work of thinking about their real needs rather than their wishes—keeping people safe from a pandemic, for example, rather than facilitating a premature return to dorm life. It is useful to articulate and work through such conflicts. I am proposing something like a mission statement, but for care. You might ask: for whom does my institution really care?

Critical Care in Research

Care-community theory seems quite self-evidently relevant to service and teaching, but I argue that it can also help academics rethink research, at least in the humanities. The fact that individual monographs are still the main criterion for success in many humanities fields speaks to our profession's continuing pursuit of a fantasy of autonomous achievement, a competitive, grueling race to amass the most publications. But writing is not a diachronic history of adding up the trophies one has accumulated over time. It is, rather, a synchronic composite process. For as we know, every act of writing is communal, composite work, and so even the monograph is a joint production. If we look at any publication through the lens of care theory, it spreads out into complex, weblike traces of collaborative networks, bearing the marks of readers, editors, working groups, and conference audiences.[27] For the problem isn't research in itself, but our mistaken insistence on seeing that work in terms of competitive individualism.[28]

We need critical care—a way to articulate the role of care in critical scholarship. The trophy publication approach discourages academics from imagining themselves in dialogue with others, which helps account for the problematic quality of so much academic prose, the impenetrable, static writing, not to mention the casual cruelty of so many peer review and grading practices. Care theory can provide a specific set of principles to guide us as we write and to turn our writing toward the other's needs.[29]

In chapter 6, I discussed the tradition of composite writing, in which a particular author invokes, alters, and re-presents other writers from multiple eras. While coauthored books and edited collections clearly exemplify such composite writing, I'd argue that all academic writing in the humanities already does something similar. All writing is not only marked by a web of multiple interlocutors over time but also internally constructed out of numerous voices. In the humanities, we cite multiple sources, and each citation coexists in dialogue with the others, even though they may come from different centuries and regions, their originators never able to speak in real life. The academic essay is a network that holds multiple writerly voices simultaneously in suspension. Like the jostling community of a newspaper, like the academic communities that form on Twitter, a piece of academic writing allows for mutual correction, revision, reinscription. A collection of references, a list of quotations, is analogous to a crowd, but when we select particular components and put them in relation with one another, we generate a kind of textual community.

Of course, the analogy between academic writing and a community is not exact. We cannot, for instance, consider our citations to have voluntarily affiliated with one another, inasmuch as they have no agency for such measures. The words we cite are inert abstract and textual entities that require a guiding authorial intelligence to pull them into correspondence. Yet, as we have seen, humans project our social needs onto the inanimate and work out our relationships through these proxy items, these transitional objects. Moreover, once we generate language, those texts will end up having their own interrelationships. Michel Serres offers the metaphor of bread dough with a mark cut into it. When the baker kneads and folds and stretches the dough, the mark travels, recurs and extends, creates unpredictable tracks, and so too, Serres argues, do events move through time.[30] The image is also helpful for writing. We may make the mark where we wish, but we have no control over how that mark might travel in time. A word from a novel published in 1853 can resonate with a tweet from last week, the two reverberating against one another in the space of the text that cites them both. That echo may please and sustain readers, enacting a care relation.

Indeed, in some ways, citations do behave like a care community. They are performative inasmuch as they act, and they are present in order to exert an effect. Moreover, they have to be discursively justified; as we always tell our students, you have to introduce and gloss your quotations, explaining why they're in the paper.[31] And once citations are in the paper, they have a basically egalitarian status: each is valued because it makes some contribution. Moreover, citations reside in a kind of temporal suspension, the perpetual present of the essay. Temporal suspension is true in terms of reading—as we tell our students, every time you read something it is happening again anew for you. But it is also true for writing, particularly in a digital era, as we use materials that remain suspended in a glowing, detached, endlessly available presence. History in a digital writing practice is often signaled by failure: the now-unreadable notes in an outmoded program, the backup that has disappeared, the links that have gone dead. To the extent that we can write, it is by staying in the illusion of the perpetual present. The digital elements that we select, insert, and rework create a small group, just the right size for a care community, which thrives at the midrange scale between a dyad and an institution.

Many of the rules for caregiving also govern citation. For instance, when dealing with the other—whether that other is a person or another person's words—we need to avoid projecting our own wishes onto that other and instead imaginatively work to inhabit the other's perspective. When dealing with many people or with multiple quotations, we need to treat each on a case-by-case basis, rejecting abstract manipulation that would turn them all into equivalent instances of generic problems. We can certainly disagree with what the quotations say, for critical care is important; it is the unpleasant but crucial work of disciplining and redirecting an other that constitutes genuine care when facile praise would be so much easier. In this respect, we treat our quotations as cared-fors, respecting their alterity, considering their unique selfhood, treating each one with respect, practicing motivational displacement. It was her students' failure to manage this task that motivated Fitzpatrick to write *Generous Thinking*. She found that her graduate students were unable (or unwilling) to simply sum up a reading in its own terms. It is crucial to be able to take up the other's perspective, Fitzpatrick realized, and that engrossment is also the basis of decent caregiving.[32]

But citation-as-care also produces interesting ethical reverberations. To cite someone is to create a kind of ghostly textual avatar of that person, an avatar that can move, replicate, and interact with others, but that ultimately points back to the living being who originated it. Citation confers scholarly approbation by keeping a name and ideas in circulation, even when the author is critiquing that idea: famously, there is no such thing as bad publicity. The ethical difficulty develops when the textual avatar diverges from its human originator. Anyone who has been followed around by words written decades ago knows the feeling of a long-past utterance trailing behind, stuck forever to you; you can neither shake it off nor fully claim it. But that slight embarrassment pales in comparison to deeper ethical problems. What about citing a scholar who was later unmasked as, say, a sexual predator, when that quotation will publicize a name that ought to be buried in oblivion? What happens when the textual second self has slipped out of sync due to the passage of time, as in the case of gender transition? Citing earlier work of a scholar who has transitioned would circulate a dead name and very likely do damage.

What, then, are the ethics of a situation in which a suspended, digital, ghostly textual trace nonetheless has real effects on living beings? In *Living a Feminist Life*, Sara Ahmed proposed an intriguing solution: "In this book, I adopt a strict citation policy: I do not cite any white men." Instead, Ahmed chooses to cite "feminists of color." "Citation is feminist memory," she explains. "Citation is how we acknowledge our debt to those who came before; those who helped us find our way when our way was obscured because we deviated from the paths we were told to follow."[33] Thus, Ahmed brings the canon of foundational thinkers she wants into the world. Scholars who follow Ahmad's example explicitly cite black and indigenous people of color (BIPOC) and emerging scholars in preference to elite senior white male authorities. Some scholars have called for a conscientious citational policy to recalibrate our syllabi and teaching by centering other voices or advocating for a generous citational policy that recognizes communal contributions to the field of knowledge rather than specific individuals.[34] This has been a foundational recognition for me, and it underlies my construction of *Communities of Care*'s citational canon out of popular as well as academic writing and my efforts to feature emerging voices as well as recognized authorities while working to place care communities in a rich field of racial, ethnic, and national perspectives.

While Ahmed has led the way in thinking about citation as a community whose members one can choose, her solution is problematic if it requires us to judge sources' racial or ethnic affiliation before we can cite them. Citational choice also asks us to decide whether we ought to include work by people who engaged in predatory behavior or exploitative actions. While I too wish to use citational power to amplify the work of those who are contributing constructively to the field, I prefer not to act as a gatekeeper who decides (perhaps based on limited knowledge) on others' worthiness before I cite. Rather, I prefer to work out that decision during and through the act of writing, citing those whose ideas meet the reader's needs, and engaging with their personal issues as part of that citational process. Let's treat our interaction with the citational other as an ongoing relationship (often conducted in the paratextual space of the footnotes) rather than a single stamp of approval.

In so doing, we will be working against the assumption that a citation is nothing more or less than a valuable commodity, a shiny object. In some fields, particularly the sciences, citations are treated as particles that can pile up into quantities that substantially advance a career, as measured by numerical metrics. This quantitative emphasis on one narrow component of scholarly life produces what Nicky Agate and coauthors identify as "a toxic culture predicated on scarcity, competition, and alienation from personal and institutional values." They advocate for a new emphasis on scholarly process rather than product, articulating an allegiance to shared values and working against the myth of the lone scholar. Substituting a shared values framework for a grueling individual competition can produce a more meaningful notion of academic success, they argue.[35] In the humanities, we can draw on our long-standing practice of citing others to engage their voices in a conversation carried on in the messy modes of disputation, argumentation, selective reuse, support, endorsement, and extensions. Such complex conversations should not easily be compacted into citational pebbles. Rather, we should retain the warm relational spread that frustrates attempts to manage our work, participating in Moten and Harney's undercommons academic half-life, neither fully co-opted nor totally oppositional.[36] Care requires duration. If our academic professional relations consist not of itemizable citations but of mutually satisfying relationships conducted over time, silting up layer upon layer of experiences, memories, gratitudes, hopes, conflicts, and resolutions, we have created a living community that cannot fit into the cells of a spreadsheet.

The citations matter not in themselves but as the surface traces of a deeper relationship. In prioritizing care relations, we remain aware that to cite someone is to care for that person's words, and therefore indirectly to care for the person too (so that we always remember the real person beyond the text). It is true that later unsavory revelations may reveal that person as someone to whom you no longer wish to extend care. It is also true that repeatedly citing the same people can reinforce their power instead of distributing it among deserving others. But when we understand citation as the construction of a textual community of care, we make it clear that the carer has a responsibility for those textual avatars, and in the suspended time of the text that responsibility never disappears. Perhaps we should insist on the humans behind the citations when our students reference quotations as disembodied "support" or "proof," when beginning scholars set themselves up by attacking "arguments," when people on social media attack others' words, or even when intertextuality imagines disembodied texts eddying around. Those words were written by people whom we have chosen to bring into visibility. The way we treat those words can hurt or help the people who wrote them, so we need to manage them with care.

It's also helpful to ask yourself: Who is the "other" whose needs I am trying to meet through this citation or critique? Often, we automatically want to correct the people we cite, but those earlier scholars are not really the others in question. Those scholars may never read your critique, they may have changed their minds or moved into a different field, or they may even have died. The other is actually the reader, and to meet the reader's need, we ought to offer a steadily respectful, clear critique meant to advance the argument, not take down an enemy.

Remembering the human source of arguments also can help us give better peer reviews. Academics constantly evaluate their colleagues' labors, whether grading graduate students' work or writing recommendations, readers' reports, and book reviews. These evaluations can be superlative examples of care. True care is neither being kind nor being cruel; true care is meeting the other's need by thinking deeply about how to help the work become its best self. Matthew K. Gold is right to advise us to turn to "the practices and rhetorics of care" to ensure that peer-to-peer review is not a site of alienated labor. Because people are most motivated when they feel part of a community, "the labor of peer-to-peer review, then, isn't towards an individual text but to a community. What we need to start taking stock of is community value."[37] It might be helpful if writers engaged in such scholarly evaluations explicitly imagine the object of their writing as a cared-for. As with citation, the point is to remember that there is a living other behind the text.

We might even consider certain genres to be textual versions of care communities. (Instead of Pahl's "communities in the mind," these might be "communities in the volume.") For instance, multiauthored publications like journal issues or edited collections can be conceptualized as communities of care, since they consist of a dozen or so members who are voluntarily affiliated, egalitarian contributors.[38] The main impediment to these article providers becoming an actual care community is the fleeting nature of the engagement, as well as the fact that they often are unaware of each other until the volume comes out. But if we imagine the group of contributors continuing to work together, we can see how their efforts would naturally morph into a care community. This sometimes happens with editorial boards, which do have continuity over time and occasionally meet in person.[39] Similarly, people producing an annotated scholarly edition are giving care to the original text: as they foster and restore and explain it, they subordinate themselves to the needs of that text.

All literary criticism, whatever its form, enacts care for its primary text. Every time we read attentively, carefully, generously, we are publicizing the idea that this text is a worthy resource in our culture. Every time we teach or publish on it, we are disseminating the view that this text merits and repays our attention. Moreover, as Nija Cunningham points out: "argument generates a relational context, conjuring an interlocutor." By imagining an addressee, even one that does not respond, we construct a scholarly conversation.[40] Our writing is a scene of intricate and multilayered enmeshment with our (imagined) readers, our subjects, our citations. Indeed, we establish relationality in much the same way for primary and secondary texts, for in both cases we step in when we feel needed, when the original text has a lack that we can fill, a need that we can meet. In quoting criticism, this takes the form of the gloss explicating what might have been unclear in the quote itself. In reading the primary text, it occurs when we realize we can say something that is not obvious to other readers. In reading *The Wings of the Dove*, I argue that the very silences of James's novel prod us to step in to explain what the text itself is unable to speak. We feel called upon by the fragility, the evident need for care, that a text presents. Andrew Miller has called this openness in a text "implicative," arguing that the most generative criticism is open enough to encourage a reader to elaborate on it.[41] Another way to put it, I think, is that "implicative" criticism is criticism that reaches out for a care relation—criticism that leaves something for us to do. A self-sufficient piece of writing may put us into sympathy, the passive specular state of regarding something from the outside. But implicative criticism is care-based criticism: a criticism that needs our acts to fulfill its best self.

Good criticism is motivated by a scene of care: a text that cannot speak for itself and needs us to step in. Like my readers, I daresay, I have had this feeling many times in my professional life: when I found an obscure text that, I felt, needed me to broadcast its merits; when I suddenly saw something I was convinced was new and important in a text I thought I knew well; or when I came to believe that a much-discussed narrative structure was not properly apprehended.

Good criticism can come out of deep love for a text, but it need not. Sometimes we have to fake enthusiasm because in reality we feel lukewarm or even inimical to the text we are teaching. But in the effort to meet the student's need, we perform appreciation. Teaching something over and over again, carefully explaining it each time, can performatively make us care for something we originally did not care much about. How many of us have ended up writing about a text we grew to care for because we had taught it so often, having seen the shape of an idea that we felt urged to share beyond our classroom?

As I have been stressing in this book, however, care can go badly wrong, and literary criticism is no exception. I started this book by seeing Sedgwick's reparative reading as a guide to care, and I would like to end by coming full circle to revisit paranoid reading. In Heather Love's apt summation, "paranoid reading is described as *rigid, grim, single-minded, self-defeating, circular, reductive, hypervigilant, scouringly thorough, contemptuous, sneering, risk-averse, cruel, monopolistic,* and *terrible.*"[42] The monopolistic and circular nature gives the game away: paranoid reading does not imagine an other but rounds back only onto itself. In the introduction I compared paranoid reading to the medical gaze, a coldly external diagnostic scrutiny, and I suggested that care constitutes a good example of reparative reading. After all, care is literally reparative, as it names the act of working on something broken. By contrast, paranoid reading is a self-contained whole: believing in itself as an autonomous entity, it is stuck, forced to perpetually retrace the same repetitive motions. Bad criticism demonstrates a failure to form ties, whether to the primary text or to the reader.

One form of bad critical care is critique that fails to imagine the reader at all. Such work is written for itself. Sometimes this is a critique that shows off, flaunting skills in order to browbeat the reader into dazzled admiration. Sometimes it is self-indulgent writing that has given the writer pleasure to compose without any sense of other people's needs. Sometimes it is an anxiously dutiful, dull critique that is desperate to assert competence while guarding against any criticism. The reader is either not imagined at all or only hazily sketched as an applauding crowd or a menacing army of invigilators. It is a cantilevered arm thrown out for the admiration of those on shore, with no thought of matching up with a corresponding structure reaching from the other side. The opposite is a form of writing that strives to reach a richly imagined reader, as Sedgwick does—a structure yearning for its match. Consider her title: "Paranoid Reading and Reparative Reading, or, You're So Paranoid, You Probably Think This Essay Is about You." Her attempt to please and amuse us makes us feel seen.[43]

A second form of bad critical care is writing for the judgment of other critics. This kind of criticism slashes at colleagues, ignores those who have contributed to the argument, or aims to eradicate an entire field. Let me clarify that the mere fact of an attack does not make critical work bad. Of course there are legitimate reasons to attack certain critics and fields, and an attack that boldly clarifies and incisively disputes a direction in the field can meet a reader's need very well, even if the targets dislike it. Indeed, such criticism does a service by weeding out poor ideas, clarifying controversies, and reaffirming standards.[44] In such cases it indeed qualifies as "critical care." But such an attack goes wrong if the author seems cruel and attacks a rival or deliberately ignores other critics. Such criticism is no longer meeting any other's need, although it may make its author feel gleeful. When Sedgwick criticizes Judith Butler's *Gender Trouble* and D. A. Miller's *The Novel and the Police*, she works hard to make her criticism an analysis of a critical tendency, rather than a personal accusation, by praising the works before criticizing them, contextualizing them within their oeuvres, and listing her own writing as part of the problem.[45]

Finally, the "other" can be the text under discussion, and a different form of bad critical care is the one that misrepresents and distorts the text. Here I would remind us that we need to be extra tender with a text that cannot care for itself. Bad critical care is criticism that pays no respect to the special qualities of the object of study—whether its intellectual, theoretical, formal, historical, or cultural elements—but bulldozes it into a mound that can then be triumphantly declared a mountain. Such studies often declare something and then try to prove it, without respecting the way the text itself qualifies and resists that claim. What Sedgwick does instead is to leave her analysis open. Famously, she does not flesh out reparative reading. Like Henry James, Sedgwick leaves a gap we can fill. Like Miller's implicative criticism, this is criticism that invites a response, and like the broken tool in Heidegger's theory, it is the moment when the article, so skillfully woven to that point, shows a gap that we become fully aware of it. It is a cantilevered structure that is beautifully constructed to inspire us to build out a corresponding arm, to meet her in the middle, to put in the pin that will complete the structures. "Paranoid Reading and Reparative Reading" is invitingly oblique, hopeful, lyrical, and intellectually exciting, and it has remained, for me, one of the best examples of critical care I have ever seen. Which is to say, it is a piece of criticism that cares for me, and that I can care for in return by trying to give something back, to help elaborate a part of the theory Sedgwick left for us to work out.

The forms of bad care in research I have listed are not uncommon problems—I can think of half a dozen critical works just in the last few years that evince these issues, and I have no doubt my reader can too. We all want to avoid failed bridges, webs that twist in on themselves instead of anchoring to another point, lenses that distort and narrow our vision instead of expanding it. In sharing my thinking about how to reimagine our scholarship, I'm not saying anything original: it is obvious advice to remember your reader, to not alienate people, and to be sensitive to the nature of the text. But the rubric of care gives us a way to bundle this advice together and justify it under a single claim. Care does not give us something new, but it does give us something useful: a way to consolidate what otherwise seems like disparate advice through the single, memorable reminder to meet the other's need. In this case, what all this bad criticism shares is a failure to come into relation with the other.

Speaking to the other can be hard. I think here of Fitzpatrick's savvy note about the challenge of care: real generosity can be "an often painful, failure-filled process related to what Dominick LaCapra has called 'empathetic unsettlement,' in which we are continually called not just to feel for others but to simultaneously acknowledge their irreconcilable otherness."[46] The irreconcilable otherness of the other is, after all, the basis of Levinas's ethics. But that challenging alterity is what gives good writing its shiver, the eerie sense that somewhere down the centuries or across space and time, someone out there has seen you. The past is reaching out a hand. The dead begin with a desire to speak to you.

How can we make our criticism the richest possible care? How can we write in a way that meets the needs of readers, colleagues, and text at once, a way that is simultaneously intellectually exhilarating, aesthetically pleasing, and emotionally rich? How can we invoke our colleagues' best thoughts, elucidate new aspects of the texts, and inspire our readers to climb onto the platforms we build in order to reach across to higher things?

These are questions to which I do not have an answer. I am leaving the bridge unfinished, reaching out a hand to the reader, hoping that you will take over. Nobody can be more aware than I of the many faults and failures in this ambitious project. If you like an ethic of care, it will need a lot of help from you. I have not aimed for the last word, or anything close, but I hope the very holes in this theory will speak to you with a desire to take care of them. If this book is a care relationship between me and you, the reader, I have given you my best attempt to give something like critical care, and the best return you can make is to critique it in order to build on it and make it better. This book is a cantilevered arm swung out from my shore, reaching toward yours. Reader, I am hoping you can build out to reach me, bridging our gap. Together we can create a composite text in the virtual space of reading, imagining our way across that magical gap between the two sides of the bridge, building on the silence, the emptiness, the possibilities in the middle.

NOTES

Introduction. Care Communities Today

1. Nightingale, *Notes on Nursing*, v.
2. In so doing, I follow Sara Ahmed's example, as she takes "orientation" literally in *Queer Phenomenology*.
3. Dalmiya, *Caring to Know*; Onazi, *An African Path to Disability Justice*.
4. Christoff, *Novel Relations*.
5. Fitzpatrick, *Generous Thinking*; Ruddick, "When Nothing Is Cool"; Felski, *The Limits of Critique*; Wiegman, "The Times We're In."
6. Sedgwick, "Paranoid Reading and Reparative Reading." Wiegman points out that Sedgwick published an early version of this piece in 1996 and revised it in 1997; most scholars use this 2003 version (8–9). For a perceptive account of how Sedgwick personalizes and binarizes Klein's categories, see Kurnick, "A Few Lies," 364.
7. Sedgwick, "Paranoid Reading and Reparative Reading," 150.
8. Kurnick, "A Few Lies," 365.
9. See Anderson, "Therapeutic Criticism"; Love, "Truth and Consequences"; Wiegman, "The Times We're In."
10. Sedgwick, "Paranoid Reading and Reparative Reading," 130–31.
11. Ibid., 130.
12. Ibid., 140–41.
13. I am indebted to Livia Woods for her thinking about diagnostic medical gazes and reading. See "Generations in, Generations of."
14. Jackson, "Rethinking Repair," 222. I am grateful to Matt Gold for bringing Jackson's work to my attention. See also Reaume's beautiful meditation on "the aesthetics of brokenness" as a more promising way of conceptualizing disability. "On Reclaiming Brokenness and Refusing the Violence of 'Recovery Narratives.'"
15. Clare, *Brilliant Imperfection*, 14–15.
16. See Harvey, *Tool-Being*; and Heidegger, *Being and Time*, 97–102.
17. See Armstrong's *Victorian Glassworlds* for a magnificent evocation of the meanings of the material "glass" in the nineteenth century.
18. Ahmed, *What's the Use?*
19. Jackson, "Rethinking Repair," 223.
20. Ibid. Jackson takes the term from Star and Strauss, "Layers of Silence, Arenas of Voice."
21. Noddings, "A Response to Card, Hoagland, Houston," 123.
22. Barnes, "Beyond the Dyad," 36.
23. Star and Strauss, "Layers of Silence, Arenas of Voice."
24. I am grateful to Zarena Aslami for this clever coinage (in a private communication).
25. For me, such a good breakage occurred at the 2016 Democratic National Convention, when I saw the eminent elder, male, silver-haired statesman playing the part of the supportive spouse, while everyone celebrated the middle-aged woman. Hillary Clinton looks somewhat like my mother, and I realized at that moment that I had never imagined my mother's body occupying a place of power.
26. McKeon, *The Origins of the English Novel*, xxv–xxvi.

27. McGirr, *Eighteenth-Century Characters*, 1.
28. See Armstrong, *Desire and Domestic Fiction*, but also, and more especially, *How Novels Think*.
29. Watt, *The Rise of the Novel*, 13.
30. Lynch, *The Economy of Character*, 126.
31. Lukács, *The Historical Novel*.
32. See Loose, *The Chartist Imaginary*; Vargo, *An Underground History*; Haywood, "Radical Print Culture"; and Michie, "The Novel."
33. Stout, *Corporate Romanticism*, 4.
34. Ibid., 2–4.
35. On Jellyby and Pardiggle as philanthropic types, see Goodlad, *Victorian Literature and the Victorian State*, 110–12.
36. Gallagher, "George Eliot: Immanent Victorian," 66.
37. It sounds difficult, but it's not. Readers need only a very few rudimentary markers to enable them to imagine a character. Piper, *Enumerations*, 121–30; Auyoung, *When Fiction Feels Real*.
38. Stout, *Corporate Romanticism*, 171.
39. Woloch, *The One Versus the Many*, 27, 24.
40. Ibid., 143.
41. May, *The Victorian Domestic Servant*, 4.
42. The excellent scholarship in this field includes Steinlight, *Populating the Novel*; McWeeny, *The Comfort of Strangers*; Daly, *The Demographic Imagination*; and Plotz, *The Crowd*.
43. Leah Lakshmi Piepzna-Samarasinha, for instance, offers advice to people trying to put together a care collective in *Care Work*, 69–73.
44. Teachers know this experientially. For instance, they know that it is better to pull chairs into a circle because the configuration makes students focus on each other, and performatively, the feelings follow. When students sit in parallel rows focused on the teacher, physically directed toward an external good, they are deterred from noticing each other.
45. Simone Chambers noted how a women's antiwar collective, the Seneca Peace Camp, bogged down in endless, exhausting discussions. "Feminist Discourse/Practical Discourse." See also Nancy Fraser's idea that child-care collectives could be political spaces in "Rethinking the Public Sphere," 135. However, Dean Spade argues that the reparative experience of egalitarian consensual decision-making can actually empower participants to make bolder demands, and he itemizes concrete techniques for keeping discussion on track. See *Mutual Aid*, 17–18, 67, 76–80, 84–98.
46. McGee, "Capitalism's Care Problem," 43–44.
47. See Furneaux, *Military Men of Feeling*; and Schaffer, *Romance's Rival*, 187.
48. Hobart and Kneese, "Radical Care." See also Spade, *Mutual Aid*.
49. Cohn and Passell, "A Record 64 Million Americans."
50. Roseneil and Budgeon, "Cultures of Intimacy and Care beyond 'the Family,'" 141.
51. George K. Behlmer, cited in Schaffer, *Romance's Rival*, 126.
52. See Keller and Kittay, "Feminist Ethics of Care."
53. Huang and Wu, "New Feminist Biopolitics in Ultra-Low-Fertility East Asia"; Chan, "Confucianism and Care Ethics"; Chan, *Confucian Perfectionism*, 178–80. I am grateful to Joseph Chan for explaining Confucian perfectionism, and to Johnathan Flower for sharing work in progress with me on Shinto metaphysics.
54. Dalmiya, *Caring to Know*; Onazi, *An African Path to Disability Justice*.
55. Weston, *The Families We Choose*. For a particularly thoughtful account of the difficulty in finding a language for queer relations that neither emulates heterosexual ties

nor dissolves those relationships into generic community, see Elizabeth Freeman's "Queer Belongings." Freeman connects Weston's families of choice with the kinship issues in critical race theory (302–3). For an argument for more attention to fictive kin, especially in nonheteronormative arrangements, see Weeks, Heaphy, and Donovan, *Same Sex Intimacies*. Maltino thinks about communal trans solidarity in *Trans Care*.

56. Roseneil and Budgeon, "Cultures of Intimacy and Care beyond 'the Family,'" 153–54.
57. Freeman, "Queer Belongings," 305.
58. Collins, *Black Feminist Thought*, 178–83; White, "Practicing Care at the Margins." See also two foundational early studies that demonstrated the creativity and resilience of Black care networks: Stack, *All Our Kin*; and Guttman, *The Black Family in Slavery and Freedom*.
59. Spillers, "Mama's Baby, Papa's Maybe."
60. Freeman, "Queer Belongings," 303.
61. Benjamin, "Black AfterLives Matter," 47–48.
62. Such outreach to the beloved dead will be familiar to Victorianists, given the period's fascination with spiritualism, ghost stories (especially Margaret Oliphant's extraordinary *A Beleaguered City*), and Tennyson's "In Memoriam."
63. Wilson and Hughes, "Why Research Is Reconciliation," 8.
64. Mingus, "Pods and Pod Mapping Worksheets." I was tempted to use one of these alternative terms myself but decided they all sounded too contemporary. "Web" carries a digital connotation (in spite of its tempting connection with Eliot), while "pod" sounds like science fiction and "collective" conjures a 1960s commune. I stuck with "community," in spite of its inconvenient vagueness, as the term that best establishes continuities with my Victorian texts.
65. Piepzna-Samarasinha, *Care Work*, 35.
66. Lorde, "The Master's Tools Will Never Dismantle the Master's House."
67. Spade, *Mutual Aid*.
68. Tolentino, "What Mutual Aid Can Do during a Pandemic," 24.
69. Chávez, *Queer Migration Politics*.
70. Joe Biden released a plan in July 2020 that would offer serious support for American caregivers. See Miller, Goldmacher, and Kaplan, "Biden Announces $775 Billion Plan to Help Working Parents and Caregivers," and Span, "Biden's Plan for Seniors Is Not Just a Plan for Seniors."
71. See Sered, *Until We Reckon*; and Dixon and Piepzna-Samarasinha, *Beyond Survival*. This category might also arguably include truth and reconciliation commissions, which have facilitated recovery from colonial-era traumas, most famously in South Africa. See also the resources at the Centre for Justice and Reconciliation (restorativejustice.org).
72. Sered, *Until We Reckon*, 114, 138.
73. Living Justice Press, "The Indigenous Origins of Circles."
74. Sered, *Until We Reckon*, 143.
75. Bailin, *The Sickroom in Victorian Fiction*, 25.
76. Straus, "Disability and 'Late Style' in Music," 6.
77. Thomson, *Extraordinary Bodies*.

Chapter 1. Ethics of Care and the Care Community

1. Felski, *The Limits of Critique*, 165.
2. Eliot, *Middlemarch*, 141.
3. Matthew Crawford, a philosopher who repairs motorcycles, writes that presenting his bill to his customer is a kind of care relation. "In presenting the labor bill, I am

owning my actions. I am standing behind them retrospectively. And this requires making my actions intelligible to the customer," he writes. "Work, then, is a mode of acting in the world that carries the possibility of justification through pay. When the claim I make for the value of what I have done prevails in a meeting with another free agent and I succeed in getting paid, I take this as a validation of my own take on my doings." *The World Beyond Your Head*, 154, 155.

4. Cited in Chávez, *Queer Migration Politics*, 147.

5. *All the Year Round*, 438. Another perhaps unintentionally poetic description is J.A.L. Waddell's: "a structure at least one portion of which acts as an anchorage for sustaining another portion which extends beyond the supporting pier." *Bridge Engineering*, 1917.

6. The theory was first propounded by Carol Gilligan in *In a Different Voice* (1982) and then given fuller development by Noddings in *Caring* (1984).

7. Ruddick, *Maternal Thinking*; Held, *Feminist Morality*.

8. This critique comes from Keller and Kittay, "Feminist Ethics of Care," 544.

9. Bowden, *Caring*, 8.

10. Kofman and Raghuram, "Gender and Global Labour Migrations"; Hochschild, "Global Care Chains and Emotional Surplus Value"; Yeates, "Global Care Chains."

11. Houston, "Caring and Exploitation."

12. Manne, *Down Girl*, xxi.

13. Garland Thomson, *Extraordinary Bodies*, 82–83, 88.

14. Pierrette Hondagneu-Sotelo credits maternalism to Judith Rollins in *Doméstica*, 259n3. Many scholars have noted how commonly employer-employee relations exceed professional boundaries, including Anderson, "Just Another Job?"; Himmelweit, "Caring Labor"; and Constable, "Filipina Workers in Hong Kong Homes."

15. See Narayan, "Colonialism and Its Others," 134.

16. Kipling, "The White Man's Burden," 485.

17. Ames, "An ABC for Baby Patriots." A sample: "E is our Empire / Where sun never sets; / The larger we make it / The bigger it gets." Ames's alphabet appeared in the 1880s.

18. Yeates, "Global Care Chains," 380.

19. Kittay, "When Caring Is Just and Justice Is Caring," 272.

20. Hankivsky is cited in Abu-Laban, "A World of Strangers or a World of Relationships?," 163. However, Petr Urban and Lizzie Ward contest this two-generation view, arguing that ethics of care was invested in political theory as early as the mid-1980s. See Urban and Ward, "Introducing the Contexts of a Moral and Political Theory of Care."

21. For a history of this transition to political investments, see Engster and Hamington, "Introduction," 4–5; and Keller and Kittay, "Feminist Ethics of Care."

22. Engster, *The Heart of Justice*, 2.

23. Kittay, *Love's Labor*, 68.

24. Robinson, "Care Ethics, Political Theory, and the Future of Feminism," 308.

25. See also Brison, "Personal Identity and Relational Selves," and Robinson, "Resisting Hierarchies."

26. Communitarian philosophy also tries to rethink political societies in terms of a communal ethos, but care ethicists have critiqued it for being indifferent to feminism and politically retrograde in its nostalgia for older, more exclusionary social traditions. See Kittay, "A Feminist Public Ethic of Care Meets the New Communitarian Family Policy."

27. Held, *The Ethics of Care*, 43.

28. Kittay, "Welfare, Dependency, and a Public Ethic of Care," 129. See also Held, *The Ethics of Care*, 41.

29. Ibid., 129.

30. Held, *The Ethics of Care*, 14.

31. See Raworth, *Doughnut Economics*; and Marçal, *Who Cooked Adam Smith's Dinner?*
32. Tronto, *Moral Boundaries*.
33. Noddings, *Caring*, 18, 25.
34. Noddings, *Starting*, 13.
35. Summarized from Noddings, *Caring*, chap. 1.
36. Keller and Kittay, "Feminist Ethics of Care," 542.
37. Engster, *The Heart of Justice*, 21–24.
38. Tronto's and Bubeck's definitions appear in Held's useful summary in *The Ethics of Care*, 31–32.
39. Engster's definition of care is somewhat similar to mine, although he is more specific about the desired outcomes: "Altogether, then, caring may be defined as everything we do directly to help individuals to meet their vital biological needs, develop or maintain their basic capabilities, and avoid or alleviate unnecessary or unwanted pain and suffering, so that they can survive, develop, and function in society." *The Heart of Justice*, 28–29.
40. Habermas, *The Habermas Reader*, 186.
41. Setting up a meta-list is dictatorial, Laurence Hamilton warns: "Complete lists of general human needs are archetypal examples of dictatorship of theory: they are *meta-political naturalisations of historically contingent human means and ends because they entrench a single moment in a dynamic process*." *The Political Philosophy of Needs*, 12.
42. Bérubé, *The Secret Life of Stories*, 20. As Bérubé writes, "It does not matter whether Charles Wallace Murry is a child on the autism spectrum. What matters is the web of social relations that constitutes other people's responses to Charles Wallace, and that intensifies to Meg's fierce, protective love of him" (24–25).
43. See Sered, *Until We Reckon*, and Piepzna-Samarasinha, *Care Work*, for some hard-won wisdom about the best ways to make a dialogue productive. They itemize what needs to be said, heard, overlooked, or understood without words.
44. Attentive listening is centrally important in care ethics, as Sophie Bourgault attests in her review of major care ethicists who have explicated this position. See "Democratic Practice and 'Caring to Deliberate,'" 33.
45. Almost all care ethicists grapple with issues of justice; prominent book-length treatments include Tronto, *Caring Democracy*; Engster, *The Heart of Justice*; and Sevenhuijsen, *Citizenship and the Ethics of Care*. See also Held, *The Ethics of Care*; and Kittay, *Love's Labor*.
46. In *The Birth of Theory*, Andrew Cole argues that this lineage begins when G.W.F. Hegel broke with Kant and developed the ideas of alterity and the dialectic.
47. See Wehrs and Haney, "Introduction: Levinas, Twenty-First Century Ethical Criticism, and Their Nineteenth-Century Contexts," esp. 17–21.
48. Levinas, *Totality and Infinity*, 197–200.
49. Friedman, "Introduction," xiv.
50. Levinas and Buber are not geared, however, toward specific interventions. See Perpich, "Don't Try This at Home."
51. See Harvey, *Tool-Being*; and Heidegger, *Being and Time*, 97–102. See also Shaviro, *The Universe of Things*. In a provocative piece, David Wolpe and Kinney Zalesne ask "What Would Martin Buber Think of Zoom?" as they investigate whether technology could center on relationships instead of individuals so as to raise the social media connection into an I-Thou communion.
52. Noddings, *Caring*, 21.
53. Lizzie Ward argues, however, that relationality is foundational to self-care: "The reality is that life does involve self-care on a daily basis, and more so in contexts where

access to public health and welfare resources is limited or non-existent. But the ways in which this challenge is met are through connectedness with others, in other words, our capacity to be taken care of ourselves is predicated on our connectedness to others. 'Self-care' can only be fully expressed through recognising not only one's own needs for care but also, crucially, that these will be met in relation to others." "Caring for Ourselves?," 55–56.

54. Zunshine, *Why We Read Fiction*, 17. Zunshine is summarizing Peter Carruther's theory here.

55. Hamilton, *The Political Philosophy of Needs*, 38.

56. Winnicott, "Transitional Objects and Transitional Phenomena."

57. Winnicott explains that "it must seem to the infant to give warmth, or to move, or to have texture, or to do something that seems to show it has vitality or reality of its own." Ibid., 91.

58. In *The Care of the Self*, Foucault argues that the ancient Greeks had a model of handling the self to transform it into a beautiful object, which we have lost today. I am grateful to Paul Kelleher for this insight.

59. Jackson, "Material Care," 427.

60. Jackson, "Rethinking Repair," 231–32.

61. Abram, *The Spell of the Sensuous*, 9. See also Puig de la Bellacasa, *Matters of Care*.

62. Harvey, *Animism*, xi.

63. Cited in ibid., 21.

64. On enmeshment in the natural world, see Harvey, *Animism*; and Abram, *The Spell of the Sensuous*. On the legal rights of nature, see Samuel, "Lake Erie Just Won the Same Legal Rights as People"; and Tanasescu, "When a River Is a Person." I am indebted to Annette Zimmerman for this point.

65. Latour, *Reassembling the Social*.

66. Bennett, *Vibrant Matter*.

67. Brontë, *Jane Eyre*, 372.

68. This argument is indebted to Auyoung, *When Fiction Feels Real*.

69. Puig de la Bellacasa, *Matters of Care*, 63.

70. Felski, "Latour and Literary Studies," 739.

71. Ibid., 740. See also Sara Ahmed's idea of "companion texts" as texts that offer revelations, resources, and feelings. *Living a Feminist Life*, 16.

72. Marian Barnes writes that "a key implication of recognising the significance of caring networks is that responsibilities for and to care need to be understood to operate within the network as a whole, rather than being solely in one direction—from care giver to care receiver. Responsibilities exist to other members of the network and attentiveness to the range of others contributes to the complexity of caring relationships. This in turn emphasises the importance of both dialogue and praxis to enable the learning that is necessary for ethical care. Interdependency is multidirectional" (36).

73. Some care ethicists do pay attention to communal care, but it is in a context of modern medical and institutional arrangements. Marian Barnes discusses networked care (care given by a network of family members and medical providers) and collective care (mutual care among patients or inmates) in "Beyond the Dyad." Similarly, in "Longing to Belong," Ruth Emond studies mutual care among children in residential and foster care communities.

74. Ray Pahl points out that his study of UK communities agrees exactly with prior studies in the Netherlands and in the United States that put the personal community at 18.5 people. See "Are All Communities Communities in the Mind?," 635. Claude Fischer, author of the US study, specifies that the average size of a personal network is fifteen to nineteen people. See *To Dwell among Friends*, 38. On the stability of these groups, see Spencer and Pahl, *Rethinking Friendship*, 46.

75. In a parallel case, Karen Bourrier and Kelly Hager, in "Recurring Siblings," find that families in Victorian fiction tend to be drastically smaller than in lived reality, and they cite the difficulty of handling so many characters at once as one reason.
76. Bessant, *The Relational Fabric of Community*, 16, 19, 25.
77. Delanty, *Community*, 157.
78. Pahl, "Are All Communities Communities in the Mind?," 634.
79. Poovey, *Genres of the Credit Economy*.
80. Delanty, *Community*, 4. On Anderson, see Zarena Aslami's observation in *The Dream Life of Citizens* that in the nineteenth century the state became the subject of fantasy, constructed as a hero and the object of adoration.
81. Anderson, *Imagined Communities*, 6.
82. Habermas, *The Structural Transformation of the Public Sphere*.
83. Habermas, *The Theory of Communicative Action*.
84. Calhoun, "Introduction: Habermas and the Public Sphere," 9–11.
85. Fraser, "What's Critical about Critical Theory?"
86. For an account of associational communities in the eighteenth century, see Stern, *The Social Life of Criticism*. For a sense of women's social activities in the same period, see Vickery, *The Gentleman's Daughter*. Scholars have also questioned whether there was in fact ever a public sphere of the sort that Habermas imagines. John Plotz, for instance, depicts a chaotic mess of competing discourse rather than a public sphere in the early nineteenth century. *The Crowd*, 9–10.
87. Benhabib, "The Debate over Women and Moral Theory Revisited," 186.
88. Fraser, "Rethinking the Public Sphere," 132.
89. Ibid., 123.
90. Ibid.
91. Jovchelovitch, *Knowledge in Context*, 88. Amanda Anderson has argued that Habermas's communicative ethics, in allowing for flexible, open-ended, multiple social forms, are more capacious than literary scholars normally assume. *The Way We Argue Now*, 44, 158.
92. María Puig de la Bellacasa makes a point that we actually need to stay in this tension rather than try to resolve it. *Matters of Care*, 5.
93. Held, "Care and Justice, Still," 20.
94. Sevenhuijsen, *Citizenship and the Ethics of Care*, 2.
95. Chambers, "Feminist Discourse/Practical Discourse."
96. Braaten, "From Communicative Rationality to Communicative Thinking," 142.
97. Ibid., 143.
98. Habermas, "Reconciliation through the Public Use of Reason," cited in Harvey, *Animism*, 117–18.
99. Young, *Justice and the Politics of Difference*, 96–121. Amanda Anderson points out, however, that Habermas, in stressing their social embeddedness, allows us to recognize that participants' utterances might be culturally determined. See *The Way We Argue Now*, chap. 6.
100. Fraser, "Rethinking the Public Sphere," 120.
101. Fricker, *Epistemic Injustice*.
102. See Benhabib, "Models of Public Space," 86–87.
103. The locus classicus for this analysis is Goffman, *The Presentation of Self in Everyday Life*. See also Hamington, "Politics Is Not a Game," 279.
104. Austen, *Persuasion* [1817], 38.
105. Ibid., 155.
106. Dickens, *Our Mutual Friend*, 439–41.
107. Sedgwick, "Paranoid Reading and Reparative Reading," 146–47.

108. Kafer, *Feminist, Queer, Crip*, 27. See also Samuels, "Six Ways of Looking at Crip Time." I also find Jasbir Puar's work useful for thinking about temporality, debility, and prognosis, especially "Hands Up, Don't Shoot!" and "Prognosis Time."

109. Noddings, *Caring*, 24.

110. James, *The Portrait of a Lady*, 622.

111. Esther Summerson recalls that, "while I was very ill, the way in which these divisions of time became confused with one another, distressed my mind exceedingly. At once a child, an elder girl, and the little woman I had been so happy as, I was not only oppressed by cares and difficulties adapted to each station, but by the great perplexity of endlessly trying to reconcile them." Dickens, *Bleak House*, 555.

112. Luciano, *Arranging Grief*.

113. Important queer temporality studies include Edelman, *No Future*; Halberstam, "Perverse Presentism"; Love, *Feeling Backward*; Freeman, *Time Binds*; and Muñoz, *Cruising Utopia*. See also "Queer Temporalities," a special issue of *GLQ: A Journal of Lesbian and Gay Studies*, edited by Elizabeth Freeman.

114. Chávez, *Queer Migration Politics*, 8. Delanty would regard Chávez's coalitions as examples of political consciousness and collective action, one of four main types of community (the others being communitarian organic groups, sociological searches for connection, and postmodern digital cosmopolitan networks). *Community*, 5.

115. Noddings, *Caring*, 181.

116. On the importance of discourse in care relations, see Laugier, "The Ethics of Care as a Politics of the Ordinary."

117. Jürgen Habermas himself ascribes his discursive emphasis to his childhood experience of disability. He was born with a cleft palate that necessitated surgeries and made it hard for others to understand him, an experience he credits with making him recognize the importance of communication. Habermas, "Public Space and Political Public Sphere." I am grateful to Rosemarie Garland Thomson for bringing this lecture to my attention.

118. Anderson, "What Is the Point of Equality?," 313.

119. Calhoun, "Introduction: Habermas and the Public Sphere, " 12–13.

120. Anderson, *Liberty, Equality, and Private Government*.

121. Often an explicitly voluntary community can form in reality as well. Briallen Hopper describes such a "care team" of friends forming around a mutual friend with cancer in *Hard to Love*. Leah Lakshmi Piepzna-Samarasinha describes the effort—and the liberation—involved in Loree Erickson's experiment producing a radical voluntary care collective in *Care Work*.

Chapter 2. Austen, Dickens, and Brontë: Bodies before the Normate

1. Important work on medical and disability concerns in "Sanditon" includes Jason Farr, *Novel Bodies*, and an article by Christian Lewis, "A Malady of Interpretation."

2. Bourdieu defines the habitus as naturalized practice over time, rather than mechanistic adherence to rules, free choice, or strategic decision. It simply seems like the obvious, ordinary thing to do. Its practitioner is oblivious to the social conditions that have shaped this particular action. See *Outline of a Theory of Practice*, 72–95.

3. Bailin, *The Sickroom in Victorian Fiction*, 20.

4. Smith-Rosenberg, "The Female World of Love and Ritual," 11, 12. A similar social dynamic is described in Dye and Smith, "Mother Love and Infant Death, 1750–1920."

5. Vickery, *The Gentleman's Daughter*.

6. Vargo, *An Underground History of Early Victorian Fiction*, 15.

7. Lowe, *Victorian Fiction and the Insights of Sympathy*, 241. Another sensitive reading of care ethics in Victorian literature can be found in Lauren M. E. Goodlad's analysis of E. M. Forster's *Where Angels Fear to Tread* (1905) in *The Victorian Geopolitical Aesthetic*.

8. Jane Austen, letter to Anna Austen, September 9, 1814, *Jane Austen's Letters*, 401.

9. Holmes, "Victorian Fictions of Interdependency," 30.

10. Holly Furneaux argues that the mid-Victorian cultural ideal of the gentle, nurturing soldier compensated for the shock of imagining British young men killing and being killed in the Crimean War. See *Military Men of Feeling*.

11. Ellis, *The Women of England*, 18–19.

12. Noddings, *Caring*, 37.

13. Eliot, *Middlemarch*, 211; Noddings, *Caring*, 14.

14. Cited in Semmel, *George Eliot and the Politics of National Inheritance*, 12.

15. In Eliot, "The Natural History of German Life," cited in Albrecht, "The Balance of Separateness and Communication," 392.

16. Cited in Mitchell, *Victorian Lessons in Empathy and Difference*, ix.

17. Hensley, *Forms of Empire*, 83.

18. See Foucault's *The Birth of the Clinic* for the most influential version of this history. See also Williams, *The Rich Man and the Diseased Poor*, 15–25; and Archimedes, *Gendered Pathologies*. Permeable, contagious bodies are addressed in Athena Vrettos's *Somatic Fictions* and Tina Young Choi's *Anonymous Connections*.

19. Grinnell, *The Age of Hypochondria*, 9.

20. Archimedes, *Gendered Pathologies*, 19–20; Foucault, *The Birth of the Clinic*.

21. Cited in Grinnell, *The Age of Hypochondria*, 12.

22. Archimedes, *Gendered Pathologies*, 7.

23. We can begin to see the transition in John Brown's influential *The Elements of Medicine* (1795), in which he advocated for moving away from ideas of fluids and ethers to a theory of deviations from health. While Brown still used a holistic measure—he thought that health came from the proper stimulation of nerves across the whole body—his perspective that disease was a pathological shift away from a healthy baseline prefigures the development of the normate half a century later. Grinnell, *The Age of Hypochondria*, 10.

24. Davis, "Introduction: Normality, Power, and Culture," 2.

25. Ibid.

26. "Since *Enforcing Normalcy* was published, the dates of some of the earliest uses of the words associated with 'normalcy' have been pushed back. The OED (2008) moved the earliest written source for 'normal' from 1840 to 1777. The origin of the word 'norm' moved from 1855 to 1821, and 'normality' moved from 1849 to 1848," writes Essaka Joshua in *Physical Disability in British Romantic Literature* (16). The 2020 update of the 2003 online edition of the OED continues to find earlier usages, listing an 1839 use of "normality" and incidences of "normal" meaning "typical" from 1598, 1706, and the 1820s, although it notes that this meaning only becomes common after 1840. What seems clear is that there were some scattered earlier uses, but that Davis is correct that it became standard only in the second half of the nineteenth century. (The updates to the third edition of the OED are available, by subscription, at https://public.oed.com/updates/.)

27. Ibid., 3.

28. Garland Thomson, *Extraordinary Bodies*, 8.

29. Ibid., 7.

30. See Thomson, *Freakery*; Tromp, *Victorian Freaks*; Durbach, *Spectacle of Deformity*; and Craton, *The Victorian Freak Show*.

31. Davis, "Introduction: Normality, Power, and Culture," 2.

32. Davis, *Enforcing Normalcy*, 25.

33. See Deutsch and Nussbaum, "*Defects.*" Scholars of eighteenth-century and Romantic disability include Emily Stanback, Essaka Joshua, Paul Kelleher, Travis Chi Wing Lau, and Jason Farr. See also Bradshaw, "Foreword," in *Disabling Romanticism*, vii–viii; Titchkosky, "Normal." Roy Porter's *Bodies Politic* is a locus classicus for these early somatic ideas.

34. Lau, "Before the Norm?"

35. Puar's idea of debility, in which economic or political agents cause the weakening of a population, is slightly different from the way I use it here, in which debility is not caused by an adverse agent but baked into the structures of inequity governing a society.

36. Lauren Berlant, "Slow Death (Sovereignty, Obesity, Lateral Agency)," 754.

37. Aslami, "Ability."

38. Cited in Frawley, *Invalidism and Identity*, 16.

39. Archimedes, *Gendered Pathologies*, 2.

40. Alex Tankard points out that "the vast majority of disabled Victorians owed their impairment" to tuberculosis, a disease so widespread as to even become fashionable. *Tuberculosis and Disabled Identity*, 5.

41. Williams, *The Rich Man and the Diseased Poor*, 7–14.

42. Goodman, *How to Be a Victorian*, esp. 164–74.

43. Frawley, *Invalidism*, 23.

44. Ibid., 4, 5.

45. Psychiatrist Kelli Harding sums up research that enmeshment in community has significant health advantages in *The Rabbit Effect*.

46. Krienke, "Now What? Surviving Serious Illness in the Nineteenth-Century."

47. We might think of Florence Nightingale's hospital administration at Scutari, a standardized, sanitized space for mass treatments, compared with Mary Seacole's hotel, a homey space where she could care for her beloved soldiers individually.

48. Wright, *Reading for Health*, 26.

49. Krienke, "Now What? Surviving Serious Illness in the Nineteenth-Century."

50. See Anders, "Locating Convalescence in Victorian England"; and Krienke, "The 'After-Life' of Illness." See also Frawley, "Introduction"; and Frawley, *Invalidism and Identity*.

51. Hodgkinson, *The Origins of the National Health Service*, 215–34.

52. Austen, "Sanditon," 334.

53. In "Before the Norm?," Lau similarly appreciates the prenormate disability mode's sense of the quotidian and urges us to theorize it "in ways that demonstrate its reciprocity and even co-constituency with what we might consider the 'social.'"

54. Austen, "Sanditon," 313.

55. Livia Arndal Woods argues that in nineteenth-century obstetrics, medical examiners' external scrutiny conflicted with women's "somatic reading" practice, sensing their own internal bodily experience. See "Generations in, Generations of."

56. Corfield, *Power and the Professions in Britain*, 19.

57. Ibid. See also Perkin, *The Rise of Professional Society*.

58. Cohen, *Professional Domesticity*.

59. See Shuman, *Pedagogical Economies*.

60. See Corfield, *Power and the Professions in Britain*; and Pionke, *The Ritual Culture of Victorian Professionals*, for a study of the rituals through which such forms of power were recognized.

61. Kucich, *The Power of Lies*, 166.

62. Spade sees mutual aid as a democratic, antiauthoritarian system that empowers ordinary people and militates against the regime of expertise. Spade, *Mutual Aid*, 16.

63. Fraser, *The Evolution of the British Welfare State*.

64. Goodlad, *Victorian Literature and the Victorian State*, 34.
65. Ibid., 82.
66. Ibid., 40–49. See also Gregory Vargo's point that radical working-class activists opposed the New Poor Law on the grounds that national resources had been stolen from laborers, who deserved its restitution. *An Underground History of Early Victorian Fiction*, 39–54.
67. For instance, the Medical Order of 1842 and the General Consolidated Order of 1847 tried to systematize medical relief and improve doctors' qualifications, workload, and payments, but these reforms were not thoroughly adopted until the 1860s. Hodgkinson, *The Origins of the National Health Service*, 335.
68. Peterson, *The Medical Profession in Mid-Victorian London*, 2; Hodgkinson, *The Origins of the National Health Service*, 335–336.
69. Penner and Sparks, "Introduction," 3.
70. Hodgkinson, *The Origins of the National Health Service*, 696. See also Stone, *The Disabled State*.
71. Frawley, *Invalidism*, 52, 55.
72. N. D. Jewson, cited in ibid., 54.
73. On Victorian professionalism, see Perkin, *The Rise of Professional Society*; and Gooch, *The Victorian Novel, Service Work*.
74. Bailin, *The Sickroom in Victorian Fiction*, 24–25.
75. See Lawrence Rothfield's reading of Lydgate's problematic clinical attitude in *Vital Signs*; see also Sparks, *The Doctor in the Victorian Novel*.
76. Eliot, *Middlemarch*, 454–55.
77. Bailin, *The Sickroom in Victorian Fiction*, 11.
78. For Victorian testimony about daily conditions in the sickroom, see Julia Stephen's *Notes from Sick Rooms* and Harriet Martineau's *Life in the Sickroom*, as well as Florence Nightingale's *Notes on Nursing*. These texts testify to concern for making the sickroom pleasant, with fresh air, cleanliness, and amusements.
79. Bailin, *The Sickroom in Victorian Fiction*, 25.
80. Noddings, *Caring*, 37.
81. For instance, Charlotte Brontë's experience of nursing her siblings (particularly her addicted brother Branwell) appears to have been traumatic. Marchbanks, "A Costly Morality."
82. See Kristine Swenson's study of female medical workers in the second half of the nineteenth century, *Medical Women in Victorian Fiction*.
83. Nixon, *Kept from All Contagion*.
84. Puar, "Coda: The Cost of Getting Better."
85. Berlant, "Slow Death (Sovereignty, Obesity, Lateral Agency)," 754. A relevant theory of precarity due to our mutual dependence can be found in Butler, *Frames of War*.
86. Favret, "Everyday War," 620.
87. Wiltshire, *Jane Austen and the Body*, 164.
88. Austen, *Persuasion*, e10, 11.
89. Lynch, "Introduction," x–xvi. See also Wiltshire, *Jane Austen and the Body*, 163–64.
90. Austen, *Persuasion*, 181.
91. Ibid., 32.
92. Ibid., 82–83.
93. When Lady Russell reminds Anne of her family in Bath, "Anne would have been ashamed to have it known, how much more she was thinking of Lyme, and Louisa Musgrove, and all her acquaintance there, how much more interesting to her was the home and the friendship of the Harvilles and Captain Benwick, than her own father's house." Austen, *Persuasion*, 101.

94. Ibid., 105–6.
95. Ibid., 96.
96. Ibid., 95.
97. Ibid., 128.
98. Ibid.
99. Ibid., 74.
100. Pinch, *Strange Fits of Passion*, 157.
101. Austen, *Persuasion*, 124.
102. Ibid., 126–27.
103. Mary makes this claim in the letter in which she announces Louisa's engagement to Captain Benwick—another love that developed through nursing. Ibid., 134.
104. Dickens, "A Christmas Carol," 38.
105. Ibid., 38–40.
106. Ibid.
107. I am grateful to Lindsay Lehman for pointing this out.
108. Dickens, "A Christmas Carol," 57.
109. Ibid., 64.
110. Ibid., 96–99.
111. Ibid., 80. I have argued that Jenny Wren, in *Our Mutual Friend*, is not necessarily disabled, inasmuch as her legs and back do not preclude her from doing anything she wants to do, and a similar case could be made for Tiny Tim: these are children who get around with crutches, but that does not mean they are disabled. See Schaffer, "Disabling Marriage," 206.
112. Rodas, "Tiny Tim, Blind Bertha, and the Resistance of Mrs. Mowcher," 67–68.
113. Dickens, "A Christmas Carol," 34. Scrooge has a cold: see ibid., 43.
114. Ibid., 40.
115. Ibid., 39.
116. Ibid., 92.
117. Dickens insists, for instance, that Jo in *Bleak House* represents a larger population. Jo's death is not just his own, for poor children are "dying thus around us, every day." *Bleak House*, 734.
118. Dickens, "A Christmas Carol," 39.
119. Ibid., 113, 116.
120. Ibid., 116.
121. Ibid.
122. Ibid., 118.
123. Harrison, "The Paradox of Fiction and the Ethics of Empathy."
124. Dickens, "A Christmas Carol," 118.
125. See chronology in Gordon, *Charlotte Brontë*, 345–46.
126. See Bolt, Rodas, and Donaldson, *The Madwoman and the Blindman*.
127. Rodas has argued in "'On the Spectrum'" that Jane is autistic. After all, she was "like nobody" at Gateshead, "an uncongenial alien" whom they could not love (Brontë, *Jane Eyre*, 15–16). While this risks an anachronistic diagnosis of a fictional character, it also opens up the possibility of reading *Jane Eyre* as an inspirational early account of what it feels like to live on the spectrum.
128. Brontë, *Jane Eyre*, 7, 452.
129. Ibid., 437.
130. Gabbard, "From Custodial Care to Caring Labor."
131. Brontë, *Jane Eyre*, 435.
132. Ibid., 445.

133. Brontë, *Villette*, 253.
134. Ibid., 402.
135. Ibid., 107.
136. Austen, "Sanditon," 298.
137. Ibid., 295.
138. Ibid., 319.

Chapter 3. Global Migrant Care and Emotional Labor in Villette

1. There were, of course, plenty of stories of migration before and after *Villette*; what Brontë does that seems fairly new to me is to focus specifically on the caregiver as global migrant. On nineteenth-century migration narratives, see McDonagh and Sachs, "Special Article Cluster: New Work on Literature and Migration."
2. I am grateful to Jason Rudy for bringing *Clara Morison* to my attention.
3. Gilbert and Gubar, *The Madwoman in the Attic*, 416.
4. Brontë, *Villette*, 342. Further references will be noted parenthetically in the text.
5. Gilbert and Gubar, *The Madwoman in the Attic*, 416; Anderson, *The Powers of Distance*, 55.
6. Scribner ("Liberalism and Inner Life") also points out that Lucy does not have the interiority we expect in a novel.
7. Gooch, *The Victorian Novel, Service Work*, 2.
8. Kotchemidova, "From Good Cheer to 'Drive-by Smiling,'" 13.
9. May, *The Victorian Domestic Servant*, 4.
10. Hoffer, "'She Brings Everything to a Grindstone,'" 194.
11. Ibid.; see also Hoffer, "Employment Relations and the Failure of Sympathy."
12. Dickens, *Little Dorrit*, 434.
13. Hochschild, *The Managed Heart*, 7.
14. Dalley and Rappoport, "Introducing Economic Women," 2.
15. Schroeder ("A Thousand Petty Troubles") shows the potential of "emotional labor" to help read Victorian narratives of female domestic development in her discussion of *North and South*.
16. Dickens, *David Copperfield*, 275.
17. Ibid., 278.
18. There are male workers who write their own vocational tales, as in Trollope's *Three Clerks* (1857), but until George Moore published *Esther Waters* in 1894, few other well-known British novels centered on women in service.
19. Brontë, *The Letters of Charlotte Brontë*, vol. I, 191.
20. Ibid., 193.
21. Ibid., 266.
22. Ibid., 195.
23. For a thoughtful reading of this scene, see Aslami, "Ability," 551–54.
24. Branwell died in September 1848, Emily in December 1848, and Anne in May 1849.
25. Marchbanks, "A Costly Morality," 60.
26. For readings of the "Choseville" name and Ginevra's tendency to substitute "chose" for words she can't remember, see McDonagh, "Rethinking Provincialism"; and Badowska, "Choseville."
27. Anderson, *The Powers of Distance*, 58.
28. Rebecca Rainof explores a comparable dynamic, although she ascribes it to middle age, not work, in *The Victorian Novel of Adulthood*.

29. Brontë, *The Letters of Charlotte Brontë*, vol. III, 74.
30. Badowska, "Choseville," 1513.
31. Nail, *The Figure of the Migrant*, 13.
32. See DeLucia and Shields, *Migration and Modernities*.
33. This dynamic has been thoroughly charted in Wagner, *Victorian Settler Narratives*; Kranidis, *The Victorian Spinster and Colonial Emigration*; and Hammerton, *Emigrant Gentlewomen*.
34. Aviv, "The Cost of Caring"; Sassen, "Global Cities and Survival Circuits," 35; Hondagneu-Sotelo, *Doméstica*, x.
35. In "Emigrant Spinsters and the Construction of Englishness," Longmuir argues for Taylor's strong influence on Lucy Snowe. Hammerton depicts Taylor as an aggressive, energetic, plainspoken woman whose personality did not resemble Lucy Snowe's, although she may have suggested some of Lucy's actions.
36. Kranidis, *The Victorian Spinster and Colonial Emigration*, 154–64. In "Skirting the Issues," however, Marni Stanley points out that women tended to minimize their own discomfort in travel narratives.
37. Hughes, "The Affective World of Charlotte Brontë's 'Villette,'" 712.
38. Ehrenreich and Hochschild, "Introduction," 10.
39. Hochschild, "Love and Gold," 28.
40. Parreñas, *Servants of Globalization*, 150.
41. Hondagneu-Sotelo, *Doméstica*, 66.
42. In modern economic thinking, service work simply refers to work that produces immaterial relations rather than material goods. It includes jobs in the financial, professional, educational, nursing, entertainment, clerical, legal, informational, advertising, and literary sectors, and it features "affective labor," which, like Hochschild's emotional labor, is work that makes another person feel better. See Gooch, *The Victorian Novel, Service Work*, 21; and Hardt, "Affective Labor." However, *Villette* contrasts two types of service work—intimate personal physical care versus public performance—thus showing how a fictional case can offer a different definition of an economic category.
43. Bayley, "The English Miss, German *Fraulëin*, and French *Mademoiselle*," 174.
44. Ibid., 185.
45. Tucker, "Race: Tracing the Contours of a Long Nineteenth Century."
46. Nott and Gliddon cited M. Thierry's theory that the Belgians were related to the Welsh and the Armoricans—in other words, that they were racially different from the Saxons in England. *Types of Mankind*, 91.
47. Pamela Gilbert traces the difficulties of using color as a reliable marker in mid-Victorian racial thinking. *Victorian Skin*, chap. 7, "Inscriptions."
48. White, "Geography, Literature, and Migration," 3.
49. Knox, *The Races of Men*, 8.
50. Ayşe Çelikkol argues that Brontë endorses cosmopolitanism throughout her *oeuvre*, citing the sympathetic figures of Hunsden in *The Professor* and Robert Moore in *Shirley*. See *Romances of Free Trade*, 104–8.
51. Anderson, *The Powers of Distance*, 30. See also Agathocleous, *Urban Realism and the Cosmopolitan Imagination*; Agathocleous and Rudy, "Victorian Cosmopolitanisms"; and Buzard, *Disorienting Fiction*.
52. The racial theorists of the mid-Victorian period had an answer for this problem: Nott and Gliddon argued that some races were already biologically cosmopolitan because they had been historically intermingled from ages past. *Types of Mankind*, 67.
53. See, for instance, Bonfiglio, "Cosmopolitan Realism"; Clarke, "Charlotte Brontë's *Villette*, Mid-Victorian Anti-Catholicism"; Lawson and Shakinovsky, "Fantasies of National

Identification in *Villette*"; and Wong, "Charlotte Brontë's *Villette* and the Possibilities of a Postsecular Cosmopolitan Critique."

54. See White, "Geography, Literature, and Migration"; and Mardorossian, "From Literature of Exile to Migrant Literature." This idea was first and most influentially formulated by Homi Bhabha in *The Location of Culture*.

55. Wagner, "Becoming Foreign in the Victorian Novel," 81.

56. Cooper, "Introduction," xliii.

57. Buzard, *Disorienting Fiction*, 247.

58. On Brontë's persistent interest in identifying women with slavery, see Meyer, *Imperialism at Home*. Patrick Brontë escaped an impoverished Irish laboring childhood to achieve a Cambridge degree and career as a clergyman in England. His history may have shaped Charlotte's sense of foreignness, alterity, and identity. For the way Irishness affected the Brontës, see Eagleton, *Heathcliff and the Great Hunger*; and Ellis, "The Brontës' Very Real and Raw Irish Roots."

59. Bayley, "The English Miss, German *Fraulëin*, and French *Mademoiselle*," 180.

60. Ibid., 174.

61. Lawson and Shakinovsky, "Fantasies of National Identification in *Villette*," 932.

62. Bhabha, *The Location of Culture*, 185.

63. Noddings, *Caring*, 17.

64. Sometimes this feeling helps assuage the longing for the families left behind or substitutes for less satisfactory adult relations in a new place. See Zelitzer, *The Purchase of Intimacy*, 174–80.

65. Interestingly, Lucy's response is typical of modern immigrant babysitters, who often feel that the mothers need to interact with their children more and discipline them more strictly. Hondagneu-Sotelo, *Doméstica*, 146, 153.

66. Kucich, "Passionate Reserve and Reserved Passion," 917–18.

67. Shuttleworth, *Charlotte Brontë and Victorian Psychology*, 228; see also Gilbert and Gubar, *The Madwoman in the Attic*, 401. More recent analyses include May, "Lucy Snowe, a Material Girl?," 47–48, 60; Badowska, "Choseville," 1513; Kucich, "Passionate Reserve and Reserved Passion," 923; Hughes, "The Affective World of Charlotte Brontë's 'Villette,'" 721.

68. May, "Lucy Snowe, a Material Girl?," 60.

69. Hochschild, *The Managed Heart*, 34.

70. Rivas, "Invisible Labors," 77.

71. Frame, "Dinner and Deception."

72. Hochschild, *Managed Heart*, 23.

73. Wharton, "The Psychosocial Consequences of Emotional Labor," 174.

74. Gooch, *The Victorian Novel, Service Work*, 174.

75. For an analysis of maternalism, see chapter 1, note 6.

76. Hondagneu-Sotelo, *Doméstica*, 171.

77. Ibid., 32.

78. On the isolation of the migrant, see Wagner, "Becoming Foreign in the Victorian Novel."

79. Anderson, *The Powers of Distance*, 60.

80. Rivas, "Invisible Labors," 75.

81. Ibid., 79.

82. Hondagneu-Sotelo, *Doméstica*, 198.

83. Hoffer, "'She Brings Everything to a Grindstone,'" 197; Bayley, "The English Miss, German *Fraulëin*, and French *Mademoiselle*," 181.

84. At the opera, M. Paul hisses (in Helen Cooper's translation): "You seem sad, submissive, dreamy, but you are not those things; I will describe you: Savage! your soul is on

fire, lightning in your eyes." Lucy retorts, "Yes, I have fire in my soul, and I have reason to!" (586).

85. In Kincaid's *Lucy*, the name Lucy derives from Lucifer, the devil. Lucy Potter is allowed a level of rebelliousness that Lucy Snowe cannot own.

86. Gilbert and Gubar, *The Madwoman in the Attic*, 425–26; Vrettos, *Somatic Fictions*, 68.

87. Hondagneu-Sotelo, "Blow-Ups and Other Unhappy Endings," 55–56.

88. Ibid.

89. Ibid., 65.

90. Hondagneu-Sotelo, *Doméstica*, 66.

91. Her union with M. Paul promises to be an example of "vocational marriage," a marriage that gives the woman meaningful work. A vocational marriage remained an acceptable alternative in fiction until midcentury. Schaffer, *Romance's Rival*.

92. Davis, "'I Seemed to Hold Two Lives,'" 202–3.

93. Previous interlocutors, Ginevra and Dr. John, were inadequate in this regard, for they tended to overlook and ignore Lucy's particular personality, confirming her invisibility. Paulina and Mrs. Bretton were better, but they entered Lucy's life too infrequently to make a difference.

94. Davis, "'I Seemed to Hold Two Lives,'" 204.

95. Particularly notable examples of such direct addresses to the reader can be found on pages 50, 77, 82, 173, and 273.

96. Hughes, "The Affective World of Charlotte Brontë's 'Villette,'" 716.

97. Kittay, "When Caring Is Just and Justice Is Caring," 272.

Chapter 4. Beyond Sympathy: The State of Care in Daniel Deronda

1. Brontë, *Jane Eyre*, 230.
2. Eliot, "The Natural History of German Life," 110.
3. Bodenheimer, *The Real Life of Mary Ann Evans*, 259, 263.
4. Greiner, *Sympathetic Realism in Nineteenth-Century British Fiction*, 16. On the specular distantiation in Smith's model, see Degooyer, "'The Eyes of Other People'"; and Kelleher, "The Man within the Breast."
5. Yousef, *Romantic Intimacy*, 5.
6. Ablow, *The Marriage of Minds*, 3.
7. In "Moving Accidents," James Chandler argues that sensibility entered the novel as a way of borrowing from theater.
8. Skinner, *Sensibility and Economics in the Novel*, 1–2.
9. Festa, *Sentimental Figures of Empire*, 16.
10. See Skinner, *Sensibility and Economics in the Novel*; see also Rowland, "Sentimental Fiction," 199–200.
11. Of course, empathy is still a powerful rhetorical tool today. See Blankenship, *Changing the Subject*.
12. Festa, *Sentimental Figures of Empire*, 17.
13. Pinch, *Strange Fits of Passion*, 11. In a later article, Pinch argues that in fact sensibility and Romanticism shared a strong emphasis on feeling. Although scholars have traditionally treated sensibility as a cruder movement supplanted by the deeper writings of Romanticism, Pinch argues that "it may be more accurate to see Sensibility as a literary movement that preceded, enabled, *and* coexisted with Romanticism." Pinch, "Sensibility," 50.

14. Pinch, *Strange Fits of Passion*, 2. Pinch argues that Romantic-era writing mediates between these positions, as in her analysis of Charlotte Smith's sonnets as both powered by her claim to unique private experience and given currency by her usage of widespread literary conventions; Smith's melancholy is thus both her own authentic history and her capacity to inhabit a shared recognizable state.

15. Yousef, *Romantic Intimacy*, 24.

16. Rae Greiner is the critic who argues most strongly for Adam Smith's continued influence on Victorian thought. I concur that Smith remained influential and also agree with Greiner that this does not mean that Victorians were unproblematically accepting his ideas.

17. Collins, "G. H. Lewes Revised."

18. Pinch, "Sensibility," 59.

19. Andrew Miller discusses Evangelicism's vision of Christian duty as a profoundly socially enmeshed objective. This idea shaped the childhoods of major Victorian thinkers. Miller, *The Burdens of Perfection*, 20–21.

20. Carlyle, *Sartor Resartus*, 148.

21. Bailin, *The Sickroom in Victorian Fiction*, 11.

22. See, for instance, Festa, *Sentimental Figures of Empire*; Greiner, *Sympathetic Realism in Nineteenth-Century British Fiction*; Nandrea, *Misfit Forms*; Kaplan, *Sacred Tear*; Bown, "Introduction: Crying over Little Nell"; Blair, "'Thousands of Throbbing Hearts.'"

23. Mason, "Feeling Dickensian Feeling."

24. Austen, *Emma*, 71.

25. Tennyson, "Enoch Arden."

26. Tennyson, "Tears, Idle Tears."

27. Noddings, *Caring*, 21.

28. Johnson, *Equivocal Beings*.

29. Fosco uses his status as a "Man of Sentiment" to excuse his crimes. For instance, he congratulates himself for his willingness to murder Anne Catherick on the grounds that it is a kind act, securing her a blessed release from pain. Collins, *The Woman in White*, 627, 632.

30. Lindhé, "The Paradox of Narrative Empathy and the Form of the Novel."

31. Bloom, *Against Empathy*.

32. Eliot, *Middlemarch*, 278.

33. Cvetkovich, *Mixed Feelings*. Pamela Gilbert offers a useful summary of Tompkins and other critics while contemplating sentimental fiction's applicability to Victorian fiction in "Ouida and the Canon."

34. In "Facing Ethics," Hina Nazar points out that it was Eliot who brought the Young or Left Hegelians to Britain through her translations of David Strauss and Ludwig Feuerbach. See Isobel Armstrong's fascinating discussion of how Eliot used Spinoza's ideas to extend Adam Smith's idea of sympathy and to insist on its corporeal nature in "George Eliot, Spinoza, and the Emotions"; see also Nemoianu, "The Spinozist Freedom of George Eliot's *Daniel Deronda*," and Atkins, *George Eliot and Spinoza*.

35. Cited in Parker, *Ethics, Theory, and the Novel*, 82. Eliot wrote in a letter that "with the ideas of Feuerbach I everywhere agree." Cited in Newton, *George Eliot*, 4.

36. Anger, "George Eliot and Philosophy," 80.

37. Graver, *George Eliot and Community*, 12.

38. Elizabeth Deeds Ermarth stresses the importance of alterity to Eliot in "George Eliot's Conception of Sympathy." See. also Argyros, *Without Any Check of Proud Reserve*.

39. Gilligan, *In a Different Voice*, 69, 130–31.

40. See Nazar, "Facing Ethics," 437–50.

41. Toker, "Vocationalism and Sympathy in *Daniel Deronda*," 569.

42. Eliot, *Daniel Deronda*, 304–5. Future references will be noted parenthetically in the text.

43. Bodenheimer, *The Real Life of Mary Ann Evans*, 265; Jaffe, *Scenes of Sympathy*, 131–32; Albrecht, "The Balance of Separateness and Communication"; Anderson, *The Powers of Distance*; Ablow, *The Marriage of Minds*, 94; During, "The Concept of Dread," 82. My critique of sympathy in *Daniel Deronda* is also indebted to Hoffman, "Eliot against Eliot-ian Sympathy."

44. Levine, "Daniel Deronda: A New Epistemology," 63.

45. Hertz, "Some Words in George Eliot," 289.

46. During, "The Concept of Dread," 78.

47. I have discussed such a case in "Disabling Marriage." Other restorative disabled characters include Thurston Benson in *Ruth*, Ralph Touchett in *Portrait of a Lady*, and Phineas Fletcher in *John Halifax, Gentleman*.

48. Ragussis, *Figures of Conversion*, 272–73.

49. Noddings, *Caring*, 177.

50. Ibid.

51. Chase, "The Decomposition of the Elephants," 222.

52. Ibid., 217.

53. For homoerotic readings of *Daniel Deronda*, see Levine, "Daniel Deronda: A New Epistemology," 62; and Stewart, *Dear Reader*, 308.

54. Eliot is quoting from Milton's *Samson Agonistes*.

55. Noddings, *Caring*, 181.

56. See During, "The Concept of Dread," 82–83; Ragussis, *Figures of Conversion*, 286.

57. Held, *Feminist Morality*, 204.

58. Tucker, *A Probable State*, 119–21.

59. Semmel, *George Eliot and the Politics of National Inheritance*, 6.

60. Vargo, *An Underground History of Early Victorian Fiction*, 44.

61. Swaert, "'Individualism' in the Mid-Nineteenth Century," 78–81.

62. Gagnier, "The Law of Progress and the Ironies of Individualism," 316.

63. Other important studies included Frederic Seebohm's *English Village Community* (1883) and Jacob Burckhardt's *The Civilization of the Renaissance in Italy* (1878, English translation). For a more detailed account of this Victorian fantasy of organic community, see Schaffer, *Romance's Rival*, 91–93.

64. Graver, *George Eliot and Community*, 1.

65. Semmel, *George Eliot and the Politics of National Inheritance*, 135.

66. Zygmunt Bauman points out the unrelentingly positive connotations of "community" in *Community*, 1. Raymond Williams famously addressed the myth of the always-past golden age in *The Country and the City*.

67. Bell, "Communitarianism."

68. Taylor, "Atomism," 206.

69. Hamilton, *The Political Philosophy of Needs*, 42.

70. See Kittay's critique, "A Feminist Public Ethic of Care Meets the New Communitarian Family Policy," and part III of Weiss and Friedman's *Feminism and Community*.

71. Bowden, *Caring*; Engster, *The Heart of Justice*.

72. Kittay, *Love's Labor*, 109.

73. Henry, *The Life of George Eliot*, 210.

74. See Hall, McClelland, and Rendall, *Defining the Victorian Nation*.

75. Some care ethicists do call for a transnational political model of care: see Bowden, *Caring*, and Engster, *The Heart of Justice*. However, Eliot is trying a different thought

experiment: can one create a new state on the basis of care? In imagining the formation of a nation, her writing is more aligned with Hobbes, Locke, and Rousseau than with care ethicists who advocate for methods for existing states to satisfy needs for child care, elder care, and disability care.

Chapter 5. Care Meets the Silent Treatment in The Wings of the Dove

1. Calhoun, "Introduction: Habermas and the Public Sphere," 13.
2. Lech Harris describes a parallel phenomenon: the way Victorian oral narration is sublimated and distributed in modernist style ("Elliptical Orality").
3. Quoted in Seltzer, *Henry James and the Art of Power*, 82.
4. Kaplan, *Henry James*, 83.
5. Daugherty, "Henry James and George Eliot"; see also Ricks, "The Novelist as Critic."
6. As we shall see, Yonge also refashions and depoliticizes national space. Nancy Armstrong argues in *Desire and Domestic Fiction* that the realist novel works to depoliticize matters by making them seem like merely personal choices.
7. James, "Daniel Deronda: A Conversation," 312.
8. James, "Preface to the New York Edition," 5.
9. Bailin, *The Sickroom in Victorian Fiction*, 20.
10. Spunt, "Pathological Commodification, Contagious Impressions, and Dead Metaphors," 171. See also Tankard, *Tuberculosis and Disabled Identity*; and Byrne, *Tuberculosis and the Victorian Literary Imagination*. Jennifer MacLure makes a similar point about the ambiguity of Esther's disease, which is and yet is not smallpox.
11. For discussions of the deathbed scene in Victorian literature, see Bailin, *The Sickroom in Victorian Fiction*; Lutz, *Relics of Death*; Wood, *Dickens and the Business of Death*; and Stewart, *Death Sentences*. For explanations of the iconography of consumption, see Tankard, *Tuberculosis and Disabled Identity*; Byrne, *Tuberculosis and the Victorian Literary Imagination*; and Sontag, *Illness as Metaphor*.
12. Byttebier, "'None of the Effect of an Invalid.'"
13. James, *The Wings of the Dove*, 197. Subsequent references will be noted parenthetically in the text.
14. Diana Fuss and Joel Sanders note an additional irony by pointing out that museum seating, which was keyed to the viewer's comfort early on, began in the 1890s to function instead to train the viewer to focus on art and ignore the body. Milly's Bronzino appears to be in a private house, not a museum, but the dynamic is the same: Milly's somatic experience, the sense of suffering and discomfort we would expect in a person with a terminal condition, is never more absent than in this scene where she is being retrained to view her own approaching dissolution solely as an aesthetic spectacle. She is absolutely unconscious of her own body in the moment when she apprehends her coming death as a purely visual event. Fuss and Sanders, "An Aesthetic Headache."
15. Byttebier, "'None of the Effect of an Invalid,'" 165–66.
16. James, "Preface to the New York Edition," 12.
17. Woloch, *The One Versus the Many*, 24; James, "Preface to the New York Edition," 14.
18. Seltzer, *Henry James and the Art of Power*, 95.
19. Cameron, *Thinking in Henry James*, 150.
20. Kurnick, "What Does Jamesian Style Want?," 219.
21. Ibid., 218.
22. Ibid., 214.
23. Quoted in Nussbaum, *Love's Knowledge*, 162.

24. Nussbaum does see James's characters as exemplary figures, although she does not address *The Wings of the Dove*.
25. Moses, "Henry James's Suspended Situations," 116.
26. Bowden, *Caring*, 11.
27. Moses, "Henry James's Suspended Situations," 128–29.
28. Charon, *Narrative Medicine*.
29. Bersani, *A Future for Astyanax*, 146.
30. See Holland, *The Expense of Vision*, for an explanation of how Kate's father has influenced her tendency to suspension and silence.
31. Noddings, *Caring*, 24.
32. Charon, *Narrative Medicine*, 134.
33. Noddings, *Caring*, 32.
34. Auchard, *Silence in Henry James*, 85.
35. Teahan, "The Abyss of Language in *The Wings of the Dove*," 204.
36. Charon, *Narrative Medicine*, 134.
37. Auchard, *Silence in Henry James*, 101.
38. Jameson, "Remarks on Henry James," 301–2.
39. Nussbaum, *Love's Knowledge*, 162.
40. Cross, "The Ethics of Tact in *The Wings of the Dove*," 403.

Chapter 6. Composite Fiction and the Care Community in The Heir of Redclyffe

1. Elias, "Context Rocks!" 583.
2. See Sedgwick, "Paranoid Reading and Reparative Reading," 130. For queer and crip temporalities, see Kafer, *Feminist, Queer, Crip*, 27; Samuels, "Six Ways of Looking at Crip Time"; Freeman, *Time Binds*; Muñoz, *Cruising Utopia*; and "Queer Temporalities," a special issue of *GLQ*. Jasbir Puar writes about temporality, debility, and prognosis in "Hands Up, Don't Shoot!" and "Prognosis Time."
3. Cited in Stern, *The Social Life of Criticism*, 167.
4. Woolf, *A Room of One's Own*; Leavis, *The Great Tradition*; Bloom, *A Map of Misreading* (1971), cited in Allen, *Intertextuality*, 141.
5. Graham Allen explains, for instance, that when Elizabeth Barrett Browning appropriates the love sonnet for her female speaker, she is playing with genre in a way that Bloom's theory cannot recognize (*Intertextuality*, 143).
6. Dimock, "A Theory of Resonance," 1061.
7. Connolly, "The Death of the Author."
8. Booth, *The Ethics of Fiction*, 135.
9. Kristeva, "Word, Dialogue, and Novel," 37.
10. Miller, *Subject to Change: Reading Feminist Writing*, cited in Allen, *Intertextuality*, 155.
11. Barthes, "The Death of the Author," 142.
12. Orr, *Intertextuality*, 62.
13. Ibid., 171.
14. For a different perspective on the historicity of intertextuality, see Frow, "Intertextuality and Ontology."
15. Mitchell, "Charlotte M. Yonge and the Concept of Conservative Community."
16. Palmer, "Assuming the Role of Editor," 61–62.
17. Yonge's relation with Dyson is discussed in both Battiscombe, *Charlotte M. Yonge: The Story of an Uneventful Life*, and Coleridge, *Charlotte Mary Yonge, Her Life and Letters*,

but a more modern summary can be found in Clare Simmons's "Introduction" to *Clever Woman*, 9–10.

18. Jay, "Charlotte Mary Yonge and Tractarian Aesthetics," 47.
19. Richardson, *Women of the Church of England*, 212.
20. Walton, *Imagining Soldiers and Fathers*, 16.
21. Palmer, "Assuming the Role of Editor," 61–62. See *The Letters of Charlotte Mary Yonge*, 67–68.
22. Richardson, *Women of the Church of England*, 212.
23. Hughes, "SIDEWAYS!," 2.
24. Brake, *Subjugated Knowledges*, 13–18
25. Havens, *Revising the Eighteenth-Century Novel*, 2.
26. McDowell, *The Women of Grub Street*, 184, cited in Lee, *Failures of Feeling*, 87. One such writer, for instance, "saw herself as born into a network of dependencies, and did not consciously differentiate herself from the other elements of that web."
27. Brewer, *The Afterlife of Character*, 10.
28. Stern, *The Social Life of Criticism*, 2–3.
29. Ibid., 4.
30. Peterson, "Introduction," 5.
31. Ehnenn, *Women's Literary Collaboration*, 3.
32. Marcus, *Between Women*, 34.
33. Beetham, "Periodical Writing," 222; Ehnenn, *Women's Literary Collaboration*, 26–28.
34. Peterson, *Victorian Autobiography*, 22.
35. Yonge, *The Letters of Charlotte Mary Yonge*, 67–68.
36. Bourrier and Hager, "Recurring Siblings."
37. For another interesting investigation into contemporaneity in nineteenth-century fiction, see Michie, "Hard Times, Global Times," and "Victorian(ist) 'Whiles' and the Tenses of Historicism."
38. Hingston, "Interdependence, Incarnation, and Disability," 189. Although Hingston is specifically discussing *The Pillars of the House*, the remark could apply to any of the family chronicles.
39. Budge, *Charlotte M. Yonge*. See also Landow, *Victorian Types, Victorian Shadows*.
40. Peterson, *Victorian Autobiography*, 26–27.
41. Schaffer, chap. 3, "Preservation: The Daisy and the Chain," in *Novel Craft*, 91–118.
42. Goldhill, *The Buried Life of Things*, 143.
43. Ibid., 148.
44. In *The Pillars of the House*, when the Underwood family is restored to its ancestral holdings, the members rush to restore the family church rather than spending money on themselves.
45. See Dennis, "Introduction," xviii.
46. Yonge, *The Heir of Redclyffe*, 37. Subsequent references will be noted parenthetically in the text.
47. Gore, "'The Right and Natural Law of Things,'" 124–25.
48. Another 1850s novel about young men who marry sisters, Anthony Trollope's *The Three Clerks* (1858), shows how fiction structured by bureaucracy, rather than care communities, would work. Richard Menke has described the way Trollope presents his characters as generic, stable articles, set into predestined grooves—a far cry from *Heir*'s fluid care dynamics, which are characterized by reversals, surges of feeling, unexpected results, and emotional alliances and rivalries. *Telegraphic Realism*, 5–61.

49. Simone Chambers gives the Seneca Peace Camp as an example in "Feminist Discourse/Practical Discourse."
50. Shakinovsky, "Domestic History and the Idea of the Nation," 79.
51. Stout, *Corporate Romanticism*, 13.
52. Budge, "Realism and Typology."
53. Colón, "Realism and Parable."
54. Dennis identifies Hollywell's genre as "domestic realism." "Introduction," vii–viii.
55. Jay, "Charlotte Mary Yonge and Tractarian Aesthetics," 52.
56. On *I Promessi Sposi* as an important intertext for *Heir*, see Mitchell, "Charlotte M. Yonge: Reading, Writing, and Recycling Historical Fiction."
57. Jay, "Charlotte Mary Yonge and Tractarian Aesthetics," 54.
58. Christabel Coleridge "quotes a letter in which Yonge refers to 'Mrs. Keble's favourite part is the Mondenfelsen time,' glossing it in a footnote: 'The time when Guy was banished to Redclyffe, in imitation of the banishment of Sintram to the Rocks of the Moon.'" *Charlotte Mary Yonge, Her Life and Letters*, 191.
59. See ibid., 111. T.H.S. Escott wrote that, other than de la Motte Fouqué, "Yonge had studied no modern author but Sir Walter Scott. In his character and books she saw the mirror of knightly manhood, the inspiration of the noblest human duty, and exemplars of personal courage." "The Young Idea 'Twixt Square and Thwackum," 687. See also *The Churchman*, "The Author of The Heir of Redclyffe," 46–48.
60. Coleridge, *Charlotte Mary Yonge, Her Life and Letters*, 93, 113.
61. Regarding Yonge's rewritings of Austen, see Schaffer, *Romance's Rival*, 142–44.
62. In a letter she wrote in 1850 while composing the novel, Yonge calls the family the Dashwoods. Yonge, *The Letters of Charlotte Mary Yonge*, 73–74.
63. Chadwick, *The Spirit of the Oxford Movement*, 57.
64. Nel Noddings, *Starting at Home*, 16–18.
65. Ibid., 13.
66. Ian Duncan argues that in *Guy Mannering* Scott invents the romance genre, in which a private individual's development parallels (but also conflicts with) the development of the modern nation. Duncan, *Modern Romance and Transformations of the Novel*, 7–15. However, Katie Trumpener argues that in *Guy Mannering* Scott imagines a historical actor who is oblivious to the larger forces shaping his destiny, for he acts from private feeling rather than as a representative of a historical force. Trumpener, *Bardic Nationalism*, 185.
67. The one exception is Guy's impecunious uncle, a musician with a gambling problem, but he hardly counts as a real underclass.
68. Genette, *Palimpsests*, 1–5.
69. Sedgwick, "Tales of the Avunculate"; see also Cleere, *Avuncularism*.
70. Rowling's influences include *The Lord of the Rings*, the Narnia series, the Christ story, the myth of King Arthur, Austen, Dickens, school stories like *Tom Brown's Schooldays*, E. Nesbit, Dorothy Sayers, *Pilgrim's Progress*, *Wuthering Heights*, Roald Dahl, *Star Wars*, and fantasy literature of the 1960s and 1970s, including Lloyd Alexander's Prydain Chronicles, Susan Cooper's The Dark Is Rising series, Diana Wynne Jones's *Charmed Life*, and Ursula Le Guin's Earthsea quartet.
71. Rody, "Burning Down the House," 316, 317. However, in *Minor Characters Have Their Day*, Jeremy Rosen argues that minor character narratives hew to a predictable narrative. Like Scott's postcolonial romances and Keen's romances of the archive, Rosen's minor character elaboration encourages us to feel delighted at the liberation of a previously silenced figure. In all three cases, the past is made to serve a liberal fantasy of vindication and redemption.
72. Woolf, *A Room of One's Own*, 65.

Epilogue. Critical Care

1. Fitzpatrick, *Generous Thinking*, 209.
2. See, for instance, Katrine Marçal's wonderfully entitled *Who Cooked Adam Smith's Dinner?* Supritha Rajan's *A Tale of Two Capitalisms* explains how the sacralized home became the opposite of the commercial arena.
3. Felski, *The Limits of Critique*, 182; Ruddick, "When Nothing Is Cool," 72. Felski and Ruddick want a literary criticism that works to protect love, integrity, and interiority. In "The Hows and Whys of Public Humanities," Devoney Looser recounts how speaking to popular audiences reaffirmed her sense of positive joy, which had been degraded by skeptical, negative academic norms.
4. Rebekah Taussig offers vivid examples of the disruptive and demoralizing effect of well-meaning interference in "I've Been Paralyzed since I Was Three."
5. In Taussig's words: "Human beings are complicated, and communication can be nuanced. 'No, please don't. This is making me uncomfortable' isn't always expressed through language. You have to pay attention to the human person in front of you. What signals are they giving you? What expression do you see on their face? Even if this isn't intuitive for you, pay attention to their eyes—are they avoiding your gaze or looking toward you like they want to engage? If you really can't tell, you can ask, but if someone says, 'No thank you,' listen. You might get it wrong sometimes, but please don't let the discomfort of 'messing up' make you throw up your hands and leave this conversation." Tausig, "I've Been Paralyzed Since I Was Three."
6. Piepzna-Samarasinha, *Care Work*.
7. Chávez, *Queer Migration Politics*.
8. Crunk Feminist Collective, "Self-Care Is Crunk," 443.
9. Harney and Moten, *The Undercommons*, 26.
10. Burton and Turbine, "'We're Not Asking for the Moon on a Stick.'"
11. Noddings, "Caring in Education." Scherto Gill confirms that Noddings's view of education was not communal but rather fundamentally dyadic, a "relationship between two individuals." Gill, "Caring in Public Education."
12. hooks, *Teaching Community*, 91.
13. Cited in Fitzpatrick, *Generous Thinking*, 53.
14. Kittay, "A Theory of Justice as Fair Terms of Social Life," 68.
15. Fitzpatrick, *Generous Thinking*, 33.
16. Risam, "Diversity Work and Digital Care Work in Higher Education."
17. Carr, "Mentoring Midcareer Colleagues"; Miller, "Mentoring the Mentor."
18. Fitzpatrick, *Generous Thinking*, 4.
19. Fitzpatrick acknowledges concern about an injured person being generous to someone who permitted her to be harmed, but she does not recommend any way to curb that behavior, only remarking generally that "we must consider the limitations of the notion of generosity I am describing." Ibid., 70.
20. Manne, *Down Girl*.
21. Nowviskie, "On Capacity and Care."
22. Losh, "Home Inspection."
23. Dohe, "Critical Practice in Digital Library Communities." Dohe is referencing Eugene, "To Be of Use."
24. Risam, "Diversity Work and Digital Care Work in Higher Education"; Zuroski, "#BIPOC18 and the Undercommons of Enlightenment."
25. Fitzgerald interrogates the way a corporate, neoliberal, privatizing university can use "community" to cover its shortcomings and asks us to engage in genuine collaboration instead. See "Sustainability, Solidarity, and Community in Higher Education."
26. For Fitzpatrick's discussion of the different missions of the university, see ibid., 8.

27. In noting our shared practices, I am building on the important work of HuMetricsHSS, which aims to rethink the values of scholarly lives, stressing such factors as communal and local enmeshment in the humanities and social sciences. HuMetricsHSS: Humane Metrics Initiative, "Values Framework," https://humetricshss.org/our-work/values/.

28. Fitzpatrick agrees that our fidelity to competitive individualism undermines the communal nature of the educational enterprise. Fitzpatrick, "Sustainability, Solidarity, and Community in Higher Education," 27.

29. Dabashi describes her cohort's practice of cooperative and recuperative critical modes in "Introduction to 'Cultures of Argument,'" 950.

30. Serres, *Rome*, 68–70.

31. This is true at least of American humanities citational practices, with which I am primarily familiar. See Eric Hayot's useful sketch of different cultural citational norms in *The Elements of Academic Style*, 39–40.

32. Fitzpatrick, *Generous Thinking*, 1–2.

33. Ahmed, *Living a Feminist Life*, 15–16.

34. See, for instance, the work of Eve Tuck, a scholar of indigenous culture who ran a "Citation Practices Challenge" for a year, inspired by Ahmed. On citation usage to reform teaching practices, see Eidinger, "Cultivating a Conscientious Citation Practice." On generous and inclusive citation, see Hayot, *The Elements of Academic Style*, 163.

35. Agate et al. are co-PIs on the Humane Metrics in Humanities and Social Sciences (HuMetricsHSS) initiative.

36. Harney and Moten, *The Undercommons*; see also Risam, "Academic Generosity, Academic Insurgency."

37. Gold, "Issues of Labor, Credit, and Care."

38. Some good examples of collaborative authors advocating for collective writing: the coauthors of the *Care Manifesto*, the Warwick Research Collective, and the Bigger Six Collective.

39. Meetings can trigger editorial boards' community spirit because they facilitate members' awareness of their role as carers for the journal.

40. Cunningham, "Scenes of Argument," 997.

41. Miller, *The Burdens of Perfection*, 30. Miller looks for relational readings, but he stresses someone's relation to an exemplary other, making it an emulatory relationship rather than a relation of care. (Care is different, because it is founded on need rather than aspiration.)

42. Love, "Truth and Consequences," 237.

43. For more on the need for engagement with the reader, see Sword, *Stylish Academic Writing*, 8.

44. An exemplary article of this sort is John Kucich's "The Unfinished Historicist Project." I also admire the style of Ethan Kleinberg, Joan Wallach Scott, and Gary Wilder's *Theses on Theory and History*.

45. Sedgwick, "Paranoid Reading and Reparative Reading," 129, 144.

46. Fitzpatrick, *Generous Thinking*, 42.

WORKS CITED

Ablow, Rachel. *The Marriage of Minds: Reading Sympathy in the Victorian Marriage Plot*. Stanford University Press, 2007.
Abram, David. *The Spell of the Sensuous: Perception and Language in a More-than-Human World*. Pantheon Books, 1996.
Abu-Laban, Yasmeen. "A World of Strangers or a World of Relationships? The Value of Care Ethics in Migration Research and Policy." In *Rooted Cosmopolitanism: Canada and the World*, edited by Will Kymlicka and Kathryn Walker, 156–77. University of British Columbia Press, 2012.
Agate, N., R. Kennison, S. Konkiel, et al. "The Transformative Power of Values-Enacted Scholarship." *Humanities and Social Sciences Communications* 7:165 (2020). https://doi.org/10.1057/s41599-020-00647-z.
Agathocleous, Tanya. *Urban Realism and the Cosmopolitan Imagination in the Nineteenth Century: Visible City, Invisible World*. Cambridge University Press, 2011
Agathocleous, Tanya, and Jason Rudy, eds. "Victorian Cosmopolitanisms." *Victorian Literature and Culture* 38:2 (2010).
Ahmed, Sara. *Queer Phenomenology: Orientations, Objects, Others*. Duke University Press, 2006.
———. *Living a Feminist Life*. Duke University Press, 2017.
———. *What's the Use? On the Uses of Use*. Duke University Press, 2019.
Albrecht, Thomas. "The Balance of Separateness and Communication: Cosmopolitan Ethics in George Eliot's *Daniel Deronda*." *ELH* 79:2 (Summer 2012): 389–416.
Allen, Graham. *Intertextuality*. Routledge, 2000.
All the Year Round, vol. II, 3rd series (November 9, 1889): 438. https://www.google.com/books/edition/All_the_Year_Round/T782AQAAMAAJ?hl=en&gbpv=1&dq=cantilever+bridge+definition&pg=PA438&printsec=frontcover.
Ames, Mrs. Ernest. "An ABC for Baby Patriots." In *Empire Writing: An Anthology of Colonial Literature*, edited by Elleke Boehmer, 277–81. Oxford University Press, 1998.
Anders, Eli. "Locating Convalescence in Victorian England." Remedia, November 7, 2014. https://remedianetwork.net/2014/11/07/locating-convalescence-in-victorian-england/.
Anderson, Amanda. *The Powers of Distance: Cosmopolitanism and the Cultivation of Detachment*. Princeton University Press, 2001.
———. *The Way We Argue Now: A Study in the Cultures of Theory*. Princeton University Press, 2006.
———. "Therapeutic Criticism." *Novel* 50:3 (2017): 321–28.
Anderson, Benedict. *Imagined Communities: Reflections on the Origin and Spread of Nationalism*. Verso, 1983.
Anderson, Bridget. "Just Another Job? The Commodification of Domestic Labor." In *Global Woman: Nannies, Maids, and Sex Workers in the New Economy*, edited by Barbara Ehrenreich and Arlie Russell Hochschild, 104–14. Henry Holt & Co., 2002.

Anderson, Elizabeth. "What Is the Point of Equality?" *Ethics* 109:2 (January 1999): 287–337.

———. *Liberty, Equality, and Private Government.* Tanner Lectures in Human Values. Delivered at Princeton University, March 4–5, 2015. https://tannerlectures.utah.edu/Anderson%20manuscript.pdf.

Anger, Suzy. "George Eliot and Philosophy." In *The Cambridge Companion to George Eliot*, edited by George Levine, 76–97. Cambridge University Press, 2001.

Archimedes, Sondra M. *Gendered Pathologies: The Female Body and Biomedical Discourse in the Nineteenth-Century English Novel.* Routledge, 2005.

Armstrong, Isobel. *Victorian Glassworlds: Glass Culture and the Imagination, 1830–1880.* Oxford University Press, 2008.

———. "George Eliot, Spinoza, and the Emotions." In *George Eliot: A Companion*, edited by Amanda Anderson and Harry E. Shaw, 294–308. John Wiley & Sons, Ltd., 2013.

Argyros, Ellen. *"Without Any Check of Proud Reserve": Sympathy and Its Limits in George Eliot's Novels.* Studies in Nineteenth-Century British Literature. Peter Lang, 1999.

Armstrong, Nancy. *Desire and Domestic Fiction: A Political History of the Novel.* Oxford University Press, 1990.

———. *How Novels Think: The Limits of Individualism, 1719–1900.* Columbia University Press, 2006.

Aslami, Zarena. *The Dream Life of Citizens: Late Victorian Novels and the Fantasy of the State.* Fordham University Press, 2012.

———. "Ability." *Victorian Literature and Culture* 46:3/4 (Fall/Winter 2018): 551–54.

Atkins, Dorothy. *George Eliot and Spinoza.* Salzburg Studies in English Literature, 1978.

Auchard, John. *Silence in Henry James: The Heritage of Symbolism and Decadence.* Pennsylvania State University Press, 1986.

Austen, Jane. Letter to Anna Austen, September 9, 1814. In *Jane Austen's Letters*, 2nd ed., edited by R. W. Chapman. Oxford University Press, 1952.

———. *Emma* [1816]. Oxford University Press, 2003.

———. *Persuasion* [1817], edited by James Kinsley and Deidre Shauna Lynch. Oxford World's Classics, 2004.

———. "Sanditon" [1817]. In *Northanger Abbey, Lady Susan, The Watsons, and Sanditon*, edited by Claudia Johnson. Oxford University Press, 2003.

———. *Persuasion* [1818], edited by Gillian Beer. Penguin, 1998.

Auyoung, Elaine. *When Fiction Feels Real: Representation and the Reading Mind.* Oxford University Press, 2018.

Aviv, Rachel. "The Cost of Caring." *The New Yorker*, April 11, 2016, 57–63.

Badowska, Ewa. "Choseville: Brontë's *Villette* and the Art of Bourgeois Interiority." *PMLA* 120:5 (2005): 1509–23.

Bailin, Miriam. *The Sickroom in Victorian Fiction: The Art of Being Ill.* Cambridge University Press, 1994.

Barnes, Marian. "Beyond the Dyad: Exploring the Multidimensionality of Care." In *Ethics of Care: Critical Advances in International Perspective*, edited by Marian Barnes, Tula Brannelly, Lizzie Ward, and Nicki Ward, 31–43. Policy Press, 2015.

Barthes, Roland. "The Death of the Author." In Barthes, *Image Music Text*, translated by Stephen Heath, 142–49. Hill & Wang, 1977.

Battiscombe, Georgina. *Charlotte M. Yonge: The Story of an Uneventful Life*. Constable, 1943.
Bauman, Zygmunt. *Community: Seeking Safety in an Insecure World*. Polity Press, 2001.
Bayley, Susan N. "The English Miss, German *Fraulëin*, and French *Mademoiselle*: Foreign Governesses and National Stereotyping in Nineteenth- and Early-Twentieth-Century Europe." *History of Education* 43:2 (2014): 160–86.
Beetham, Margaret. "Periodical Writing." In *The Cambridge Companion to Victorian Women's Writing*, edited by Linda H. Peterson, 221–35. Cambridge University Press, 2015.
Bell, Daniel. "Communitarianism." In *The Stanford Encyclopedia of Philosophy: Fall 2013 Edition*, edited by Edward N. Zalta. Published October 4, 2001, updated January 25, 2012. http://plato.stanford.edu/archives/fall2013/entries/communitarianism/.
Benhabib, Seyla. "Models of Public Space: Hannah Arendt, the Liberal Tradition, and Jürgen Habermas." In *Habermas and the Public Sphere*, edited by Craig Calhoun, 73–98. MIT Press, 1992.
———. "The Debate over Women and Moral Theory Revisited." In *Feminists Read Habermas: Gendering the Subject of Discourse*, edited by Johanna Meehan, 181–203. Routledge, 1995.
Benjamin, Ruha. "Black AfterLives Matter: Cultivating Kinfulness as Reproductive Justice." In *Making Kin Not Population*, edited by Adele E. Clarke and Donna Haraway, 41–65. Prickly Paradigm Press, 2018.
Bennett, Jane. *Vibrant Matter: A Political Ecology of Things*. Duke University Press, 2010.
Berlant, Lauren. "Slow Death (Sovereignty, Obesity, Lateral Agency)." *Critical Inquiry* 33:4 (2007): 754–80.
Bersani, Leo. *A Future for Astyanax: Character and Desire in Literature*. Little, Brown & Co., 1969.
Bérubé, Michael. *The Secret Life of Stories: From Don Quixote to Harry Potter, How Understanding Intellectual Disability Transforms the Way We Read*. New York University Press, 2016.
Bessant, Kenneth C. *The Relational Fabric of Community*. Palgrave Macmillan, 2018.
Bhabha, Homi. *The Location of Culture*. Routledge, 1994.
Bigger Six Collective. "Coda: From Coteries to Collectives." *Symbiosis* 23:1 (Spring 2019): 139–40.
Blair, Kristie. "'Thousands of Throbbing Hearts': Sentimentality and Community in Popular Victorian Poetry: Longfellow's Evangeline and Tennyson's Enoch Arden." *19: Interdisciplinary Studies in the Long Nineteenth Century* 4 (2007). http://doi.org/10.16995/ntn.455.
Blankenship, Lisa. *Changing the Subject: A Theory of Rhetorical Empathy*. Utah State University Press, 2019.
Bloom, Paul. *Against Empathy: The Case for Rational Compassion*. HarperCollins, 2016.
Bodenheimer, Rosemarie. *The Real Life of Mary Ann Evans: George Eliot, Her Letters and Fiction*. Cornell University Press, 1994.
Bolt, David, Julia Miele Rodas, and Elizabeth Donaldson, eds. *The Madwoman and the Blindman: Jane Eyre, Discourse, Disability*. Ohio State University Press, 2012.

Bonfiglio, Richard. "Cosmopolitan Realism: Portable Domesticity in Brontë's Belgian Novels." *Victorian Literature and Culture* 40:2 (2012): 599–616.
Booth, Wayne. *The Ethics of Fiction*. University of California Press, 1988.
Bourdieu, Pierre. *Outline of a Theory of Practice*, translated by Richard Nice. Cambridge University Press, 1977.
Bourgault, Sophie. "Democratic Practice and 'Caring to Deliberate': A Gadamerian Account of Conversation and Listening." In *Care Ethics, Democratic Citizenship and the State*, edited by Petr Urban and Lizzie Ward, 31–51. Palgrave, 2020.
Bourrier, Karen, and Kelly Hager, "Recurring Siblings." Presentation at North American Victorian Studies Association, Phoenix, Arizona, November 2–5, 2016.
Bowden, Peta. *Caring: Gender-Sensitive Ethics*. Routledge, 1997.
Bown, Nicola. "Introduction: Crying over Little Nell." *19: Interdisciplinary Studies in the Long Nineteenth Century* 4 (2007). http://doi.org/10.16995/ntn.453.
Braaten, Jane. "From Communicative Rationality to Communicative Thinking: A Basis for Feminist Theory and Practice." In *Feminists Read Habermas: Gendering the Subject of Discourse*, edited by Johanna Meehan, 139–61. Routledge, 1995.
Bradshaw, Michael. *Disabling Romanticism*. Palgrave, 2016.
Brake, Laurel. *Subjugated Knowledges: Journalism, Gender, and Literature in the Nineteenth Century*. New York University Press, 1994.
Brewer, David A. *The Afterlife of Character, 1726–1825*. University of Pennsylvania Press, 2005.
Brison, Susan J. "Personal Identity and Relational Selves." In *The Routledge Companion to Feminist Philosophy*, edited by Ann Garry, Serene J. Khader, and Alison Stone, 218–30. Routledge, 2017.
Brontë, Charlotte. *Jane Eyre* [1847], edited by Margaret Smith. Oxford University Press, 2000.
———. *Villette* [1853], edited by Helen M. Cooper. Penguin, 2004.
———. *The Letters of Charlotte Brontë*, vol. I, *1829–1847*, edited by Margaret Smith. Clarendon Press, 1995.
———. *The Letters of Charlotte Brontë*, vol. III, *1852–1855*, edited by Margaret Smith. Clarendon Press, 2004.
Budge, Gavin. "Realism and Typology in Charlotte M. Yonge's *The Heir of Redclyffe*." *Victorian Literature and Culture* 31:3 (2003): 193–223.
———. *Charlotte M. Yonge: Religion, Feminism, and Realism in the Victorian Novel*. Peter Lang, 2007.
Burton, Sarah, and Vikki Turbine. "'We're Not Asking for the Moon on a Stick': Kindness and Generosity in the Academy." Discover Society, July 3, 2019. https://discoversociety.org/2019/07/03/were-not-asking-for-the-moon-on-a-stick-kindness-and-generosity-in-the-academy/.
Butler, Judith. *Frames of War: When Is Life Grievable?* [2009]. Verso Books, 2016.
Buzard, James. *Disorienting Fiction: The Autoethnographic Work of Nineteenth-Century British Novels*. Princeton University Press, 2005.
Byrne, Katherine. *Tuberculosis and the Victorian Literary Imagination*. Cambridge University Press, 2011.
Byttebier, Stephanie. "'None of the Effect of an Invalid': The Trials of Empathy in Henry James's *The Wings of the Dove*." *Henry James Review* 35:2 (Summer 2014): 157–74.

Calhoun, Craig. "Introduction: Habermas and the Public Sphere." In *Habermas and the Public Sphere*, edited by Craig Calhoun, 1–49. MIT Press, 1992.

Cameron, Sharon. *Thinking in Henry James*. University of Chicago Press, 1989.

The Care Collective (Andreas Chatzidakis, Jamie Hakim, Jo Littler, Catherine Rottenberg, and Lynne Segal). *The Care Manifesto: The Politics of Independence*. Verso, 2020.

Carlyle, Thomas. *Sartor Resartus* [1833–1834], edited by Peter Sabor and Kerry McSweeney. Oxford University Press, 2008.

Carr, Jean Ferguson. "Mentoring Midcareer Colleagues." *Profession* (Winter 2020). https://profession.mla.org/mentoring-midcareer-colleagues/.

Çelikkol, Ayşe. *Romances of Free Trade: British Literature, Laissez-Faire, and the Global Nineteenth Century*. Oxford University Press, 2011.

Chadwick, Owen. *The Spirit of the Oxford Movement: Tractarian Essays*. Cambridge University Press, 1990.

Chambers, Simone. "Feminist Discourse/Practical Discourse." In *Feminists Read Habermas: Gendering the Subject of Discourse*, edited by Johanna Meehan, 163–79. Routledge, 1995.

Chan, Joseph. *Confucian Perfectionism: A Political Philosophy for Modern Times*. Princeton University Press, 2014.

Chan, Sin Yee. "Confucianism and Care Ethics." In *The Routledge Companion to Feminist Philosophy*, edited by Ann Garry et al., 556–67. Routledge, 2017.

Chandler, James. "Moving Accidents: The Emergence of Sentimental Probability." In *The Age of Cultural Revolutions: Britain and France, 1750–1820*, edited by Colin Jones and Dror Wahrman, 137–70. University of California Press, 2002.

Charon, Rita. *Narrative Medicine: Honoring the Stories of Illness*. Oxford University Press, 2006.

Chase, Cynthia. "The Decomposition of the Elephants: Double-Reading Daniel Deronda." *PMLA* 93:2 (March 1978): 215–27.

Chávez, Karma. *Queer Migration Politics: Activist Rhetoric and Coalitional Possibilities*. University of Illinois Press, 2013.

Choi, Tina Young. *Anonymous Connections: The Body and Narratives of the Social in Victorian Britain*. University of Michigan Press, 2015.

Christoff, Alicia Mireles. *Novel Relations: Victorian Fiction and British Psychoanalysis*. Princeton University Press, 2019.

The Churchman. "The Author of *The Heir of Redclyffe*." *The Churchman*, January 11, 1879, 46–48.

Clare, Eli. *Brilliant Imperfection: Grappling with Cure*. Duke University Press, 2017.

Clarke, Micael M. "Charlotte Brontë's *Villette*, Mid-Victorian Anti-Catholicism, and the Turn to Secularism." *ELH* 78:4 (2011): 967–89.

Cleere, Eileen. *Avuncularism: Capitalism, Patriarchy, and Nineteenth-Century English Culture*. Stanford University Press, 2004.

Cohen, Monica F. *Professional Domesticity: Women, Work, and Home*. Cambridge University Press, 1998.

Cohn, D'vera, and Jeffrey S. Passell. "A Record 64 Million Americans Live in Multigenerational Households." Pew Research Center, April 5, 2018. https://www.pewresearch.org/fact-tank/2018/04/05/a-record-64-million-americans-live-in-multigenerational-households/.

Cole, Andrew. *The Birth of Theory*. University of Chicago Press, 2014.
Coleridge, Christabel. *Charlotte Mary Yonge, Her Life and Letters*. Macmillan, 1903.
Collins, K. K. "G. H. Lewes Revised: George Eliot and the Moral Sense." *Victorian Studies* 21:4 (Summer 1978): 463–92.
Collins, Patricia Hill. *Black Feminist Thought: Knowledge, Consciousness, and the Politics of Empowerment*. Routledge, 2000. https://uniteyouthdublin.files.wordpress.com/2015/01/black-feminist-though-by-patricia-hill-collins.pdf.
Collins, Wilkie. *The Woman in White* [1859–1860], edited by Julian Symons. Penguin, 1986.
Colón, Susan E. "Realism and Parable in Charlotte Yonge's *The Heir of Redclyffe*." *Journal of Narrative Theory* 40:1 (Winter 2010): 29–52.
Connolly, Brian. "The Death of the Author: Historians and Citation." Public Seminar, May 17, 2018. http://www.publicseminar.org/2018/05/the-death-of-the-author/.
Constable, Nicole. "Filipina Workers in Hong Kong Homes: Household Rules and Relations." In *Global Woman: Nannies, Maids, and Sex Workers in the New Economy*, edited by Barbara Ehrenreich and Arlie Russell Hochschild, 115–41. Henry Holt & Co., 2002.
Cooper, Helen M. "Introduction." In Charlotte Brontë, *Villette*, edited by Helen M. Cooper, xi–li. Penguin, 2004.
Corfield, Penelope J. *Power and the Professions in Britain 1700–1850*. Routledge, 1995.
Covert, Bryce. "Biden's Quietly Radical Care Plan." *New York Times*, August 2, 2020. https://www.nytimes.com/2020/08/02/opinion/biden-child-care.html.
Craton, Lillian. *The Victorian Freak Show: The Significance of Disability and Physical Differences in 19th-Century Fiction*. Cambria Press, 2009.
Crawford, Matthew B. *The World Beyond Your Head: On Becoming an Individual in an Age of Distraction*. Farrar, Straus and Giroux, 2015.
Cross, Samuel. "The Ethics of Tact in *The Wings of the Dove*." *Novel* 43:3 (Fall 2010): 401–23.
Crunk Feminist Collective. "Self-Care Is Crunk." In *Debates in the Digital Humanities 2019*, edited by Lauren F. Klein and Matthew K. Gold, 442–44. University of Minnesota Press, 2019. https://dhdebates.gc.cuny.edu/read/untitled-f2acf72c-a469-49d8-be35-67f9ac1e3a60/section/21fdd83a-382b-475e-ae60-bb8111b349c7#ch42.
Cunningham, Nia. "Scenes of Argument," *PMLA* 135:5 (2020): 995–1001.
Cvetkovich, Ann. *Mixed Feelings: Feminism, Mass Culture, and Victorian Sensationalism*. Rutgers University Press, 1992.
Dabashi, Pardis. "Introduction to 'Cultures of Argument': The Loose Garments of Argument." *PMLA* 135:5 (2020): 946–55.
Dalley, Lana L., and Jill Rappoport. "Introducing Economic Women." In *Economic Women: Essays on Desire and Dispossession in Nineteenth-Century British Culture*, edited by Lana L. Dalley and Jill Rappoport, 1–22. Ohio State University Press, 2013.
Dalmiya, Vrinda. *Caring to Know: Comparative Care Ethics, Feminist Epistemology, and the Mahābhārata*. Oxford University Press, 2016.
Daly, Nicholas. *The Demographic Imagination and the Nineteenth-Century City: Paris, London, New York*. Cambridge University Press, 2015.
Daugherty, Sarah B. "Henry James and George Eliot: The Price of Mastery." *Henry James Review* 10:3 (Fall 1989): 153–66.

Davis, Helen H. "'I Seemed to Hold Two Lives': Disclosing Circumnarration in *Villette* and *The Picture of Dorian Gray*." *Narrative* 2:2 (2013): 198–220.
Davis, Lennard J. *Enforcing Normalcy: Disability, Deafness, and the Body*. Verso, 1995.
———. "Introduction: Normality, Power, and Culture." In *The Disability Studies Reader*, 4th ed., edited by Lennard J. Davis, 1–16. Routledge, 2013.
Degooyer, Stephanie. "'The Eyes of Other People': Adam Smith's Triangular Sympathy and the Sentimental Novel." *ELH* 85:3 (Fall 2018): 669–90.
Delanty, Gerard. *Community*, 3rd ed. Routledge, 2018.
DeLucia, JoEllen, and Juliet Shields, eds. *Migration and Modernities: The State of Being Stateless, 1750–1850*. Edinburgh University Press, 2019.
Dennis, Barbara. "Introduction." In Charlotte Yonge, *The Heir of Redclyffe*, vii–xxv. Oxford University Press, 1997.
Deutsch, Helen, and Felicity Nussbaum. *"Defects": Engendering the Modern Body*. University of Michigan Press, 2000.
Dickens, Charles. "A Christmas Carol" [1843]. In *A Christmas Carol and Other Christmas Writings*. Penguin, 2003.
———. *Dombey and Son* [1846–1848]. Modern Library, 2003.
———. *David Copperfield* [1849–1850], edited by Jeremy Tambling. Penguin, 1996.
———. *Bleak House* [1853], edited by Nicola Bradbury. Penguin, 2003.
———. *Little Dorrit* [1857], edited by Helen Small. Penguin, 1998.
———. *Our Mutual Friend* [1865]. Penguin, 1997.
Dimock, Wai Chee. "A Theory of Resonance." *PMLA* 112 (1997): 1060–71.
Dixon, Ejeris, and Leah Lakshmi Piepzna-Samarasinha, eds. *Beyond Survival: Strategies and Stories from the Transformative Justice Movement*. AK Press, 2020.
Dohe, Kate. "Critical Practice in Digital Library Communities." *In the Library with the Lead Pipe*, February 20, 2019. http://inthelibrarywiththeleadpipe.org/2019/digital-libraries-critical-practice-in-communities/.
Duncan, Ian. *Modern Romance and Transformations of the Novel*. Cambridge University Press, 1992.
Durbach, Nadja. *Spectacle of Deformity: Freak Shows and Modern British Culture*. University of California Press, 2010.
During, Lisbeth. "The Concept of Dread: Sympathy and Ethics in *Daniel Deronda*." In *Renegotiating Ethics in Literature, Philosophy, and Theory*, edited by Jane Adamson, Richard Freadman, and David Parker, 65–83. Cambridge University Press, 1998.
Dye, Nancy Schrom, and Daniel Blake Smith, "Mother Love and Infant Death, 1750–1920." *Journal of American History* 73:2 (September 1986): 329–53.
Eagleton, Terry. *Heathcliff and the Great Hunger*. Verso, 1996.
Edelman, Lee. *No Future: Queer Theory and the Death Drive*. Duke University Press, 2004.
Ehnenn, Jill R. *Women's Literary Collaboration, Queerness, and Late-Victorian Culture*. Ashgate, 2008.
Ehrenreich, Barbara, and Arlie Russell Hochschild. "Introduction." In *Global Woman: Nannies, Maids, and Sex Workers in the New Economy*, edited by Barbara Ehrenreich and Arlie Russell Hochschild, 1–13. Henry Holt & Co., 2002.

Eidinger, Andrea. "Cultivating a Conscientious Citation Practice." *Unwritten Histories*, May 7, 2019. http://www.unwrittenhistories.com/cultivating-a-conscientious-citation-practice/.
Elias, Amy J. "Context Rocks!" *PMLA* 134:3 (May 2019): 579–87.
Eliot, George. "The Natural History of German Life" [1856]. In *George Eliot: Selected Essays, Poems, and Other Writings*, edited by A. S. Byatt and Nicholas Warren, 107–39. Penguin, 1990.
———. *Middlemarch* [1871–1872], edited by Rosemary Ashton. Penguin, 1994.
———. *Daniel Deronda* [1876]. Oxford University Press, 2014.
Ellis, Samantha. "The Brontës' Very Real and Raw Irish Roots." *Irish Times*, January 11, 2017. https://www.irishtimes.com/culture/books/the-bront%C3%ABs-very-real-and-raw-irish-roots-1.2932856.
Ellis, Sarah Stickney. *The Women of England: Their Social Duties, and Domestic Habits*. Appleton & Co., 1843.
Emond, Ruth. "Longing to Belong: Children in Residential Care and Their Experiences of Peer Relationships at School and in the Children's Home." *Child and Family Social Work* 19:2 (August 13, 2012). https://doi.org/10.1111/j.1365-2206.2012.00893.x.
Engster, Daniel. *The Heart of Justice: Care Ethics and Political Theory*. Oxford University Press, 2007.
Engster, Daniel, and Maurice Hamington. "Introduction." In *Care Ethics and Political Theory*, edited by Daniel Engster and Maurice Hamington, 1–18. Oxford University Press, 2015.
Ermarth, Elizabeth Deeds. "George Eliot's Conception of Sympathy." *Nineteenth-Century Fiction* 40:1 (June 1985): 23–42.
Escott, T.H.S. "The Young Idea 'Twixt Square and Thwackum." *The Fortnightly* 92 (1912): 675–89.
Eugene, Toinette M. "To Be of Use." *Journal of Feminist Studies in Religion* 8:2 (1992): 138–47.
Farr, Jason. *Novel Bodies: Disability and Sexuality in Eighteenth-Century British Literature*. Bucknell University Press, 2019.
Favret, Mary. "Everyday War." *ELH* 72:3 (Fall 2005): 605–33.
Felski, Rita. "Latour and Literary Studies" *PMLA* 130:3 (2015): 737–42.
———. *The Limits of Critique*. University of Chicago Press, 2016.
Festa, Lynn. *Sentimental Figures of Empire in Eighteenth-Century Britain and France*. Johns Hopkins University Press, 2006.
Fischer, Claude S. *To Dwell among Friends*. University of Chicago Press, 1982.
Fitzpatrick, Kathleen. *Generous Thinking: A Radical Approach to Saving the University*. Johns Hopkins University Press, 2019.
———. "Sustainability, Solidarity, and Community in Higher Education." *Educause Review*, August 26, 2019. https://er.educause.edu/articles/2019/8/sustainability-solidarity-and-community-in-higher-education#fnr4.
Foucault, Michel. *The Birth of the Clinic: An Archaeology of Medical Perception* [1963]. Vintage, 1994.
———. *The Care of the Self*. Vol. 3 of *The History of Sexuality*. Penguin, 1984.

Frame, Edward. "Dinner and Deception." *New York Times*, August 22, 2015. http://www.nytimes.com/2015/08/23/opinion/sunday/dinner-and-deception.html?smprod=nytcore-ipad&smid=nytcore-ipad-share&_r=0.

Fraser, Derek. *The Evolution of the British Welfare State: A History of Social Policy since the Industrial Revolution*. Palgrave Macmillan, 1992.

Fraser, Nancy. "Rethinking the Public Sphere: A Contribution to the Critique of Actually Existing Democracy." In *Habermas and the Public Sphere*, edited by Craig Calhoun, 109–42. MIT Press, 1992.

———. "What's Critical about Critical Theory?" In *Feminists Read Habermas: Gendering the Subject of Discourse*, edited by Johanna Meehan, 21–55. Routledge, 1995.

Frawley, Maria H. "Introduction." In Harriet Martineau, *Life in the Sickroom* [1844]. Broadview Press, 2003.

———. *Invalidism and Identity in Nineteenth-Century Britain*. University of Chicago Press, 2004.

Freeman, Elizabeth. "Queer Belongings: Kinship Theory and Queer Theory." In *A Companion to Lesbian, Gay, Bisexual, Transgender, and Queer Theory*, edited by George Haggerty and Molly McGarry, 295–314. Blackwell, 2007.

———, ed. "Queer Temporalities." Special issue of *GLQ: A Journal of Lesbian and Gay Studies* 13:2/3 (Winter/Spring 2007).

———. *Time Binds: Queer Temporalities, Queer Histories*. Duke University Press, 2010.

Fricker, Miranda. *Epistemic Injustice: Power and the Ethics of Knowing*. Oxford University Press, 2009.

Friedman, Maurice. "Introduction." In *Between Man and Man* by Martin Buber, xiii–xxi. Macmillan 1965.

Frow, John. "Intertextuality and Ontology." In *Intertextuality: Theories and Practices*, edited by Michael Worton and Judith Still, 45–55. Manchester University Press, 1990.

Furneaux, Holly. *Military Men of Feeling: Emotion, Touch, and Masculinity in the Crimean War*. Oxford University Press, 2016.

Fuss, Diana, and Joel Sanders. "An Aesthetic Headache: Notes from the Museum Bench." JSA: News, June 12, 2015. http://joelsandersarchitect.com/an-aesthetic-headache-notes-from-the-museum-bench-with-diana-fuss/.

Gabbard, D. Christopher. "From Custodial Care to Caring Labor: The Discourse of Who Cares in *Jane Eyre*." In *The Madwoman and the Blindman: Jane Eyre, Discourse, Disability*, edited by David Bolt, Julia Miele Rodas, and Elizabeth Donaldson, 91–110. Ohio State University Press, 2012.

Gagnier, Regenia. "The Law of Progress and the Ironies of Individualism in the Nineteenth Century." *New Literary History* 31:2 (2000): 315–36.

Gallagher, Catherine. "George Eliot: Immanent Victorian." *Representations* 90 (Spring 2005): 61–74.

Garland Thomson, Rosemarie. *Freakery: Cultural Spectacles of the Extraordinary Body*. New York University Press, 1996.

———. *Extraordinary Bodies: Figuring Physical Disability in American Culture and Literature*. Columbia University Press, 1997.

Genette, Gérard. *Palimpsests: Literature in the Second Degree*, translated by Channa Newman and Claude Dobinsky. University of Nebraska Press, 1997.

Gilbert, Pamela. "Ouida and the Canon." In *Ouida and Victorian Popular Fiction*, edited by Jane Jordan and Andrew King, 37–51. Ashgate, 2013.

———. *Victorian Skin: Surface, Self, History*. Cornell University Press, 2019.

Gilbert, Sandra M., and Susan Gubar. *The Madwoman in the Attic: The Woman Writer and the Nineteenth-Century Literary Imagination*. Yale University Press, 1979.

Gill, Scherto. "Caring in Public Education." *Forum* 61:2 (2019): 200. http://doi.org/10.15730/forum.2019.61.2.199.

Gilligan, Carol. *In A Different Voice: Psychological Theory and Women's Development*. Harvard University Press, 1982.

Goffman, Erving. *The Presentation of Self in Everyday Life*. University of Edinburgh Social Sciences Research Centre, 1956.

Gold, Matthew K. "Issues of Labor, Credit, and Care in Peer-to-Peer Review Processes." Presentation at the MLA convention, Chicago, January 5, 2019, available at The Lapland Chronicles, http://blog.mkgold.net/2019/01/05/issues-of-labor-credit-and-care-in-peer-to-peer-review-processes/.

Goldhill, Simon. *The Buried Life of Things: How Objects Made History in Nineteenth-Century Britain*. Cambridge University Press, 2015.

Gooch, Joshua. *The Victorian Novel, Service Work, and the Nineteenth-Century Economy*. Palgrave Macmillan, 2015.

Goodlad, Lauren M. E. *Victorian Literature and the Victorian State: Character and Governance in a Liberal Society*. Johns Hopkins University Press, 2004.

———. *The Victorian Geopolitical Aesthetic: Realism, Sovereignty, and Transnational Experience*. Oxford University Press, 2015.

Goodman, Ruth. *How to Be a Victorian: A Dawn-to-Dusk Guide to Victorian Life*. Penguin, 2013.

Gordon, Lyndall. *Charlotte Brontë: A Passionate Life*. W. W. Norton, 1994.

Gore, Clare Walker. "'The Right and Natural Law of Things': Disability and the Form of the Family in the Fiction of Dinah Mulock Craik and Charlotte M. Yonge." In *Queer Victorian Families: Curious Relations in Literature*, edited by Duc Dau and Shale Preston, 116–33. Routledge, 2015.

Graver, Suzanne. *George Eliot and Community: A Study in Social Theory and Fictional Form*. University of California Press, 1984.

Greiner, Rae. *Sympathetic Realism in Nineteenth-Century British Fiction*. Johns Hopkins University Press, 2012.

Grinnell, George C. *The Age of Hypochondria: Interpreting Romantic Health and Illness*. Palgrave Macmillan, 2010.

Guttman, Herbert G. *The Black Family in Slavery and Freedom, 1750–1925*. Vintage Books, 1977.

Habermas, Jürgen. *The Structural Transformation of the Public Sphere: An Inquiry into a Category of Bourgeois Society* [1962], translated into English by Thomas Burger. MIT Press, 1991.

———. *The Theory of Communicative Action*, 2 vols. [1981]: *Reason and the Rationalization of Society*, vol. 1, and *Lifeworld and System: A Critique of Functionalist Reason*, vol. 2, both translated into English by Thomas McCarthy. Beacon Press, 1984, 1987.

———. "Reconciliation through the Public Use of Reason: Remarks on John Rawls's Political Liberalism." *Journal of Philosophy* 92:3 (1995): 109–31.

———. *The Habermas Reader*, edited by William Outhwaite. Polity Press, 1996.
———. "Public Space and Political Public Sphere: The Biographical Roots of Two Motifs in My Thought." Commemorative lecture, Kyoto, November 11, 2004. http://ikesharpless.pbworks.com/f/Kyoto_lecture_Nov_2004,+Jurgen+Habermas.pdf.
Halberstam, Judith. "Perverse Presentism: The Androgyne, the Tribade, the Female Husband, and Other Pre-Twentieth Century Genders." Chapter 2 in *Female Masculinity*, 45–73. Duke University Press, 1998.
Hall, Catherine, Keith McClelland, and Jane Rendall. *Defining the Victorian Nation: Class, Race, Gender, and the Reform Act of 1867*. Cambridge University Press, 2000.
Hamilton, Laurence A. *The Political Philosophy of Needs*. Cambridge University Press, 2003.
Hamington, Maurice. "Politics Is Not a Game: The Radical Potential of Care." In *Care Ethics and Political Theory*, edited by Daniel Engster and Maurice Hamington, 272–92. Oxford University Press, 2015.
Hammerton, A. James. *Emigrant Gentlewomen: Genteel Poverty and Female Emigration, 1830–1914*. Rowman & Littlefield, 1979.
Harding, Kelli. *The Rabbit Effect: Live Longer, Happier, and Healthier with the Groundbreaking Science of Kindness*. Atria Books, 2019.
Hardt, Michael. "Affective Labor." *boundary 2* 26:2 (1999): 89–100.
Harney, Stefano, and Fred Moten. *The Undercommons: Fugitive Planning and Black Study*. Autonomedia, 2013.
Harris, Lech. "Elliptical Orality: Rhetoric as Style in Conrad." *Victorian Studies* 61:2 (Winter 2019): 240–47. https//doi.org/10.2979/victorianstudies.61.2.08.
Harrison, Mary-Catherine. "The Paradox of Fiction and the Ethics of Empathy: Reconceiving Dickens's Realism." *Narrative* 16:3 (2008): 256–78.
Harvey, Graham. *Tool-Being: Heidegger and the Metaphysics of Objects*. Open Court Publishing, 2002.
———. *Animism: Respecting the Living World*. Hurst & Company, 2005.
Havens, Hilary. *Revising the Eighteenth-Century Novel: Authorship from Manuscript to Print*. Cambridge University Press, 2019.
Hayot, Eric. *The Elements of Academic Style: Writing for the Humanities*. Columbia University Press, 2014.
Haywood, Ian. "Radical Print Culture: From Chartism to Socialism." In *The Routledge Companion to Victorian Literature*, edited by Dennis Denisoff and Talia Schaffer, 171–81. Routledge, 2020.
Heidegger, Martin. *Being and Time*, translated by John Macquarrie and Edward Robinson. Harper & Row, 1962.
Held, Virginia. *Feminist Morality: Transforming Culture, Society, and Politics*. University of Chicago Press, 1993.
———. *The Ethics of Care: Personal, Political, and Global*. Oxford University Press, 2006.
———. "Care and Justice, Still." In *Care Ethics and Political Theory*, edited by Daniel Engster and Maurice Hamington, 19–36. Oxford University Press, 2015.
Henry, Nancy. *The Life of George Eliot: A Critical Biography*. Wiley, 2012.
Hensley, Nathan K. *Forms of Empire: The Poetics of Victorian Sovereignty*. Oxford University Press, 2016.
Hertz, Neil. "Some Words in George Eliot: Nullify, Neutral, Numb, Number." In *Languages of the Unsayable: The Play of Negativity in Literature and Literary Theory*,

edited by Sanford Budick and Wolfgang Iser, 280–97. Stanford University Press, 1987.

Himmelweit, Susan. "Caring Labor." *Annals: American Academy of Political and Social Science* 561:1 (1999): 27–38.

Hingston, Kylee-Ann. "Interdependence, Incarnation, and Disability in Charlotte Yonge's *The Pillars of the House*." *Journal of Disability and Religion* 22:2 (May 2018): 187–98.

Hobart, Hiʻilei Julia Kawehipuaakahaopulani, and Tamara Kneese. "Radical Care: Survival Strategies for Uncertain Times." *Social Text* 38:1 (142) (March 1, 2020): 1–16. https://doi.org/10.1215/01642472-7971067.

Hochschild, Arlie Russell. *The Managed Heart: The Commercialization of Human Feeling* [1983], 2nd ed. University of California Press, 2003.

———. "Global Care Chains and Emotional Surplus Value." In *On the Edge: Living with Global Capitalism*, edited by Will Hutton and Anthony Giddens, 130–46. Random House, 2001.

———. "Love and Gold." In *Global Woman: Nannies, Maids, and Sex Workers in the New Economy*, edited by Barbara Ehrenreich and Arlie Russell Hochschild, 15–30. Henry Holt & Co., 2002.

Hodgkinson, Ruth G. *The Origins of the National Health Service: The Medical Services of the New Poor Law, 1834–1871*. University of California Press, 1967.

Hoffer, Lauren N. "'She Brings Everything to a Grindstone': Sympathy and the Paid Female Companion's Critical Work in *David Copperfield*." *Dickens Studies Annual* 41 (2010): 191–213.

———. "Employment Relations and the Failure of Sympathy in Hardy's *Desperate Remedies* and *The Mayor of Casterbridge*." *Victorians Institute Journal* 41 (2013): 185–218.

Hoffman, Meechal. "Eliot against Eliot-ian Sympathy: Reconsidering "the Extension of Our Sympathies" in *Romola* and *Daniel Deronda*." In "Acting Social: The Relational Nineteenth-Century Novel." PhD manuscript, Graduate Center, CUNY.

Holland, Laurence B. *The Expense of Vision: Essays on the Craft of Henry James*. Johns Hopkins University Press, 1982.

Holmes, Martha Stoddard. "Victorian Fictions of Interdependency: Gaskell, Craik, and Yonge." *Journal of Literary Disability* 1:2 (2007): 29–41.

Hondagneu-Sotelo, Pierrette. "Blow-Ups and Other Unhappy Endings." In *Global Woman: Nannies, Maids, and Sex Workers in the New Economy*, edited by Barbara Ehrenreich and Arlie Russell Hochschild, 55–69. Henry Holt & Co., 2002.

———. *Doméstica: Immigrant Women Cleaning and Caring in the Shadows of Affluence*. University of California Press, 2007.

hooks, bell. *Teaching Community: A Pedagogy of Hope*. Routledge, 2003.

Hopper, Briallen. *Hard to Love: Essays and Confessions*. Bloomsbury Publishing, 2019.

Houston, Barbara. "Caring and Exploitation." *Hypatia* 5:1 (Spring 1990): 115–19.

Huang, Yu-Ling, and Chia-Ling Wu. "New Feminist Biopolitics in Ultra-Low-Fertility East Asia." In *Making Kin Not Population*, edited by Adele E. Clarke and Donna Haraway, 125–44. Prickly Paradigm Press, 2018.

Hughes, John. "The Affective World of Charlotte Brontë's 'Villette.'" *Studies in English Literature* 40:4 (Autumn 2000): 711–26.

Hughes, Linda K. "SIDEWAYS! Navigating the Material(ity) of Print Culture." *Victorian Periodicals Review* 47:1 (2014): 1–30.
HuMetricsHSS: Humane Metrics Initiative. "Values Framework," https://humetricshss.org/our-work/values/.
Jackson, Steven J. "Rethinking Repair." In *Media Technologies: Essays on Communication, Materiality, and Society*, edited by Pablo J. Boczkowski, Kirsten A. Foot, and Tarleton Gillespie, 221–39. MIT Press, 2014.
———. "Material Care." In *Debates in the Digital Humanities 2019*, edited by Lauren F. Klein and Matthew K. Gold, 427–30. University of Minnesota Press, 2019.
Jaffe, Audrey. *Scenes of Sympathy: Identity and Representation in Victorian Fiction*. Cornell University Press, 2000.
James, Henry. "Daniel Deronda: A Conversation" [1876]. Reprinted in F. R. Leavis, *The Great Tradition*. Doubleday Anchor, 1954, 300–319.
———. *The Portrait of a Lady* [1881], edited by Roger Luckhurst. Oxford Worlds Classics, 2009.
———. *The Wings of the Dove* [1902], edited by Millicent Bell. Penguin, 2008.
———. "Preface to the New York Edition" [1909]. Reprinted in *The Wings of the Dove*, 3–20. Penguin, 2008.
Jameson, Frederic. "Remarks on Henry James." *Henry James Review* 36:3 (Fall 2015): 296–306.
Jay, Elisabeth. "Charlotte Mary Yonge and Tractarian Aesthetics." *Victorian Poetry* 44:1 (2006): 43–59.
Johnson, Claudia. *Equivocal Beings: Politics, Gender, and Sentimentality in the 1790s*. University of Chicago Press, 1995.
Joshua, Essaka. *Physical Disability in British Romantic Literature*. Cambridge University Press, 2020.
Jovchelovitch, Sandra. *Knowledge in Context: Representations, Community, and Culture*. Routledge, 2007.
Kafer, Alison. *Feminist, Queer, Crip*. Indiana University Press, 2013.
Kaplan, Fred. *Sacred Tears: Sentimentality in Victorian Literature*. Princeton University Press, 1987.
———. *Henry James: The Imagination of Genius*. William Morrow, 1992.
Kelleher, Paul. "The Man within the Breast: Sympathy, Deformity, and Moral Subjectivity in Adam Smith's *The Theory of Moral Sentiments*." In *Inventing Agency: Essays on the Literary and Philosophical Production of the Modern Subject*, edited by Claudia Brodsky and Eloy LaBrada, 173–200. Bloomsbury, 2017.
Keller, Jean, and Eva Feder Kittay. "Feminist Ethics of Care." In *The Routledge Companion to Feminist Philosophy*, edited by Ann Garry, 540–55. Routledge, 2017.
Kipling, Rudyard. "The White Man's Burden" [1899]. In *Literature and Culture at the Fin de Siècle*, edited by Talia Schaffer, 485–86. Longman, 2007.
Kittay, Eva Feder. "Welfare, Dependency, and a Public Ethic of Care." *Social Justice* 25:1 (Spring 1998): 123–45.
———. *Love's Labor: Essays on Women, Equality, and Dependence*. Routledge, 1999.
———. "A Feminist Public Ethic of Care Meets the New Communitarian Family Policy." *Ethics* 111:3 (April 2001): 523–47.

Kittay, Eva Feder. "When Caring Is Just and Justice Is Caring." In *The Subject of Care: Feminist Perspectives on Dependency*, edited by Eva Feder Kittay and Ellen K. Feder, 257–76. Rowman & Littlefield, 2002.

———. "A Theory of Justice as Fair Terms of Social Life." In *Care Ethics and Political Theory*, edited by Daniel Engster and Maurice Hamington, 51–71. Oxford University Press, 2015.

Kleinberg, Ethan, Joan Wallach Scott, and Gary Wilder. *Theses on Theory and History*, May 2018. https://theoryrevolt.com/.

Knox, Robert. *The Races of Men: A Fragment*. H. Renshaw, 1850.

Kofman, Eleonore, and Parvati Raghuram. "Gender and Global Labour Migrations: Incorporating Skilled Workers." *Antipode* 38:2 (March 2006): 282–303.

Kotchemidova, Christina. "From Good Cheer to 'Drive-by Smiling': A Social History of Cheerfulness." *Journal of Social History* 39:1 (2005): 5–37.

Kranidis, Rita S. *The Victorian Spinster and Colonial Emigration: Contested Subjects*. St. Martin's Press, 1999.

Krienke, Hosanna. "The 'After-Life' of Illness: Reading against the Deathbed in Gaskell's *Ruth* and Nineteenth-Century Convalescent Devotionals." *Victorian Literature and Culture* 45 (March 2017): 35–53. doi:10.1017/S1060150316000425.

———. "Now What? Surviving Serious Illness in the Nineteenth-Century," University of Oxford, Diseases of Modern Life, January 8, 2018. https://diseasesofmodernlife.web.ox.ac.uk/article/now-what-surviving-serious-illness-in-the-nineteenth-century.

Kristeva, Julia. "Word, Dialogue, and Novel." In *The Kristeva Reader*, edited by Toril Moi, 35–61. Columbia University Press, 1986.

Kucich, John. "Passionate Reserve and Reserved Passion." *ELH* 52:4 (1985): 913–37.

———. *The Power of Lies: Transgression in Victorian Fiction*. Cornell University Press, 1994.

———. "The Unfinished Historicist Project: In Praise of Suspicion." *Victoriographies* 1:1 (2011): 58–78.

Kurnick, David. "What Does Jamesian Style Want?" *Henry James Review* 28:3 (2007): 213–22.

———. "A Few Lies: Queer Theory and Our Method Melodramas." *ELH* 87:2 (Summer 2020): 349–74.

Landow, George. *Victorian Types, Victorian Shadows: Biblical Typology in Victorian Art, Literature, and Thought*. Routledge & Kegan Paul, 1980.

Latour, Bruno. *Reassembling the Social: An Introduction to Actor-Network-Theory*. Oxford University Press, 2005.

Lau, Travis Chi Wing. "Before the Norm?" *Disability Studies Quarterly* 37:3 (2017). http://dsq-sds.org/article/view/5939/4695.

Laugier, Sandra. "The Ethics of Care as a Politics of the Ordinary." *New Literary History* 46:2 (Spring 2015): 217–40.

Lawson, Kate, and Lynn Shakinovsky. "Fantasies of National Identification in *Villette*." *Studies in English Literature* 49:4 (2009): 925–44.

Leavis, F. R. *The Great Tradition* [1948]. New York University Press, 1963.

Lee, Wendy Anne. *Failures of Feeling: Insensibility and the Novel*. Stanford University Press, 2019.

Levinas, Emmanuel. *Totality and Infinity: An Essay on Exteriority*, translated by Alphonso Lingis. Duquesne University Press, 1961.
Levine, George. "Daniel Deronda: A New Epistemology." In *Knowing the Past: Victorian Literature and Culture*, edited by Suzy Anger, 52–74. Cornell University Press, 2001.
Lewis, Christian. "A Malady of Interpretation: Performance of Hypochondria in Jane Austen." forthcoming in *Nineteenth-Century Studies*.
Lindhé, Anna. "The Paradox of Narrative Empathy and the Form of the Novel, or What George Eliot Knew." *Studies in the Novel* 48:1 (Spring 2016): 19–42.
Living Justice Press. "The Indigenous Origins of Circles and How Non-Natives Learned about Them." http://www.livingjusticepress.org/index.asp?Type=B_BASIC&SEC ={0F6FA816-E094-4B96-8F39-9922F67306E5}.
Longmuir, Anne. "Emigrant Spinsters and the Construction of Englishness in Charlotte Brontë's *Villette*." *Nineteenth-Century Gender Studies* 4:3 (Winter 2008). http://www.ncgsjournal.com/issue43/longmuir.htm.
Loose, Margaret. *The Chartist Imaginary: Literary Form in Working-Class Political Theory and Practice*. Ohio State University Press, 2014.
Looser, Devoney. "The Hows and Whys of Public Humanities." *Profession* (Spring 2019). https://profession.mla.org/the-hows-and-whys-of-public-humanities/.
Lorde, Audre. "The Master's Tools Will Never Dismantle the Master's House." Comments at "The Personal and the Political" panel, Second Sex Conference, October 29, 1979. Reprinted in Audre Lorde, *Sister Outsider: Essays and Speeches*, 110–14. Crossing Press, 1984. http://s18.middlebury.edu/AMST0325A/Lorde_The _Masters_Tools.pdf.
Losh, Elizabeth. "Home Inspection: Mina Rees and National Computing Infrastructure." *First Monday* 23:3 (March 5, 2018). https://doi.org/10.5210/fm.v23i3.8282.
Love, Heather. *Feeling Backward: Loss and the Politics of Queer History*. Harvard University Press, 2009.
———. "Truth and Consequences: On Paranoid Reading and Reparative Reading." *Criticism* 52:2 (Spring 2010): 235–41.
Lowe, Brigid. *Victorian Fiction and the Insights of Sympathy: An Alternative to the Hermeneutics of Suspicion*. Anthem Press, 2007.
Luciano, Dana. *Arranging Grief: Sacred Time and the Body in Nineteenth Century America*. New York University Press, 2007.
Lukács, Georg. *The Historical Novel* [1937], translated by Hannah Mitchell and Stanley Mitchell. University of Nebraska Press, 1983.
Lutz, Deborah. *Relics of Death in Victorian Literature and Culture*. Cambridge University Press, 2015.
Lynch, Deidre Shauna. *The Economy of Character: Novels, Market Culture, and the Business of Inner Meaning*. University of Chicago Press, 1998.
———. "Introduction." In *Persuasion* [1817], edited by James Kinsley and Deidre Shauna Lynch, x–xvi. Oxford World's Classics, 2004.
MacLure, Jennifer. "Undiagnosing Esther: The Productive Ambiguity of Disease in Bleak House." *Dickens Studies Annual* 51:1 (2020): 95–122.
Malatino, Hil. *Trans Care*. University of Minnesota Press, 2020.
Manne, Kate. *Down Girl: The Logic of Misogyny*. Oxford University Press, 2017.

Marçal, Katrine. *Who Cooked Adam Smith's Dinner?* Pegasus Books, 2016.
Marchbanks, Paul. "A Costly Morality: Dependency Care and Mental Difference in the Novels of the Brontë Sisters." *Journal of Literary and Cultural Disability* 4:1 (2010): 55–72.
Marcus, Sharon. *Between Women: Friendship, Desire, and Marriage in Victorian England*. Princeton University Press, 2007.
Mardorossian, Carine M. "From Literature of Exile to Migrant Literature." *Modern Language Studies* 32:2 (Autumn 2002): 15–33.
Martineau, Harriet. *Life in the Sickroom* [1844], edited by Maria H. Frawley. Broadview Press, 2003.
Mason, Emma Jane. "Feeling Dickensian Feeling." *Interdisciplinary Studies in the Long Nineteenth Century* (April 2007). https://doi.org/10.16995/ntn.454.
May, Leila S. "Lucy Snowe, a Material Girl? Phrenology, Surveillance, and the Sociology of Interiority." *Criticism* 55:1 (Winter 2013): 43–68.
May, Trevor. *The Victorian Domestic Servant*. Bloomsbury, 2008.
McDonagh, Josephine. "Rethinking Provincialism in Mid-Nineteenth-Century Fiction: *Our Village* to *Villette*." *Victorian Studies* 55:3 (2013): 399–424.
———, and Jonathan Sachs, eds. "Special Article Cluster: New Work on Literature and Migration." *Modern Philology* 118:2 (November 2020): 204–76.
McGee, Micki. "Capitalism's Care Problem: Some Traces, Fixes, and Patches." *Social Text* 38:1 (142) (March 1, 2020): 39–66. https://doi.org/10.1215/01642472-7971091.
McGirr, Elaine M. *Eighteenth-Century Characters: A Guide to the Literature of the Age*. Palgrave Macmillan, 2007.
McKeon, Michael. *The Origins of the English Novel, 1600–1740*. John Hopkins University Press, 2002.
McWeeny, Gage. *The Comfort of Strangers: Social Life and Literary Form*. Oxford University Press, 2016.
Menke, Richard. *Telegraphic Realism: Victorian Fiction and Other Information Systems*. Stanford University Press, 2008.
Meyer, Susan. *Imperialism at Home: Race and Victorian Women's Fiction*. Cornell University Press, 1996.
Michie, Elsie. "The Novel." In *The Routledge Companion to Victorian Literature*, edited by Dennis Denisoff and Talia Schaffer, 22–32. Routledge, 2020.
Michie, Helena. "Victorian(ist) 'Whiles' and the Tenses of Historicism." *Narrative* 17:3 (2009): 274–90.
———. "Hard Times, Global Times: Simultaneity in Anthony Trollope and Elizabeth Gaskell." *SEL* 56:3 (2016): 605–26.
Miller, Andrew H. *The Burdens of Perfection: On Ethics and Reading in Nineteenth-Century British Literature*. Cornell University Press, 2008.
Miller, Claire Cain, Shane Goldmacher, and Thomas Kaplan. "Biden Announces $775 Billion Plan to Help Working Parents and Caregivers." *New York Times*, July 21, 2020. https://www.nytimes.com/2020/07/21/us/politics/biden-workplace-childcare.html.
Miller, Nancy K. "Mentoring the Mentor." *Avidly*, January 7, 2020. http://avidly.lareviewofbooks.org/2020/01/07/mentoring-the-mentor/.

Mingus, Mia. "Pods and Pod Mapping Worksheets." Berkeley Area Transformative Justice Collective, June 2016. https://batjc.wordpress.com/pods-and-pod-mapping-worksheet/.
Mitchell, Rebecca N. *Victorian Lessons in Empathy and Difference*. Ohio State University Press, 2011.
Mitchell, Rosemary. "Charlotte M. Yonge: Reading, Writing, and Recycling Historical Fiction in the Nineteenth Century." *Nineteenth-Century Contexts* 31:1 (2009): 31–43.
———. "Charlotte M. Yonge and the Concept of Conservative Community." In *Charlotte M. Yonge: Writing the Victorian Age*, edited by Clare Walker Gore, Clemence Shultze, and Julia Courtney. Palgrave Macmillan, forthcoming.
Moses, Omri. "Henry James's Suspended Situations." *Modern Philology* 108:1 (August 2010): 116–50.
Muñoz, José Esteban. *Cruising Utopia: The There and Then of Queer Futurity*. New York University Press, 2009.
Nail, Thomas. *The Figure of the Migrant*. Stanford University Press, 2015.
Nandrea, Lorrie. *Misfit Forms: Paths Not Taken by the British Novel*. Fordham University Press, 2015.
Narayan, Uma. "Colonialism and Its Others: Considerations on Rights and Care Discourses." *Hypatia* 10:2 (Spring 1995): 133–40.
Nazar, Hina. "Facing Ethics: Narrative and Recognition from George Eliot to Judith Butler." *Nineteenth-Century Contexts* 33:5 (December 2011): 437–50.
Nemoianu, Virgil Martin. "The Spinozist Freedom of George Eliot's *Daniel Deronda*." *Philosophy and Literature* 34:1 (April 2010): 65–81.
Newton, K. M. *George Eliot: Romantic Humanist*. Macmillan, 1981.
Nightingale, Florence. *Notes on Nursing: What It Is, and What It Is Not*. Harrison, 1860.
Nixon, Kari. *Kept from All Contagion: Germ Theory, Disease, and the Dilemma of Human Contact in Late-Nineteenth-Century Literature*. State University of New York Press, 2020.
Noddings, Nel. *Caring: A Feminine Approach to Ethics and Moral Education*. University of California Press, 1984.
———. "A Response to Card, Hoagland, Houston." *Hypatia* 5:1 (Spring 1990): 123.
———. *Starting at Home: Caring and Social Policy*. University of California Press, 2002.
———. "Caring in Education." *The Encyclopedia of Informal Education*. 2005. http://infed.org/mobi/caring-in-education/.
Nott, J. C., and George R. Gliddon. *Types of Mankind: or, Ethnological Researches*. Lippincott, Crambo & Co., 1854.
Nowviskie, Bethany. "On Capacity and Care." October 4, 2015. http://nowviskie.org/2015/on-capacity-and-care/. Revised and reprinted in *Debates in the Digital Humanities 2019*, edited by Lauren F. Klein and Matthew K. Gold, 424–26. University of Minnesota Press, 2019.
Nussbaum, Martha Craven. *Love's Knowledge: Essays on Philosophy and Literature*. Oxford University Press, 1990.
Onazi, Ocho. *An African Path to Disability Justice: Community, Relationships, and Obligations*. Springer, 2020.
Orr, Mary. *Intertextuality: Debates and Contexts*. Polity Press, 2003.

Pahl, Ray. "Are All Communities Communities in the Mind?" *Sociological Review* 53:4 (November 2005): 621–40.

Palmer, Beth. "Assuming the Role of Editor." In *The Cambridge Companion to Victorian Women's Writing*, edited by Linda H. Peterson, 59–72. Cambridge University Press, 2015.

Parker, David. *Ethics, Theory, and the Novel*. Cambridge University Press, 1994.

Parreñas, Rhacel Salazar. *Servants of Globalization: Women, Migration, and Domestic Work*. Stanford University Press, 2001.

Penner, Louise, and Tabitha Sparks. "Introduction." In *Victorian Medicine and Popular Culture*, edited by Louise Penner and Tabitha Sparks, 1–8. Pickering and Chatto, 2015.

Perkin, Harold. *The Rise of Professional Society: England since 1880*. Routledge, 1989.

Perpich, Diane. "Don't Try This at Home: Levinas and Applied Ethics." In *Totality and Infinity at 50*, edited by Scott Davidson and Diane Perpich, 127–52. Duquesne University Press, 2012.

Peterson, Linda. *Victorian Autobiography: The Tradition of Self-Interpretation*. Yale University Press, 1986.

———. "Introduction." In *The Cambridge Companion to Victorian Women's Writing*, edited by Linda H. Peterson, 1–14. Cambridge University Press, 2015.

Peterson, M. Jeanne. *The Medical Profession in Mid-Victorian London*. University of California Press, 1978.

Piepzna-Samarasinha, Leah Lakshmi. *Care Work: Dreaming Disability Justice*. Arsenal Pulp Press, 2018.

Pinch, Adela. *Strange Fits of Passion: Epistemologies of Emotion, Hume to Austen*. Stanford University Press, 1996.

———. "Sensibility." In *Oxford Companion to the Romantic Age*, edited by Nicholas Roe, 49–61. Oxford University Press, 2005.

Pionke, Albert D. *The Ritual Culture of Victorian Professionals: Competing for Ceremonial Status 1838-1877*. Routledge, 2016.

Piper, Andrew. *Enumerations: Data and Literary Study*. University of Chicago Press, 2018.

Plotz, John. *The Crowd: British Literature and Public Politics*. University of California Press, 2000.

Poovey, Mary. *Genres of the Credit Economy: Mediating Value in Eighteenth- and Nineteenth-Century Britain*. University of Chicago Press, 2008.

Porter, Roy. *Bodies Politic: Disease, Death, and Doctors in Britain, 1650-1900*. Reaktion Books, 2001.

Puar, Jasbir. "Prognosis Time: Toward a Geopolitics of Affect, Debility, and Capacity." *Women and Performance* 19:2 (2009): 161–72.

———. "Coda: The Cost of Getting Better." *GLQ* 18:1 (2011): 149–58.

———. "Hands Up, Don't Shoot!" *The New Inquiry*, September 15, 2017.

Puig de la Bellacasa, María. *Matters of Care: Speculative Ethics in More than Human Worlds*. University of Minnesota Press, 2017.

Ragussis, Michael. *Figures of Conversion: "The Jewish Question" and English National Identity*. Duke University Press, 1995.

Rainof, Rebecca. *The Victorian Novel of Adulthood: Plot and Purgatory in Fictions of Maturity*. Ohio University Press, 2015.

Rajan, Supritha. *A Tale of Two Capitalisms: Sacred Economics in Nineteenth Century Britain*. University of Michigan Press, 2015.
Raworth, Kate. *Doughnut Economics: Seven Ways to Think Like a 21st Century Economist*. Random House, 2017.
Reaume, A. H. "On Reclaiming Brokenness and Refusing the Violence of 'Recovery Narratives.'" *Open Book*, June 17, 2020. http://open-book.ca/Columnists/On-Reclaiming-Brokenness-and-Refusing-the-Violence-of-Recovery-Narratives.
Richardson, Jerusha D. *Women of the Church of England*. Chapman Hall, 1908.
Ricks, Christopher. "The Novelist as Critic." In *The Oxford Handbook of the Victorian Novel*, edited by Lisa Rodensky, 634–62. Oxford University Press, 2013.
Risam, Roopika. "Diversity Work and Digital Care Work in Higher Education." *First Monday* 23:3 (March 5, 2018). https://firstmonday.org/ojs/index.php/fm/article/view/8241/6651.
———. "Academic Generosity, Academic Insurgency." *Public Books*, November 27, 2019. https://www.publicbooks.org/academic-generosity-academic-insurgency/.
Rivas, Lynn May. "Invisible Labors: Caring for the Independent Person." In *Global Woman: Nannies, Maids, and Sex Workers in the New Economy*, edited by Barbara Ehrenreich and Arlie Russell Hochschild, 70–84. Henry Holt & Co., 2002.
Robinson, Fiona. "Care Ethics, Political Theory, and the Future of Feminism." In *Care Ethics and Political Theory*, edited by Daniel Engster and Maurice Hamington, 293–312. Oxford University Press, 2015.
———. "Resisting Hierarchies through Relationality in the Ethics of Care." *International Journal of Care and Caring* 4:1 (2020): 11–23.
Rodas, Julia Miele. "Tiny Tim, Blind Bertha, and the Resistance of Mrs. Mowcher: Charles Dickens and the Uses of Disability." *Dickens Studies Annual* 34 (2004): 51–97.
———. "'On the Spectrum': Rereading Contact and Affect in *Jane Eyre*." In *The Madwoman and the Blindman: Jane Eyre, Discourse, Disability*, edited by David Bolt, Julia Miele Rodas, and Elizabeth Donaldson, 51–70. Ohio State University Press, 2012.
Rody, Caroline. "Burning Down the House: The Revisionary Paradigm of Jean Rhys's *Wide Sargasso Sea*." In *Famous Last Words: Changes in Gender and Narrative Closure*, edited by Alison Booth, 300–325. University Press of Virginia, 1993.
Rosen, Jeremy. *Minor Characters Have Their Day: Genre and the Contemporary Literary Marketplace*. Columbia University Press, 2016.
Roseneil, Sasha, and Shelley Budgeon. "Cultures of Intimacy and Care beyond 'the Family': Personal Life and Social Change in the Early 21st Century." *Current Sociology* 52:2 (March 1, 2004): 135–59.
Rothfield, Lawrence. *Vital Signs: Medical Realism in Nineteenth-Century Fiction*. Princeton University Press, 1992
Rowland, Ann Wierda. "Sentimental Fiction." In *The Cambridge Companion to Fiction in the Romantic Period*, 191–206. Cambridge University Press, 2008.
Ruddick, Lisa. "When Nothing Is Cool." In *The Future of Scholarly Writing: Critical Interventions*, edited by Angelika Bammer and Ruth-Ellen Boetcher Joeres, 71–85. Palgrave Macmillan, 2015. Also published in abridged form in *The Point*, December 7, 2015, https://thepointmag.com/criticism/when-nothing-is-cool/.
Ruddick, Sara. *Maternal Thinking: Towards a Politics of Peace*. Women's Press Ltd., 1990.

Samuel, Sigal. "Lake Erie Now Has Legal Rights, Just Like You." *Vox*, February 26, 2019. https://www.vox.com/future-perfect/2019/2/26/18241904/lake-erie-legal-rights-personhood-nature-environment-toledo-ohio.

Samuels, Ellen. "Six Ways of Looking at Crip Time." *Disability Studies Quarterly* 37:3 (2017). https://dsq-sds.org/article/view/5824/4684.

Sassen, Saskia. "Global Cities and Survival Circuits." In *The Global Dimensions of Gender and Carework*, edited by Mary K. Zimmerman, Jacquelyn S. Litt, and Christine E. Bose, 30–38. Stanford University Press, 2006.

Schaffer, Talia. *Novel Craft: Victorian Domestic Handicraft and Nineteenth-Century Fiction*. Oxford University Press, 2011.

———. *Romance's Rival: Familiar Marriage in Victorian Fiction*. Oxford University Press, 2016.

———. "Disabling Marriage: Communities of Care in *Our Mutual Friend*." In *Re-Plotting Marriage: Engagement and Wedlock in the Long Nineteenth Century*, edited by Jill Galvan and Elsie Michie, 192–210. Ohio State, 2018.

Schroeder, Janice. "'A Thousand Petty Troubles': Margaret Hale's Emotional Labor in *North and South*." *Women's Writing* 27:4 (2020): 461–72. https://doi.org/10.1080/09699082.2020.1775773.

Scribner, Abby. "Liberalism and Inner Life: The Curious Cases of *Mansfield Park* and *Villette*." *Novel* 53:3 (November 1, 2020): 317–40.

Sedgwick, Eve Kosofsky. "Tales of the Avunculate." In *Tendencies*, 52–72. Duke University Press, 1993.

———. "Paranoid Reading and Reparative Reading, or, You're So Paranoid, You Probably Think This Introduction Is About You." In *Touching Feeling: Affect, Pedagogy, Performativity*, edited by Eve Sedgwick, 123–51. Duke University Press, 2003.

Seltzer, Mark. *Henry James and the Art of Power*. Cornell University Press, 1984.

Semmel, Bernard. *George Eliot and the Politics of National Inheritance*. Oxford University Press, 1994.

Sered, Danielle. *Until We Reckon: Violence, Mass Incarceration, and a Road to Repair*. New Press, 2019.

Serres, Michel. *Rome: The First Book of Foundations*, translated by Randolph Burks. Bloomsbury, 2015.

Sevenhuijsen, Selma. *Citizenship and the Ethics of Care: Feminist Considerations on Justice, Morality, and Politics*, translated by Liz Savage. Routledge, 1998.

Shakinovsky, Lynn. "Domestic History and the Idea of the Nation in Charlotte Yonge's *The Heir of Redclyffe*." In *Antifeminism and the Victorian Novel*, edited by Tamara Silvia Wagner, 77–93. Cambria Press, 2009.

Shaviro, Steven. *The Universe of Things: On Speculative Realism*. University of Minnesota Press, 2014.

Shuman, Cathy. *Pedagogical Economies: The Examination and the Victorian Literary Man*. Stanford University Press, 2000.

Shuttleworth, Sally. *Charlotte Brontë and Victorian Psychology*. Cambridge University Press, 1996.

Simmons, Clare A. "Introduction" to Charlotte M. Yonge, *The Clever Woman of the Family* [1865], 7–26. Broadview Press, 2001.

Skinner, Gillian. *Sensibility and Economics in the Novel, 1740–1900: The Price of a Tear*. Palgrave Macmillan, 1999.

Smith-Rosenberg, Carroll. "The Female World of Love and Ritual: Relations between Women in Nineteenth-Century America." *Signs* 1:1 (Autumn 1975): 1–29.

Sontag, Susan. *Illness as Metaphor* and *AIDS and Its Metaphors*. Farrar, Straus and Giroux, 2013.

Spade, Dean. *Mutual Aid: Building Solidarity during This Crisis (and the Next)*. Verso, 2020.

Span, Paula. "Biden's Plan for Seniors Is Not Just a Plan for Seniors." *New York Times*, November 27, 2020. https://www.nytimes.com/2020/11/27/health/biden-senior-citizens.html.

Sparks, Tabitha. *The Doctor in the Victorian Novel: Family Practices*. Routledge, 2009.

Spencer, Liz, and Ray Pahl. *Rethinking Friendship: Hidden Solidarities Today*. Princeton University Press, 2006.

Spillers, Hortense J. "Mama's Baby, Papa's Maybe: An American Grammar Book." *Diacritics* 17:2 (Summer 1987): 64–81. https://people.ucsc.edu/~nmitchel/hortense_spillers_-_mamas_baby_papas_maybe.pdf.

Spunt, Nicola Ivy. "Pathological Commodification, Contagious Impressions, and Dead Metaphors: Undiagnosing Consumption in *The Wings of the Dove*." *Henry James Review* 34:2 (Summer 2013): 163–82.

Stack, Carol. *All Our Kin: Strategies for Survival in a Black Community*. Basic Books, 1974.

Stanley, Marni. "Skirting the Issues: Addressing and Dressing in Victorian Women's Travel Narratives." *Victorian Review* 23:2 (1997): 147–67.

Star, Susan Leigh, and Anselm Strauss. "Layers of Silence, Arenas of Voice: The Ecology of Visible and Invisible Work." *Computer Supported Cooperative Work* 8 (1999): 9–30.

Steinlight, Emily. *Populating the Novel: Literary Form and the Politics of Surplus Life*. Cornell University Press, 2018

Stephen, Julia. *On Being Ill; with Notes from Sick Rooms* [1885]. Wesleyan University Press, 2012.

Stern, Kimberly J. *The Social Life of Criticism: Gender, Critical Writing, and the Politics of Belonging*. University of Michigan Press, 2016.

Stewart, Garrett. *Death Sentences: Styles of Dying in British Fiction*. Harvard University Press, 1984.

———. *Dear Reader: The Conscripted Audience in Nineteenth-Century British Fiction*. Johns Hopkins University Press, 1996.

Stone, Deborah A. *The Disabled State*. Temple University Press, 1984.

Stout, Daniel M. *Corporate Romanticism: Liberalism, Justice, and the Novel*. Fordham University Press, 2017.

Straus, Joseph N. "Disability and 'Late Style' in Music." *Journal of Musicology* 25:1 (2008): 3–45.

Swaert, Koenraad W. "'Individualism' in the Mid-Nineteenth Century (1826–1860)." *Journal of the History of Ideas* 23:1 (January/March 1962): 78–81.

Swenson, Kristine. *Medical Women in Victorian Fiction*. University of Missouri Press, 2005.

Sword, Helen. *Stylish Academic Writing*. Harvard University Press, 2012.

Tanasescu, Mihnea. "When a River Is a Person: From Ecuador to New Zealand, Nature Gets Its Day in Court." *The Conversation*, June 19, 2017. https://theconversation

.com/when-a-river-is-a-person-from-ecuador-to-new-zealand-nature-gets-its-day-in-court-79278.

Tankard, Alex. *Tuberculosis and Disabled Identity in Nineteenth-Century Literature: Invalid Lives*. Palgrave Macmillan, 2018.

Taussig, Rebekah. "I've Been Paralyzed since I Was Three. Here's Why Kindness toward Disabled People Is More Complicated than You Think." *Time*, August 31, 2020. https://time.com/5881597/disability-kindness/?fbclid=IwAR09ghKSqfuSXO_-r-f-kxT4GSOLcQJbyrZMAfWYLUJn-7ay18FC5uoogIc.

Taylor, Charles. "Atomism." In *Philosophy and the Human Sciences: Philosophical Papers 2* [1985], 187–210. Reprint, Cambridge University Press, 1985.

Teahan, Sheila. "The Abyss of Language in *The Wings of the Dove*." *Henry James Review* 14 (Spring 1993): 204–14.

Tennyson, Alfred Lord. "Tears, Idle Tears," from *The Princess* [1857]. Available at: https://www.poetryfoundation.org/poems/45384/the-princess-tears-idle-tears.

———. "Enoch Arden" [1864]. Available at: http://www.everypoet.com/archive/poetry/Tennyson/tennyson_contents_enoch_arden.htm.

Titchkosky, Tanya. "Normal." In *Keywords for Disability Studies*, edited by Rachel Adams, Benjamin Reiss, and David Serlin, 130–33. New York University Press, 2015.

Toker, Leona. "Vocationalism and Sympathy in *Daniel Deronda*." *Victorian Literature and Culture* 32:2 (2004): 565–74.

Tolentino, Jia. "What Mutual Aid Can Do during a Pandemic." *New Yorker*, May 11, 2020, 24. https://www.newyorker.com/magazine/2020/05/18/what-mutual-aid-can-do-during-a-pandemic.

Tromp, Marlene. *Victorian Freaks: The Social Context of Freakery in Britain*. Ohio State University Press, 2008.

Tronto, Joan C. *Moral Boundaries: A Political Argument for an Ethic of Care*. Routledge, 1993.

———. *Caring Democracy: Markets, Equality, and Justice*. New York University Press, 2013.

Trumpener, Katie. *Bardic Nationalism: The Romantic Novel and the British Empire*. Princeton University Press, 1997.

Tuck, Eve. "Citation Practices Challenge." *Critical Ethnic Studies* (April 2015). http://www.criticalethnicstudiesjournal.org/citation-practices/.

Tucker, Irene. *A Probable State: The Novel, the Contract, and the Jews*. University of Chicago Press, 2000.

———. "Race: Tracing the Contours of a Long Nineteenth Century." In *The Routledge Companion to Victorian Literature*, edited by Dennis Denisoff and Talia Schaffer, 330–41. Routledge, 2020.

Urban, Petr, and Lizzie Ward. "Introducing the Contexts of a Moral and Political Theory of Care." In *Care Ethics, Democratic Citizenship, and the State*, edited by Petr Urban and Lizzie Ward, 1–27. Palgrave Macmillan, 2020.

Vargo, Gregory. *An Underground History of Early Victorian Fiction: Chartism, Radical Print Culture, and the Social Problem Novel*. Cambridge University Press, 2017.

Vickery, Amanda. *The Gentleman's Daughter: Women's Lives in Georgian England*. Yale University Press, 1998.

Vrettos, Athena. *Somatic Fictions: Imagining Illness in Victorian Culture*. Stanford University Press, 1995.
Waddell, J.A.L. *Bridge Engineering*, vol. 2. John Wiley and Sons, 1923.
Wagner, Tamara Silvia, ed. *Victorian Settler Narratives: Emigrants, Cosmopolitans, and Returnees in Nineteenth-Century Literature*. Pickering & Chatto, 2011.
———. "Becoming Foreign in the Victorian Novel: International Migration in *Little Dorrit* and *Villette*." *Journal of Victorian Culture* 26:1 (2021): 72–88.
Walton, Susan. *Imagining Soldiers and Fathers in the Mid-Victorian Era: Charlotte Yonge's Models of Manliness*. Ashgate, 2010.
Ward, Lizzie. "Caring for Ourselves? Self-Care and Neoliberalism." In *Ethics of Care: Critical Advances in International Perspective*, edited by Marian Barnes, Tula Brannelly, Lizzie Ward, and Nicki Ward, 45–56. Policy Press, 2015.
Warwick Research Collective. "Collectivity and Crisis in the Long Twentieth Century." *MLQ* 81:4 (December 2020): 465–89.
Watt, Ian. *The Rise of the Novel: Studies in Defoe, Richardson, and Fielding*. University of California Press, 1957.
Weeks, Jeffrey, Brian Heaphy, and Catherine Donovan. *Same Sex Intimacies: Families of Choice and Other Life Experiments*. Routledge, 2001.
Wehrs, Donald R., and David P. Haney. "Introduction: Levinas, Twenty-First Century Ethical Criticism, and Their Nineteenth-Century Contexts." In *Levinas and Nineteenth-Century Literature: Ethics and Otherness from Romanticism through Realism*, edited by Donald R. Wehrs and David P. Haney, 15–41. Rosemont Publishing, 2009.
Weiss, Penny A., and Marilyn Friedman, eds. *Feminism and Community*. Temple University Press, 1995.
Weston, Kath. *The Families We Choose: Lesbians, Gays, Kinship*. Columbia University Press, 1991.
Wharton, Amy S. "The Psychosocial Consequences of Emotional Labor." *Annals: American Academy of Political and Social Science* 561:1 (1999): 158–76.
White, Julie Ann. "Practicing Care at the Margins: Other-Mothering as Public Care." In *Care Ethics and Political Theory*, edited by Daniel Engster and Maurice Hamington, 208–24. Oxford University Press, 2015.
White, Paul. "Geography, Literature, and Migration." In *Writing Across Worlds*, edited by Russell King, John Connell, and Paul White, 1–19. Routledge, 1995.
Wiegman, Robin. "The Times We're In: Queer Feminist Criticism and the Reparative 'Turn.'" *Feminist Theory* 15:1 (2014): 4–25.
Wilkie, Christina. "Biden Announces $775 Billion Plan to Fund Universal Child Care and In-Home Elder Care." CNBC, July 21, 2020. https://www.cnbc.com/2020/07/21/biden-to-unveil-775-billion-plan-to-fund-child-care-and-elder-care.html.
Williams, A. Susan. *The Rich Man and the Diseased Poor in Early Victorian Literature*. Macmillan, 1987.
Williams, Raymond. *The Country and the City*. Chatto & Windus, 1973.
Wilson, Shawn, and Margaret Hughes. "Why Research Is Reconciliation." In *Research and Reconciliation: Unsettling Ways of Knowing through Indigenous Relationships*, edited by Shawn Wilson, Andrea V. Breen, and Lindsay DuPré, 5–20. Canadian Scholars, 2019.
Wiltshire, John. *Jane Austen and the Body*. Cambridge University Press, 1992.

Winnicott, D. W. "Transitional Objects and Transitional Phenomena—A Study of the First Not-Me Possession." *International Journal of Psychoanalysis* 34 (1953): 89–97.

Woloch, Alex. *The One Versus the Many: Minor Characters and the Space of the Protagonist in the Novel.* Princeton University Press, 2003.

Wolpe, David, and Kinney Zalesne. "What Would Martin Buber Think of Zoom?" *Los Angeles Review of Books*, July 20, 2020, https://lareviewofbooks.org/short-takes/martin-buber-think-zoom/.

Wong, Daniel. "Charlotte Brontë's *Villette* and the Possibilities of a Postsecular Cosmopolitan Critique." *Journal of Victorian Culture* 18:1 (2013): 1–16.

Wood, Claire. *Dickens and the Business of Death.* Cambridge University Press, 2015.

Woods, Livia Arndal. "Generations in, Generations of: Pregnancy in Jane Austen." *Women's Writing* 26:2 (2019): 132–48. https://doi.org/10.1080/09699082.2019.1534649.

Woolf, Virginia. *A Room of One's Own* [1929]. Harcourt Brace Jovanovich, 1981.

Wright, Erika. *Reading for Health: Medical Narratives and the Nineteenth-Century Novel.* Series in Victorian Studies, edited by Joseph McLaughlin. Ohio University Press, 2016.

Yeates, Nicola. "Global Care Chains: Critical Reflections and Lines of Enquiry." *International Feminist Journal of Politics* 6:3 (September 2004): 369–91.

Yonge, Charlotte M. *The Letters of Charlotte Mary Yonge (1823–1901)*, edited by Charlotte Mitchell, Ellen Jordan, and Helen Schinske, 67–68. http://discovery.ucl.ac.uk/13734/3/Yongesecondbatchto1859.pdf.

———. *The Heir of Redclyffe* [1853]. Oxford University Press, 1997.

———. *The Clever Woman of the Family* [1865]. Broadview Press, 2001.

Young, Iris Marion. *Justice and the Politics of Difference.* Princeton University Press, 1990.

Yousef, Nancy. *Romantic Intimacy.* Stanford University Press, 2013.

Zelitzer, Viviana A. *The Purchase of Intimacy.* Princeton University Press, 2005.

Zunshine, Lisa. *Why We Read Fiction: Theory of Mind and the Novel.* Ohio State University Press, 2006.

Zuroski, Eugenia. "#BIPOC18 and the Undercommons of Enlightenment." Conference paper delivered at "Activism in Academia III," Center for Humanities, CUNY Graduate Center, New York, April 10, 2019.

INDEX

Ablow, Rachel, 128
Abram, David, 42
academia: care in, 26–27, 189–90, 197–98; and egalitarianism, 56; and gatekeeping, 211; labor of, 203–4; and measuring value, 242n27; and peer review, 213. *See also* citational practices; education
academic writing, 43, 187, 208
actor-network theory, 42
affiliation, 57–58, 76–77, 130, 136–37. *See also* care
Against Empathy (Bloom), 125
Agate, Nicky, 211
agency, 81
Ahmed, Sara, 5–6, 210–11, 242n34
Albrecht, Thomas, 128
All the Year Round (journal), 30
American Civil War, 31
Anderson, Amanda, 89, 94–95, 101, 110, 128, 225n91
Anderson, Benedict, 45, 52, 56
Anderson, Elizabeth, 55
"angel in the house" figure, 14–15, 21, 31, 62, 71, 114
Anger, Suzy, 126
animism, 41–42
Archimedes, Sondra M., 65, 68
Armstrong, Nancy, 8
Aslami, Zarena, 68
Auchard, John, 152, 156
"Aurora Leigh," 63
Austen, Jane, 60, 62, 75, 86, 123, 180
authenticity, 47, 50–51, 85, 91, 106, 108–9, 191, 199–200
authorial influence, 162–65, 180–81, 183. *See also* intertextuality
autism, 84, 230n127

Badowska, Ewa, 95
Bailin, Miriam, 22, 61, 73–74, 122, 143
Bakhtin, Mikhail, 164
"Barnacle, The," 166–67
Barnes, Marian, 6, 224n72–224n73
Barthes, Roland, 164

Bayley, Susan, 99
Bell, Daniel, 135
Bellacasa, María Puig de la, 43
Benjamin, Ruha, 17
Bennett, Jane, 42
Berlant, Lauren, 68
Bersani, Leo, 148–49
Bérubé, Michael, 36
Bhabha, Homi, 104
Bildungsroman, 104, 193
binocular vision, 7, 10, 89, 185–86. *See also* characters
Bird-David, Nurit, 42
Birth of the Clinic, The (Foucault), 67
Black Lives Matter protests, 18–19
Bleak House (Dickens), 9, 13, 53, 56–57, 121, 125
Bloom, Paul, 125, 162–63, 177, 183
Bodenheimer, Rosemarie, 118, 128
bodies: centrality of, 156; and decline, 4, 79; and emotion, 76; experiential knowledge of, 70; and identity, 68, 132–33; ignorance of, 237n14; organization of, 14; perceptions of, 23, 64–66, 76; rhythms of, 52. *See also* debility; extraordinary bodies; ordinary bodies
Booth, Wayne, 63, 163
Bourdieu, Pierre, 17, 61, 226n2
Bourrier, Karen, 169
Bowden, Peta, 30, 136, 149
breakage, 5, 7–8, 219n25
Brontë, Charlotte, 51, 83–86, 88, 93, 95, 100, 102, 116–18, 231n1. *See also specific works*
Brontë, Emily, 93
Brontë, Patrick, 233n58
Bronzino, Agnolo, 237n14
Brown, John, 227n23
Browning, Elizabeth Barrett, 238n5
Bubeck, Diemut, 34–35
Buber, Martin, 38, 223n51
Budge, Gavin, 169, 178
Burton, Sarah, 197
Buzard, James, 102
Byttebier, Stephanie, 145–46

[267]

INDEX

Cameron, Sharon, 147
care: active forms of, 1, 5–6, 10, 19, 34, 117, 127, 133, 194, 204; bad forms of, 34, 36, 58–59, 113, 130, 181, 191–92, 195, 215–16; communal forms of, 3, 12, 17, 58–59, 224n73; and critique, 190, 194–95, 213; definitions of, 3, 24, 30, 34–35, 38, 202, 222n5, 223n39; as dynamic, 7, 10, 48, 173, 191; failures of, 25, 141, 144; and feelings of caring, 104; and gender, 15, 21, 73; institutionalization of, 69; and literary style, 147–49, 160; perceptions of, 14–15, 28–30, 32, 54, 61–62, 145; and politics, 119, 236–37n75; responsibility for, 21, 78, 80, 89–90, 136, 203–4, 224n72; rhetoric of, 31, 146; and sentiment, 123; and sympathy, 118, 139; and textuality, 141–42. *See also* affiliation; care communities; caregiving; care readings; discourse; egalitarianism; needs; nursing; paid care; performativity; self-care; sympathy; temporality; unpaid care
care communities: absence of, 156–57, 192; in academia, 26–27, 197–98, 208; and affiliation, 57–58, 76–77, 130, 136–37; citations as, 208–10, 212; classrooms as, 99, 132, 198–200; and criminal justice reform, 19; formation of, 13, 24, 60–62, 145, 212; and intertextuality, 165; limits of, 14, 21–22, 57; and literary style, 147–49; and mass care, 69; and medical professionalism, 71, 77–78, 87; and ordinary bodies, 83–84; organization of, 3, 12, 15–16, 43, 49–59, 159, 171, 173–74, 193–94; power of, 74, 76, 160, 183; and the public sphere, 46–47, 49, 57; as reading mode, 45, 157, 187, 189. *See also* care; care relationships; public sphere
caregiving: as distinct from caring, 5; as reciprocal, 136; roles of, 11, 88, 95, 98; and textuality, 142. *See also* care
care readings, 26, 133–34, 187. *See also* care; reading
care relationships, 7, 10, 31–41, 69, 99, 104, 113, 131–32, 140, 153, 187–88. *See also* care communities
Caring (Noddings), 127
Carlyle, Thomas, 122, 135
Carr, Jean Ferguson, 204

"Casabianca" (Hemans), 123–24
Chalmers, Thomas, 72
Chambers, Simone, 220n45
characters: assumptions about, 88; disability readings of, 36; and emotional splits, 91–92; as extradiegetic, 160; as fluid beings, 167; identification with, 39, 169; in minor roles, 10–11, 91–92, 148, 240n71; as the modern subject, 8; as outward-facing, 58; reader perceptions of, 2, 7, 45, 122, 148, 155, 189; theories of, 7–10; as types, 8–10, 12, 80, 82–83, 94, 161, 177, 185. *See also* binocular vision; subjectivity
Charon, Rita, 149
Chartist fiction, 9
Chase, Cynthia, 132
Chávez, Karma, 19, 53–54, 196
Christian and Civic Community of Towns, The (Chalmers), 72
"Christmas Carol, A" (Dickens), 79–83, 122–24, 138
Christoff, Alicia, 2–3
citational practices, 187, 190, 208–12, 242n31. *See also* academia
Clara Morison (Spence), 88, 90, 95, 97
Clare, Eli, 4
class distinctions, 62, 71, 77–78, 181
Clever Woman of the Family, The (Yonge), 57
Cobbett, William, 125
Cohen, Monica, 71
Coleridge, Christabel, 168
collectivism, 9–10, 147–48
Collins, Wilkie, 66, 74
Colón, Susan, 178
colonialism, 31, 102
communitarianism, 135–36, 166, 222n26
communities: forms of, 135–36; organization of, 12, 19, 26, 48; and politics, 46–47; romanticization of, 18. *See also* care communities
composite writing, 26, 159, 166–68, 179, 181, 186–88, 208
Connolly, Brian, 163
Contagious Diseases Act, 72
Continental philosophy, 38
Cooper, Helen, 101
Corfield, Penelope J., 71
corporate personhood, 9
cosmopolitanism, 101–2, 132, 143

COVID-19 pandemic, 18–19, 95
Cranford (Gaskell), 62
Crawford, Matthew, 221n3
crip time, 52, 162. *See also* temporality
Cross, Samuel, 158
Crunk Feminist Collective, 196–97
Cunningham, Nija, 213

Daisy Chain, The (Yonge), 169–70
Dalley, Lana, 92
Dalmiya, Vrinda, 2, 16
Daniel Deronda (Eliot), 62, 117–19, 125, 127, 132–34, 136–37, 142–43, 148, 192
David Copperfield (Dickens), 66
Davis, Helen, 114
Davis, Lennard, 65, 67
deathbeds, 143, 157
"Death of the Author, The" (Barthes), 164
debility, 68, 75–76, 82, 84, 228n35. *See also* bodies
Deerbrook (Martineau), 74
dehumanization, 11, 15, 41
de la Motte Fouqué, Friedrich, 177, 180–81
Dickens, Charles, 9–11, 13, 22, 51, 62, 66, 74, 80, 83, 121, 179. *See also specific works*
digital humanities, 206–7
digital media, 20, 41, 44–45, 169, 187–88, 207, 223n51. *See also* social media
Dimock, Wai Chee, 163
disability: depictions of, 79–80, 82, 84, 130, 175, 230n111; as an identity, 36–37; stigma of, 66; understandings of, 67–68, 228n53
disability readings, 36, 81
discourse: and care, 13, 123; failures of, 176, 182–83, 205; importance of, 54–55, 140; and interaction, 200; and money, 145–46; and regulation, 26. *See also* care; silence
disease: depictions of, 155–56; diagnosis of, 144, 152; forms of, 142; understandings of, 64–65, 67
disindividuation, 25, 78, 80, 82, 95, 99. *See also* individuality
doctors: and care communities, 71, 83, 145; consultations with, 175; distrust of, 60, 64, 73–74, 86; as social connections, 153, 171. *See also* medical professionalization
Dohe, Kate, 207
Dombey and Son (Dickens), 12, 15, 51, 54–56, 61, 90, 179, 181

doulia, 136
Duncan, Ian, 240n66
During, Lisbeth, 129–30
Dyson, Marianne, 166

economic pressures, 16, 22, 33, 44, 75, 105, 108
education, 105–6, 132, 194–203, 207, 220n44. *See also* academia
egalitarianism, 32, 55–56, 131, 147, 191, 199, 205
Ehnenn, Jill, 168
Elements of Medicine, The (Brown), 227
Elias, Amy J., 160
Eliot, George: and care communities, 62; influence of, 25, 63, 127–28, 158, 165; and politics, 137–38, 143; style of, 148; and sympathy, 117–18, 126
Ellis, Sarah Stickney, 62
Emma (Austen), 124
emotional labor, 25, 90–95, 107, 111, 117–18, 145, 152, 158, 191, 231n15. *See also* labor; service work
empathetic unsettlement, 216–17
Enforcing Normalcy (Davis), 67, 227n26
English identity, 100–102, 104, 132
engrossment, 105
Engster, Daniel, 32, 136
"Enoch Arden" (Tennyson), 123
epistemic injustice, 49, 55
eroticism, 132–33, 151
ethics of care, 2–3, 20–23, 28–33, 42–43, 63, 118, 127, 136, 193, 206–7, 223n44, 224n73
Eustace Diamonds, The (Trollope), 90
Evangelicalism, 122
extraordinary bodies, 24, 67, 84, 94, 192. *See also* bodies; freak; ordinary bodies

Families We Choose, The (Weston), 16–17
family relations, 183
Favret, Mary, 75
feelings: and actions, 51; assumptions of, 88; expression of, 47–48, 93; pathology of, 117. *See also* sentiment; sympathy
Felix Holt (Eliot), 137
Felski, Rita, 28, 43
feminine service ideals, 14–15, 21. *See also* gender roles
femininity, 30, 91, 116

feminism, 46, 162, 210–11
Feminist Morality (Held), 30
Festa, Lynn, 120
Feuerbach, Ludwig, 126, 235n34
Figure of the Migrant, The (Nail), 96
Fitzpatrick, Kathleen, 189, 196, 203–7, 210, 216, 241n19
Flaubert, Gustave, 74
Foucault, Michel, 67, 164
fourth wall, 141, 160
Frame, Edward, 107
Fraser, Nancy, 46, 220n45
Frawley, Maria, 73
freak, 66–67, 84. *See also* extraordinary bodies; normate; ordinary bodies
Freeman, Elizabeth, 17
Fricker, Miranda, 49
Friedman, Maurice, 38
Friedman, Susan Stanford, 162
Fuss, Diana, 237n14

Gallagher, Catherine, 9–10
Galton, Francis, 65
Garland-Thomson, Rosemarie, 65
Gaskell, Elizabeth, 62, 73–75, 125
Gemeinschaft und Gesellschaft (Tönnies), 135
gender roles, 1, 9, 14–15, 30–31, 46, 57, 62–63, 73, 91. *See also* feminine service ideals
generosity, 117, 205–7
Generous Thinking (Fitzpatrick), 206–7, 210
Genette, Gérard, 164, 184
germ theory, 75
Gilbert, Sandra, 89, 111
Gilligan, Carol, 30, 46, 63, 127
Glenn, Evelyn Nakano, 110
Gold, Matthew K., 213
Goldhill, Simon, 170
Gooch, Joshua, 109
Goodman, Ruth, 68
Greiner, Rae, 119
Gubar, Susan, 89, 111
Guy Mannering (Scott), 176, 180–81, 240n66

Habermas, Jürgen, 24, 29, 35, 45–55, 68, 119, 138, 140, 156, 193, 225n91. *See also* public sphere
habitus, 61, 226n2
Hager, Kelly, 169

Hamilton, Laurence, 40, 136
Hankivsky, Olena, 32
Hard Times (Dickens), 62, 90
Harney, Stefano, 197, 212
Harrison, Mary-Catherine, 82
Harry Potter series, influences on, 187, 240n70
Harvey, Garham, 42
Havens, Hilary, 167
Hegel, G.W.F., 40, 126
Heidegger, Martin, 4–5, 38–39, 157, 216
Heir of Redclyffe, The (Yonge), 54, 160, 171, 176–78, 181–82, 184
Held, Virginia, 29–30, 32–33, 48, 134
Hemans, Felicia, 123
Henry, Nancy, 137–38
Hensley, Nathan, 64
Hertz, Neil, 128
Hingston, Kylee-Anne, 169
Historical Novel, The (Lukács), 8–9
History of the Protestant Reformation (Cobbett), 134–35
Hobart, Hi'ilei Julia, 15
Hobbes, Thomas, 236–37n75
Hochschild, Arlie Russell, 25, 91, 107. *See also* emotional labor
Hodgkinson, Ruth, 72–73
Hoffer, Lauren, 90–91
Holmes, Martha Stoddard, 62
Homo Economicus, 119
Hondagneu-Sotelo, Pierrette, 109–10, 113
hooks, bell, 202–3
Houston, Barbara, 31
Hughes, John, 97, 115
Hughes, Linda, 166
Hume, David, 119, 126

Imagined Communities (Anderson), 45
individuality, 8–10, 29, 69, 121, 135, 183, 185, 190–91. *See also* disindividuation
industrialization, 11, 100
industrial novels, 9, 138
interrelationality, 1–3, 6, 29, 78–79, 149, 190, 195, 203
intertextuality, 162–65, 187. *See also* authorial influence; textuality
In the Wake (Sharpe), 17
invalidism, 68, 142
I Promessi Sposi (Manzoni), 179–80, 182
isolation, 110, 144–47, 175

INDEX [271]

Jackson, Steven, 4–5, 41
Jaffe, Audrey, 121, 128
James, Henry, 62, 140–43, 147–49, 157, 160, 165, 216
Jameson, Frederic, 157
Jane Eyre (Brontë), 11–12, 15, 42, 56, 83–84, 93, 114, 117, 127, 230n127
Jay, Elisabeth, 178
Johnson, Claudia, 124
justice, 1, 18–19, 21, 34, 37, 136, 139, 206, 221n71, 223n45. *See also* epistemic injustice; restorative justice

Kafer, Alison, 52
Keble, John, 166, 171, 181
Keller, Jean, 34
Kincaid, Jamaica, 88, 97, 100, 105
King, Martin Luther, Jr., 1
Kipling, Rudyard, 31
Kittay, Eva Feder, 29, 32–34, 136, 203
Klein, Melanie, 3
Kneese, Tamara, 15
Knox, Robert, 101
Kotchemidova, Christine, 90
Kranidis, Rita, 97
Krienke, Hosanna, 69
Kristeva, Julia, 164
Kucich, John, 71, 106
Kurnick, David, 4, 147–48

labor: boundaries of, 110; conditions of, 6, 11, 14, 62, 68, 71, 88, 203; language of, 93; and migration, 96, 98; precarity of, 112, 206; relations of, 14, 80, 206. *See also* emotional labor
LaCapra, Dominick, 216–17
Latour, Bruno, 42
Lau, Travis Chi Wing, 67
law, 37, 99
Law and the Lady, The (Collins), 66
Lawson, Kate, 104
Leavis, F. R., 162
"Letter from a Birmingham Jail" (King), 1
Levinas, Emmanuel, 38–39, 217
Lewes, George Henry, 121, 128
Life in the Sickroom (Martineau), 68
Lindhé, Anna, 125
literary criticism, 1–2, 7, 58, 187, 213
literary style (as care), 147–49, 160

Little Dorrit (Dickens), 62, 66, 90, 107–8, 115
Living a Feminist Life (Ahmed), 210–11
Locke, John, 236–37n75
Longmuir, Anne, 96
Lorde, Audre, 18
Love, Heather, 214
Lowe, Brigid, 61
Luciano, Dana, 53
Lucy (Kincaid), 88, 97
Lukács, Georg, 8–9
Lynch, Deidre Shauna, 8

Madame Bovary (Flaubert), 74
Manne, Kate, 31, 205
Manzoni, Alessandro, 179–80
Marchbanks, Paul, 94
Marcus, Sharon, 168
marriage, 85, 166, 172, 193, 234n91, 239n48
Martineau, Harriet, 68, 74
maternalism, 30–31, 89, 109–10, 222n14. *See also* motherhood
Maternal Thinking (Ruddick), 30
May, Leila, 106
McAleavey, Maia, 169
McDowell, Paula, 167
McGee, Micki, 15
McKeon, MIchael, 8
Medical Act of 1858, 72
medical professionalization, 60, 64, 71–74, 77–78, 83–86, 88, 145, 153, 160, 227n23. *See also* doctors
melodrama, 9
memory, 44, 75, 210–11. *See also* nostalgia
Menke, Richard, 239n48
mental illness, 84
miasma theory, 64–65
Michael Armstrong, Factory Boy (Trollope), 138
Middlemarch (Eliot), 9, 62, 73–74, 90, 92, 125
migration, 88, 95–96, 98, 102–4, 139, 231n1
Miller, Andrew, 214
Miller, Nancy, 164, 204
Mill on the Floss, The (Eliot), 127
Minor Characters Have Their Day (Rosen), 240n71
misogyny, 31

missionary discourse, 102
Mitchell, Rosemary, 165–66
mobility, 96, 108, 116
modernism, 26, 140, 159, 237n2
modernity, 8, 86, 96, 140–41, 159, 177, 237n2
Monthly Packet, The, 166
Morris, William, 135
Moses, Omri, 148–49
Moten, Fred, 197, 212
motherhood, 30, 133–34. *See also* maternalism
Mothers in Council, 166
Mothers' Union, 166

Nail, Thomas, 96
narrative form, 89–90, 93, 95, 193
National Health Service, 73
nationhood, 45, 119, 134, 139, 236–37n75
"Natural History of German Life, The" (Eliot), 118
Nazar, Hina, 235n34
needs, 35–36, 61, 151, 175, 191–92, 202, 207, 215. *See also* care
neoliberalism, 163, 196
New Poor Law Act of 1834, 71–73, 80, 122, 138, 229n66
"New Women" novels, 75
Nightingale, Florence, 1, 57, 74–75, 228n47
Noddings, Nel, 29–30, 34, 52, 63, 105, 124, 127, 132, 200
normate, 64, 67, 85, 227n26, 228n53. *See also* freak
nostalgia, 88, 135, 166. *See also* memory
Novel Craft (Schaffer), 170
novels: history of, 7–8, 115; reader's relation to, 158; as a space of community, 45; utility of, 64, 157
Nowviskie, Bethany, 206–7
nuclear family norm, 16
nursing: as a career, 75, 85, 93 (*see also* paid care); depictions of, 74–75; and gender, 1, 57, 62; perceptions of, 122, 144; practices of, 171; and shifts in medicine, 64. *See also* care
Nussbaum, Martha, 157
Nussey, Ellen, 83

object relations, 40–41. *See also* subjectivity
Oliphant, Margaret, 73, 167–68
Oliver Twist (Dickens), 74

Onazi, Oche, 2, 16
One Versus the Many, The (Dickens), 11
ordinary bodies, 24, 67–68, 70, 79, 81–84. *See also* bodies; extraordinary bodies; freak
Orr, Mary, 164
Our Mutual Friend (Dickens), 9, 51, 230n111

Pahl, Ray, 44, 207, 213
paid care, 30–33, 51–52, 64, 73, 85, 90–95, 116–17, 145–46, 159–60, 191, 221n70. *See also* care; nursing
Palmer, Beth, 166
panpsychism, 42
paranoid reading, 3–4, 23, 52, 162, 214–15. *See also* reading; reparative reading
Parreñas, Salazar, 98
Penner, Louise, 72
performativity, 17, 25, 50, 107, 109, 117, 148–49, 200, 205, 214. *See also* care
periodical culture, 166
Persuasion (Austen), 50, 75–76, 79, 82
Peterson, Linda, 167–68
Philip, M. NourbeSe, 17
Phineas Finn (Trollope), 137
Phineas Redux (Trollope), 137
Piepzna-Samarasinha, Leah Lakshmi, 18, 196
Pinch, Adela, 78, 120–21, 234n13, 235n14
placelessness, 104
plagiarism, 162–65. *See also* authorial influence; intertextuality
poetic misprision, 177
Poor Miss Finch (Collins), 74
Poovey, Mary, 44
Portrait of a Lady, The (James), 53, 57, 62, 142–43, 157
postcolonialism, 104
postmodernism, 96, 116
Powers of Distance, The (Anderson), 94–95
practical kinship, 17
Prime Minister, The (Eliot), 138
privacy, 93, 147, 159
private sphere, 29, 46–47, 49, 58, 71, 94, 134, 137, 139, 194. *See also* public sphere
psychoanalysis, 47–48
psychology, 88–89
Puar, Jasbir, 68, 75, 228n35

public sphere, 24, 29, 45–48, 50, 52, 55, 57–58, 119, 134, 137–38, 193–94, 225n86. *See also* Habermas, Jürgen; private sphere
Pugin, A.W.N., 135

queer families of choice, 16–17
queer relations, 220n55
queer temporality, 53, 162. *See also* temporality

race: and colorlessness, 165; and identification, 132; justice and, 18–19; perceptions of, 101, 103, 116; and sympathy, 128; theories of, 100, 106, 232n52; and whiteness, 7
Rappoport, Jill, 92
readers: as care communities, 157; expectations of, 114, 144, 215; mobilization of, 138; and relationship to characters, 141, 155; subjectivity of, 82, 193, 213; and sympathy, 121
reading: as collective, 183; as a form of care, 26; as interactive, 122, 178–79; modes of, 2, 25, 89, 93, 122, 160 (*see also* care readings; paranoid reading; reparative reading); structures of, 141; and sympathy, 125–26; theories of, 3–12
Readings, Bill, 203
realist novels, 175
religion, 43, 69, 102, 111, 122, 134–36, 170, 177–78, 181
reparative reading, 3–5, 7–8, 11, 214–16. *See also* paranoid reading; reading
Restoration, the, 170
restorative justice, 19, 47
Rhys, Jean, 187
Riffaterre, Michael, 164
Risam, Roopika, 203–4
Rivas, Lynn May, 107, 111
Robinson, Fiona, 32
Rodas, Julia Miele, 81, 84, 230n127
Rody, Caroline, 187
romance genre, 250n66
Romance's Rival (Schaffer), 69
Romanticism, 120, 234n13
Rosen, Jeremy, 240n71
Rousseau, 236–37n75
Rowe, Aimee Carrillo, 29
Rowland, Ann Wierda, 120
Rowling, J. K., influence on, 187, 240n70

Ruddick, Sara, 30, 196
Ruskin, John, 135
Ruth (Gaskell), 62, 74–75

Sanders, Joel, 237
"Sanditon" (Austen), 60, 64, 67, 70–71, 75
Scott, Sir Walter, 8–9, 176, 180
Second Reform Bill of 1867, 138
Sedgwick, Eve Kosofsky, 3, 52, 162, 186, 214–16, 219n6
self-care, 39–41, 114, 223n53. *See also* care
Seltzer, Mark, 147
Semmel, Bernard, 135
Sense and Sensibility (Austen), 180, 183
sensibility, 120, 234n13
sentiment, 25, 118, 123, 141, 148–49, 193. *See also* feelings; sympathy
Sered, Danielle, 19
Serres, Michel, 209
service work, 11, 90, 92, 103, 107, 115, 232n42. *See also* emotional labor
Sevenhuijsen, Selma, 48
sexual repression, 89
Shakinovsky, Lynn, 104, 176
Sharpe, Christina, 17
Shirley (Brontë), 83
Shuttleworth, Sally, 106
silence, 26, 140, 149–55, 157–58, 182–83, 214. *See also* discourse
Sintram (de la Motte Fouqué), 180, 183
slavery, 16, 96, 102, 120, 233n58
Smith, Adam, 119, 126, 128, 235n16
Smith-Rosenberg, Carroll, 61
social media, 20, 207, 223n51. *See also* digital media
social networks, 17–21, 29–32, 38, 61, 70, 77–78, 119–20, 131, 140, 150, 157, 167–68, 172, 196–97
social problem novel, 9
social spaces, 78
sociological readings, 90–95
Spade, Dean, 18
Sparks, Tabitha, 72
spatiality, 90, 172
Spence, Catherine Helen, 88
Spinoza, Baruch, 126, 235n34
Spunt, Nicola Ivy, 144
Star, Susan Leigh, 6
Stern, Kimberly, 167
Stout, Daniel M., 9–10, 176
Stowe, Harriet Beecher, 138

Straus, Joseph, 23
Strauss, Anselm, 6
Strauss, David, 126, 235n34
Structural Transformation of the Public Sphere, The (Habermas), 45
subjectivity, 9–10, 29, 32, 40–42, 63, 78, 88–89, 103, 106–9, 115, 149, 161, 167, 178, 185, 190, 210. *See also* characters
sympathy: demonstration of, 125, 148–49, 154; limits of, 118, 127, 129, 139, 205; and race, 128; reading for, 7–8, 25, 125–26; rhetoric of, 120; and social bonds, 119; theory of, 119, 126. *See also* care; feelings; sensibility; sentiment
synchronic historicism, 163

TallBear, Kim, 17
Taussig, Rebekah, 241n4–241n5
Taylor, Charles, 135–36
Taylor, Mary, 96
Teahan, Sheila, 154
"Tears, Idle Tears" (Tennyson), 124
temporality, 52–54, 161–62, 183, 212, 534
Tennyson, 123–24
textuality, 142, 163, 179, 187. *See also* intertextuality
Theory of Communicative Action, The (Habermas), 46
Thomson, Rosemarie Garland, 24, 31, 66–67
Three Clerks, The (Trollope), 239n48
Toker, Leona, 127
Tönnies, Ferdinand, 135
tool-being theory, 4–5, 38–39, 157, 216
Trial, The (Kafka), 169
Trollope, Anthony, 73, 90, 137–38, 168, 239n48
Trollope, Frances, 138
Tuck, Eve, 242n34
Tucker, Irene, 134
Turbine, Vikki, 197

Uncle Tom's Cabin (Stowe), 31, 122, 138
unpaid care, 30, 116. *See also* care; paid care
urbanization, 90

Vanity Fair (Thackeray), 90
Vargo, Gregory, 61
vibrant matter, 42
Vickery, Amanda, 61

Victorian culture: class stratification, 11, 21; communal social relations, 13–15, 26, 61–63, 134–35; interventionism, 121–22, 193; invalidism, 68; women's service work, 90–93. *See also* industrialization; urbanization
Victorian thinking: on bodies, 23, 68; colonialist rhetoric, 31, 96, 102; literary marketplace, 166–68; racial theory of, 100–101, 232n52
Villette (Brontë), 25, 51, 83–85, 88, 93–98, 100–101, 105, 112–16, 132, 139, 146, 231n1
visibility, 6, 19, 107, 110–11, 113, 115, 123, 234n93

Waddell, J.A.L., 222n5
Wagner, Tamara Silvia, 102
Walton, Susan, 166
Ward, Lizzie, 223n53
Watt, Ian, 8
Way We Live Now, The (Trollope), 138
Weston, Kath, 16–17
Wharton, Amy, 108
White, Paul, 100
"White Man's Burden, The" (Kipling), 31
Wide Sargasso Sea (Rhys), 187
Williams, Susan, 68
Wings of the Dove, The (James), 53–55, 62, 140–43, 146–48, 150–51, 155–57, 159, 182, 193, 214
Winnicott, Donald, 40
Wives and Daughters (Gaskell), 62, 125
Woloch, Alex, 10–11, 147, 162
Woman in White, The (Collins), 66
Women Novelists of Queen Victoria's Reign (collaborative), 168
Woolf, Virginia, 162, 183, 187
Wright, Erika, 69

Yonge, Charlotte: and caregiving, 165–66, 173; within her own writing, 185–86, 192; influence of, 62, 159; style of, 170, 172, 182, 188; and typology, 169; writing career of, 166–69, 171. *See also specific works*
Young, Iris Marion, 48
Yousef, Nancy, 120

Zionism, 134, 137, 143, 192
Zong! (Philip), 17
Zunshine, Lisa, 39–40

A NOTE ON THE TYPE

THIS BOOK has been composed in Miller, a Scotch Roman typeface designed by Matthew Carter and first released by Font Bureau in 1997. It resembles Monticello, the typeface developed for The Papers of Thomas Jefferson in the 1940s by C. H. Griffith and P. J. Conkwright and reinterpreted in digital form by Carter in 2003.

Pleasant Jefferson ("P. J.") Conkwright (1905-1986) was Typographer at Princeton University Press from 1939 to 1970. He was an acclaimed book designer and AIGA Medalist.

The ornament used throughout this book was designed by Pierre Simon Fournier (1712-1768) and was a favorite of Conkwright's, used in his design of the *Princeton University Library Chronicle*.

GPSR Authorized Representative: Easy Access System Europe - Mustamäe tee 50, 10621 Tallinn, Estonia, gpsr.requests@easproject.com